Explorers of the Nile

Explorers of the Nile

The Triumph and the Tragedy of a
Great Victorian Adventure

TIM JEAL

faber and faber

First published in 2011
by Faber and Faber Limited
Bloomsbury House
74–77 Great Russell Street
London WC1B 3DA

Typeset by Donald Sommerville
Printed and bound by CPI Group (UK) Croydon, CR0 4YY

A CIP record for this book
is available from the British Library

ISBN 978-0-571-24975-6

2 4 6 8 10 9 7 5 3

To my daughters,
Jessica, Lucy and Emily

Contents

List of Illustrations

———— ∞∞∞ ————

List of Plates

A medieval reconstruction of Ptolemy's map of the world, in *The Discovery of the Nile* by Gianni Guadalupi, from a map in the Vatican Library, Rome
Richard Burton depicted as an Afghan peddler in Isabel Burton's *The Life of Captain Sir Richard F. Burton* (1893).
John Speke and James Grant at Mutesa's court. From Speke's *Journal of the Discovery of the Source of the Nile*.
A naked Mutesa drawn by Speke in one of his sketchbooks, now at the Royal Geographical Society. *RGS*
Speke portrayed standing at the Ripon Falls source, by the artist James Watney Wilson. *RGS*
African birds drawn by Speke. *RGS*
Samuel Baker and Florence von Sass in a storm on Lake Albert, an engraving from Samuel Baker's *The Albert Nyanza* (1874).
Obbo warriors perform a war dance, a water colour by Samuel Baker, in the Baker family collection.
Baker's sketch of himself in danger of being trampled by an elephant, in the Baker family collection.
James Gordon Bennett Jr., editor of the *New York Herald*, by 'Nemo' (Constantine von Grimm), chromolithograph, *Vanity Fair*, 15 November 1884.
Stanley and his men crossing the Makata swamp, a magic lantern slide in a private collection.
Hats worn by Livingstone and Stanley at the time of their meeting, now in the RGS.
Stanley watches a phalanx dance by Chief Mazamboni's warriors, during the Emin Pasha Relief Expedition, an illustration in Stanley's *In Darkest Africa* (1890).

Livingstone's remains being carried to the coast by his men, a magic lantern slide from *The Life and Work of David Livingstone*, published by the London Missionary Society (1900).

David Livingstone in 1866. *London Missionary Society*
Richard Burton posing in Arab clothes, by Ernest Edwards, April 1865, in *David Livingstone and the Victorian Encounter with Africa. National Portrait Gallery*
Richard Burton in his tent in Somaliland, a photograph in Isabel Burton's *The Life of Captain Sir Richard F. Burton* (1893).
John Hanning Speke as a young officer in India, an oil painting reproduced in Harry Johnston's *The Nile Quest* (1903).
Speke before his great journey, a photograph in Mary Lovell's *A Rage to Live* (1998).
Speke's memorial in Kensington Gardens.
Samuel Baker in his African hunting attire, Baker family collection.
Florence von Sass before her marriage to Samuel Baker, from Richard Hall's *Lovers on the Nile*.
The Royal Geographical Society outing during the meeting of the British Association in Bath, 1864, a photograph in the David Livingstone Centre.
Henry Stanley aged twenty-eight, two years before he 'found' Dr Livingstone, a photograph in the estate of the late Quentin Keynes.
Chuma and Susi, Dr Livingstone's servants. *London Missionary Society*
Some of Stanley's principal Wangwana carriers on his great trans-Africa journey, a photograph in the Royal Museum of Central Africa.
Karl Peters, the German explorer and imperialist. © *Getty Images*
Princess Salme, sister of the Sultan of Zanzibar. *Author's Collection*
Captain T. M. S. Pasley RN. *Author's Collection*

James S. Jameson, a photograph in *The Story of the Rear-Column of the Emin Pasha Relief Expedition*, ed. Mrs J. S. Jameson (1890).

Major Edmund Barttelot, a photograph in W. G. Barttelot's *The Life of Edmund Musgrave Barttelot* (1890).

Stanley (aged forty-six) and Anthony Swinburne, a photograph in the Royal Museum of Central Africa.

Captain Frederick Lugard soon after claiming Uganda for Britain, a photograph in Margery Perham's *Lugard: The Years of Adventure 1858–1898* (1956).

Kabarega of Bunyoro in old age, a photograph in Alan Moorehead's *The White Nile* (1960).

Henry Stanley in 1892 with his close friend Sir William Mackinnon of the Imperial British East Africa Company, a photograph in the Royal Museum of Central Africa.

Major-General Sir Horatio Kitchener at the time of the battle of Omdurman, a photograph in Philip Magnus's *Kitchener: Portrait of an Imperialist* (1958).

Marchand's emissaries approach Kitchener's ship, a photograph in J. O. Udal's *The Nile in Darkness: A Flawed Unity 1863–1899* (2005).

Commandant Jean-Baptiste Marchand, from an oil painting in the Musée de l'Armée, Paris.

Sir Harold MacMichael, Britain's top civil servant in Sudan 1926–33.

List of Maps

Introduction

In the middle of the nineteenth century the whereabouts of the Nile's source was still the planet's most elusive secret, as it had been since the days of the Pharaohs. When Alexander the Great was shown the temple of Ammon in Luxor, the first question he asked is said to have been: 'What causes the Nile to rise?' Indeed, a longing to find answers to the twin mysteries of the location of the river's source, and why it always flooded in summer rather than in winter, had drawn Alexander to Egypt as powerfully as any military, commercial or political reason.[1] From 30 BC Egypt was ruled by Rome. A Roman proverb – *Facilius sit Nili caput invenire* ('It would be easier to find the source of the Nile') was still current in nineteenth-century Europe as a handy epithet to hurl at impractical dreamers of all sorts. In AD 66, the Emperor Nero – surprisingly, a keen geographer – had sent an expedition upriver, led by two centurions, with instructions to find the legendary headwaters. Two thousand miles from the Mediterranean (half-way between the river's mouth and its unknown source), the centurions were defeated by an immense swamp extending for hundreds of miles. This was the mosquito-infested Sudd, where under the blazing sun a maze of shifting channels was blocked by floating islands of papyrus and interlaced aquatic plants.

Over the millennia the Nile mystery remained unsolved. How, people asked, could the river flow unfailingly every day of the year, for 1,200 miles through the largest and driest desert in the known world without being replenished by a single tributary? Small wonder that its annual inundation of the Nile Delta in the hottest month of the year caused awe and no little anxiety in case the mysterious sources might one day fail and Egypt perish. Yet, despite the passionate curiosity of successive generations, 2,000 years would pass without any significant new discovery being made on the White Nile. To the south of Latitude 9.5° North (the position of the Bahr el-Ghazal and the Sudd), mid-nineteenth-century maps would still show the main channel dwindling away into a tracery of ever more hesitant dots.

The world's longest river has two main branches: the White Nile, which flows 4,230 miles from its remotest central African sources to the Mediterranean, and the Blue Nile, which rises high up on the Ethiopian plateau and flows for 1,450 miles before it joins the White Nile at Khartoum. By then the White Nile has already flowed for nearly 2,500 miles.[2]

During the first two decades of the seventeenth century, two Spanish Jesuit priests, Pedro Paez and Jeronimo Lobo, reached the headwaters of the Blue Nile. The Scot James Bruce ignored their achievement and published a popular account of his own identical 'discovery' made 150 years later. From that time it would be suspected that the annual flood on the lower Nile between July and October was due to monsoon rains falling on the Ethiopian highlands and cascading with spectacular force down a succession of rapids towards the parent stream via the Blue Nile and other rivers.

But on the White Nile itself, there would be no comparable discoveries, although this far longer river provided water all the year round, even during the months of winter and spring when the Blue Nile and the Atbara were dried-up riverbeds. Despite Egypt's absolute dependence on the continuous flow of the White Nile, by the early 1850s not a single one of the succession of Greek, Italian, Maltese and French traders and adventurers who had attempted to locate the source for two decades had managed to journey further south than the position of the present town of Juba 750 miles south of Khartoum.

At first sight it seems incredible that in the era of the steam engine, the galvanic battery, telegraphic communication and accurate chronometers, the Nile continued to keep its secrets. But there were many excellent reasons for the lack of progress in the great quest: 'fever' and other unexplained tropical illnesses decimated expeditions, cataracts blocked the upper river, tsetse

fly killed beasts of burden and made wheeled transport impossible, porters deserted, the rainy season turned whole regions
into quagmires, and local conflicts stirred up by the slave trade
caused many chiefs to shower strangers with spears and poisoned
arrows rather than with gifts.

But between 1856 and 1876, the White Nile would at last
yield up its secrets to an idiosyncratic group of exceptionally
brave British explorers, who would solve the mystery of the
source bit by bit – despite many illnesses, including loss of sight
and hearing, and in one instance, for a time, the use of both legs.
They also suffered the ravages of flesh-eating ulcers, malaria,
colonic haemorrhage and deep spear wounds. Ironically, after
their journeys were over, almost all would disagree profoundly
about which one of them had won the crown.

Fifty years ago, Alan Moorehead's international bestseller about
the search for the source of the Nile was published. Although,
in the decades since *The White Nile* first appeared, a mass of
previously unknown facts relating to the search have come to
light, both in manuscript and in published form, no full-scale
attempt has been made until now to write a further book on the
subject, in which the new material is used to deepen and redraw
the characters and relationships of the original Nile explorers,
to re-examine their journeys, and to reassess up to the present
day the enduring and tragic consequences of nineteenth-century
exploration of the Nile basin. New information exists that
sheds light on all the above subjects, but also on more personal
matters, ranging from Speke's alleged betrayal of Burton, to how
Baker acquired the mistress he took to Africa, to whether Speke
had an affair with a Ugandan courtier, and to whether the real
Livingstone and the real Stanley resembled their portrayals in
The White Nile. I give a full account of related books and my
own researches at the end of this volume on pages 438–42.

Today, the mid-nineteenth-century explorers are often assumed
to have been motivated by an avaricious desire to exploit Africans

and Africa for commercial gain, or for the dubious satisfaction of wielding power over the powerless. In reality, a decade before the discovery of diamonds at Kimberley and nearly twenty years before gold was found on the Witwatersrand, the motives of men like Burton, Speke and Grant were quite different from those of the European administrators, soldiers and traders who went out to Africa in the 1880s and 1890s when the Scramble for Africa was in progress. In the 1850s and 1860s love of adventure played a greater part in motivating men to risk their lives to make 'discoveries' than did the desire to carve out markets. Indeed, a longing to escape from what Stanley called 'that shallow life in England where a man is not permitted to be real and natural', first drew him and the rest to Africa.[3]

Only 'the Dark Continent' and other wild places appeared to offer to high-spirited individuals in the industrialised countries a chance to escape from the factories, offices and counting houses of the expanding cities. Most would have empathised with Rimbaud's oft-quoted lament before he left Europe for Harar in Ethiopia: 'What a life this is! True life is elsewhere.' Samuel Baker wrote of longing to be 'a wandering spirit' and to plunge 'into the Unknown'.[4] When Speke had been granted periods of leave from the Indian Army, he had travelled to the mountains of Tibet or to Somalia rather than return to the tame tea cups and social chit-chat of England. An early missionary in Nyasaland (Malawi) put his finger on an essential part of the appeal of Africa. 'The sense of individuality is the main attraction. In the constant whirl of civilization the personal element is somewhat lost in the mass. Out in the forests of Africa you are the man amongst your surroundings.'[5]

Burton echoed these sentiments but went a Nietzschean step further. 'Man wants to wander,' he declared, 'and he must do so, or he shall die.' Famously, he described for the benefit of a friend: 'Starting in a hollowed log of wood – some thousand miles up a river, with an infinitesimal prospect of returning! I ask myself "Why?" and the only echo is "damned fool! . . . The Devil drives."'[6] Many other explorers relished living on the razor's edge and typically experienced long depressions on coming home after prolonged periods exposed to danger.

For a former workhouse boy like Henry Morton Stanley, Africa offered a chance to transform himself and assume a fresh identity with a new mission in life. Riding into the bush on his white stallion on his way to find Dr Livingstone, he was quite literally a man re-made, with his old, unwanted persona and nationality (even his name) discarded. In Africa, he declared, the human spirit is 'not repressed by fear, nor depressed by ridicule and insults ... [but] soars free and unrestrained ... [and] imperceptibly changes the whole man'.[7]

Then there was the urgent hunger for discovery which all these men felt – an intensified form of the innate curiosity of all humans. 'Discovery is mostly my mania,' confessed Burton.[8] This 'mania' seemed at times to consign explorers to membership of a separate species, set apart by extreme purposefulness and an extraordinary capacity to suffer and take risks. But the 'mania' was not always masochistic or even purely egotistical. Speke described how his determination to be an explorer had 'led on from shooting, collecting, mapping and ranging the world generally' to the point where he felt himself 'gradually wedded with geographical research'.[9] 'Wedded' was a strong word, and Speke would indeed be utterly single-minded about making precise scientific observations even when this demanded that he sit up all night in bad weather waiting for a break in the clouds to calculate his lunar angles. Stanley was also determined to make his maps accurate at a heavy personal cost.

Along with undoubted dreams of personal glory through best-selling books and social advancement, most of the Nile explorers harboured a genuine belief that they were making geographical discoveries for the benefit of the human race at large and not just for themselves. Whether or not fame would ultimately be theirs, the achievement of reaching any long-pursued lake, river or spring bestowed a joy that was almost religious. Believing that he was looking down at the principal reservoir of the Nile, the normally brash Baker thanked God that: 'I had been the humble instrument permitted to unravel this portion of the great mystery . . . I felt too serious to vent my feelings in vain cheers for victory.'[10] Of all the explorers, David Livingstone seemed least affected by the desire to achieve personal glory. He wrote: 'When one travels with the specific object of ameliorating the condition of the natives every act becomes ennobled . . . the sweat of one's brow is no longer a curse when one works for God.'[11] Yet even Livingstone longed to 'cut out' his rivals by finding the Nile's source and restoring his reputation as the world's greatest explorer.

When Baker saw Speke and Grant emerge from central Africa on the upper Nile, gaunt and sun-browned, their clothes in tatters after three years of travelling, he cried out spontaneously: 'Hurrah for Old England!' Simple patriotism was certainly a great spur to these explorers at a time when Britain was master of the seas and the undisputed 'workshop of the world'. Speke told a friend that he had gone back to Africa because he 'would rather die a hundred times' than wake up and learn that 'any foreigner should have taken from Britain the honour of discovery'.[12] But he did not mean to stake out territory for Britain. His pride was in being the first, as he thought, to have made a particular discovery ahead of the explorers of other nations.

Yet the explorers' motives would shift and change as time passed. While the Nile mystery was being solved between 1856 and 1877, humanitarians, sportsmen and adventurers were in the ascendant along the river and in Equatorial Africa. Thereafter political interests intruded, and came to dominate. Samuel Baker returned to Africa to fight the slave trade but also to extend the territory of the *khedive* of Egypt, and Henry Stanley sailed for West Africa to launch steamships on the Congo and build a road and trading posts for King Leopold II of Belgium. Meanwhile the journeys of Hermann von Wissmann and Karl Peters would be used to justify Germany in claiming the greater part of East Africa. By then de Brazza's rivalry with Stanley had led the French government to earmark a vast territory along the north bank of the Congo.

*

It was suggested by Malawi's first 'President for Life', Dr Hastings Banda, that the whole idea of European explorers making 'discoveries' was insulting and absurd. 'There was nothing to discover,' said Dr Banda, 'we were here all the time.'[13] And of course African eyes had looked upon all the great lakes and rivers for countless generations before any European explorer ever managed to do the same. Yet no African knew the extent of the watersheds of the Nile, Congo or Niger, nor understood how Africa's lakes and rivers were connected. The distances that had to be travelled before conclusions could be reached about such matters ran into thousands of miles, and the same problems that had made travel so difficult for Europeans also existed for Africans, who, even if they had learned where the Nile's or Congo's sources were situated, would not have had access to the chronometer watches, sextants and artificial horizons that would have enabled them to place the headwaters on an accurate map.

Chief Kasembe, when asked by Livingstone about the direction of a local river and its source, replied: 'We let the streams run on, and do not enquire whence they rise or whither they flow.' Another chief declined to talk about a nearby lake on the grounds that it was 'only water – nothing to be seen'. Questions about such matters struck many Africans as suspicious and pointless.[14] In the case of places that had not been visited before, most villagers judged that there would probably be supernatural reasons for this, and that such places were best avoided.

It is true that few European explorers gave adequate recognition in their books either to the geographical information they obtained from Arab-Swahili slave traders or to the essential role played by the Africans who accompanied them and made their journeys possible by carrying the trade goods used to buy food *en route* and pay chiefs for the right to pass through their territories. Africans also acted as interpreters, guards and guides. But some explorers *did* give credit where it was due. Livingstone often praised his men despite their frequent desertions and thefts. Speke sided with his porters against Burton in a long-running dispute over alleged misbehaviour, and Stanley often paid tribute

to his men in print. 'Their names should be written in gold,'
he wrote of the brave crewmen who volunteered to accompany
him in a small boat on the uncharted waters of Lake Victoria.[15]
The most famous African leaders of caravans, such as Sidi
Mubarak Bombay and Abdullah Susi acquired their experience
and expertise on many journeys – Bombay having served Speke
twice, before working for Stanley, and Susi having been freed
from a slave caravan by Livingstone, and then working for
eight years for him, before serving Stanley on the Congo. Most
explorers owed their lives to their porters, often several times,
but to suppose that such men, in different circumstances, might
have taken equivalent risks on their own account in order to
make similar geographical discoveries, would be fanciful.

Richard Burton once complained that:

The Anglo-African traveller in this section of the nineteenth century
is an overworked professional . . . expected to survey and observe, to
record meteorology and trigonometry, to shoot and stuff birds and
beasts, to collect geological specimens and theories . . . to advance the
infant study of anthropology, to keep accounts, to sketch, to indite a
copious legible journal . . . and to forward long reports which shall
prevent the Royal Geographical Society napping through its evenings.[16]

All this work had to be done against a background of very
real danger. In the middle of the nineteenth century, when few
European travellers entered the East African interior, three had
been murdered there – and this was at the very time when Speke
and Burton set out for Lake Tanganyika, and when Livingstone
began his last journey. The Nile explorers only had to study the
fate of the earlier West African explorers to know that whole
expeditions had died of malaria. During Mungo Park's 1805
expedition, forty out of forty-four Europeans had perished, with
Park himself being murdered. In Richard Lander's expedition on
the same river thirty years later, thirty-eight men succumbed out
of forty-seven, and Lander died of the after-effects of a bullet
wound. Between 1853 and 1856, Livingstone demonstrated
that quinine aided resistance to malaria – though all Stanley's
white companions perished on successive journeys, and the

same fate would befall V. L. Cameron's two European colleagues.

The courage and resourcefulness of the Nile explorers and their capacity for transcending ordinary human limitation was demonstrated again and again during their epic twenty-year quest. Speke in 1861, on his magnificent journey from Unyanyembe to Buganda, faced repeated illness, months of forced detention and robbery, and the mass desertion of his porters. In 1868, David Livingstone was deserted by all but three of his men, but still had the temerity to set out for Lake Bangweulu in the midst of the rainy season.[17] In 1877, when many of Stanley's men were starving on the lower Congo, and had lost the will to live, he led by example and inspired them to struggle on, shooting the rapids and saving themselves.

Daring to complete death-defying quests chimed with the Victorians' passion for medieval chivalry, and with the Christian idea of redemption through suffering which resonated so deeply with them. So the modern penchant for calling men like David Livingstone and Henry Stanley self-destructive or perverse would have caused great surprise to most of their contemporaries, for whom the discovery of the Nile's source was an event as momentous as the moon landings would be when witnessed a century later. Nor is it appropriate to stigmatise these extraordinary men for possessing the exploitative vices of a later generation of European adventurers and settlers. (That change in attitudes in the last quarter of the nineteenth century is the subject of later chapters in this book.)

In retrospect it is possible to see the search for the source of the Nile as the last flowering of the spirit of adventure before 'Great Power' competition, and the 'scramble' for colonies, elbowed aside extraordinary individuals, and replaced them with government expeditions marching ever faster along the jingoistic path that led, at journey's end, to the final death of adventure in the mud of the Western Front.

Tim Jeal
London, 2011

PART I

SOLVING THE MYSTERY

ONE

Blood in God's River

In March 1866, David Livingstone, wearing his trademark peaked cap, landed at Mikindani Bay on the East African coast and strode inland followed by thirty-five porters and a bizarre assortment of baggage animals, consisting of four buffaloes, six camels, four donkeys and six mules. The day was fiercely hot, and Dr Livingstone and his polyglot following of coastal Africans, Indian sepoys and mission-educated freed slaves were soon struggling along a valley choked with rank grass that towered above their heads and made them feel as if they were being smothered.[1] By a characteristic piece of bad luck, the doctor had chanced to step ashore at one of the few points on the coast where dense jungle stretched far into the interior. Soon the undergrowth became thicker, and his men were obliged to use their axes to hack a path wide enough for the swaying camels to negotiate. Within hours the overloaded animals were being bitten by tsetse fly. As they weakened and slowed, the porters beat them to restore their energy. When Livingstone objected, the first mutinous voices were raised against him. His troubles were just beginning.[2]

Just over a year earlier – despite being a decade or more older than his principal rivals – the 53-year-old medical missionary turned explorer had been commissioned by the Royal Geographical Society, the world's principal sponsor of exploration, to do nothing less extraordinary than solve the planet's greatest remaining geographical mystery by finding the River Nile's headwaters. In recent years, other explorers, notably John Speke, Richard Burton and Samuel Baker, had claimed to have reached the river's source, or at least one of its main reservoirs; but there was no consensus among geographers about whether any had proved his case. So Sir Roderick Murchison, the elderly President of the RGS, had decided in Livingstone's self-approving phrase, 'to take the true scientific way of settling the matter' by inviting him 'to ascertain the watershed'.[3] Had Sir Roderick chosen anyone else, Dr Livingstone, who prided himself on travelling 'beyond every other man's line of things',[4] would have thought it anything but 'the true scientific way'. In fairness to him, no other explorer had spent anything approaching his twenty-one years in Africa, nor come close to overhauling the vast mileage he had tramped.

But while he had never suffered from false modesty, Livingstone, who had started life as a child factory worker in a Scottish textile mill and had lived in a single tenement room with his parents and four siblings, had not taken his selection for granted. The affluent members of the RGS were a snobbish crowd, who thought former Nonconformist missionaries socially *infra dig* – even should one of them miraculously qualify as a medical doctor – so Dr Livingstone had been touched by Sir Roderick's loyalty. Although the two men had been friends for a decade, and Murchison had backed the doctor's epic trans-Africa journey – the first crossing of the continent by a European – Livingstone was painfully conscious that the fame and adulation he had enjoyed in the 1850s had not survived the deaths and disasters of his more recent Zambezi Expedition. His objective on that later occasion had been to prove that European traders and missionaries could navigate the Zambezi in steamships, and live and work safely near the Victoria Falls – 'discovered' by him in 1855. But despite an immense expenditure of money, time and effort, this ill-starred expedition had merely underlined the complete impracticability of its aims. The Zambezi – far from being, as he had promised it would be, 'God's Highway' into the interior 'for Christianity and commerce' – had turned out to be a malarial maze of shifting sandbanks leading to a chain of cataracts, whose local name 'Kebrabassa', meaning 'where the work ends', had proved to be cruelly apt. As disillusion had turned to anger, most of Livingstone's expedition colleagues had either resigned or quarrelled with him in public. Several died of malaria, as had his wife, Mary, along with five missionaries, two of their wives and three of their children. Even more disastrous in the eyes of the press, had been the death of the first Anglican bishop ever to make south central Africa his field of work, due entirely to Dr Livingstone's passionate appeal to him to come out there.

After his triumphant crossing of Africa, Livingstone had been lauded in the press not simply as a sublime explorer, but as a great missionary, 'a saintly and truly apostolic preacher of Christian truth'.[5] In the aftermath of the Zambezi Expedition, 'saintly' was the last adjective likely to be applied to him by any journalist. But if anything could help the doctor to atone for past failures, it was going to be an enterprise demanding extremes of selflessness and courage, as the Nile search undoubtedly would. The fact that he might very well die in Africa, if he accepted Murchison's invitation, had not tempered his eagerness to say yes. In truth, finding the source meant more to him than the restoration of his reputation – desirable though that undoubtedly was. Despite possessing many human weaknesses – and vanity was not the least – David Livingstone loved Africa and Africans, and saw his geographical quest as offering an unrepeatable chance to serve the continent and its people.

'Men may think I covet fame,' he told a friend, '[but] the Nile sources are valuable only as a means of enabling me to open my mouth with power among men. It is this power which I hope to apply to remedy an enormous evil.'[6] The 'evil' was the East African slave trade, which was then being energetically expanded by the coastal Arab-Swahili and by the Portuguese colonists of Mozambique. But if Livingstone could survive, and return as the discoverer of the Nile's source, he believed his agenda would be adopted by politicians with the consequence being a naval blockade of the East African coast and the closure of Zanzibar's slave market. Yet Livingstone's obsession with the Nile had other dimensions: such as its historical and scriptural significance.

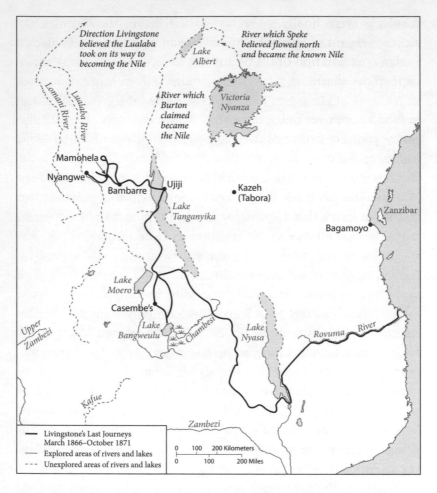

The Nile's Central African Watershed as Livingstone believed it to be
in the late 1860s.

'For more than sixteen hundred years,' he told his elder
daughter, Agnes, 'Emperors, Kings, Philosophers – all the great
men of antiquity – longed to know whence flowed the famous
river and longed in vain.'[7] But the Biblical resonance of the search
impressed him even more than its antiquity: 'An eager desire to
discover any evidence of the great Moses having visited these
parts bound me, spell bound me, I may say, for if I can bring to
light anything to confirm the Sacred Oracles, I shall not grudge
one whit all the labour expended.'[8] As he explained to Agnes,

if success were finally to be his: '[I will have] shown myself a worthy servant of Him who has endowed me to be an explorer.'[9] Such a confirmation of his usefulness to God would put worldly fame in the shade.

In June 1870, over four years after leaving the coast, Livingstone was at the very centre of Africa in the tiny village of Mamohela, which, as the crow flew, was about a thousand miles both from the east coast and from the west. Never had he felt so close to achieving his goal: 'I had a strong presentiment during the first three years that I should never live through the enterprise, but it weakened as I came near the end of the journey.'[10] He made this astonishingly self-confident statement about nearing the completion of his work, despite just having taken a year to travel 250 miles to Mamohela from the western shores of Lake Tanganyika. But now, he believed, the delays and disappointments were over. Only fifty miles lay between him and the banks of a mighty river, which local people called the Lualaba. Its width, they said, was two miles or more, and it was studded with tree-covered islands. Livingstone was tantalised. Because of its size and its location at the heart of Africa, and because it was said to flow north for hundreds of miles, it *had to be the Nile*. The only alternative was the Congo. But this seemed most unlikely. The 200 miles of the Congo, which had to-date been navigated from the Atlantic, had taken explorers not south-east, but *north*-east, away from the river on which he hoped to embark. So unless the Congo changed course completely, it could have no connection with the Lualaba.

Two years before, Livingstone had been exploring in an area 500 miles to the south of his present position, and had investigated a hitherto 'undiscovered' lake (Bangweulu), from which he was sure the Lualaba rose. 'The discovery [of the Nile's source] is unquestionably mine,' he had informed Agnes at the time.[11] Now, in order to prove that the Lualaba really was what he said it was, he needed to trace it downstream all the way to the Sudan and Egypt – a journey of more than 5,000 miles. But once he had bought canoes and was paddling down the river, the current would do much of the work. So what could stop him now, when he longed with every fibre of his being to finish his work? A lot as it happened.

In June 1870, just as he expected his problems to decline, they multiplied. All African explorers depended upon porters to carry the trade goods they needed in order to buy food and pay tolls to pass through the territories of individual chiefs. Indeed, without these goods, a traveller in Africa died, or, if he wished to go anywhere, was compelled to depend upon the charity of Arab-Swahili slave traders, who were most unlikely to be going just where he wanted. By mid-1870, most of Livingstone's original thirty-five porters, and all of the further twenty-four he had recruited in the interior, had died or deserted. So dependence on Arabs seemed inevitable.

On 26 June, he entered in his journal: 'With only three attendants, Susi, Chuma and Gardner, I started off to the north-west for the Lualaba.' He had been reduced to this pathetic number, because, on that same day, six of the nine men, who had been with him till then, had deserted, taking most of his trade goods with them. But fifty miles was not far, so perhaps he would be able to manage this distance with his three 'faithfuls', and without Arab help.

In the opening days of his journey, he was surprised to find local people friendly, although he was passing close to villages which Arab-Swahili slave traders had burned. It was the rainy season, and many streams flowed into the path he was travelling along, making it resemble a small river. A species of palm with long thick leaf-stalks had colonised the valley he now entered, obliging him to follow a track created by elephant and buffalo. In consequence, he and his men often fell into elephants' footprints up to their thighs. The going was so rough that Livingstone, a keen naturalist, was unable to write descriptions of the many birds and monkeys he was seeing for the first time.

Caught in the open, for hours on end, in drenching rain, he was obliged each evening to strip off his clothes, and dry them by a smoky fire in whatever hut he had managed to beg from villagers for himself and his men. Another bout of pneumonia, like one he had suffered eighteen months earlier, would very likely be the end of him.[12] Malaria had prostrated him many times, but now he was more worried about his worsening bowel and digestive problems.[13] Whenever his food was coarse, as it was at present, his piles bled heavily. His damaged teeth made so little impression on green maize and elephant meat that his stomach was left with too much to do. The result was constant heartburn. Many of his molars were so loose that he was obliged to perform extractions, employing 'a strong thread with what sailors call a clovehitch', and then 'striking the thread with a heavy pistol'.[14]

After a few days of independent travel, he was struggling to progress at all, and fell in with some slave traders, who suspected that he was only in Manyema to spy on them. Livingstone parted with beads and cloth from his depleted store, and obtained the assistance of additional porters, as well as their leaders' grudging consent to his accompanying them. 'They hated me,' he admitted, 'and tried to get away . . . I however kept up, and on the fourth day passed through nine villages destroyed by the worthies, who did not wish me to see more of their work.' One of these Arabs was stabbed to death in the night by a local African in revenge for the enslavement of his relatives.[15] Fortunately, at this point, Livingstone met up with Muhammad Bogharib, a less brutal slave trader, with whom he had often travelled in the past. Bogharib warned him that he would never reach the Lualaba by heading north-west. Instead he should swing south-west to allow for a loop in the river.

Livingstone did his best to follow Bogharib westward, but thick mud made each step an ordeal. When he was not slipping and falling in the rain, he was fording small rivers, 'neck deep'. In many places 'trees had fallen across the path forming a breast-high wall, which had to be climbed over'.[16] Ahead, the whole country was flooded. Livingstone pressed on for a few more days, but then, in mid-July, he wrote despairingly in his journal: 'For the first time in my life my feet failed me . . . Instead of healing quietly as heretofore, when torn by hard travel, irritable eating ulcers fastened on both feet.' He blamed his inability ever to dry his shoes. Having only three attendants, Livingstone knew there was no question of his being carried. So he had no choice but to limp back to Bambarre (Kabambare), the nearest significant Manyema town, which was also an Arab-Swahili slave-trading depot. He arrived there on 22 July 1870, numb with misery at his failure to reach the river.

For weeks the pain of his ulcers kept him awake at night, as did 'the wailing of slaves tortured with these sores'. The ulcers, he noted, 'eat through everything – muscle, tendon and bone, and often lame permanently if they do not kill'. With good reason he feared he might never recover. When placing either foot on the ground, 'a discharge of bloody ichor [sic] flowed'. The Arabs used crushed malachite to treat ulcers, or a salve of beeswax and sulphate of copper. The malachite, though it did not cure him, after many applications seemed at least to contain the spread of the sores.[17]

This was an Arab settlement. So, hating the slave trade as much as he did, it was cruelly ironic that Livingstone should have to remain on affable terms with slavers, who routinely murdered anyone resisting enslavement. Forty Manyema were killed one day, nine another, a hundred the day after that.[18] And so it went on. Often Livingstone saw smoke curling above burning villages, and heard distant shots. His one consolation was the thought that his written descriptions of the mayhem might one day compel the British government to act against the trade. The heartlessness of it provoked some of his most haunting descriptions, written while he was immobilised in Bambarre, close to many recently captured men, women and children. 'The strangest disease I have seen in this country seems really to be broken-heartedness, and it attacks free men who have been captured and made slaves.' He questioned many captives who were wasting away, apparently without physical cause. 'They ascribed their only pain to the heart, and placed a hand correctly on the spot, though many think that organ stands high up under the breast bone.'[19]

An Arab-Swahili slave trader murders a sick slave
(from *Livingstone's Last Journals*).

Livingstone's ability to be the friend of a man like Muhammad Bogharib owed a lot to his realisation that Arab treatment of domestic slaves was relatively mild. So, while the process by which Africans were torn from their homes was unspeakably brutal, and although they endured terrible suffering on their land and sea journeys to Zanzibar and the Gulf, Livingstone saw mitigation in the fact that their treatment on arrival was often better than that meted out to workers in British factories. His explanation of this paradox was that the Arabs were not yet thoroughly dominated by the profit motive – as were the plantation owners of the American Deep South. 'When society advances, wants multiply; and to supply these, the slaves' lot becomes harder. The distance between master and man increases as the lust of gain is developed.'[20]

All around him in Manyema, elephants were being shot, and chiefs forced to surrender their ivory. The trade in slaves was inextricably entwined with that in ivory, and Livingstone knew that the European passion for ivory piano keys, and for ivory knife-handles, had led to a vast increase in the number of slaves needed to carry tusks to the coast. So, in his eyes, responsibility for events in Manyema did not rest solely on Arab-Swahili shoulders. Nor could he find it in himself to dislike all Arabs. When he had been gravely ill a few months earlier, Muhammad Bogharib had nursed him and saved his life.[21]

The Arabs justified maltreating the Manyema by claiming that they were cannibals. Taking the side of Africans, as Livingstone always did, he remained sceptical. Even after surprising a Manyema man carrying a severed human finger, wrapped in a leaf, he was unconvinced that people were killed deliberately for magical or alimentary reasons.[22] He thought the Manyema 'a fine-looking race', and declared: 'I would back a company of Manyema men to be far superior in shape of head and generally in physical form too, against the whole Anthropological Society.'[23] Bogharib's men – and indeed his own – were terrified of being killed and eaten whenever large numbers of Manyema assembled. 'Poor things,' wrote Livingstone of these local people, 'no attack is thought of, if it does not begin on our side.'[24] As for cannibalism, he saw no need for it. 'The country abounds with food – goats, sheep, fowls, buffaloes and elephants: maize, sorghum . . . and other farinaceous eatables.'[25] Yet when James, one of his six deserters, was killed and eaten close to Bambarre, there was no denying his fate.[26] Other compelling evidence came Livingstone's way, unbidden. Slaves, who had died from hunger or disease, were being exhumed and then cooked and eaten. Reluctantly Livingstone conceded: 'I think they are cannibals, but not ostentatiously so.'[27] But the red parrot feathers, which many men wore in their hair, were nothing if not 'ostentatious', though they had struck him as charming until he had learned that a warrior only qualified to wear one if he had first killed a man.[28] Yet even when realising that Manyema were selling each other to the slavers, Livingstone never lost his conviction that they 'retained their natural kindness of disposition', and were never 'ferocious without cause', unless 'abused by Ujijians' or other intruders.[29] (The Ujijians were slave traders based at Ujiji on Lake Tanganyika.)

While confined to his hut, Livingstone longed for news of home, but no letters ever came for him via Ujiji, with the arrival of successive caravans.[30] At times he despaired of leaving for the Lualaba. 'This is the sorest delay I ever had,' he wrote in his journal, and he had experienced many in the past. His friend Muhammad Bogharib offered to go with him to the river when he was better, but Livingstone needed more than a temporary escort. He desperately required new men to replace his deserters. And because Bogharib stood to lose money in the ivory trade if he parted with any carriers, Livingstone offered the equivalent of £270 – a vast sum.[31] But this was to plan far ahead – until his feet healed, he would have to resign himself to many more months as an object of curiosity to the people of Bambarre. Though remarkably patient with villagers who stared, he drew the line when locals 'came and pushed off the door of my hut with a stick while I was resting, as we should do with a wild beast [in a] cage'. Occasionally, moments of pure comedy delighted him: as when he washed his hair and the watching audience fled, having mistaken the soapy lather for his brains being taken out for a wash.[32]

As 1870 dragged by, Livingstone immersed himself in the Bible, which he read through a total of four times.[33] He also pondered for days at a time Greek theories about the Nile's source. Homer had called the river, 'Egypt's heaven-descended spring', and because it flowed for 1,200 miles through the largest and driest desert in the world, at the hottest time of year, without requiring replenishment from a single tributary, Livingstone also thought it God-given and miraculous. At times, during his months of sickness, he lived in a trance-like state, with the Nile occupying what he called his 'waking dreams'.[34] It comforted him to rehearse a roll call of the ancients, who had 'recorded their ardent desire to know the fountains'. They too had had to endure frustration:

Alexander the Great, who founded a celebrated city at the river's mouth, looked up the stream with the same desire to know the springs, and so did the Caesars. The great Julius Caesar is made by Lucan to say that he would give up the civil war if he might but see the fountains of this far-famed river. Nero Caesar sent two centurions to examine the 'Caput Nili'.[35]

The centurions, according to Seneca – another name on Livingstone's reading list – travelled with their 200 soldiers further up the Nile than anyone would manage until the mid-nineteenth century, ascending the river as far as the Bahr el-Ghazal (a White Nile tributary, briefly thought to be the main channel) and the marshes of the Sudd. Braving tribesmen's attacks, overpowering heat and clouds of mosquitoes, they came at last through the shimmering haze 'to immense swamps, the end of which neither the natives knew, nor is it possible for anyone to hope to know'.[36] It would be 1841 – almost 2,000 years later – before the Egyptian ruler, Muhammad Ali, sent an expedition that succeeded in penetrating the Sudd's 300-mile maze of papyrus-choked channels. Only one of the nineteenth-century explorers, who subsequently struggled upstream through the Sudan and Equatoria, won more than faint praise from the exacting Dr Livingstone.

None rises higher in my estimation than Miss Tinné, who after the severest domestic afflictions, nobly persevered in the teeth of every difficulty ... [she] came further up the river than the centurions sent by Nero Ceasar [she had passed Gondokoro and reached Rejaf], and showed such indomitable pluck as to reflect honour on her race.[37]

Alexine Tinné, Holland's richest heiress, lost her mother and an aunt to fever while navigating the Bahr el-Ghazal. When Livingstone was penning his praise for her, he had no means of knowing that she had already been hacked to death by Tuaregs, during a valiant attempt to reach the Nile's source by crossing the Sahara, and then heading east through Chad to strike the river, she hoped, near its head.[38] As for Livingstone's fellow Britons, Richard Burton, John Speke and Samuel Baker – he wrote little about these younger rivals, except to criticise them. For why praise explorers, who seemed certain to be 'cut out' by his Bangweulu 'Nile' sources, which were so far south of their entire sphere of operation?

Livingstone's confidence that the Lualaba was the Nile received an unexpected boost while he was confined to his dark and smoky hut in Bambarre. Two Arab ivory traders arrived in mid-August, after a long journey that had taken them to Katanga and beyond. Their names were Josut and Moenpembé and what they said electrified the sick man. Their information was that Lake Bangweulu was not the only source of the Lualaba. A nearby spring, to the west of the lake, gave rise to a river, which, after joining with the waterway that issued from Bangweulu, flowed on northward as the Lualaba. So there were *two* sources of the Lualaba. The Arabs also announced that near to these north-facing sources, there were two additional springs, whose waters flowed to the south. What thrilled Livingstone was their account's uncanny resemblance to what had been written about the Nile's source by Herodotus, ancient Greece's most famous historian.

In 457 BC, Herodotus had visited Egypt and travelled up the Nile as far as the first cataract, eager to discover whatever he could about the river's origins. He would be largely disappointed. From a variety of Egyptian and Greek travellers, he learned that the river probably came from far to the west, from the country we now know as Chad, but no convincing detail was volunteered. On returning home, Herodotus wrote: 'Not one writer of the Egyptians, or of the Libyans, or of the Hellenes, who came to speak with me, professed to know anything, except the scribe of the sacred treasury of Athene at the city of Sais in Egypt.'[39] But this one scribe made up for the vagueness of the historian's other informants. Between two mountains, he said, could be found 'the fountains of the Nile, fountains which it is impossible to fathom: half the water runs northward into Egypt; half to the south'. Although Herodotus had sensed that 'the scribe did not seem to be in earnest', Livingstone believed he had been. This was because the scribe's version tallied so closely with Josut's and Moenpembé's. There was one difference. The scribe had mentioned two mountains between the four sources, whereas the Arabs had mentioned 'a mound between them, the most remarkable in Africa'.⁴⁰ But, in Livingstone's opinion, this difference seemed too small to worry about. A remarkable mound was likely to be a colossal feature: perhaps a range of mountains. Nor was he being naive to have believed the Arabs. The oral accounts of travellers often turned out to be true, and he knew already that the sources of the Zambezi, and the Kafue, were within a hundred miles of Bangweulu – so two southward-flowing rivers existed in reality.

The presence of mountains near the northward-flowing sources delighted Livingstone for another reason. In about AD 150, the Greek astronomer and geographer, Claudius Ptolemaeus – Ptolemy, as he is generally known – had stated, in his *Geography*, that after marching for twenty-five days into the interior from somewhere near Mombasa, a traveller would arrive at 'the snowy range of mountains from whence the Nile draws its twin sources'. Ptolemy had this information from the report of a Greek trader, Diogenes, who, on returning from a voyage to India a century earlier, had landed on the East African coast, where he claimed to have reached the sources after a twenty-five-day march. This would not have taken him far inland. More likely, he had heard from Arab traders that, while in the interior, they had learned about the existence of sources close to snow-peaks known as the Mountains of the Moon.⁴¹ Livingstone found this compelling:

What we moderns can claim is rediscovery . . . The headwaters of the Nile are gathered into two or three arms, very much as was depicted by Ptolemy . . . [he] was not believed because his sources were between 10 and 12 north latitude.

This was, of course, where Livingstone had found Lake Bangweulu and where Josut and Moenpembé had just been.⁴² The recuperating explorer found this additional Greek endorsement of his own view of the Nile's sources wonderfully reassuring.

By 10 October, Livingstone's ulcers were starting to heal, and for the first time since 22 July he was able to leave his hut. Just as he was making plans to move on, he heard that the leader of a trading party from Ujiji had reported that a second caravan was *en route* for Manyema 'with letters and perhaps people for me'.⁴³

Clearly, he would have to wait till they came, before heading for the river. And wait he did, very reluctantly, until 4 February the following year. 'I am in agony for news from home; all I feel sure of now is that my friends will want me to finish my work.'[44] Also on the 4th, ten men arrived who had been sent from the coast by Dr John Kirk, the acting British Consul at Zanzibar. Livingstone was enraged to find that these new arrivals were slaves and not freemen. Almost at once these men, who were owned by Indian coastal traders (known as *banians*), told him they would not move except for higher wages, and claimed that Consul Kirk had instructed them to force him back to Zanzibar as soon as possible. Only when Livingstone threatened the men's leaders with his pistol would they agree to march.[45]

Even after reading about the public rows on the Zambezi Expedition, it would have amazed the Rev. Dr Livingstone's contemporaries to know that he sometimes threatened to shoot Africans. In fact he had once fired at Susi, one of his three longest-serving attendants, who had been with him since 1863, and still was. Susi's offence had been to seize Livingstone's hand roughly, and to refuse to let it go. So Livingstone had fired at him, and had very fortunately missed. This incident would be cut from the published version of Livingstone's *Last Journals* by the clergyman editor appointed by his family, as would many others which showed his 'faithfuls' in an unflattering light.

There being no law or magistrate higher than myself, I would not be thwarted if I could help it . . . They would like me to remain here and pay them for smoking the *bange* [cannabis], and deck their prostitutes with the beads which I give them regularly for their food.[46]

Despite the reputation for devoted behaviour which they would later enjoy in Britain, his followers were as different from the members of a Sunday School as it would be possible to imagine.

It is doubtful whether any of his men understood why he was prepared to travel in the rainy season, risking his life and theirs. Why did the direction of rivers matter so much? Why could he not rest more and enjoy his life? There is no evidence that Livingstone ever tried to explain. Before he left Bambarre, two of his favourites, Chuma and Gardner, brought him close to despair by taking part in an Arab attack on local Manyema. Gardner actually returned, dragging after him a woman he had captured. Chuma came 'caricolling [*sic*] in front of the party . . . mimicking shooting'.[47] Chuma had been a boy of ten when released by Livingstone from a slave gang near Lake Nyasa (Malawi) in 1861, and, like Gardner, had spent several years at the Nassick Mission School in Bombay, having been left there by Livingstone in 1864. 'Christian boys from Nassick,' Livingstone shouted at them both, '[should] not need to be told not to murder.' Chuma countered that in 1863, in the Shire Highlands, Livingstone had fought the Ajawa (Yao) and had shot at them. 'Yes,' Livingstone retorted, 'to make slaves free, but you want to make free people slaves.'[48] (The Yao had been allies of Portuguese slave traders.)

As he was preparing to leave Bambarre, several of the men who had deserted him the previous June asked to be taken back. Mabruki (another Nassick pupil) was allowed to stay, but Livingstone told Ibrahim and Simon 'to be off or [he] would certainly shoot them'. Simon had admitted to two murders and Ibrahim to numerous thefts, so their master's fury with them was understandable.[49] He left for the Lualaba on 16 February 1871, with Muhammad Bogharib's caravan and his own fourteen men.

The grass and mud are grievous, but my men lift me over the waters . . . The country is everywhere beautiful and undulating: light green grass covers it all, save at the brooks . . . Grass tears the hands and wets the extremities.[50]

Early in the journey, Katomba, a slave-trading associate of Bogharib, presented Livingstone with an eighteen-inch-tall female gorilla. He judged this motherless infant: 'The most intelligent and charming of all the monkeys I have seen. She holds out her hand to be lifted and carried, and if refused makes her face [resemble] a bitter human, weeping.' It dismayed Livingstone not to be able to take her with him. 'I fear that she will die . . . from people plaguing her.'[51] The rains had not quite ended, but there was sunshine too, and as so often in the past, Livingstone enjoyed the beauty of villages nestling between tree-covered hills.

Soon after dawn, he loved to see people sitting outside their huts around a fire when the low rays of the sun were just appearing.

The various-shaped leaves of the forest all around their village are bespangled with myriads of dewdrops. The cocks crow vigorously and strut and ogle; the kids [goats] gambol and leap on the backs of their dams . . . thrifty wives often bake their new clay pots in a fire, made by lighting a heap of grass roots . . . The beauty of this morning scene of peaceful enjoyment is indescribable.[52]

Yet Livingstone was accompanying people who could change in an instant this peaceful tableau to one of death and misery. Days later, Livingstone was thankful to be travelling independently again. In exchange for his double-barrelled gun, Katomba lent him seven men. Since Bogharib had left him to go in search of slaves and ivory, the extra men would be indispensable.[53] Livingstone's main problem was a dearth of canoes, which began to worry him seriously as he came within six miles of the river. The nearest vessels were said to be about five days' journey away across a region criss-crossed with shallow rivers. On 11 March he was told by Amur, yet another slave trader, that there was no point in trying to progress along the Lualaba unless he could muster 200 guns. All the people for miles around, said Amur, hated strangers and 'wanted a white one to eat!'[54] Of course, Livingstone ignored this warning. He knew very well that most of the slavers wanted to drive him back eastwards, away from their profitable new slave frontier.

Crossing many streams that flowed into the Lualaba – now three miles distant – he was depressed to meet a party of slavers with eighty-two captives and twenty tusks. He travelled the final miles to the river with this party's leaders, Abed bin Salim and Hassani, who when questioned, swore to him that they 'never began hostilities'. 'They began nothing else,' he countered in his journal. 'The prospect of getting slaves overpowers all else, and blood flows in horrid streams.'[55] Although the last day of March was an unforgettable one for Livingstone, he described the river clinically and without emotion in his journal:

I went down to take a good look at the Lualaba here [at the town of Nyangwe]. It is narrower than it is higher up, but still a mighty river, at least 3,000 yards broad, and always deep: it can never be waded at any point . . . It has many large islands . . . The current is about two miles an hour away to the north.[56]

During the three days following his first sight of the Lualaba's wide expanse of smooth and slow-moving brown water, he made numerous attempts to buy canoes from local people, but all failed. Four days later, a local Manyema chief agreed to sell him a dugout large enough to hold him and all his men. But the one that actually arrived turned out to be able to carry no more than three people.[57] The Manyema's refusal to sell canoes and dugouts was entirely rational. They feared that if strangers were to cross the river they would extend the slave trade to the left bank. But, as Livingstone realised, this reluctance was already encouraging the slavers to take dugouts by force. Only Dr Livingstone, the man of peace, was being denied what he so desperately needed. He described: 'Waiting wearily and anxiously [while] the owners of canoes say, "Yes, yes; we shall bring them," but do not stir.' His lack of progress obliged Livingstone to ask his followers to build him a wooden house, so that he could leave the vermin-ridden hut he had been loaned.[58]

The ten men who had recently arrived from Zanzibar – and whom he had been shocked to learn were slaves – now began to make life even harder for their master by telling the local Manyema: 'He does not wish slaves and ivory, but a canoe in order to kill Manyema.' Livingstone soon discovered that slavers, like Hassani and Abed, had 'aided [his] men in propagating the false accusation'. Not surprisingly, the Arab-Swahili wanted to stop Livingstone spying on them as they extended their activities north and west of Nyangwe. As for his followers, their attitude was easy to understand. No African or Arab had ever followed the Lualaba downstream for more than 100 miles north of Nyangwe, and it scared all Livingstone's men to contemplate venturing into an unknown region, peopled by tribes who had every reason to hate new arrivals. Understandably, his men wanted to return home at once, rather than die in this remote and frightening place.

By mid-May Livingstone still had no canoe, and now Abed added to his anxieties by telling him he had overheard his men – the recent arrivals from Zanzibar – plotting to kill him. 'He advised me strongly not to trust myself to them anymore.' Since they admitted that they had shot three men and had been capturing and selling people, Livingstone realised that this was good advice.[59] But without these ten slaves, how could he finish his work? He could hardly travel thousands of miles with four men. As usual, when he was worried, Livingstone's bowels started to plague him.

His next venture was to try to buy dugouts from the Wenya people, who lived on the left bank. But the Arabs chose this moment to buy up all the Wenya vessels that had until then been available for sale, 'nine large canoes – and I could not secure one'.[60] Eventually, on 5 July, in desperation, he offered Dugumbé, a leading slave trader in Nyangwe, £400 to provide him with ten porters to replace the mutinous slaves sent by Consul Kirk from Zanzibar. But even this vast sum could not persuade Dugumbé to help a man, whom the Arab was sure would one day expose his bloody record, if given the chance. In mid-month, Livingstone was finally reduced to pleading. 'I have goods at Ujiji . . . take them all and give me men to finish my work . . . do not let me be forced to return now I am so near the end of my undertaking.' But Dugumbé merely said he would consult his associates and report back.[61] The Arab had still not answered Livingstone by 15 July, the day on which an event took place in Nyangwe that changed everything.

One of the only places where Livingstone had felt able to forget his worries had been Nyangwe's market, where up to 3,000 people came to buy and sell. That day there were half that many, but he found it no less enjoyable to watch the market women, old and young, laughing and joking as they bartered their earthen pots for cassava, palm-oil, salt, pepper, and relishes

Massacre of the Manyema women in Nyangwe
(from *Livingstone's Last Journals*).

for their food. Local fish of many varieties were also for sale, and Livingstone loved the bustle: children carrying squawking fowls, a pig breaking free, sellers throwing up their hands after failing to convince a potential customer of the value of a goat or sheep. The weather was so hot and sultry that he did not stay as long as usual. As he was leaving, he was surprised to see five Arab-Swahili in their white robes come into the market carrying guns. Until now, whenever he had been in this place, the Arabs had respected the local custom never to bring arms there. Livingstone was shaken to note that three of these armed men worked for Dugumbé; but while he was considering whether to reprove them, they began firing into the throng, killing people at point-blank range. A moment later, as screams echoed around him, other Arabs fired into a crowd of terrified people fleeing towards the creek where their canoes were moored. Pandemonium followed, with men and women flinging themselves into canoes, either swamping vessels, or making it impossible for anyone to paddle. The press of numbers in the creek soon prevented canoes from getting out into the river, away from the guns. So wounded men and women ignored the boats and scrambled into the water, hoping to swim against the current to an island a mile away. In horror Livingstone watched overloaded canoes sinking, and the long line of heads making for the island beginning to thin out, as one by one the swimmers drowned. The firing had been so frenzied near the creek that the Arabs had actually shot several of their own number there. They later reckoned that 400 were shot or drowned. Livingstone suspected this was an underestimate. 'No-one will ever know the exact loss on this bright and sultry morning; it gave me the impression of being in Hell.'

While people were still drowning, Dugumbé arrived at the creek and 'put people into one of the deserted vessels to save those in the water'. But since his men had started the firing, Livingstone was not mollified by these humane acts. He knew the attacks had been concerted 'to make an impression in the country as to the importance and greatness of the newcomers'. Even while Dugumbé had been saving people from the water, men under the orders of Tagamoio, an associate of his, continued the reign of terror on land 'shooting right and left like fiends'. Although Dugumbé claimed to have told Tagamoio to stop, he continued the slaughter into the following day, burning twenty-seven villages around Nyangwe. Livingstone wrote in anguish:

Who could accompany the people of Dugumbé and Tagamoio . . . and be free from blood-guiltiness? . . . The open murder perpetrated on hundreds of unsuspecting women fills me with unspeakable horror.

It was now out of the question for him to go anywhere with Arabs. But could Livingstone trust his ten slaves and four loyal men to stay with him on a journey of thousands of miles down the Lualaba, contending with cataracts, and facing hostile people on the banks day after day? When his Zanzibari slaves told him next day they would prefer to follow Tagamoio and capture slaves, Livingstone knew that his situation was hopeless.

The terrible scenes of man's inhumanity to man brought on severe headache . . . I was laid up all yesterday afternoon with depression at the bloodshed . . . I cannot stay here in agony.

David Livingstone left for Ujiji with his fourteen men and an unknown number of women on 20 July. He had been delayed at the last moment by one of his slaves, who had pretended to be ill, so that he and his fellows gained 'time to negotiate for women with whom they had cohabited'. Disgusted by his followers, and traumatised by the killings, against his will Livingstone was turning his back on the river that had carried all his hopes. On the very edge of achieving something more wonderful than all his past achievements combined, everything had been snatched from him. The best he could hope for was to reach Lake Tanganyika and Ujiji in three or four months' time, and from there send letters to Zanzibar appealing for new and more carefully chosen men and supplies to be sent from the coast. With luck, they might arrive ten months after a caravan had departed with his letters. After that it might be another six months or more before he was back at Nyangwe.[62] Twenty months in all, or two years – time which his age and health told him he might not have.

Once again he was struggling through an immense and impenetrable forest, where the light of the sun was filtered by the canopy to a dim haze. In the semi-darkness, the sense of isolation was overwhelming – as was the constant fear. Livingstone felt as if he were running the gauntlet, with hidden spearmen waiting to strike on either side, believing that 'if they killed [him] they would be revenging the death of relations'. How ironic if the man who longed to expose the traders should die because mistaken for one of them.

From each hole in the tangled mass we looked for a spear; and each moment expected to hear the rustle which told of deadly weapons hurled. I became weary with the constant strain of danger, and – as I suppose happens with soldiers on the field of battle – not courageous, but perfectly indifferent whether I were killed or not.

Then one morning, when he was threading his way along 'a narrow path with a wall of dense vegetation touching each hand, a large spear almost grazed [his] back, and stuck firmly into the soil'.[63] Another spear whipped by less than a foot ahead of him. He and his men fired into the foliage, but hit no one.

Though he meant to do everything in his power to return to Manyema, Livingstone feared he might never see the Lualaba

'A large spear . . . stuck firmly into the soil'
(from *Livingstone's Last Journals*).

again. In the meantime, the world's geographers would be left knowing that there was, at the heart of Africa, an immense northward-flowing river, the ultimate direction of which they could only guess at.

TWO

A Great Misalliance

In November 1853, eighteen years before Dr Livingstone stumbled away from the Lualaba in despair, a man whom the doctor would come to detest for what he called 'his bestial immorality',[1] booked in at Shepheard's Hotel in Cairo. His name was Lieutenant Richard Francis Burton, and he intended, while recovering from dysentery, to work on a mould-breaking travel book. His hope – even expectation – was that its subject would make him famous.[2] While writing up his recent Arabian adventure, Burton had no premonition that before he left Cairo the geographical goals of his 'mania for discovery' – as he himself described his wanderlust – would have changed decisively.[3]

During a year's leave from the 18th Regiment of Bombay Native Infantry, the 32-year-old officer had completed the pilgrimage to Mecca disguised as a Muslim peddler of medicines and horoscopes. Whether he would have been killed if unmasked is far from certain, although Burton meant to give that impression. His book could only create a sensation if he appeared to have risked a public beheading, or a knife in the back. Before setting out, he had not only chosen his identity as an Afghan Sufi, but to be safe had arranged to be circumcised.[4] His voluntary subjection of himself to this painful procedure would not stop critics calling his pilgrimage a theatrical sham.

In truth, the *hajj* had been successfully completed only forty years earlier by the Swiss explorer, Johann Ludwig Burckhardt, who had entered Mecca dressed as a Muslim merchant, and had published no fewer than four fat volumes about the experience. Over the centuries, numerous self-professed converts to Islam had made the journey openly as Westerners, in perfect safety. But Burton's passion for disguise – which his gift for languages facilitated – ran very deep. While working for General Napier's intelligence section in Sindh, India, he had already assumed a false identity as an Iranian traveller in fine linens. For a man who was alienated from his British origins, missions requiring him to assume alternative identities had helped him reinvent himself as 'Ruffian Dick', a perpetual maverick and outsider. He would claim that while staying at Shepheard's in Cairo, he wore his Arab clothes to dismay his fellow-European guests into thinking they were under the same roof as an Arab. They would have disapproved even more had they known that 'the Arab' was really an Englishman, who had recently visited a nearby brothel, where, as he told a friend, he had participated in 'a precious scene of depravity . . . beating the Arabian Nights all to chalks!'[5]

Though born in the respectable seaside town of Torquay on England's south coast, Burton had spent much of his childhood and adolescence travelling from town to town in France, Italy and Sicily at the whim of his hypochondriac father, who, after retiring early from the British Army as a lieutenant-colonel, had left England for the sake of his health. This was not improved when his two teenage sons took to visiting local brothels and having love affairs with married women. On several occasions the threat of scandal caused sudden departures from otherwise pleasant places.

Richard, who was Joseph Burton's second son, was sent briefly to England: at first to a third-rate private school in Brighton and later to Trinity College, Oxford, where he deliberately contrived his own sending down to stop his father forcing him into Holy Orders. Burton's experiences in his native land had convinced him that he would never feel comfortable with his fellow-countrymen. In India, he had been equally ill at ease in the company of civil servants of the East India Company and their wives, and scornfully described middle-class 'society' in the sub-continent as being 'like that of a small county town suddenly raised to the top of a tree [where it] lost its head accordingly'.[6]

By becoming fluent in Hindustani, Marathi and Gujerati, he got to know the local people, and at the same time gained promotion in his regiment. He studied with *munshis* (Indian teachers), and was not displeased when his visits to their homes led to his being called a 'white nigger'.[7] He liked to shock respectable people, provided it caused no lasting offence to his military superiors. Most officers – and he was no exception – had Indian mistresses; but since this fact was never mentioned in public, it carried no stigma. Burton despised ostentatious piety and deplored attempts made by missionaries to convert colonised peoples. Yet he was no liberal, and his respect for Indian culture did not stop him kicking servants and boasting of 'well deserved beatings'. In truth, he believed in British superiority and was a convinced imperialist.[8]

Outwardly sure of himself, his opinions were often contradictory or ambivalent. Indeed, Burton regretted that his peripatetic early life had left him rootless and unattached. He believed that if his father had only sent him to Eton, he would have found his passage through life far easier.

In consequence of being brought up abroad, I never thoroughly understood English society, nor did society understand me . . . it is a real advantage to belong to some parish . . . In the contrary condition you are a waif, a stray; you are a blaze of light without a focus.[9]

He found his 'parish' and his 'focus' by entering the Arab world, and through dangerous journeys like the pilgrimage to Mecca.

Yet despite his fluency in Arabic, Persian and Sanskrit, and his justifiable pride in being an outstanding Arabist, he could never fully take on the mental, as well as the physical, clothing of a true Bedouin. His enjoyment of being in the desert, and dressing as an Arab, weakened his sense of his English self but did not replace it. He neither converted to Islam nor gave up his military career, despite his continuing need to escape from 'civilised life' and from the social conventions of his class. The result was a dissatisfaction with himself that was only appeased by visiting wild places.[10]

'Man wants to wander and he must do so, or he shall die,' he wrote while still in Cairo.[11] Because he was dismayed to have no new adventure in prospect, he was overjoyed when an old friend, Dr John Stocks, who had served with him as a medical officer in Sindh, arrived at Shepheard's Hotel with news that the Royal Geographical Society wanted to sponsor an expedition to Somaliland (later Somalia). Burton wrote at once to Dr Norton Shaw, the RGS's secretary, whom he knew already, thanks to the society's sponsorship of his journey to Mecca, and confided his keenness to lead any future expedition to Somaliland. In parentheses Burton mentioned to Shaw that the Bombay government would have sent an exploring expedition to East Africa a year before, if the man appointed to lead it had not suddenly pulled out because of 'not relishing the chance of losing his cod'. It was said that the Somalis were 'in the habit of cutting them off and hanging them as ornaments round their arms'. This alarmist talk did not bother *him*, Burton assured Shaw, and since he expected to have recovered his health within a few months, he would be ready to start for Somaliland early in 1854 after the hot season was over. But that was not all. What he wished to do too, he explained, was go on to Zanzibar from Somaliland and then head eastward into the African interior.

'You will ask why I now prefer Zanzibar to Arabia,' he went on, before explaining that a German missionary called Krapf had recently 'arrived (in Cairo) from Zanzibar with [talk of his] discoveries about [the source] of the White Nile, Kilimanjaro & Mts of Moon which reminds one of a "de Lunatico". I have not seen him,' Burton admitted, 'but don't intend to miss the spectacle'.[12] Despite the humorously dismissive tone of his letter, Burton was madly excited by Krapf's remarks. Like Livingstone, he knew all about Ptolemy's report of Diogenes' claim to have located 'the Mountains of the Moon, from which the lakes of the Nile receive the snows'.[13] And now this German missionary, Dr Johann Ludwig Krapf, was asserting that in May 1848 his missionary colleague, Johann Rebmann, had become the first European to see a snowy mountain peak in sub-Saharan Africa. Its local name was Kilimanjaro, and it was 175 miles inland from the coast. In the following year, Krapf gained a distant view of Mount Kenya, another snow-mountain, a hundred miles to the north-west. Then Burton heard something really startling that Krapf was telling people. 'When in Ukumbani [the area of both mountains], I heard of a mighty inland sea, the end of which was not to be reached after a hundred days'.[14] So there were two snow mountains in East Africa and also a lake – or possibly two – again as Ptolemy had stated – perhaps fed by glacier water flowing from the as yet undiscovered 'Mountains of the Moon', placed by the Greek geographer just south of the lakes. Mounts Kilimanjaro and Kenya were said by the missionaries not to give rise to any rivers, but the existence of snow-clad summits south of the equator seemed to point to the probable existence of other tall mountains, perhaps an entire range.

Burton suggested to Shaw that these recent discoveries could turn Krapf into his [Burton's] 'John the Baptist'. This blasphemous comparison of himself with Christ would have entertained Burton, as would its arrogant subtext that he would now complete what the missionary had merely started.[15] Krapf did not stay long in Cairo, and it is doubtful whether Burton actually met him. So he would not learn for several years that in Masailand, with his colleague Rebmann, Krapf had narrowly escaped being killed by a group of Masai warriors who had butchered their African porters almost to a man.[16] But, at this date, Burton did at least know that, in 1844, a young French naval officer, Lieutenant M. Maizan, journeying inland from the coast, had been caught, tied to a tree, mutilated and then beheaded by tribesmen – another clear indication that trying to reach the Nile's source from Mombasa or Zanzibar, rather than directly upstream from Egypt, was unlikely to be problem-free.[17]

So why not try the direct route up the Nile? Throughout recorded history it had been blocked by the swamps of the Sudd. But in 1841, the Egyptian viceroy, Muhammad Ali Pasha, a modernising Francophile, had sent an expedition of several boats commanded by Selim Bimbashi, a corpulent Turkish captain, who, accompanied by his favourite concubine and a eunuch, had forced a way through the floating islands of aquatic vegetation, and had then sailed on to Gondokoro, 700 miles south of Khartoum as the crow flies.[18] The Upper Nile had thus become viable for traders, missionaries, big-game hunters and adventurers. So, for two decades, a motley group of people launched a series of uncoordinated attempts to reach the source. Because they lacked proper funding, exploration had to be fitted in with trading or with sporting pursuits. Andrew Melly, a Liverpool businessman, had plenty of money, but he made his Nile attempt purely for pleasure in the company of his son, his daughter and his wife. Their tinned salmon, champagne and other provisions had been purchased at Fortnum & Mason, and they had no intention of risking their lives. Even so, Melly died of fever at Shendi near Khartoum in 1850.[19]

Most of the Europeans who travelled south at this time were Frenchmen and Italians hoping to get rich in the ivory trade. Instead, the majority died of malaria. More successful was a determined Maltese trader, technically a British subject. By 1851 the moustachioed, cane-carrying Andrea De Bono employed 400 men as porters and boatmen in his ivory company. Occasionally he would capture a lion and sell it to a zoo or menagerie. De Bono's enemies swore that he and his nephew bought and sold human beings as well as exotic animals. At this time, De Bono moved his headquarters south from the slaving town of Khartoum to distant Gondokoro, described by one traveller as 'that Babylon of prostitution'.[20] From this stinking, rat-infested string of slave and ivory camps beside the Nile, De Bono, and his friends and business partners, launched themselves up the river. But a combination of cerebral malaria, cataracts and hostile Africans defeated them. In 1853, while Richard Burton was writing his book in Cairo, entirely unknown to him De Bono travelled up the Nile once again and passed through the land of the Bari and the Obbo to within eighty miles of Lake Albert. A few years later, Jules Verne would pay tribute to the Maltese trader's achievement in his adventure novel, *Five Weeks in a Balloon,* by having one of his characters look down through binoculars and spot De Bono's initials, which he had carved on a rock on an island, near Fola Rapids. 'It is the signature of the traveller who has gone farthest up the course of the Nile!'[21] Although other attempts were soon made – several ending tragically – De Bono's most southerly point would not be bettered until 1860 when the extraordinary Italian polymath, Giovanni Miani – who had written operas and been a professional wood carver before starting to trade in ivory – struggled as far south as modern Nimule, near the present Ugandan border, before being forced back by illness and an attack by Madi tribesmen.[22] Miani would die in 1872, aged sixty-one, still trading on the upper Nile and its tributaries. His last written words were: 'Adieu so many great hopes: the dreams of my life.'[23] Since De Bono and Miani did not know precisely how close they had been to making significant discoveries, the world would remain ignorant of their achievements.

Blissfully unaware of what had been happening on the upper Nile, Burton stayed on in Cairo for three leisurely months, only leaving in mid-January 1854. On reaching India in mid-February, he delayed till April before submitting to the Bombay government his application for leave of absence and permission to explore Somaliland, and then head south and travel into the interior from Zanzibar. Since it was not unusual for favoured officers to be given paid leave in which to make journeys likely to increase the company's knowledge of the lands bordering its territories, he was not surprised when the required permission was formally confirmed by the East India Company in London, and a grant of £1,000 was promised.[24] But he was appalled to be given only a year's leave of absence since this would make it all but impossible to attempt his all-important second objective: a journey into the heart of the continent from Zanzibar to find the Nile's source. How disappointed he was can easily be imagined after reading this declaration in his application to the Bombay government. Despite the maddeningly pedantic style of the communication, his passionate desire to solve the age-old mystery shines through:

It may be permitted me to observe that I cannot contemplate without enthusiasm, the possibility of bringing my compass to bear upon the Jebel Hamar, those 'Mountains of the Moon' ... a range white with eternal snows even in the blaze of the African summer, supposed to be the father of the mysterious Nile ... a tract invested with all the romance of wild fable and hoar antiquity, to this day the [most] worthwhile subject to which human energy could be devoted. For unnumbered centuries, explorers have attempted the unknown source of the 'White River' by voyaging and travelling and literally against the stream. I shall be the first to try by a more feasible line to begin with the head.[25]

The thought of finding the Nile's source now became for Burton 'the *mot de l'énigme*, the way to make the egg stand upright, the rending of the veil of Isis'. and, of course, the way to become a great deal more famous than his journey to Mecca was ever likely to make him.[26] But that would have to wait till he could persuade his employer to grant him more time. But a year might nevertheless be long enough to bring back a wealth of new information about Somaliland and its people – enough, perhaps, to persuade the grandees of the East India Company to send him to find the Nile's source.

To prepare for his expedition, Burton arrived at the coaling station of Aden, on the southern Arabian coast, in advance of the men he had chosen as expedition members. Later, he would claim that it was entirely due to advice tendered by the over-cautious British Political Resident, Brigadier James Outram, that he decided to journey without his fellow officers into south-eastern Ethiopia to visit Harar, which was then considered to be Islam's fourth most holy city, after Mecca, Medina and the Dome of the Rock in Jerusalem.[27] In truth, he had never intended to take any colleague with him, and had always planned to claim sole credit for becoming the first European to enter this fiercely religious place, which was said to be closed to foreign visitors and therefore dangerous to enter. That Burton was eager to upstage his companions in a reprise of his Mecca adventure would not have mattered if one of them had not been destined to become his partner on his next and far more important East Africa journey, targeting the Nile's source.

Burton had wanted to take to Somaliland his friend Dr John E. Stocks, a military surgeon, who is thought to have circumcised him before his trip to Mecca. But Stocks, who lived hard – 'an excellent chap, but a mad bitch' according to his friend – died of a sudden cerebral haemorrhage, and so Burton was left looking for a last-minute replacement.[28] He had already chosen Lieutenant William Stroyan of the Indian Navy, and Lieutenant G. E. Herne, who had both worked on the Sindh survey with him. Then pure chance delivered to him the man who would be his nemesis, and whose well-merited place in the pantheon of the world's greatest explorers Burton would later work so hard to obliterate. Right on cue, Lieutenant John Hanning Speke – 'Jack' to his friends – stepped ashore on a hot day in mid-September 1854 at Steamer Point, Aden, from a P&O steamship from Calcutta. One of the greatest misalliances in history was about to begin, without either party having the least presentiment of trouble ahead.

THREE

A Rush of Men Like a Stormy Wind

———— ◁◁◁◁◁ ————

Most of Richard Burton's many biographers have seen John Hanning Speke as a being inferior to their own complex and multi-talented subject in virtually every respect.[1] But Burton himself did not make the same mistake. Almost twenty years after the two men had first met – by which time Burton would have long since come to detest the man and his memory – he could still vividly recall the favourable impression which Speke had made upon him.

A man of lithe, spare form, about six feet tall, blue-eyes, tawny-maned; the old Scandinavian type, full of energy and life, with a highly nervous temperament, a token of endurance, and long wiry, but not muscular limbs that could cover the ground at a swinging pace.[2]

Jack Speke's willowy figure, his fair-skinned, fresh-faced good looks, and his assured but reserved manner, contrasted strikingly with Burton's swarthy, almost oriental appearance, and his dark-eyed, melodramatic presence. As tall as Speke, and broader shouldered, Burton, with his high cheekbones, black hair and luxuriant moustache, looked exotic and foreign – rather gypsy-like – although he sprang from the English upper-middle-class, as did the new arrival. Burton's face often bore an expression of ferocious cynicism, which one of his recent biographers has attributed to resentment of his superiors in India for failing to appreciate his merits.[3] His heavy brows and darkly brooding expressions sometimes led acquaintances, and even friends, to call his appearance Satanic.[4] But it was the sociable Richard Burton, and not his fiercely combative *doppelgänger*, who greeted Speke under the dark cliffs of Aden's extinct volcano.

Jack Speke had just been to see Brigadier Outram, who, as Political Resident of this recently snatched British outpost, ruled it with paternal zeal, and had conscientiously refused the young officer permission to cross the Gulf of Aden to hunt game in Somaliland and Ethiopia because 'the Somalis were the most savage of all African savages' and would very likely kill him.[5] But if Lieutenant Speke could persuade Lieutenant Burton to take him with him on his expedition, then Outram would be delighted to change his mind and even ask the East India Company to allow him to serve on full pay.

Later, Burton would claim that in 1854 Speke had been an inexperienced greenhorn, who had arrived unprepared, with no knowledge of Somaliland or its language. He would also mock the younger man (at twenty-seven, Speke was six years his junior) for having brought with him 'all manner of cheap and useless chow-chow, guns and revolvers, swords and cutlery, which "the simple-minded negro of Africa" would have rejected with disdain'. Burton next derided Speke's attempt to engage as guides 'the first mop-headed ... donkey boys' he encountered.[6] Yet, in reality, far from accepting Speke out of pity as he later made out he had, Burton was eager to have him on the expedition, and appealed to Outram to 'allow [him] to enrol Lieut. Speke'.

The more he learned about Speke, the more Burton realised that his innocent, enthusiastic manner masked a loner's steely self-reliance. Something else struck him about the outwardly easy-going officer. Although he joked about being a *Masti Bengali* ('a bumptious Bengal-man'), for all his humorous self-deprecation, 'he had a way as well as a will of his own', after being 'for years his own master'.[7] While on leave from the 46th Regiment of Bengal Native Infantry, Speke had not gone home to England but had travelled in the unexplored mountains of Tibet with a couple of servants, mapping the country and collecting specimens of wildlife for the museum he had created in his father's house. He was an exceptional shot, and a capable soldier, having served in General Sir Colin Campbell's brigade during the Sikh Wars.[8] Unlike Burton, he drank little alcohol, and on his Tibetan journeys had risen 'with the freezing dawn, walked in the burning sun all day, breaking his fast upon native bread and wild onions, and passed the night in the smallest of "rowtie" tents'.⁹ As Burton conceded, Jack Speke had rare gifts such as 'an uncommonly acute eye for country – by no means a usual accomplishment even with the professional surveyor'.¹⁰

While they were still in Aden, Burton and his new expedition member had a conversation that would have momentous consequences. The subject was 'Krapf's snow mountains'. Burton confided to Speke that within a year or two, he meant to travel westward from Zanzibar into the African interior to find the Nile's source. Although Speke was surprised to learn that his leader was planning anything so ambitious, he declared an existing interest of his own. Ever since seeing the Mountains of the Moon depicted in a reproduction of Ptolemy's famous map, he said he had deduced that these snow peaks must feed the Nile, just as the Himalayas' glaciers fed the Ganges. But though Burton must have been struck by what the new arrival said, his discovery that their minds were running on similar lines did not cause him to invite Speke to go with him to the mysterious city of Harar. From now on, however, Speke knew that in order to be chosen for a future expedition to the Nile's source, he was going to have to seem to be on friendly terms with Burton, whatever he might secretly feel about him.¹¹

In the meantime, it vexed Speke to have nothing to do while Stroyan and Herne were being sent to Berbera with orders to detain the Emir of Harar's caravan should Burton be held captive in the 'forbidden city'. So rather than be left kicking his heels, Speke 'volunteered to travel in any direction [his] commandant might think proper to direct'. Burton decided to send him to a region known as the Wadi Nogal, where he was to collect specimens of flora and fauna, and buy camels for the journey south to Zanzibar.¹² Since collecting specimens was what he would have been doing had Brigadier Outram allowed him to go to Somaliland on his own, Speke was mollified, until Burton ordered Herne, Stroyan and him to wear Arab clothing. Speke's huge turban and long close-fitting gown were intolerably hot, and because he looked so odd in them they seemed likely to endanger his life rather than preserve it. But because Burton believed that he would never be allowed to enter Harar unless disguised, 'he thought it better,' wrote Speke sardonically, that 'we should appear as his disciples'.[13]

Somaliland and the Horn of Africa.

Burton had laughed at Speke's donkey boys; but if Speke had engaged them, they could hardly have performed worse as guides than Sumunter and Ahmed, the duo chosen to be his *abbans* by Burton. From time immemorial in Somaliland, guides for foreigners had been called *abbans* – the word meaning protector, as well as guide. Since the only language Speke shared with Sumunter was Hindustani, in which neither of them was even moderately fluent, communication was haphazard. In no time, Sumunter tried to fleece Speke so blatantly that the young officer was forced to stand and defend his 'date and rice bags with his gun'. Various locals were then incited to join in robbing him. Soon Speke knew he was never going to reach the Wadi Nogal. But, realising that his present mission was really a test of his fitness to be chosen to accompany Burton on any future Nile expedition, Speke kept up his journal and pressed on with his collecting, eventually securing a new species of snake, some rare fossils and numerous antelope heads and specimens of indigenous birds.[14]

After two months of what Speke described as 'this useless journey', he rejoined his colleagues at the coast and sailed to Aden to re-supply for the expedition's second and more important phase. Although Speke was eager to forget his humiliation by his insubordinate *abban*, Burton decided that Sumunter must be prosecuted, since he had treated other travellers in the same way. The *abban* was duly tried, found guilty, and sentenced to two months in prison. After the trial, Burton sounded off in public about the system of *abban*-ship being ripe for abolition.[15] Both the *abban*'s trial and Burton's remarks caused great indignation among Somalis in Aden and news of the vengeful behaviour of the British officers spread swiftly to Berbera and the Somali coast. Colonel R. L. Playfair (Outram's political assistant) would later describe Burton's criticism of *abban*-ship *as* 'the *termina causa* of all the mishaps which befell the expedition'.[16]

But for the moment, Speke was worried only by his failure to reach the Wadi Nogal. He felt all the worse because Burton had successfully entered Harar and had returned to tell the tale – or as much of it as he thought consistent with striking a heroic pose. Unknown to Speke, Harar had disappointed his commander architecturally, culturally, and as 'a forbidden city'. Far from being threatened and imprisoned, Burton had been allowed to leave the decaying place as freely as he had been permitted to enter it. If Burton had ever let Speke know that he judged his own mission a failure, Speke would have been less upset by his leader's condescending remarks about his failure to reach the wretched Wadi Nogal.

Nor did Speke have any idea that Burton's experiences on the way to Harar had destroyed an important part of his self-image:

namely his faith in his talent for disguising himself as 'a native'. On this occasion, his Somali servants had rumbled him with ease and had broadcast his identity to strangers along the way.[17] Rather than become a figure of fun, Burton had rapidly discarded his turban. If he could not pass himself off as a Somali, he would fail hopelessly among darker-skinned Africans, so in future he knew he would have to travel as a British officer. Some years later he admitted with uncharacteristic honesty that he had gone to Harar principally 'for display of travelling *savoir faire*' but he had actually 'displayed' the reverse.[18]

'Privately and *entre nous*,' he told Norton Shaw of the RGS, thinking of the epic journey which he hoped would follow this one, 'I want to settle the question of Krapf and "eternal snows". There is little doubt of the White Nile being thereabouts. And you will hear with pleasure that there is an open route through Africa to the Atlantic. I heard of it at Harar.'[19]

Burton arrived at Berbera on 7 April 1855 in time for him and his companions to link up with the Ogaden caravan, before it headed south from Berbera in the second week of April. Yet most unfortunately, soon after his arrival, he changed his mind about doing this, preferring to run the risk of going south on his own. The reason he gave for remaining encamped outside Berbera was the desirability of hanging on there long enough to take delivery of the 'instruments and other necessaries [arriving] by the mid-April mail from Europe'. But another consideration influenced him more. This was his desire 'to witness the close of the Berbera fair' – a memorable event, to be sure, attended by thousands of buyers and sellers of slaves, camels, ivory, cloth, metal, beads and rhinoceros horn, but hardly a spectacle worth risking life and limb to see.[20]

So, while the immense Ogaden caravan was snaking away southward – with several thousand camels, 500 chained slaves, and 3,000 head of cattle – the four British officers remained in their tents, strung out in a line by the small seaside village of Kurrum outside Berbera.[21] Here, they continued to make leisurely preparations for their eventual departure. Behind a superficial friendliness, the local people hid a deep antipathy. In their eyes, the Englishmen had come to collect information about the slave trade, probably in preparation for its suppression – an outcome certain to impoverish the whole region. Many locals were still smarting from Burton's public criticism of the system of *abban*-ship. But neither he, nor any of his officers, suspected that they were in danger. Speke knew perfectly well that Somalis visiting Aden were considered so dangerous that the authorities regularly disarmed them, but bizarrely neither he nor Burton considered posting more than two sentries at night. It seemed inconceivable to them that the locals would dare attack them and bring upon themselves a naval blockade of the port of Berbera.[22] How wrong the young Englishmen were.

At about 2.00 a.m. on 19 April, their camp was invaded by about 200 armed Somalis. 'Hearing a rush of men, like a stormy wind', Burton sprang up, and yelled at a servant to bring his sabre. Herne was sent out into the darkness to investigate and darted back into the tent having fired a few shots at the advancing attackers with his Colt. In his separate tent, Speke heard Burton calling to Stroyan to get up, and he also heard shots, but at first he thought these were being fired at imaginary intruders by trigger-happy sentries. But hearing footsteps immediately outside, he leapt from his bed and sprinted to Burton's tent. While trying to do the same, Stroyan was slashed across the head with a sword, and then killed by a single spear-thrust to the heart.[23]

Burton and Herne, in their shared tent, were soon fighting for their lives as Somalis fired shots into the canvas and threw heavy javelins through the entrance. Although Burton was a formidable swordsman, his sabre was no help, and as Speke arrived with his revolver, it fell to him to defend the tent. Herne's powder was exhausted and he could neither find his flask, nor any alternative weapon.[24]

At this point, Speke, who had been keeping the attackers back from the entrance with his Adams five-shot revolver, was hit on the knee by a stone. Because his view was obstructed by the fly of the tent, he ducked down under this flap to get a clearer view of his assailant. Misconstruing his sudden movement, Burton roared at him: 'Don't step back, or they'll think we are running.'[25] Enraged by what he thought was a veiled accusation of cowardice, Speke, according to his own account, 'stepped boldly to the front and fired at close quarters into the first man before [him]'. He did the same, he said, to two more men in his path, and then placed the muzzle of his gun 'against the breast of the largest man before him and pulled the trigger, but pulled in vain; the cylinder would not rotate'. Just then a club struck his chest, knocking him to the ground. 'In another instant . . . a dozen Somalis were on top of [him].'[26]

Burton thought Speke had panicked and had no idea that he had dashed ahead, firing left and right, in response to his spur-of-the-moment words. Terrible things were about to happen to both men, but, for Speke, Burton's rebuke would be his most painful recollection.[27] As the Somalis tried to flatten the tent, intending to tangle Burton and Herne in its folds, the two Englishmen dashed out, Burton slashing right and left with his sabre. In the darkness, Burton mistook his Somali factotum for an attacker and was about to cut him down when the man's cry of alarm made his master freeze. 'That instant's hesitation allowed a spearman to step forward, and leave his javelin in my mouth,' wrote Burton. The spear entered on one side of Burton's face and came out on the other, cleaving the roof of his mouth and smashing out two molars. Struggling against increasing faintness caused by pain and loss of blood, Burton somehow reached the shore where a vessel – whose crew had brought him mail from Aden two days earlier – remained moored. Here at last the javelin was removed from his mouth and his wound was dressed.[28]

On the ground, gasping for breath, with men binding his hands behind his back, Speke could feel fingers exploring around his genitals:

I felt as if my hair stood on end; and not knowing who my opponents were, I feared that they belonged to a tribe called Eesa, who are notorious for the unmanly mutilations they delight in. Indescribable was my relief when I found that the men were in reality feeling whether, after an Arab fashion, I was carrying a dagger between my legs . . .[29]

At dawn, the Somalis pillaged the camp, while Speke was held by a rope. Later, he described how, without warning, the man keeping him tethered 'stepped up close to me, and coolly stabbed me with his spear'. Further jabs were aimed at his shoulder, one narrowly missing his jugular. He only prevented a stab to the heart by blocking it with his tied wrists, which were cut to the bone deflecting the weapon's point. The next lunge was to his thigh, and he heard the spearhead grind against the bone. To save himself, Speke grabbed the spear, but a whack on the arm with a club sent it clattering to the ground. He saw his captor:

. . . [drop] the rope-end, walk back a dozen paces, and rush on me with savage fury, plunging his spear through the thick part of my right thigh into the ground, passing it between the thigh-bone and the large sinew below . . . Seeing that death was inevitable if I remained lying there a moment longer, I sprang upon my legs, and gave the miscreant such a sharp back-hander in the face with my double-bound fists that he lost his presence of mind and gave me a moment's opportunity to run away . . . I was almost naked and quite bare upon the feet, but I ran over the shingly beach towards the sea like wildfire. The man followed me a little way, but finding I had the foot of him, threw his spear like a javelin, but did not strike me . . . he then gave up the chase. Still I had at least forty more men to pass, who were scattered about the place, looking for what property they could pick up . . . However I dodged them all by turns . . . bobbing as they threw their spears after me, until I reached the shore.[30]

Burton would describe Speke's escape as 'in every way wonderful', which it certainly was.[31] The three surviving officers (Herne being the only one unscathed) sailed for Aden the following day in the small sailing vessel, to which they had managed to stagger after the attack. During the voyage, Stroyan's corpse began to smell so offensively that the crew persuaded Burton to bury him at sea, rather than bring him back to Aden, as he had wished.[32] The death of a colleague, who had been a friend in India, was very painful for Burton. Not least because it

Speke's escape from his captors (frontispiece of Speke's
What Led to the Discovery of the Source of the Nile).

was obvious to all that, if he had stuck to his original plan to join
the Ogaden caravan, Stroyan would still be alive, and he and
Speke would not be lying wounded on the vessel's poop deck. On
Speke's arrival in the colony, the civil surgeon looked at the deep
wounds and lacerations to his limbs, which were now contracted
into grotesque positions, and predicted that it would take three
years for him to recover fully. The same surgeon expected Burton
to heal more swiftly. In fact Speke would be walking with a stick
by the time he sailed for England three weeks later, and Burton
would be an invalid for several months.[33]

Speke's resentment against Burton for implying that he had
been retreating at the height of the attack was not his only
complaint against his leader. As expedition leader, Burton had
taken possession of his junior officer's diary and, although
Speke could hardly object to a copy being sent to the Bombay
authorities, he knew that Burton was an author and suspected
that he might make personal use of the copy he had retained. He
was also shocked when Burton told him that he was bound by his
instructions to send to the Calcutta Museum of Natural History
all the animals' heads and other specimens he had collected.

Speke had hoped at least to send duplicates to his own private museum in his father's house.[34] Yet it could be said in Burton's favour that he was at least trying his hardest to get back the £510, which Speke had lost, along with a further thousand lost by other expedition members in the destruction of their camp. Speke was always aware of the need to keep on good terms with his leader in order to be invited to accompany him on his next expedition. So he did not reproach Burton for failing to negotiate a penny of compensation from the East India Company.

While at Kurrum, Speke had heard of the existence of a vast inland lake, which 'the Somali described as equal in extent to the Gulf of Aden'.[35] This information made him all the keener to keep in with Burton – although there could be no denying that their Somaliland expedition had been such 'a signal failure from inexperience' that it had probably damaged their reputations too much to make funding a new journey a practical proposition.[36] Yet Burton had at least reached Harar, so *his* credibility had not been entirely ruined. Yet even supposing Burton managed to gain support in the right quarters, Speke doubted whether his former leader would want to return to Africa with a man who had written no books, knew no Arabic, and had failed to reach the objective he had been set.

FOUR

About a Rotten Person

When Richard Burton arrived in England on sick leave in June 1855, the two volumes of his *Pilgrimage to El-Medinah and Meccah* were in the shops and had just received the kind of press that normally makes an author well known for life. But circumstances were far from normal, with public attention riveted by the Crimean War and the cholera, starvation, dysentery and official incompetence that were together killing more British soldiers than the enemy. Britain and France were at war with Russia in defence of threatened Turkey and their own interests in the eastern Mediterranean. Though Burton had returned from Africa marked for life by a livid facial scar, he wanted to go and fight. Not that patriotism fully explained his ardour.

He had just been severely censured by Aden's new British ruler, Brigadier William Coghlan, for his 'want of caution and vigilance' as leader of the Somali Expedition.[1] Fearing that Coghlan's report could blight his chances of returning to Africa, he decided that a stint in the Crimea might persuade the Bombay government to view him more favourably. The best he could manage was a staff appointment with Beatson's Horse, a lawless brigade of Turkish irregulars. However, within three months – during which Burton saw no action – he and the brigade's other British officers failed to stop their ill-disciplined Turks, Syrians and Albanians clashing with French troops, their allies. General Beatson was forced to resign, and Burton, as his chief staff officer, had no choice but to follow him home.[2] Yet at this apparently disastrous moment, luck came to his rescue in a most unexpected way.

Dr James Erhardt, a missionary colleague of Dr Krapf and Johann Rebmann, sent a map of a gigantic slug-shaped central African lake to the secretary of the Church Missionary

Society, who forwarded it to the Royal Geographical Society, where it was discussed at meetings in late November and early December 1855 – the very time when Burton had just come home. Although the geographers' general opinion of this map – which was based on the testimony of Arab-Swahili slave traders – was that it incorrectly conflated a southern lake with one, or possibly two lakes further to the north, its implications for the search for the Nile's source were electrifying.[3] Because Burton knew the RGS's secretary, Dr Norton Shaw, he had been kept abreast of the Society's evolving plans, and so was in pole position to apply for the leadership of a new East African expedition. Indeed, Burton's letter of application reached the Society two days before their Expeditions' Committee resolved on 12 April 1856 to send an exploring party 'to ascertain . . . the limits of the Inland Sea or Lake . . . [and, if possible, achieve] the determination of the head sources of the White Nile'.[4] By the time Burton wrote again, a week after this meeting, it was evident that he had already been informed *sub rosa* that the RGS meant to back him. At any rate, he felt confident enough to discuss with them a pivotal matter – which was whether to go alone, or accompanied. He plumped for the latter option, because 'it would scarcely be wise to stake success upon a single life . . . I should therefore propose as my companion, Lt. Speke of the B.A. [Bengal Army]'.[5]

If Speke had been in a position to hear that Burton had made him his first choice at this historic moment, he would have been amazed. But he was out of contact in the Crimea, and currently stationed at Kertch as second in command of the Turkish contingent of the 16th Regiment of Infantry. But, as he told a friend at this time, he had no interest in the war and 'was dying to go back and try again [at the Nile]', but doubted whether he would ever be given the chance.[6] So when he eventually received the good news from Norton Shaw, he was planning a hunting expedition in the Caucasus Mountains.[7]

Although still smarting from the accusation of cowardice and the theft of his specimens, Speke did not hesitate to accept

Burton's invitation. His former commander – as he was aware – 'knew nothing of astronomical surveying, of physical geography, or of collecting specimens of natural history', so he was confident that his own practical skills would be invaluable.[8]

It is not easy to judge what the two men thought of one another before they began their second journey. This is because, after it, every word they wrote (and they wrote a good many) would be coloured by their great falling out. Burton's own version of why he invited Speke to accompany him is highly suspect:

The history of our companionship is simply this: – As he had suffered with me in purse and person at Berbera in 1855, I thought it but just to offer him the opportunity of renewing an attempt to penetrate into Africa. I had no other reasons. I could not expect much from his assistance; he was not a linguist – French and Arabic being equally unknown to him – nor a man of science, nor an accurate astronomical observer.[9]

This flatly contradicts Burton's later admission that Speke had possessed 'an uncommonly acute eye for country – by no means a usual accomplishment even with the professional surveyor'. It is, of course, inconceivable that Burton would have chosen someone to accompany him on the most important journey of his life, simply because he had suffered misfortune on an earlier occasion. If a better-qualified man had been available, Burton would have chosen him without hesitation. But Speke had much to offer. Even after they had fallen out, Burton would still feel compelled to praise his 'noble qualities of energy, courage and perseverance', and would pay tribute to his skill in 'geodesy', demonstrated by his use of a watch, the sun and a compass to fix the position of geographical features on a map.[10] Burton also knew that Speke understood how to measure the moon's position, relative to other stars, in order to determine longitude – another exceptionally useful accomplishment. But perhaps what weighed most with him was his memory of the miraculous way in which Speke had escaped what had looked to be certain death. This feat had required outstanding physical fitness, and an unbreakable will.

Such qualities apart, what did Burton think of him as a person? Certainly, Jack Speke was not as well educated as he was, neither having been to a university nor having written books and mastered numerous languages. Speke's parents – though they could have afforded the fees of a leading public school – had sent him as a boarder to unremarkable Barnstaple Grammar School, fifty miles from their estate in Somerset. Like many of his contemporaries at famous schools, Speke did little work, often cutting class and preferring country pursuits to Latin and Greek.[11] But though his teenage delinquencies were no match for Burton's youthful love affairs, the pair still had one significant formative experience in common. Both had grown up in households where the mother was the dominant parent.

Speke's reclusive father, William, although rich and head of a family that had owned land in Somerset since Norman times, had refused to stand for parliament, even when urged to do so by William Pitt, the prime minister, who was a neighbouring land-owner. All he asked was to be left in peace to manage his estate, as had generations of his stay-at-home forebears. This slightly dull county family was certainly not one that might have been expected to produce, out of the blue, a man destined to rip the veil from the heart of Africa. Jack was the second of William's four sons, but would be the only one sufficiently favoured by his mother to be given her maiden name, Hanning, as one of his forenames. Indeed she always addressed him as Hanning, his second name, in preference to John or Jack.[12] Georgina was an heiress with ambitions for her family. In later years, when 'Hanning' went abroad, it would be she, rather than her husband, who would correspond with her favourite son's publisher and with the RGS on his behalf.[13] In a letter to John Blackwood, his publisher, Speke describes 'leaving the mammy strings ... [for] the life of a vagabond', implying that his journeying sprang from the need to escape his mother's control.[14]

Richard Burton's equally strong-minded mother, Martha – besides influencing him more than his professional invalid of a father – was fascinated by young tearaways like her remittance-man half-brother – another Richard Burton. Her son Richard definitely believed that his own 'madcap adventures . . . developed a secret alliance between them . . . Like all mothers she dearly loved the scamp of the family.'[15] Georgina Speke also seems secretly to have admired high-spirited misbehaviour. A curious passage was deleted by Blackwood from the proofs of Speke's first book, in which the explorer advised an African monarch how to increase his chances of impregnating his wives. The young ruler, he suggested, should limit the number of times he had sex and 'refrain from over-indulgences, which destroy the appetite in early youth'. There were plenty of youths in Europe and elsewhere, Speke explained, who, 'because of the foolish vanity their mothers and nurses have of having forward boys increase their veins in size by over-exertion, and thereby decrease their power'.[16]

The routine depiction of Speke by Burton's biographers as a dullard, with no interest in sex, is given the lie by dozens of risqué passages cut by Blackwood from proof versions of his books. Speke described the cuts disapprovingly as 'this gelding business'.[17] 'If you persist in gelding me,' he told Blackwood, 'I shall think you more barbarous than even the Somalis.'[18] Nevertheless, Fawn Brodie, one of Burton's most respected biographers, stated that 'Speke at thirty-three was inhibited and prudish'.[19] In fact, aged thirty-three he wrote to an officer friend, describing in graphic detail how Somali women's vaginas were 'stitched across to prevent intrusion until the bridegroom feels inclined to consummate the marriage'.[20]

Speke is said by one biographer to have accused Burton of making sexual advances to him. The evidence is flimsy.[21] Certainly Burton was possessed by a passionate sexual inquisitiveness, and had probably had homosexual experiences in India, but he had also kept Indian mistresses and had loved one of them deeply.[22] Nor did he suddenly lose interest in women while in Africa. On arrival in Aden, after the Berbera disaster, he had been found by the Acting Civil Surgeon to be suffering from syphilis caught from prostitutes in Egypt.[23] And Speke's behaviour towards

African women in Uganda will show that he too was by no means devoid of heterosexual feelings.

Burton, as the more experienced and celebrated traveller, wanted a colleague who would always do as he was asked and never challenge him. On their Somaliland trip, he had been struck by Speke's 'peculiarly quiet and modest aspect' and by his 'almost childlike simplicity of manner'. Only later would he detect beneath Speke's unassuming exterior 'an immense and abnormal fund of self-esteem, so carefully concealed, however, that none but his intimates suspected its existence'.[24] Speke would locate the abnormality elsewhere. As he confided to Norton Shaw several years later: 'He used to snub me so unpleasantly when talking about anything that I often kept my own counsel – Burton is one of those men who never can be wrong and will never acknowledge an error.'[25]

Burton from the start recognised Jack Speke as a risk-taker like himself – someone who instead of going home on furlough had travelled alone to Tibet to shoot bears. Risk had drawn Speke to Somaliland, which he knew to be dangerous, as was his desire to shoot Ethiopian elephants. The two men had seemed to have an identical desire to flee the monotony of everyday life.

In October 1856, soon after Speke's acceptance of Burton's invitation, an event took place which changed his hitherto temperate view of his leader. In Somaliland Burton had taken charge of his companion's journal as expedition property, and now, at last, Speke was able to see what he had done with it. Burton's book about the Somali Expedition: *First Footsteps in East Africa: or, An Exploration of Harar* was published just as the two men were making their final preparations for departure. It contained a thirty-seven-page appendix, insultingly entitled 'Diary and Observations made by Lieutenant Speke, when attempting to reach the Wady Nogal'. Adding insult to injury, Burton commented that though Speke had been 'delayed and persecuted by his "protector" [*abban*], and threatened with war, danger, and destruction, his life was never in danger'.[26] Even worse, Burton had printed for public consumption (with one minor change) the words of his warning that had upset Speke so much at the time of the Berbera attack: 'Don't step back or they will think we are retiring.'²⁷ The whole diary had been heavily cut, and then re-jigged in the third person, but kept in diary form, strongly suggesting that Speke was so illiterate that his work had needed to be completely re-written – an insinuation that would eventually be disproved by Speke's extremely readable books. Burton's overlong and invariably overwritten *oeuvres* – although containing many excellent passages – are very hard to get through in their entirety. Speke did not find writing easy, but, unlike Burton, he did at least achieve – with the help of his editors – a fluent and gripping narrative style by writing exactly as he spoke.²⁸

Though enraged by *First Footsteps in East Africa,* Speke concealed his hurt feelings. Nor did he for a moment consider resigning from an expedition which promised to make them both famous. Even when his anger was fanned by a review of *First Footsteps* – forwarded to them *en route* for Africa – Speke still did not tell Burton what he was thinking. Laurence Oliphant, a writer and traveller who was a member of the RGS Expeditions' Committee and an acquaintance of both men, had reviewed Burton's book in *Blackwood's Magazine,* and had focussed on the author's cavalier treatment of diaries, written by 'so able an explorer as Mr Speke'. The able explorer's observations, wrote Oliphant, deserved 'to have been chronicled at greater length and thrown into a form which would have rendered them more interesting to the general reader'.²⁹

Speke was not a conceited man, but he had a strong sense of his own dignity, and this had been injured by Burton's condescension. He never understood that Burton's frequent lurches from sincerity into cynicism and back again in his books, and in his conversation, were symptoms of an insecure need to assume an attitude rather than risk ridicule by speaking sincerely. A friend declared that Burton enjoyed 'dressing himself, so to speak, in wolf's clothing, in order to give an idea that he was worse than he really was'.³⁰ It would never have occurred to

Speke that there could be any point in acquiring a reputation for wildness and eccentricity, as a substitute for more reputable achievements. When the pair reached Zanzibar, Speke wrote a letter to his mother, only a fragment of which survives. It includes the sentence: 'Wishing I could find something more amusing to communicate than such rot about a rotten person.' He then told his mother that he doubted whether Burton had actually been to Mecca or Harar.[31]

While steaming across the Indian Ocean towards Zanzibar, Burton did not tell Speke that he had become engaged to be married before leaving England. The girl's parents were unlikely to give their consent and the engagement therefore had to remain secret. But if Speke *had* known about this romantic event, he might have looked upon Burton with a little more sympathy. In truth, the self-created 'Ruffian Dick' had felt isolated, even vulnerable on the brink of a journey from which he might never return. His mother was dead; his brother had returned to Ceylon; and his sister was preoccupied with her children and her husband. The parents of the two women he had loved – one of whom had been a cousin – had rejected him as a man without money or prospects. Nor had his failure in Somaliland helped his self-esteem, so despite the critical success of his account of his journey to Mecca, he knew that his entire future hinged on the outcome of his new African venture. So it was a blessing that at this time of high anxiety, his personal life offered new hope.

In 1850, he had met nineteen-year-old Isabel Arundell, who had promptly fallen in love with him. She was not strikingly beautiful, had no fortune and her membership of an aristocratic Catholic family seemed unlikely to help his career. But after they chanced to meet again in August 1856, they contrived further meetings and in early October Burton proposed. Before leaving for Africa, he gave her a poem he had written, entitled 'Fame', which told the infatuated Isabel more about Burton's ambitions as an explorer than about his love for her. Indeed there is no evidence that he had fallen in love. He would be far from chaste in the months to come.[32] But there was no doubt that *he* had never been loved so much before. Here at last was someone who would care whether he lived or died, and if it was to be the latter would venerate his memory – a comforting thought to take to Africa.

So in Zanzibar, where the duo arrived on 2 December, neither man had the measure of the other. Burton had no idea that his companion was still brooding over *First Footsteps*, and Speke had no clue that Burton was a man with strong emotional needs and self-doubts. Yet they were embarking on a dangerous venture which friendship and understanding would have made far easier to endure.

FIVE

Everything Was to be Risked for This Prize

Sighting the African coast from the sea, Jack Speke, who rarely enthused about scenery, was mesmerised by the white coral sands, vivid blueness of the ocean, 'and green aquatic mangrove growing out into the tidal waves'.[1] Soon the minarets of Zanzibar's mosques pierced the skyline above the barrack-like Sultan's palace and the grey-stone consulates. Next, a spidery tangle of ships' masts and rigging came into view as the breeze wafted seaward the scent of cloves, mixed less pleasingly with the odour of tar, hides, copra and rotting molluscs. A corpse floated near the foreshore which Burton remarked did not discourage 'the younger blacks of both sexes from swimming and disporting themselves in an absence of costume which would startle even Margate'. He was soon delighted to find that prostitutes were easily procurable in Stone Town.[2] A hundred thousand people – Arabs, *banians*, slaves, freemen, dark-skinned Swahili-speaking Afro-Arabs, and a few hundred consular and trading Europeans – were crammed onto the island.

The two men had arrived on 20 December at the start of what Speke matter-of-factly described as 'the very worst season of the year for commencing a long inland journey'. At present, the interior was tinder dry, but within weeks the rains would arrive, inundating tracks and paths, and turning vast tracts of country into a quagmire.[3] So they decided to wait several months before setting out for the 'slug-shaped' lake. This gave them time to seek out Johann Rebmann at his mission near Mombasa, in the hope of persuading the discoverer of Mount Kilimanjaro to join their expedition. But he found Burton 'facetious' and also suspected that he would use unjustified force against Africans during the march to the lake.[4] But though declining to accompany the

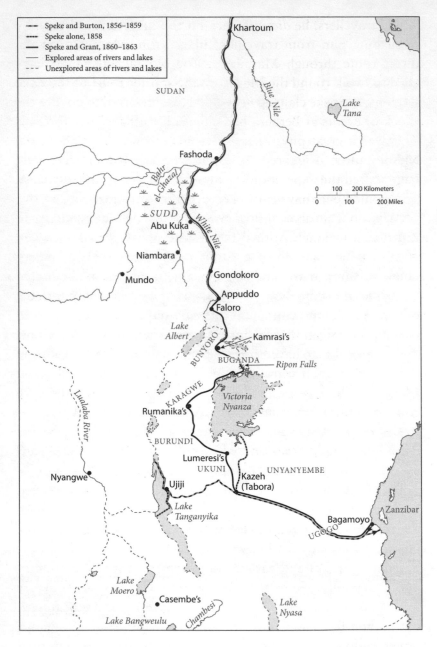

Journeys of Burton and Speke, and of Speke and Grant.

young travellers, he *did* influence Burton in one crucial way: by dissuading him from travelling inland from Mombasa on the direct route through Masailand. The old Burton would have tried to 'walk round the Masai' on the shorter route to the Lake Regions, as Speke claimed *he* would have preferred to do. But the shock of events at Berbera had changed 'Ruffian Dick' forever.[5] This was a great pity, since, if Rebmann's warnings about the Masai had been ignored, Speke and Burton would very likely have shared the expedition's greatest discovery at an early stage and would never have embarked upon their disastrous feud.

Back on Zanzibar the poor health of the British Consul, Lieutenant-Colonel Atkins Hamerton, gave notice of what African fever could do to a man over the years. Though dying, Hamerton hoped to shock the would-be explorers into going back to India while they still could. So he took them to the local prison to make the acquaintance of one hapless convict, chained so tightly to a gun that he could not stand up or lie down. This man's crime was to have beaten a drum, while Lieutenant Maizan (the young French traveller) had been tortured, mutilated and then beheaded in a macabre ceremony.[6] Though shocked, Speke and Burton knew there could be no turning back

A notable difference between the pair became apparent while they were still on Zanzibar. Everywhere they went slaves of both sexes and all ages could be seen in streets and alleys. Burton guessed there were 25,000 of them on the island – some owned by locals, some in transit to the Gulf, and others for sale.[7] Speke was the more shocked of the two by what he saw at the slave market:

The saddest sight was the way in which some licentious-looking men began a cool, deliberate inspection of a certain divorced culprit who had been sent back to the market for inconstancy to her husband. She had learnt a sense of decency during her conjugal life, and the blushes on her face now clearly showed how her heart was mortified at this unseemly exposure, made worse because she could not help it.[8]

By contrast, Burton gazed with detachment at the 'lines of negroes [as they] stood like beasts', later describing what he called 'hideous black faces some of which appeared hardly human'.⁹ Burton took pride in refusing, as he put it, 'to adorn this subject with many a flower of description; the atrocities of the capture, the brutalities of the purchase'. He was convinced that Britain, through a treaty agreed in 1845 with Seyyid Said, the former Sultan of Zanzibar, was making the lives of slaves worse by using the Royal Navy – 'the sentimental squadron', as he called the Indian Ocean Anti-Slavery Flotilla – to stop their export. The price of a slave was ten times higher in Oman than in East Africa, and, as Burton pointed out, the more valuable a human chattel was, the better he or she was cared for. So any policy stopping the export trade, and thus keeping more slaves in Africa, lowered their price, and so harmed the slaves themselves. Slavery in Africa, argued Burton, had not been invented by 'foreigners', such as his beloved Arabs, but by the Africans themselves, who regularly fought 'internal wars, whose main object is capturing serviles [sic]'. He seemed blind to the fact that the treatment of domestic slaves, however benign, could not justify their brutal capture, or their long and often fatal journey to the coast.¹⁰ Speke did not analyse the situation intellectually, but knew on an intuitive level that the entire trade – both domestic and export – should be suppressed because of the suffering and desolation it caused. Burton thought Africans contemptible and to blame for their misfortunes, despite his enthusiasm for recording their habits and customs. But while at times Speke could also write insultingly about them, he came to like and admire them.¹¹

The expedition started with Burton committing a major error of judgement. With sole responsibility for buying the expedition's supplies from Zanzibar's Indian merchants, and only half the funding he had hoped for, he had to buy wisely. He purchased from Ladha Damha (or Damji), a leading merchant, excellent presents for chiefs: sprigged muslin for turbans, embroidered hats and coats, and white and pink Venetian beads. But regarding the all-important basic trade goods, he later confessed he had 'made the mistake of ignorance of not laying in an ample store of American domestics [versatile sheeting fabric known locally as Merikani

Naval vessels at Zanzibar (from Stanley's *How I Found Livingstone*).

cloth], and a greater supply of beads'.[12] Basic trade goods were essential for buying food and paying for the right of passage through the territory of African chiefs. So to have skimped on these essential commodities was folly. His initial failure to recruit enough porters led him to leave behind the expedition's portable boat. This was another bad mistake. 'She would indeed have been a Godsend,' he admitted later, 'sparing us long delay, great expense and a host of difficulties and hardships.'[13] But, leaving Zanzibar, Burton felt euphoric.

Of the gladdest moments in human life is the departure upon a distant journey into unknown lands. Shaking off with one mighty effort the fetters of habit, the leaden weight of routine, the cloak of carking care, and the slavery of Civilization, man feels once more happy. The blood flows with the fast circulation of youth, excitement gives a new vigour to the muscles.[14]

Just before leaving, he and Speke visited the young Sultan Majid, who over sweetmeats and glasses of sherbet, alarmed them by suggesting that they take a field gun.[15] The route they meant to follow to the lake had been pioneered by Arab-Swahili slave traders twenty years earlier, and although Hamerton

warned them that 'contact with slave-dealers had increased
African cupidity and diminished hospitality', the two explorers
believed that because Africans were now accustomed to seeing
travellers, they would be unlikely to harm them if they stuck to
the known path.[16]

Burton's RGS instructions required him 'to penetrate inland'
to the 'unknown lake' – which was of course only 'unknown' to
Europeans. Many Arabs had stood on its shores since Sayf bin
Said el-Muameri had reached it in 1825. Burton was tasked by
the RGS 'to proceed northward towards the range of mountains
[Mountains of the Moon] marked upon our maps as containing
the probable source of the "Bahr el Abiad" [White Nile], which
it will be your next great objective to discover'.[17] Burton believed
that any man succeeding in linking mountains and river should
'justly be considered among the greatest benefactors of this age
of geographical science'. But because the celebrated German
explorer of the Sahara, Heinrich Barth, had told him 'that no
prudent man would pledge himself to discover the Nile sources',
he timidly redefined his mission as being 'to ascertain the limits
of the Sea of Ujiji [Tanganyika], to learn the ethnography of its
tribes, and determine the export of the produce of the interior'.[18]
It would be nine months before he discussed the source of the
Nile again with Speke, although both men knew very well that
they would be judged by how much they contributed to the
solution of the world's greatest geographical mystery.

The success or failure of expeditions depended not just on the
tenacity of individual explorers, but as much on the experience
and motivation of their African guides, porters and servants. By
great good luck, Burton and Speke had managed to employ Sidi
Mubarak Bombay, who would become the expedition's principal
factotum. When only twelve, Bombay had been captured
between Kilwa and Lake Nyasa by Arab-Swahili slave traders,
and then sold to an Indian merchant, who had taken him to
work for him in Sindh, where he had learned Hindustani. After
the merchant's death, Bombay was freed and sailed to Zanzibar,
where the two explorers met him. Since Burton and Speke both

knew Hindustani, communication with Bombay was easy. Even before the journey started Speke wrote that he had 'become much attached to Bombay' and asserted that he had never met any black man as honest, generous and conscientious as he was.[19] They had engaged at the same time another man also destined to become one of East Africa's great caravan leaders, Mabruki (later known as Mabruki Speke), a member of the Yao tribe like Bombay.

Sidi Mubarak Bombay.

On condition that Burton paid each man five Maria Theresa dollars a month,[†] the Sultan of Zanzibar agreed to lend him a dozen Baluchi soldiers – originally from Baluchistan to the north-west of Sindh – and a one-eyed *jemadar* (native officer) to command them. An Indian merchant called Rush Ramji rented to the expedition nine slaves, whose 'only object' according to Burton was to capture further slaves. Rather surprisingly, he condoned this ambition, insisting that he 'had no power to prevent [his] followers purchasing slaves'. But Burton would at least refuse to accept slaves as presents. He had already chosen

† The local silver currency in Zanzibar, worth about £1 sterling for five coins.

as personal servants and 'cook boys', Valentine and Gaetano, half-Portuguese and half-Indian teenagers, who could sew, cook and speak Kiswahili.

The entire caravan was under the orders of its *cafilah-bashi* or headman, Said bin Salim, whose father was an Omani Arab and his mother an African. He carried 'a two-handed blade fit for Richard of England', could recite poetry in Arabic and would soon fall out with Burton, though not with Speke. Said bin Salim brought along four slaves as his personal servants: three females, including 'Halimah, his acting wife, and one boy'.[20] The total recruited on Zanzibar was thirty-one, not counting Speke and Burton. Said bin Salim was sent ahead to the mainland to try to recruit 140 porters. He would only manage to engage thirty-six at the coast, but within a month the expedition's numbers would rise to 132, thanks, in part, to some men who had failed to present themselves at the coast unexpectedly turning up a month later, inland. Thirty baggage asses were also acquired by Said bin Salim.[21]

The expedition's principals sailed from Zanzibar to the mainland in mid-June 1857 on the Sultan's 18-gun corvette, which Colonel Hamerton had borrowed to ensure that the two young officers would arrive rested on Africa's shores. Since he was dying, the consul's concern for their well-being was greatly to his credit.[22] Hamerton knew that many British explorers had died in Africa earlier in the century: among them Mungo Park and Richard Lander, both murdered on the Niger; Gordon Laing killed near Timbuktu, and Hugh Clapperton dying from dysentery at Sokoto. James Tuckey and fourteen of the thirty men who had volunteered to go with him beyond the first cataracts on the Congo had succumbed to fever before travelling a hundred miles. According to Mr Frost, Hamerton's physician, the consul mistrusted Burton and feared he would be a poor leader. Frost claimed that Hamerton murmured to Speke, at the moment of parting: 'Good luck, Speke; you know I would not travel with that man under any condition.'[23]

Speke and Burton and their people were landed at Kaole Point, eighty miles south of Bagamoyo, on 16 June 1857. Ten days later, after watching his protégés' heavily laden caravan lumber out of the cantonments into the bush, Colonel Hamerton sailed for Zanzibar. He died on board nine days later.

Preceded by the Sultan's blood-red flag, which was carried at the head of all Zanzibar caravans, the column marched along the coast for several miles before heading inland, led by the Baluchis, armed with archaic muzzle-loaders and German cavalry sabres. Immediately behind them, the main body of porters straggled for several hundred yards, their seventy-pound loads chafing backs and shoulders not yet hardened to them. They were carrying not only cloth and beads, but tinned food, tea, coffee, sugar, a box of cigars, a tent, camp beds, chairs, carpenters' tools, books, a table and a chest of scientific instruments. Within a fortnight, all of the expedition's three chronometers were out of commission due to nothing worse than a few sharp jolts. Evidently these precious clocks had not been swaddled in cotton wool and carried by the most reliable porters. This was a serious oversight since without the help of at least one chronometer synchronised to Greenwich Mean Time, longitudes were going to be very hard to calculate, which in turn would make it impossible to furnish the RGS with accurate maps, unless either of the white officers could show rare ingenuity.

Speke marched ahead of the column, while Burton brought up the rear, riding on one of the expedition's thirty donkeys, most of which were girthed with coir rope, tied too loosely to prevent their 200-pound loads from slipping. So 'they rushed against one another, bolted, shied, and threw their impediments'.[24] If the beasts were anarchic, so too were the men. Being used to obedient soldiers, both Speke and Burton found their Nyamwezi porters and their concubines and hangers-on hard to manage. The problem of how best to prevent thefts and desertions became a conundrum they never could solve.

An open plain dotted with termite mounds and baobab trees stretched westwards for a hundred miles and would have to be crossed before they reached the cooler terrain of the Usagara Mountains. For several days they marched beside the Kingani river (the Ruvu) on whose banks villagers grew sweet potato, tobacco and rice. Soon jungle and swamp replaced these cultivated fields. Hours of fiery sunshine alternated with brief but violent tropical showers which soaked them to the skin. At night, the air was muggy and clouds of mosquitoes tormented them. Away from the villages, zebra and kudu could be seen grazing. Eleven days after leaving the coast, Burton rose one morning feeling 'weak and depressed, with aching head, burning eyes and throbbing extremities'. He was oppressed by a conviction that he would fail in everything. Speke had already shaken off the same symptoms, and was providing meat for the entire expedition with his gun.[25]

During their earlier foray along the coast, Speke had felt that Burton was unreasonable not to hold up their caravan for longer periods so that he could shoot hippopotami. But though Burton had little interest in hunting and shooting, he did acknowledge that it was part of an explorer's duty to shoot and stuff birds and beasts as specimens, and this function, it had been agreed – along with surveying and mapping – would be performed by Speke.[26] Thanks to Isabel Burton's later efforts to present her husband as an early opponent of blood sports and shooting, most of his biographers have applauded their subject's disapproval of killing except for the pot. In fact Burton had brought two huge double-barrelled elephant rifles to Africa. One was lost in a river, but he would have used the other, he said, 'to attack the herds of elephant' in the forests of Ugogo, if he had had 'strength enough [and] time'. In his personal armoury he also had an 8-bore by W. Richards, a .22-inch 'pea' rifle, an air gun, two revolvers and a crossbow.[27]

'Sensible men, who went out to India, took one of two lines,' Burton wrote in his memoir, 'they either shot, or they studied languages.' So he could hardly have disapproved of Speke – as has been suggested – for having adopted one of the 'two lines' open to a 'sensible man'. After they had quarrelled, Burton would claim that Speke had enjoyed eating the embryos of the pregnant animals he had shot, implying that his love of shooting was perverted. In fact Burton never saw his companion eat an embryo, but founded his allegation on a single passage written by Speke in *Blackwood's Magazine*, in which African superstitions in regard to pregnancy were mentioned, but nothing was included to suggest that Speke had any interest in eating embryos.[28]

In reality, Burton must have found Speke's prowess with his rifle reassuring as they entered country where hyena and leopard posed a danger to the expedition's donkeys. The terrain became increasingly menacing:

The black greasy ground, veiled with thick shrubbery, supports in the more open spaces screens of tiger and spear-grass, twelve and thirteen feet high, with every blade a finger's breadth ... The footpaths are crossed by lianas thick as coir cables ... The earth, ever rain-drenched, emits the odour of sulphuretted [*sic*] hydrogen, and in some parts the traveller might fancy a corpse to be hidden behind every bush.

While crossing an endless plain, 'burnt tawny by the sun' and spotted with 'calabashes, palmyras, and tamarinds', distant blue hills could be seen. Burton reflected sadly that in Africa 'grace and beauty are seldom seen for long without a sudden change to a hideous grotesqueness'.[29]

As his disapproval of Africa increased, so too did his dislike of its inhabitants:

Their character may be briefly summed up: a futile race of barbarians, drunken and immoral; cowardly and destructive; boisterous and loquacious; indolent, greedy and thriftless. Their redeeming points are a tender love of family, which displays itself by the most violent 'kin-grief', and a strong attachment to an uninviting home.

Ignorant of the existence of the ruins of African-built Great Zimbabwe and the artefacts of West Africa, Burton declared that the sub-Saharan continent 'lacked antiquarian and historic interest'. Along the way, he sneered at 'filthy heaps of the rudest hovels, built in holes in the jungle', and pronounced East Africa 'revolting'. Although Burton measured Africans' penises, as part of his research, and asked intimate questions about the duration of the 'deed of kind', he had no interest in the way *they* viewed *him*, and he resented their stares. Burton categorised these as 'the stare furtive ... the stare curious or intelligent, which generally was accompanied by irreverent laughter regarding our appearance ... the stare greedy ... the stare drunken, the stare pugnacious and finally the stare cannibal'.[30]

Mganga, or medicine man.   The porter.   The Kirangozi, or guide.

Muinyi Kidogo.   Mother and child.

Burton's drawings of the heads of Africans, from *The Lake Regions*.

In comparison Speke was a model of sympathy: 'Poor creatures! They had come a long way to see us, and now must have a good long stare; for where was there ever a Mzungu [white person] here before?' He was even prepared to let people touch his hands and hair. When Henry Morton Stanley later visited places where Speke had spent time, chiefs reminisced about Speke and 'descanted his virtues'. [31] This is not to suggest that Burton was always aloof. One particular group of African women (and there would be others) won over the sardonic traveller.

Though destitute of petticoat or crinoline they were wholly unconscious of indecorum. It is a question that by no means can be answered in the affirmative that real modesty is less in proportion to the absence of toilette. These 'beautiful domestic animals' graciously smiled when in my best Kinyamwezi I did my devoir to the sex; and the present of a little tobacco always secured for me a seat in the undress circle.[32]

The Ladies' Smoking Party, from Burton's *The Lake Regions*.

After twenty-two days travelling through dense jungle, inter-spersed with 'barrens of low mimosa and dreary savannahs', the two Britons suffered their first severe attacks of malaria. Apart from the usual headaches, nausea, lassitude, weakness, inability to stand up, and alternating burning heat and freezing cold,

Burton endured visions of 'animals of grisliest form, hag-like women and men with heads protruding from their breasts', and during this 'fever-fit [had] a queer conviction of divided identity, never ceasing to be two persons that generally thwarted and opposed each other'. When he fell ill, he usually claimed in his journal that Speke was also prostrated and 'suffering even more severely'. In reality, Burton was the one who was sick for the greater part of the time they were together, while Speke always recovered rapidly and completely. In almost all Burton's references to 'my companion' in his *Lake Regions of Central Africa,* Speke is represented either as being gravely ill, or convalescing. On this early occasion, in mid-July 1857, Burton claimed that Speke was prostrated by 'a fainting-fit which strongly resembled a sun-stroke, and which seemed permanently to affect his brain'.[33] This was patently untrue.

Just after Speke was supposed to have suffered brain damage, the chronometers were found to be useless. In this alarming situation, it was Speke who came up with a way to calculate longitude without the aid of a chronometer set to Greenwich Mean Time. Longitude could only be worked out if the difference between local time and GMT was established, and was then converted into space on the map – a one hour difference in time corresponding to a 15 degree difference in longitude. Speke succeeded in calculating GMT by using 'lunar distances', which involved measuring with a sextant the angle between the moon and a selected star. That angle is the same at any place on the surface of the earth facing the moon at a unique instant of time. Armed with his angle, Speke could thumb through a Nautical Almanac, containing listings of such angles and their associated GMT. He also used 'a rude pendulum' – which consisted of a 4-ounce rifle-ball at the end of a 39-inch string 'attached to a three-edged file as a pivot' – to confirm his observations. Each swing of the pendulum recorded a second, so he could tell how much time had elapsed between his separate observations.[34] Rarely generous to Speke, Burton admitted that 'my companion' used his 'sextant and other instruments with a resolution and a pertinacity that formed his characteristic merits. Night after night, at the end of the burning march, he sat for hours in the chilling dews, practising lunars.'[35] Nevertheless, Speke let slip to Norton Shaw that Burton had refused to assist him, making his task far harder. 'Although I can take a lunar observation in 5 minutes with anyone simply noting the time and observations; yet without that assistance & having only two sextants & no stand, I find I can do nothing.'[36] Burton seems to have been scared to place himself in any situation in which Speke might show superior aptitude. On their return, he would deride him as 'unfit for any other but a subordinate capacity'. But to preserve this view of Speke, he had to pretend that 'celestial observation' was less important on an exploring expedition than his own chronicling of 'the ethnography of the tribes'.[37]

On 7 August 1857 Speke and Burton left the low-lying and unhealthy town of Zungomero glad to have increased their number of porters by forty-one, and thankful to be only a day's march from the foothills of the Usagara Mountains. They were both so ill they could only just sit on their donkeys. But both hoped that the higher ground would mean an escape from 'the fiery and oppressive heat of the river valley into the pure sweet mountain air'. Yet, on the way, food was in very short supply, and they were 'saddened by the sight of clean-picked skeletons, and here and there the swollen corpses of porters who had perished in this place by starvation'. Next they came upon victims of smallpox, 'and the sight made a terrible impression', wrote Burton. 'Men staggering on, blinded by disease, mothers carrying on their backs infants as loathsome as themselves. The poor wretches would not leave the path, as every step in their state of failing health was precious.'[38]

The cooler weather on the hills was a blessing but the nights were damp and dew-drenched and the ascent 'was painful, the path winding along the shoulders of stony and bushy hills'. Between the three ranges of the Usagara, the path descended into deep valleys, like that of 'the Mukondokwa [river] which spread out in swamps nearly two miles broad'. On paths slippery with mud, they came across columns of 'black pismire ants', which in no time 'fastened themselves to the foot or ankle', inflicting bites that burned 'like a pinch of a red hot needle'. Then their old relapsing fever returned, severely enough to force Burton to 'beg Jack to send me back a hammock from the halting-place'. Within days, the normally sprightly Speke was delirious, and, according to Burton, 'became so violent that I had to remove his weapons'. Dire though this sounded, two nights later Speke 'came to himself and proposed to advance'. A short illness indeed.[39]

Ahead, 5,700 feet above sea level, towered the third and most westerly range of the Usagara Mountains. 'Trembling with ague, with swimming heads, ears deafened by weakness, [Burton and Speke] contemplated with dogged despair the perpendicular scramble.'[40] Six days later, on 10 September, 'by resting after every few yards, and by clinging to our supporters, we reached the summit of the Pass Terrible', and five days later saw far below, the plateau of Ugogo stretching away to the west. Descending, they were threatened by a small group of spear-wielding Africans. The Baluchis fell on them bravely. 'Spears and daggers flashed in the sun, and cudgels played with a threshing movement that promised many a broken head.' Though the attack was beaten off, Burton believed that had his men been facing more serious odds they would have run away and saved themselves. 'There was not a soul to stand by Jack and me except ourselves,' he reflected sombrely.[41] At this time, when Burton was still too weak to walk unassisted, the Baluchis decided to stage a strike in order to force their leaders to kill the expedition's goats, despite the fact that every day Speke was in the bush shooting partridge and guinea fowl for them to eat. Speke countered the strike by ordering a march.

This brought them to reason, for hitherto they thought we should be afraid to go without them . . . Finding themselves left behind, they forgot their wrath and followed us. On the way they found Captain Burton lying by the roadside prostrate with fever, and taking compassion on him, brought him into camp.

An incident now took place which deepened Speke's mistrust of Burton. Because a third of the expedition's thirty donkeys had by this juncture been killed by the tsetse fly, there was an urgent need to recruit more porters. The only men not already carrying burdens were members of a group of slaves called by Burton 'the sons of Ramji' because they had been leased to the expedition by Rush Ramji, Ladha Damha's clerk. These men justifiably considered themselves superior to ordinary slaves, since they were all either interpreters, guides or *askari* (soldiers). They were adamant that they had not been engaged to carry loads, which led Burton to consider them spoilt and above themselves. But needing their help, if he were to avoid jettisoning his precious books, he promised to pay them if they would act as carriers. When Speke pointed out to Burton that he would find it hard to honour his promise, given the expedition's stretched finances, his leader simply whispered to him that 'Arabs made promises in this way, but never kept them; and, moreover, slaves of this sort never expected to be paid.' Speke countered angrily that Tibet had been ruined by officers not keeping faith with porters. A few days later, they happened upon, and hired, a group of fifteen carriers, who had been abandoned by their caravan after a quarrel. If this extraordinary piece of luck had not come their way, the sons of Ramji would have carried Burton's baggage for a hundred miles before being cynically cheated. A serious row between the two officers would then have wrecked the expedition before anything substantial could be achieved.[42]

On 7 November 1857, after weeks spent crossing Ugogo's dusty, lifeless winter jungle, Burton and Speke entered the Arab trading settlement of Kazeh (Tabora) with their caravan to the sound of 'booming horns and muskets ringing like saluting mortars'. They had marched about 600 miles in 134 days. A welcoming party of half-a-dozen white-robed Arabs led them to a pleasant *tembe* (a house with a veranda and inner courtyard) which was placed at their disposal for the duration of their stay.

The two men had a letter of introduction to a leading Indian trader, Musa Mzuri, but in his absence his Arab agent, Snay bin Amir, who was a rich ivory and slave dealer in his own right, overwhelmed Burton with gifts of goats, bullocks, coffee, tamarind cakes and other delicacies. 'Striking indeed,' wrote Burton, 'was the contrast between the open-handed hospitality and the hearty good-will of this truly noble race, and the niggardliness of the savage and selfish African – it was heart of flesh after heart of stone.'[43] Snay from now on would spend every evening conversing in Arabic with Burton, who described his host as well-read, with 'a wonderful memory, fine perceptions and [being] the stuff of which friends are made . . . as honest as he was honourable'. In fact he was a slave trader – an occupation anything but honourable. When David Livingstone accepted help from such men, he did so from necessity, with deep regret, because he loved Africans and knew he had to survive in order to expose their exploiters, whereas Burton despised Africans and the anti-slavery humanitarians who espoused their cause.[44] A few years later, Burton still thought of the Kazeh Arabs as his friends, and denounced Speke as heartless, because, during his next expedition, he refused to assist Snay bin Amir against Manwa Sera, the African king of the Nyamwezi. But Speke preferred Manwa Sera as a man, and thought him perfectly entitled, as the local African ruler, to levy a tax on Snay and his fellow traders.[45]

Kazeh.

Snay had visited 'the great Lake Tanganyika and the northern kingdoms of Karagwah and Uganda'. Because Speke could not understand Arabic, he found himself excluded from fascinating information until he began to feed questions for Snay to Bombay in Hindustani, for him to repeat to the Arab in Kiswahili before translating his replies back into Hindustani for his master.[46] While Burton was confined to his *tembe* with fever, Speke – with Bombay interpreting – learned from the Arabs that there were three lakes and not the single immense slug shown on the German missionaries' map. To the south was Nyasa (Lake Malawi), to the west the Ujiji lake (Lake Tanganyika), and to the north 'the sea of Ukerewe' (Lake Victoria), which might be largest of all. From the Ukerewe lake's position, due south of the White Nile, Speke reckoned it was more likely to be the source of the Nile than was the Ujiji lake, which the RGS's instructions had named as their objective.[47] But, though the Ukerewe 'sea' was slightly closer than the Ujiji lake, Snay warned them that the journey to it would be too dangerous to attempt.

While they were at Kazeh, Burton became gravely ill and Speke feared he would die if they did not leave at once for a healthier place. Burton wanted to stay on with Snay but on 5 December he had to admit he was 'more dead than alive' and ought to go.[48] Shortly before they left, when Burton seemed very briefly to be a little stronger, the pair discussed Snay's geographical information, with Speke in favour of visiting the northern lake, despite the added danger. Burton overruled him. 'Captain Burton preferred going west,' Speke wrote curtly in his journal. And because Burton was still rational, although unable to walk, as commander of the expedition he had to be obeyed.[49] Shortly after the sorry decision to head west had been made, Speke persuaded Burton 'to allow [him] to assume the command *pro tem*' so he could organise their removal from Kazeh.[50] By the time Speke had recruited fresh porters and collected up additional loads of cloth, beads and brass wire, Burton's health had taken another turn for the worse. Indeed, when Speke led the expedition into the next staging post *en route* to Ujiji, Burton had to be lifted from his *machilla* (litter) and 'begged Speke to take account of his effects, as he thought he would die'.[51] On 18 January 1858, Burton's 'extremities began to burn as if exposed to a glowing fire' and he sensed death approaching. Later he recalled the horror of it:

The whole body was palsied, powerless, motionless, and the limbs appeared to wither and die; the feet had lost all sensation, except a throbbing and tingling, as if pricked by a number of needle points; the arms refused to be directed by will, and to the hands the touch of cloth and stones was the same.

Burton would not be able to move his limbs for ten days, and it would be eleven months before he would walk unassisted. Until then he had to be carried by six slaves – eight when the path was difficult.[52] Lake Tanganyika was 200 miles distant, which seemed certain to be a gruelling ordeal for him, even on a litter.

At last on 13 February, after fording three small rivers, the caravan struggled through several miles of tall grass and then climbed a stony hill. As they reached the summit, Speke's ailing donkey died under him. For two weeks he had been suffering from ophthalmia with both eyes inflamed and sore and his vision so seriously impaired that he needed to be led when riding. Just behind him, Burton's sweating carriers arrived at the top of the hill supporting their master in his *machilla*. On catching sight of a streak of light far below, Burton asked Bombay what this was. He replied unemotionally: 'I am of opinion that that is the water.' After being carried a few yards more, Burton gained his first uninterrupted view of Lake Tanganyika. Fringed by 'a ribbon of glistening yellow sand [lay] an expanse of the lightest, softest blue, in breadth varying from thirty to thirty-five miles and sprinkled by the crisp east wind with tiny crescents of snowy foam'. Beyond the lake were 'steel-coloured mountains capped with pearly mist'.[53] In his state of near blindness, Speke was devastated that 'the lovely Tanganyika Lake could be seen in all its glory by everybody but myself'.

Arriving at Ujiji, the lakeside Arab slave-trading settlement, the explorers were told that the lake measured 300 miles from north to south – in fact it is just over 400, making it the world's longest. Burton's guess that it was about thirty-five miles across at its widest point was a slight underestimate.

Although they were the first Europeans to have reached any of Africa's great lakes, and had done so despite repeated attacks of fever, partial blindness, and in Burton's case paralysis of his legs, both men knew that a lot more had to be done to confer greatness on their journey. After all, an unspecified number of Arab and Nyamwezi slave and ivory traders had preceded them to the lake, none of whom had thought it sensible to tell people about it, or worthwhile to explore it thoroughly. Burton's RGS instructions had required him and Speke to reach Lake Tanganyika and then 'to proceed northwards' to find out whether it might in some way be linked with the White Nile and the Mountains of the Moon. If they could make decisive progress in this direction, their journey might yet be acclaimed as one of the greatest ever made on land. While they had been at Ujiji, several informants had electrified them with the news that 'from the northern extremity of the Tanganyika Lake issued a large river flowing northwards'.[54] No Arab they had spoken to had actually seen this river himself, and local Africans claimed to be ignorant of it. So visiting this river in person was of the utmost importance. This was particularly true for Burton, who had chosen to come to this lake rather than to the larger 'Sea of Ukerewe' which Speke had been in favour of exploring first.

The height of Lake Tanganyika above sea level was 1,850 feet, according to the more dependable of the expedition's two bath thermometers. (Their three specialist boiling point thermometers had all been inadvertently damaged.) Although the true height is 2,600 feet, even that level (had Burton known it) would not have reassured him. Since there were many known cataracts on the Nile – and others still to be discovered – the higher the lake, the greater the likelihood of its having some connection with the Nile. In this connection, it must have troubled Burton to know (as he did) that Kazeh, which was due south of the Ukerewe lake, was 4,000 feet above sea level, making it seem likely that the larger lake, which he had chosen not to visit, was going to be considerably higher above sea level than Lake Tanganyika. Yet Burton preferred to ignore this unwelcome probability.[55]

In truth, on his arrival at Ujiji, Burton was too ill to write or even talk, and lay prostrate on the earth floor of a hut for a fortnight, unable to move his legs. He was also suffering from ophthalmia – although not as badly as Speke. Despite his brief period in command, Speke was not prepared to make the next crucial decisions and waited for Burton to recover sufficiently for them to be able to discuss their next moves. Each day at noon, 'protected by an umbrella, and fortified with stained-glass spectacles', Speke visited Ujiji's market. Here he purchased daily supplies for the porters and other servants. Displayed for sale were fish, meat, tobacco, palm oil, artichokes, bananas, melons, sugar-cane and pulses. On certain days, slaves and ivory could also be bought.[56]

When Burton felt slightly stronger, he told Speke that they would have to hire from Hamid bin Sulayyan, an Arab slave trader, the only sailing dhow currently on the lake. Hamid lived on the far side of Tanganyika, so somebody was going to have cross in a dugout. Burton dithered because he thought this too dangerous for Speke. Nor did he trust Kannena, chief of the people living in and around Ujiji. 'Seeing scanty chance of success, and every prospect of an accident,' Burton decided to send his *factotum*, Said bin Salim, whose life he felt easy about risking. When the Arab flatly refused to undertake the mission, Speke offered to go in his place. But Burton, who still felt ill enough to die, did not want to risk leaving the expedition leaderless should Speke also perish. With slave traders active on Tanganyika's shores, all strangers were mistrusted by local Africans, especially those asking inexplicable questions about rivers. So it was brave of Speke to insist on going.[57]

On 3 March 1858, Speke embarked in a substantial dugout accompanied by Bombay to interpret, Gaetano to cook, two Baluchis to defend him, and eighteen local tribesmen to paddle. It was a puzzle how to pack everyone into so small a space along with their food and possessions. Almost immediately after they left harbour, storms forced them for three days to creep along the lake's eastern shore. 'These little cranky boats can stand no sea at all,' lamented Speke. On one occasion, when they were camped on land, the appearance of a single man with a bow led the whole party to panic and launch the boat at breakneck speed, so great was the crew's fear of being attacked. Crocodiles also inspired terror, since they were known to clamber aboard dugouts when hungry. Although Burton wrote that Speke never drank or smoked, in fact he smoked a pipe and found it soothing even in the cramped circumstances of a dugout.[58]

In the early hours of the morning of the 8th they crossed the lake and during the passage the crew refused to answer Speke when he asked the names of various headlands and bays. They feared that his unnatural inquisitiveness might lead to disaster. In fact the crossing was uneventful, and the locals welcomed them when they reached Kivira Island, a few miles from Tanganyika's western shore. When harm came to Speke, it was from an entirely unexpected quarter. After a quiet day spent smoking and story-telling with the islanders, Speke lay down to sleep in his tent. A storm blew up, waking him with its powerful gusts, and then subsiding. He lit a candle so he could see to rearrange his kit, 'and in a moment, as if by magic, the whole interior became covered by a host of small black beetles'. After failing to brush them off his clothes and bedding, he blew out the candle that had attracted them, and lay down. Although insects crawled up his sleeves, down his back and legs and into his hair, he managed to fall asleep, until woken, as he recalled:

[By] one of these horrid little insects ... struggling up the narrow channel [of the ear], until he got arrested by want of passage room. This impediment evidently enraged him, for he began with exceeding vigour, like a rabbit at a hole, to dig violently away at my tympanum ... I felt inclined to act as our donkeys once did, when beset by a swarm of bees ... trying to knock them off by treading on their own heads, or by rushing under bushes ... What to do I knew not. Neither tobacco, salt, nor oil could be found: I therefore tried melted butter; that failing, I applied the point of a penknife to his back, which did more harm than good; for though a few thrusts quieted him, the point also wounded my ear so badly, that inflammation set in, severe suppuration took place, and all the facial glands extending from that point down to the point of the shoulder became contorted . . . It was the most painful thing I ever remember to have endured . . . I could not masticate for several days and had to feed on broth alone.[59]

For many months Speke would be almost entirely deaf in this ear. Strangely, he found that his misfortune drew the inflammation away from his eyes and actually improved his sight.

Two days later the wind abated and Speke crossed to the island of Kasengé, where lived Hamid bin Sulayyan, the dhow-owning slave trader. Speke landed in hope but was soon disappointed. Not even his offer of £100 could persuade the slaver to hire out his large dhow. Africans, he maintained, could only manage paddles, and since his dhow had oars it would not be possible to lease it to Speke. He could not lend his crew to him, since he needed them for his own purposes. Nevertheless, Hamid greatly excited Speke with the news that a large river flowed out of the northern end of the lake. Sadly, Hamid had not himself been able to reach it because the behaviour of 'a barbarous boisterous tribe called Warundi' had so alarmed him. Hamid had addressed these words not to Speke but to Bombay in Kiswahili, and Bombay had then translated them into Hindustani for his employer – a process which left room for misunderstanding.

On the island, Speke was horrified when several mothers tried to sell their own children to his Baluchi soldiers for a loin-cloth or two. The destruction of normal maternal feelings brought home to him 'how foolish were all those other nations who allowed the slave trade to go on'.[60] With no reason to remain longer on this blighted island, he and his men re-crossed the lake without mishap, and were back in Ujiji after an absence of twenty-seven days.

While Speke had been away, Burton, whose health was little better, had passed the time 'chiefly in eating and drinking, smoking and dozing'. Yet he saw nothing inappropriate about making fun of an exhausted Speke on his return. 'I never saw a man so thoroughly moist and mildewed . . . his guns were grained with rust, and his fire-proof powder magazine had admitted the monsoon rain.' Speke's braving of the lake when ill and half-blind deserved better than to be dismissed by Burton in one scathing sentence, which he later published: 'I was sorely disappointed: he had done literally nothing.' In fact, though Speke had returned without the expected dhow, he gave Burton an account of the lake's shape – mainly from Hamid's information, though partly from personal observation.[61] But when Speke announced that a river flowed out of the northern end of the lake, Burton was ecstatic. Now it really seemed that Lake Tanganyika was a source of the Nile, if not *the* source. Burton's earlier decision to reject Speke's request to prioritise the larger lake now seemed vindicated.

In his journal Burton represented himself as getting healthier and Speke as being the one causing the delays, thanks to 'punching-in with a penknife a beetle which had visited his tympanum'. But ill though Burton still was, the near exhaustion of their trade cloth ruled out delaying their departure for the north end of the lake. Travelling in dugouts was no picnic for a man in good health, but would be hellish for 'a sick man, even in the best weather'. And now the rains had started again. 'I was sorry for it,' wrote Speke, 'but anybody seeing him [Burton] attempt to go would have despaired of his ever returning. Yet he could not endure being left behind.' Indeed, for Burton, reaching the northward-flowing river posed the greatest challenge of his life. 'Everything – wealth, health, and even life – was to be risked for this prize,' he declared.[62]

So when Kannena – the local chief whose canoes and assistance were essential for their success – refused to help, Burton overwhelmed him with an immense heap of trade goods, including some of his most expensive beads and a six-foot length of scarlet broadcloth 'that caused Kannena to tremble with joy' and to agree to travel with the explorers in the larger of two canoes. This craft would also accommodate Burton and thirty-three paddlers provided by Kannena. Speke was to be consigned to the smaller vessel with a mere twenty-two crewmen.

This crucial trip began in the early hours of the morning of 9 April, with Burton having to be half-dragged, half-carried for three miles over rough ground to the point of departure selected by Kannena for magical reasons. The sailors were serenaded to the shore by 'their loud-voiced wives and daughters performing upon the wildest musical instruments'. Out on the lake, Burton was soon ordering his crew not to 'splash water in shovelfuls over the canoe', and to stop trying to bump the other dugout. While resting, the sailors smoked cannabis. They had no regular halting places or routines, and often slept during cool mornings, before paddling through the heat of the day. Burton thought the local people on the banks were 'quarrelsome and violent . . . and addicted, like all their Lakist [sic] brethren, to drunkenness'. Whether sheltering from torrential rain under a sail, or being drenched as his men baled water from the bottom of the dugout, Burton was in constant pain. 'The crisis of my African sufferings took place during my voyage upon the Tanganyika Lake.'[63]

After nineteen days afloat, Burton wrote that he was 'suffering so severely from ulceration of the tongue, that articulation was nearly impossible, and this was a complete stopper to progress'. This affliction could not have come at a worse time, since, on 28 April, Burton met the three handsome sons of a local chief and heard from their lips the shocking news that the Rusizi river – despite what Speke had been told earlier – flowed *into* Lake Tanganyika rather than *out* of it. Bombay then put the matter beyond doubt by admitting that he had long suspected that he and Speke had misunderstood Hamid bin Sulayyan, who had actually meant the reverse of what they had at first believed him to have said. 'All my hopes,' confessed Burton, 'were rudely dashed to the ground.'[64]

Even though it now seemed all but certain that Lake Tanganyika could have no relationship to the Nile, it remained 'a matter of vast importance', as Burton conceded, to reach the Rusizi river in person to see with his own eyes the direction in which it flowed. So it is baffling that after saying that life itself was to be risked in order to reach the river, Burton put so little pressure on

Kannena to persuade him and his men to paddle on for six more hours, which was all it would have taken to reach the Rusizi.[65] The question of why his resolution crumbled at this vital moment is one that has not been answered. Henry M. Stanley would write in an essay on 'Our Great African Travellers', that Burton's 'struggle for the mastery over African geography ceased from this time, and Speke was permitted to come to the front [and] emerge out of the contest with honour and credit'. In Stanley's opinion this voyage on the lake revealed that Burton was no explorer but 'a traveller and "litterateur"'.[66]

When the two of them had returned to Ujiji, Speke announced that he 'wanted to finish off the navigation of the lake'. Burton brushed this aside at once and said 'he had had enough of canoe-travelling'. He assured Speke that 'our being short of cloth . . . would be sufficient excuse'. For two reasons this was a very peculiar response: the first being that very recently Said bin Salim, their *major domo*, had 'generously proposed . . . to return to the Arab depot at Kazeh, and fetch some more African money [cloth and beads] to meet the necessary expenses [for a full survey]'. The second reason, as Speke later recalled, was that while preparing to leave Ujiji 'by great good fortune some supplies were brought to us by an Arab called Mohinna [Muhinna bin Sulayman of Kazeh] . . . Help had reached us when we most required it.'[67]

Of course what Burton had meant was not that they had no cloth, but that they could plead lack of it to explain and excuse their failure. Indeed, back in Britain, Burton would tell the members of the RGS: 'I was compelled by want of supplies to desist from exploration.'[68]

The decision whether or not to return to the Rusizi was a defining one. A Livingstone or a Stanley would never have allowed a chief like Kannena to thwart him when so close to attaining a major objective. Both would either have attempted the short journey in a smaller canoe, which could have been propelled by a few men, or would have risked marching overland with a few porters. Kannena had refused to go the last few miles to the Rusizi, because the Warundi hated his people (or that was what he claimed) and might have killed them all if they had travelled to the lake's tip. When Livingstone and Stanley visited this same region a dozen years later, they experienced nothing worse than some shouting and stone-throwing by the Warundi.

According to Speke, Burton had refused Said bin Salim's offer to fetch more cloth from Kazeh because his real problem – which he had not wished to admit to – had been a total collapse of his health.[69] Burton wrote that by the end of his Tanganyika voyage his mouth ulcers had no longer obliged him to take sustenance through a straw, and that his hands had lost the numbness that for weeks had restricted his ability to write. But he had still lacked the strength to ride a donkey, and left Ujiji (as he had arrived) on a *machilla* carried by slaves. 'Only fancy what a time he has had of it,' wrote Speke to Norton Shaw – not without sympathy – 'eleven months in a bed-ridden state & being obliged to travel the whole time, more or less.' So, poor health *had* indeed lain behind Burton's decision. But this does not mean it would have been physically impossible for him to have made a final attempt to navigate the lake to its northern extremity. When the moment of choice had come he had lacked the self-destructive courage and obsessive determination of a true explorer. In the same circumstances, Livingstone, Stanley and Speke, who had volunteered, would all have been prepared to endure the pain and privation of one last desperate effort to reach the river. But the sybaritic Burton 'had had enough of canoe travelling', and that had been the end of it.[70]

While recuperating in Ujiji in early May, Burton and Speke discussed the desirability of visiting the northern lake, which the Arabs called Ukerewe. Burton, whose health was much the same, said he needed to spend a month with Snay and the other Arabs at Kazeh in order to finish his book. So Speke diplomatically suggested: 'If you are not well enough when we reach Kazeh, I will go myself, and you can employ the time taking notes from the travelled Arabs.' Burton agreed to this. But in years to come, in his desperation to make it seem that *he* had been responsible for initiating Speke's historic journey, he would write for public consumption that he had 'despatched him [Speke] from Kazeh'. He knew this was untrue. In a letter to Norton Shaw of the RGS, he stated unambiguously that: 'Captain Speke has volunteered to visit the Ukerewe Lake.'[71]

The journey to Kazeh from Ujiji took from 26 May to 20 June 1858, and during this time Burton 'again suffered severely from swelling and numbness of the extremities'. *En route*, a letter was handed to him by a trader, containing the news that his father had died nine months earlier. Though they had not been close, his loss distressed him greatly. Back at Kazeh, with its comfortable *tembes* standing among shady palms and fruit trees, Burton had to decide, once and for all, whether to go north with Speke and endure more danger and discomfort or whether to stay with his Arab friends and work on his book. He chose to do the latter. 'I was delighted with the prospect of a month's leisure for inquiry amongst the intelligent Arabs.'[72]

Speke often found Burton hard to fathom. '[Burton] did not come here to open up the country,' he told a friend disapprovingly two years later, 'but to make a book and astonish the world with his prowess. He never learnt observing . . . never protracted a bit of a map on the whole journey.'[73] By 'observing', Speke had not simply meant making scientific observations with instruments, but had been referring to the practical field skills familiar to anyone used to tracking game. As for Burton's desire to 'astonish' with his book, Speke thoroughly disapproved. A year later, he would write to his publisher: 'If there is anything you don't think exactly modest in my writings, cut it out without mercy.'[74]

For Speke, exploration was all about seeing *with his own eyes* features and places new to European geography, rather than writing down what this or that Arab had claimed he had seen on his travels. Though well-disposed towards Africans, Speke cared little for the minutiae of their customs, which Burton spent so many months describing, despite finding them repellent. Speke remarked that Burton 'had not shown himself capable of doing anything but making ethnological remarks at the dictation of the Arabs'.[75] Whenever Speke urged Burton to devote more time to exploration, he had been rebuffed. His own solo trip on the lake had been a failure – as had his journey in Somaliland. So perhaps Burton expected him to fail to reach the Ukerewe lake. After all, Snay had warned of the terrible dangers to be encountered in that direction. But this time, Speke was determined to succeed at whatever cost.

SIX

Promises and Lies

Burton seems to have grasped only at the eleventh hour that Jack Speke's mission, if successful, might one day affect him adversely. By then his 'subordinate' – as he would always describe Speke in his published accounts of their time together – was buying gifts to present to chiefs and making other preparations. Speke had not fallen out with Sheikh Said bin Salim, their Arab caravan leader, as Burton had done, and therefore wished to have this seasoned traveller by his side. The sheikh was experienced in negotiating with chiefs who demanded unreasonable quantities of trade goods for the right to pass through their territory, and Speke feared he might never reach the lake without being able to call upon such skills. But, unaccountably, Said bin Salim declined to accompany him. Back in England, Burton would claim that the sheikh had been terrified 'at the prospect of meeting death', but soon after refusing to come with him the Arab told Speke, 'in the most solemn manner, that Captain Burton positively forbade his going'.[1] In the margin beside this allegation, in his personal copy of Speke's *What Led to the Discovery of the Source of the Nile*, Burton scrawled in his spidery hand: 'The Sheikh lied. What did I gain by spoiling my own exped?'[2] His 'gain' would, of course, have been to prevent Speke 'spoiling his expedition' by outshining him. Presumably it was also to discourage him from going that Burton denied Speke's urgent request to take Ramji's men with him. They too were excellent linguists and negotiators. Burton had very recently dismissed them for insubordination, and he said they would be too expensive to re-engage for the journey to the lake. But after Speke had departed, he promptly re-employed these very same men for his own uses.

As he headed into the bush, Speke brooded on the fact that Burton 'had absolutely done his best to dissuade me from going'.[3] But eventually Speke managed to assemble a caravan of thirty-four men, with Bombay and Mabruki as his captains, a local man as his *kirangozi* or guide, Gaetano as cook, ten Baluchis as guards, and twenty local men as porters to carry gifts and trade goods. They left Kazeh in the evening of 9 July 1858.

The following night saw him and his men beyond the borders of Unyanyembe, sleeping in an African village, with Speke curled up in a smoky hut, and his men lying beside the cattle, or under the eaves of other huts.[4] Each day they would start before dawn when the air was so cold that Speke's fingers 'tingled with it'. Occasionally, he spoiled himself with 'a hearty breakfast of cold meat, potted Tanganyika shrimps, rozelle [*sic*] jelly, and coffee', which must have made a good start to a day spent travelling through 'a waterless wilderness of thorn and forest'. For a typical lunch, he ate local tomatoes and chili with a village fowl.[5] After many hours walking through such terrain, Speke always enjoyed coming to villages and seeing the women grinding grain on large slabs of granite, singing as they pounded with small stones held in both hands. The cows, he noticed, were much smaller than at Lake Tanganyika. Every evening, his porters danced and sang a song composed for the occasion. 'It embraced everybody's name connected with the caravan, but more especially Mzungu [the white man].' In the hope of getting some milk to drink and some eggs, Speke visited a female chief, whose arms were decorated with huge brass rings. After receiving this food, he was happy to let 'the sultana' – a woman of about sixty – 'manipulate' his shoes, 'the first point of notice in these barefooted climes', and then touch his trousers, waistcoat and buttons. Even his hair, 'which was likened to a lion's mane', he permitted to be touched by various courtiers. Because he agreed with Burton that few Africans believed any traveller 'so stupid as to go through danger and discomfort for exploring and science, which they simply do not understand', Speke let it be thought that he was going to the lake 'to barter cloth for large hippopotami teeth'.[6]

African village scenes.

By 29 July, nearly three weeks into his march, he was crossing hilly country with well-cultivated valleys dotted with palms. The tropical feel of the landscape told him he was nearing the lake. In fact on the very next day, 30 July, Speke saw a sheet of water several miles away that turned out to be a creek of the great Nyanza (like Nyasa, the word Nyanza denoted a large body of water). Before reaching it, they had to cross a deep, muddy watercourse frequented by hippopotami, but on 1 August he was descending from the hills and following the creek, which was wide enough to accommodate small islands. His eyes were still too sensitive for him to travel without wearing his 'French grey spectacles which so excited the crowds of sable gentry who followed the caravan [that they were soon] peering underneath [his] wide-awake to get a sight of [his] double eyes'. Soon, to get some peace, he had to take them off and close his eyes while Bombay led his donkey. Two days later, with spectacles on his nose again, Speke climbed a low hill and from its summit was overjoyed to see 'the pale blue waters of the Nyanza'.[7]

Frustratingly, he could get no accurate idea of the lake's size because Ukerewe and Mzita islands obstructed his view of the water lying beyond them to the north. But even the limited archipelago he *could* see entranced him with its sandy beaches and wooded slopes.

The islands, each swelling in a gentle slope to a rounded summit . . . [were] mirrored in the calm surface of the lake; on which I here and there detected a small black speck, the tiny canoe of some Muanza [*sic*] fisherman. On the gently shelving plain below me, blue smoke curled above the trees which here and there concealed villages and hamlets, their brown thatched roofs contrasting with the emerald green of the beautiful milk-bush.

After three weeks in the bush, the lovely margins of the immense and still unseen lake made him dizzy with excitement. To stand here, as the white discoverer of the mysterious Nyanza, which was justly called a 'sea' by the Arabs, and was entirely unknown in Europe and America, made this the most joyful moment of his life to date.

I no longer felt any doubt [he wrote later] that the lake at my feet gave birth to that interesting river, the source of which has been the subject of so much speculation, and the object of so many explorers. The Arabs' tale was proved to the letter. This is a far more extensive lake than the Tanganyika, so broad that you could not see across it, and so long that no one knew its length.[8]

At this ecstatic moment, Speke longed to venture out onto the water and would have been able to do so if Burton had not left their portable boat behind. Instead Speke had to try to acquire a vessel at this place where the Arab slave trade was rife, and where people were naturally fearful of strangers. He wanted to travel either to Ukerewe or to Mzita island and from a high point gain an uninterrupted view of the lake to the north. Unfortunately, Mahaya, the chief at Mwanza – where he had reached the Nyanza – was at daggers-drawn with Machunda, the king of Ukerewe and Mzita. This enmity would inevitably delay his collection of the necessary men and boats. Furthermore, Speke heard from Mahaya, and from an Arab trader, Mansur, that the local canoes were too frail for journeying far on the unpredictable lake. People never attempted to cross from east to west in open water, but invariably hugged the southern shore. So how big was the Nyanza? Chief Mahaya's wife swore that there was no end to it. One of her headmen tried to convey the same message by repeatedly nodding his head to the north, 'and at the same time throwing forwards his right hand and making repeated snaps of his fingers, endeavouring to indicate something immeasurable'.[9]

By calculating the temperature at which water boiled, Speke estimated the lake to be almost 4,000 feet above sea level. Since he knew that the elevation of the bed of the Nile at 5° North Latitude was less than 2,000 feet, he concluded joyfully that 'it would indeed be a marvel if this lake was not the fountain of the Nile'. The Nyanza's height certainly allowed for its waters to descend the many cataracts, which were said to exist in the river's course above the most southerly point reached by traders like De Bono.[10] And Speke had other reasons for believing that 'his' lake gave birth to 'that interesting river'. He had heard from

Arabs at Kazeh that the Mountains of the Moon were situated to the west of the Nyanza, and that several large rivers flowed into its western side from these peaks. This tallied with Ptolemy's famous map of the Nile. As for the lake's size, he had been cheered by a native of Unyanyembe who had told him that he had visited 'Kitara or Uddu-Uganda' – which Speke guessed to be at 1° North Latitude – where 'the sea was of such great extent, and where winds blew so boisterous that the canoes did not trust themselves upon it'.[11] So to sail around the lake, or to cross it from south to north, was clearly going to be a major enterprise, requiring far more time than he could spare at present. So, on 7 August, Speke started the journey back to Kazeh.

My reluctance to return may be easier imagined than described. I felt as much tantalized as the unhappy Tantalus . . . and as much grieved as any mother would be at losing her first-born, and planned forthwith to do everything that lay in my power to visit the lake again.[12]

Speke could hardly have conveyed his possessive feelings for the lake more strikingly than by comparing them to a mother's protective fears for her threatened first-born! And if the Nyanza was now *his* child, he knew very well that Lake Tanganyika was Burton's offspring, on whose behalf he would doubtless exercise all his talent for special pleading. Already Speke suspected that his leader had discouraged him from visiting the Nyanza in order to preserve the lustre of *his* Lake Tanganyika.

Passing through the agricultural districts south of the Nyanza, Speke was greeted in a friendly spirit by people who seemed to view his 'advent as a matter of good omen'. On first seeing the lake, 'the pleasure of the mere view vanished in the presence of those more intense and exciting emotions which are called up by the consideration of the commercial and geographical importance of the prospect before me'. Indeed, as he marched towards Kazeh, commercial questions preoccupied him. Pondering why these people were not more prosperous, though living in a marvellously fertile and well-watered country, Speke placed most of the blame on local wars. Indeed, on the way to the lake, his guide had insisted on a lengthy diversion to avoid such fighting. Only a 'protecting government', Speke decided, would be able to prevent the strong – whether Africans or Arabs – from always getting what they wanted from the weak. But it would be wrong, he thought, for 'any foreign European power to upset these Wahuma [local African] governments; but on the contrary I would like to see them maintained as long as possible'.

From thoughts of a benign imperial future, Speke was brought down to earth by a group of drunken spear-wielding villagers bursting into the hut where he was resting. Despite being asked to leave, they continued to try to touch him, and the Baluchis made things worse by threatening to start shooting. At this dangerous moment, Speke bravely left his hut, and, with the help of a translator, told the growing crowd outside that 'they might now stand and gaze as long as they liked'. Luckily for him, this turned out to be all they wanted to do.[13]

In the early hours of the morning of 25 August, 'under the delightful influence of a cool night and a bright moon', Speke and his men marched the last eighteen miles of their return journey to Kazeh, having completed 452 miles there and back, in forty-seven days. Kazeh's villagers hurried after the caravan, shrieking and 'lullabooing'. It was breakfast-time when Speke at last arrived at Burton's *tembe* and was invited in.

Burton was genuinely relieved to see Speke because he had heard reports of fighting near the lake. At first Speke only told his leader about the immense size of the Nyanza, and Burton responded enthusiastically to this news. But towards the end of breakfast, Speke announced that he had found the source of the White Nile. Of course he could not prove his case because he had not circumnavigated the lake, and therefore could not be sure that there were not several bodies of water to the north of Ukerewe Island. That a link existed with the Nile would inevitably remain conjectural until he could establish that the Kivira river, which was reputed to flow northwards from the lake to Gondokoro, really did so.

Yet, however sensible it might be to take one cautious step at a time, Speke's astonishing experience had catapulted him beyond the realms of strict logic. He had stood on the banks of an immense inland ocean of uncharted water and had seen great flocks of birds swoop over its waves. He had heard the wind sighing in the reeds and had felt its breath on his face, cooled (as he thought) by its passage over hundreds of miles of water. He had seen its still and glassy surface at dawn and had sensed its mysterious presence in the darkness. Most suggestive of all to him was the fact that all this water was located due south of the most southerly points yet charted on the course of the White Nile. But Burton promptly dismissed all this as foolish speculation, only condescending, after they had ceased talking, to make a brief and grudging note of Speke's route.[14]

As if struck by lightning Burton was unable to marshal arguments with which to crush Speke's effrontery. His disbelief was emotional as well as logical. How *could* his ill-educated subordinate, who had failed to reach the Wadi Nogal and had not even had the wit to hire a dhow on Lake Tanganyika, have suddenly seized the greatest geographical prize of all time? It seemed perverse, impossible and downright wrong. How could Burton even be sure that Speke had properly understood his Arab and African informants through the medium of Bombay's Hindustani? Yet, even as he fought against the possibility of Speke being right, he began to fear in his guts that he might be.

Speke for his part had offered up his discovery to his superior officer for his applause, only to receive scornful disbelief. Yet despite being stung to the quick, Speke understood his commander's terror of being upstaged. Indeed, unknown to Speke, Burton was already secretly wondering how he could contrive 'to share in the glory won by his lieutenant'.[15] But 'Ruffian Dick' seemed oblivious to the sorry fact that in order to share the discovery, he would have to applaud Speke's achievement and return with him to the lake for a longer reconnaissance. Burton not only turned down Speke's proposal to re-visit the Nyanza but refused even to consider the possibility of sailing north across the lake to Uganda to find out whether the Kivira river flowed out of the north side of the Nyanza. This was what Kazeh's principal Indian merchant, Musa Mzuri, had assured Speke that it did.

Of course, such an ambitious journey could only begin after fresh supplies had been sent from Zanzibar. And the need to wait several months for them would mean outstaying their allotted period of military leave. But in the circumstances the East India Company would almost certainly have permitted them another six months. True they were overspent, but what now seemed within their grasp was nothing less than the solution of the world's greatest geographical mystery, which had been the ultimate goal of their RGS instructions. After making their way to the unknown lake described by the missionaries, they had been required *'to proceed northwards towards the probable source of the Bahr el Abiad* [White Nile] – *your next great object to discover'* [my italics].[16]

Once again, the principal reason why Burton refused to go even as far as the Nyanza was his dire state of health.[17] But since Burton had managed to travel to and from Ujiji on a litter, he could surely have travelled to the lake in like manner? After all, the journey was no longer than the trip to Ujiji from Kazeh and, by declining, Burton was tossing away his last chance to be seen as the joint-discoverer of the Nyanza. Meanwhile, Speke was left ruefully to reflect that without the encumbrance of a sick leader, he could have gone on to Uganda with Musa Mzuri.[18]

Burton and Speke began their journey to the coast on 26 September 1858, with 152 porters recruited by the ever-resourceful Said bin Salim. By flogging them, Burton persuaded the sons of Ramji, now serving him again, to carry loads. As usual, he was being carried by six long-suffering slaves, which he calculated was at a cost thirty times greater per hour than travelling by train in Europe.[19]

Early in October, Speke was struck down by a serious illness. It began with a burning sensation that felt as if he were being branded with a hot iron above the right breast. The pain moved from there to his right lung, thence to his spleen and finally settled in the region of his liver. Bombay called this affliction the 'little irons'. It was probably caused by a species of roundworm living in the flesh of the wild animals which Speke had shot and eaten. He had horrible nightmares, in one of which 'a pack of tigers, leopards and other beasts, harnessed with a network of iron hooks, were dragging him like the rush of a whirlwind over the ground', seeming to be avenging the hundreds of wild creatures he had shot. At times he suffered violent contractions of the muscles in his limbs; and once he felt ill enough to call for pen and paper so he could write a farewell note to his family. In his delirium, Speke spilled out his resentment of Burton for his supposed accusation of cowardice at Berbera and for his treatment of his diaries. Burton ought not to have been as much surprised by this outpouring as he affected to be. Many African travellers hated the sight of one another when laid low by a variety of African fevers. In fact it was commonplace for explorers to say terrible things, not only when delirious, but when fully conscious too.[20] For instance, one of H. M. Stanley's fever-stricken white companions tried to shoot him; and on the Zambezi Dr Livingstone came to blows with his own clergyman brother.[21] But Burton would later suggest that Speke's ravings were due to a permanent character change suffered during the journey. Biddable and agreeable at the outset, Speke (so argued Burton) now wished to be the expedition's leader and brooded over imagined insults. Burton had hitherto represented him as a figure of fun, but now (though not really *now*, since Burton would write his criticisms many months later) his companion became 'crooked-minded and cantankerous', exactly the kind of self-seeking junior officer who would betray his commander.[22]

In order to put all the blame on Speke for the mutual dislike that followed his return from the lake, Burton would make out that the two of them had been good friends until the difference of opinion about the lake wrecked everything. 'Jack changed his manners to me from this date,' wrote Burton. 'His difference of opinion was allowed to alter companionship.' But Burton's 'memories' of earlier days on their journey, when an admiring Speke had brought his diary to him for correction and the two of them had read Shakespeare together, like master and pupil, were fanciful. Not only had Speke been alienated by Burton's treatment of his Somali diaries long before their Tanganyika journey, but also his down-to-earth, masculine literary tastes (he most enjoyed 'political, statistical or descriptive reading') made a scenario of reading Shakespeare together wholly implausible. Burton's most sympathetic biographer, Mary Lovell, has shown him tenderly nursing a sick and increasingly disagreeable Speke, although Speke had actually been nursed by Zawada – one of Said bin Salim's concubines. Rarely generous with money, Burton was so impressed by Zawada's gentleness that he 'liberally rewarded' her for her devotion.[23]

During their return march to Zanzibar – when Speke was also ill enough to be carried in a litter – a shocking incident occurred. The *kirangozi* taken on at Ujiji had loitered behind for several days because his slave girl had been too footsore to walk at the caravan's pace. 'When tired of waiting,' recorded Burton, 'he cut off her head for fear lest she should become gratis another man's property.' If this brutal murder had been committed in a caravan commanded by Stanley or Baker, the *kirangozi* would have been arrested and handed over to the authorities in Zanzibar or Khartoum. Livingstone would have done the same if he had managed to command the obedience of his other porters. But it seems that Burton did not do anything at all. This is puzzling since earlier he had taken away a much beaten five-year-old slave from Mabruki, and given him to the kindlier Bombay.[24] Both Europeans were still too sick to stand, and Speke was unable to keep a diary at the time. So their physical state may explain the lack of immediate punitive action. But two months later, Burton appeared to have forgotten about the crime entirely. In his report to the Secretary of State for India, he said that because this same man had 'behaved well in exhorting his followers to remain with us', he had 'rewarded the *kirangozi*'.[25]

The two explorers finally reached Zanzibar on 4 March 1859 after a futile eleventh-hour diversion to Kilwa, made at Burton's insistence despite the approach of the rains and there being a cholera epidemic in the area. Burton appears to have been looking for almost any excuse to delay his return to London, where he would clearly have to pay tribute to Speke's achievement. Back at the British Consulate Burton confessed that he sank into 'an utter depression of mind and body', in which even speaking was too much effort.[26] Without a word to Speke (at this time or later), he penned a letter to Norton Shaw, which must have been extraordinarily painful to write. Enclosing Speke's map of the Nyanza, Burton wrote:

To this [Speke's map] I would respectfully draw the attention of the committee as there are grave reasons for believing it to be the source of the principal feeder of the White Nile.[27]

Having made this brave admission, Burton was to prove incapable of ever making it again, and he compounded the dishonesty of keeping his true beliefs to himself by embarking on a long and increasingly vindictive campaign to discredit Speke. His justification was that hitting back was the only natural response to Speke's treachery. Burton's accusation, which has damned Speke's reputation ever since, was that he betrayed his erstwhile leader on his return to England – by going to the RGS alone, having promised only to go there with Burton. It was in this underhand way, said Burton, that Speke cut him out and gained for himself sole command of the next Nile expedition. This notion, that Speke behaved in a totally unprincipled way, has been believed, and repeated, by five out of six of Burton's most recent biographers, and also by the author of Speke's only biography. But was Speke really 'a cad' as one of Burton's best-known biographers has insisted he was?[28]

After sailing together from Zanzibar on 22 March 1859 on the clipper *Dragon of Salem,* the pair disembarked at Aden on 16 April, and stayed with Burton's old friend, Dr John Steinhaeuser, the civil surgeon of the colony.[29] A dozen years later, Burton would write that Steinhaeuser 'repeatedly warned me that all was not right' – implying that his friend suspected that Speke was hatching some mean-minded plan. In fact, in the same para-graph, Burton stated that, while at Aden, he and Speke 'were, to all appearance, friends'. Whatever the doctor really thought, he realised that Burton was a very sick man and recommended 'a lengthened period of rest'. So it came as no surprise to anyone that Burton was not granted a medical certificate to travel, whereas Speke was.[30] They had been three days at Aden when a warship, HMS *Furious*, docked. She was due to sail again the moment she finished coaling, so the two explorers had to decide at once whether to take up the offer of a passage up the Red Sea to Suez. Speke accepted and Burton (presumably not having any choice) declined. And now the crucial words are supposed to have been uttered, which contain Speke's alleged 'promise'. They are usually imagined to have been noted down by Burton soon after being spoken.

... the words Jack said to me, and I to him, were as follows:- 'I shall hurry up, Jack, as soon as I can,' and the last words Jack ever spoke to me on earth were, *'Good-bye, old fellow, you may be quite sure I shall not go up to the Royal Geographical Society, until you come to the fore and we appear together. Make your mind quite easy about that.'* [in italics in Volume I of *The Life of Captain Sir Richard F. Burton* compiled by Isabel Burton][31]

If all the above words were written at the same time – and there is no reason for thinking they were not – that time must have been after Speke's death in 1864, because the phrase about their being 'the last words Jack ever spoke' is integral. But 1864 was five years on from the parting in 1859, and this makes it seem unlikely that Burton would have remembered the dialogue *verbatim*. Eight years after Speke's death, Burton would allege, in support of the 'dialogue', that Speke wrote to him from Cairo in April 1859 – *en route* to England – 'reiterating his engagement and urging me to take all the time and rest that broken health required'.[32] No biographer or archivist has ever seen this letter. This is suspicious, since what appears to be a complete run of Speke's correspondence with Burton has survived in Burton's letter books, now in the British Library.[33] On balance, it seems unlikely that this key letter, which Burton would have been especially eager to preserve, ever existed. To be concerned about such things is not to split hairs. Speke's supposed 'betrayal' of

Burton at this time has been thought to prove that Speke was an unprincipled and devious man, who wronged a more trusting and honourable companion. The truth about whether Speke was indeed to blame for the bitter feud, that would do lasting damage to his reputation as a man and as an explorer, hangs to a large extent on what if anything was actually promised by him. History's favoured scenario is that Speke promised not to go to the RGS on his return to England unless accompanied by Burton, but then did exactly what he had sworn not to do – and thus secured backing for his own African expedition cutting out his former leader. That is why the evidence for the 'promise' deserves close scrutiny.

I found it surprising when reading Speke's only biography, and the six most recent lives of Burton, not to learn anything about *Speke's* version of events in Aden. It appeared that he had never written anything on that subject. But, incredibly, he *did* write his own account, which remained generally unknown until some details of it were published in 2006, in a slim volume by a retired American professor.[34] The greatest revelation in Speke's account is contained in a single sentence concerned with the very point at issue: what Burton said to him at their moment of parting. Casually, after dealing with other seemingly more important matters, Speke mentions that just before his ship sailed: 'Captain Burton said he would not go to England for many months as he intended to go to Jerusalem.' Then, after a few sentences devoted to his medical certificate, and his voyage home, Speke adds: 'A fortnight after my landing in England, Captain Burton un-expectedly arrived . . .'[35] There could hardly have been a greater contrast between the two versions! So which was true? Burton's or Speke's?

The fact that Burton's famous lines of dialogue did not appear in print until 1893, three years after Burton's death, must damage their credibility. Burton's original journals were destroyed by his widow, so cannot be used for comparison. Consequently, the famous dialogue is only to be found in Isabel's printed biography of her husband – a volume that contains many passages of dubious dialogue and numerous untruths.[36] In fact her denigration of Speke flags up the possibility that Isabel may herself have been the author (or at least the improver) of the suspect dialogue. Burton himself, however, provided the best reason for doubting the dialogue's authenticity. He had started his memorable letter to Norton Shaw (the one in which he admitted that Speke's lake could well be the source of the Nile) with the information that because of his poor health, he would be leaving Aden 'a short time' after Speke. He then added: 'Captain Speke, however, will lay before you maps & observations, & two papers, one a diary of his passage on the Tanganyika lake . . . and the other his exploration of the Ukerewe or Northern Lake.'[37] So far from expecting Speke to wait for him to return to England before going to the RGS – Burton had actually expected Speke to do the opposite. But while this seriously undermines the notion that Speke promised not to go to the RGS unless accompanied by his former leader, Burton's statement to Norton Shaw, that he would be back in London 'a short time' after Speke, torpedoes the idea that he had ever had any genuine intention of returning home via Jerusalem. So was Speke as unreliable as Burton, and did he invent the projected trip to the Holy Land?

The only reason Speke might have cooked up this story would have been to make his pledge-breaking visit to the RGS seem less dishonourable by exaggerating the length of time Burton had led him to believe he would be away from England. But since Burton actually expected Speke to go to the RGS *without him*, this idea falls to the ground. It is more likely that Burton was the liar, telling Speke he would return via Jerusalem, without having any intention of doing so. By pretending it would be many months before he would return to England, he could have hoped to lull Speke into imagining that he had plenty of time in hand, and need not hurry to the RGS the moment he landed. Then, if Burton caught the very next homeward-bound steamship, and Speke in the meantime had gone to the country to relax with his family, Burton might even arrive first at the RGS and grab command of the next expedition!

The obvious reason for doubting the truth of Speke's Jerusalem claim was that he never published it in any book or article – and therefore never had to defend it in public. But letters are in existence, showing that Speke *wanted* to publish in 1864 and only held back because his paternalist publisher, John Blackwood, and his controlling mother put him under intense pressure not to append to his forthcoming book an eight-page coda, or 'Tail', containing the Jerusalem claim along with criticisms of Burton relating to both expeditions.[38] But though at first Speke allowed the 'Tail' to be excluded, by the summer of 1864 he was agitating for it to go into the second edition of his *What Led to the Discovery of the Source of the Nile.*

Blackwood was not worried about Speke's description of his parting from Burton in Aden (and what they did or did not say to one another), but he strongly advised against entering into any public argument with Burton over his failure to pay his porters properly. Details of Burton's meanness to his African employees occupied half of the 'Tail's' eight pages. Blackwood feared that by digging up this dispute, Speke would look vindictive. The other pages had mostly been devoted to Burton's failure to grasp the immense importance of going north to Uganda before leaving Africa. Speke argued fiercely for publication of the 'Tail', but eventually his publisher managed to persuade him to exclude it from all copies, except from a few specially printed volumes to be presented to three or four members of Speke's own family.[39] But, by mid-August 1864, Speke had decided, whatever the consequences, to publish the 'Tail' in the next edition of *What Led to the Discovery of the Source of the Nile* and instructed Blackwood's chief manager, George Simpson, to include it in the second edition. He informed Simpson that 'the ladies' (his mother and his aunts) now agreed with him that 'the best policy is to speak the truth and shame the Devil' – aka Richard Francis Burton.[40] At the same time, in an attempt to reassure Blackwood, Speke told him that he would be able to 'prove all I have said'.[41] So Speke *had been* prepared to defend his claim about Jerusalem.

The only reason that the 'Tail' did not appear in a second (or any other) edition of *What Led to the Discovery of the Source of the Nile* was that Speke died before a fresh printing could be undertaken. Then, after his death, his grieving mother and brothers were in no mood to publish anything likely to involve them in a public row with Burton about unpaid porters and his shortcomings as an explorer. So for almost 150 years the 'Tail' would continue to exist only between the covers of those three or four copies.[42]

Although the odds are heavily against Speke having made a pledge to his former leader, Burton's cry of betrayal was also based on what he alleged was done in London in May and June 1859. 'I reached London on May 21st,' he would write, 'and found that everything had been done for, or rather against me.'[43] So what *had* been done?

SEVEN

A Blackguard Business

———— ◦◦◦◦ ————

According to Burton, the day after Captain Speke returned to England:

He was induced to call at the rooms of the Royal Geographical Society and to set on foot a new exploration. Having understood that he was to await my arrival in London before appearing in public, I was too late with my own project.

Although this is a bizarre distortion of what actually happened, it is an account that would broadly speaking be accepted by historians.[1]

In reality, on 8 May 1859, the day Speke landed in England, he had booked a room at Hatchett's Hotel, Piccadilly, and did not need to consider whether to contact the RGS since news of where he was staying had leaked out. Without his doing anything, a note arrived from Dr Norton Shaw inviting him to come to the monthly meeting of the RGS at Whitehall Place on the following day.[2] Speke wrote back agreeing to attend 'tomorrow's discourse'. Knowing that discussion would centre on the Nyanza, he wrote with greater caution than he had yet shown: 'I believe most firmly that the Nyanza is one source of the Nile, if not the principal one.'[3] Shaw knew from Speke's earlier letters that he, rather than the less resilient Burton, had been responsible for making all the expedition's scientific observations and maps and had independently visited the Nyanza. For this reason, he seems to have decided that Speke's arrival ahead of Burton presented the RGS with an opportunity that should be grasped. He therefore took Speke to the Belgravia house of the secretary designate of the RGS, Clements Markham – a former naval officer, traveller and occasional journalist – so the three of them could discuss, in confidence, what should be done. The upshot, in Markham's words, was that: 'We talked the whole matter over for some time, and the next day I went with him [Speke] to Sir Roderick ... [who] at once took him up.'[4] Speke may just possibly have manipulated Shaw and Markham into engineering a meeting with Sir Roderick Murchison, the President of the RGS, but it seems far more likely that the two RGS officials decided for themselves that Speke ought to meet Sir Roderick as soon as possible.

Sir Roderick Murchison.

In any case, on the 9th, Speke met Murchison, showed him his map of the Nyanza, and told him that the Kivira river fed the White Nile. 'Sir Roderick, I need only say, at once accepted my views,' wrote Speke, adding joyfully that the RGS President's parting words had been: 'Speke, we must send you out there again.'[5]

Burton arrived at Southampton docks on 20 May, and later complained that on arrival he found that 'everything had been done for, or rather against me. My companion stood forth in his true colours as an angry rival.'[6] But *was* Speke angry, and had 'everything been done against' Burton? On 19 May – soon after learning that Burton's arrival at Southampton was imminent – Norton Shaw asked Speke to prepare a paper for the regular meeting at the RGS on the 23rd. Speke replied in a courteous, rather than an angry spirit:

If a geographical paper is required to illustrate my map, I shall be very happy indeed to write one. At the same time, I think it would be unfair to Captain Burton, commandant of the expedition, if I touched upon anything not entirely relating to that branch – especially as I know that Burton has been very industrious in observing & obtaining great masses of matter appertaining to the manners, customs, & productive resources of all the country traversed by the expedition.[7]

Undoubtedly Speke wanted an expedition of his own, but this was hardly surprising given that Burton had been ill for three-quarters of the time and had made it impossible for him to explore Lake Tanganyika and the northern Nyanza with any thoroughness. Burton later argued that Speke had only resolved to go back to Africa without him because Laurence Oliphant – a talented young travel writer, reviewer and RGS committee member – had poisoned Speke's mind during a week when chance had flung them together on board HMS *Furious*, then steaming from Aden to Suez.[8] Of course Speke had not needed Oliphant to alert him to his incompatibility with Burton and his need to be master of his own destiny in future. In fact, after leaving Kazeh, Speke had written to his brother Edward, suggesting that he should come to Uganda with him.[9]

But regardless of what Speke wanted for himself, there is no firm evidence that by the time Burton reached London on 21 May the RGS's grandees had already come to a clandestine decision to send Speke to Africa without his old companion, as Burton would soon allege. Certainly, by late May Speke had met Sir Roderick Murchison, who had said he wanted to send him back to Africa at the head of his own expedition. Yet decisions of this kind were not made by the President, despite his considerable influence, but by the Expeditions' Sub-Committee. Indeed, a month after Burton had returned both he and Speke were summoned to appear before this very committee to argue in favour of their recently submitted written proposals for separate African expeditions. No doubt, Laurence Oliphant, who was a member of this three-man committee, had told his colleagues that while he and Speke had been on board HMS *Furious*, the young explorer had told him about his dislike of his former leader, and that this made it essential to invite him and Burton to submit *different* East African proposals so the committee could judge which most deserved their support.

Burton wrote: 'I was too late with my own project. This was to enter Africa via the Somali country, or by landing at the Arab town of Mombas [*sic*], whence the south-eastern watershed of the Nilotic basin might be easily determined.'[10] In reality, 'lateness' had nothing to do with the subsequent rejection of his proposed itinerary. Three years earlier he himself had declared travelling inland from Mombasa to be too dangerous, and his hairbreadth escape in Somaliland made this alternative route just as unwelcome to the RGS. Inevitably, Burton's shocking physical condition could only have been a disincentive to send him on another, very likely fatal, African journey. His future wife, Isabel, described him on his return as 'partially blind . . . a mere skeleton, with brown yellow skin hanging in bags, his eyes protruding and his lips drawn away from his teeth'. A short walk in the Botanical Gardens usually ended, she said, with him being taken away 'almost fainting in a cab'.[11]

Speke, on the other hand, was in robust health, and his proposal that he should return to the Nyanza by the route he had already pioneered, and then march along the lake's western shore to Uganda and the Kivira river, struck the committee as much more realistic. Yet, despite the fact that Burton's plans were wholly impractical, his claim that he had been prevented by Speke's treachery from embarking on a viable mission would be repeated in three of his books, in his wife's biography, and then by most of his biographers. The cumulative power of this oft repeated cry of betrayal can hardly be understated. Even Speke's solitary biographer has repeated it.[12] It has proved irresistible to follow the line of the acerbic geographer and eugenicist, Francis Galton, and see Speke as 'the conventional, solid Briton' being preferred to Burton by unimaginative Establishment figures like Murchison, who would have been sure to mistrust 'Ruffian Dick' as 'a man of eccentric genius and tastes, orientalised in character and thoroughly Bohemian'. In fact they would have backed Burton to the hilt if they had thought him likely to be a winner in Africa. But when Burton faced Laurence Oliphant and his more venerable colleagues across the well-polished committee table in Whitehall Place, he had been so ill and so unconvincing in his arguments that he had not even been able to offer an approximate starting date for his journey. His most recent and clear-sighted biographer has fairly described his proposal as 'the last despairing throw of the dice by a gambler, who knows that his luck has run out'.[13]

Two days after this uncomfortable encounter, Burton experienced another. As leader of the expedition he was awarded the Founder's Medal of the RGS in front of a large and well-dressed audience of gentlemanly geographers and travellers. A happy event, one might have thought, but because Sir Roderick Murchison spent most of his talk before the presentation praising Captain Speke rather than Captain Burton, his audience was left with the strong impression that although Burton was entitled to the medal as leader of the expedition, Speke had actually done all the work. 'A marked feature of the expedition is the journey of Captain Speke from Unyanyembe to the vast inland lake called Nyanza,' remarked Murchison, not long before drawing Burton's attention to 'the very important part which your colleague, Captain Speke, has played in the course of the African expedition headed by yourself'. The silver-haired geographer had earlier talked about the great value of Speke's observations for latitude and longitude. These unwelcome reminders of his indebtedness to his 'subordinate' compelled Burton to pay him a tribute of his own. He would never do so again.

To Captain Speke [Burton conceded] are due those geographical results to which you have alluded in such flattering terms. Whilst I undertook the history and the ethnography . . . to Captain Speke fell the arduous task of delineating an exact topography, and of laying down our positions by astronomical observations – a labour to which at times even the undaunted Livingstone found himself unequal.[14]

Yet, within a year, Burton would write in the preface to his *Lake Regions of Central Africa*,

I could not expect much from his assistance; he was not a linguist – French and Arabic being equally unknown to him – nor a man of science, nor an accurate astronomical observer . . . During the exploration he acted in a subordinate capacity, and . . . was unfit for any other but a subordinate capacity.[15]

Eventually, Burton would claim the expedition's entire achievement as his alone:

I led the most disorderly of caravans into the heart of Inter-tropical Africa, and succeeded in discovering the Tanganyika, and the southern portion of what is now called the Victoria Nyanza Lake . . . My labours thus rendered easy the ingress of future expeditions, which had only to tread in my steps.[16]

For a man who had been carried most of the way and had made not one scientific observation, this was quite a claim.

Three separate sources of disagreement had fanned the embers of mutual dislike into hatred by the end of 1859. The first concerned what each man owed to the other financially, the second arose from the publication of Speke's most recent journals, and the third sprang from a difference of opinion over the payment of the African porters who had accompanied them. The two explorers had returned to Britain in May, and as late as July Speke, at least, was still behaving towards his companion with consideration. When first approaching the Edinburgh publisher, John Blackwood, Speke explained that he wanted his diaries to appear in *Blackwood's Magazine* (a great favourite with Indian Army officers) rather than in volume form, because he did not want to bring out a book of his own before Burton could publish his *magnum opus*. 'I would on no consideration be in any kind of opposition to him,' he insisted.[17] Nor would Speke write anything offensive about Burton in the text of the published diaries, which would appear in consecutive instalments in *Blackwood's Magazine* in September and October. He could not have been expecting Burton to react with hostility, since before publication he had told Burton that he hoped his (Speke's) journals 'would be of use to him & his writings'.[18]

Yet, in the event, these two seemingly innocuous instalments enraged Burton. 'They contained,' he wrote later, 'futilities which all readers could detect. A horse-shoe or Chancellor's wig, some six thousand feet high and 180 miles in depth, was prolonged beyond the equator and gravely named "Mountains of the Moon". The Nyanza water, driven some 120 miles further north than was originally laid down from Arab information.'[19] Of course Speke's placing of the Mountains of the Moon in a crescent just to the north of the northern end of Lake Tanganyika (about 200 miles south of their actual position) separated that lake from the Nile but, since he and Burton, while navigating the lake, had been emphatically assured by numerous informants that the river at Tanganyika's northern end ran into the lake and not out of it, any relationship between Lake Tanganyika and the Nile had been shot to pieces already. In his *Lake Regions* Burton countered by placing *his* Mountains of the Moon to the north of Speke's Nyanza, blocking *it* off from the Nile, in the spirit of tit for tat, and giving the impression that the Tanganyika was more likely to be the Nile's source than the Nyanza.[20] This was despite Burton's earlier opinion expressed to Norton Shaw that the Nyanza was probably 'the source of the principal feeder of the White Nile'.

Burton's true statement that Speke had mapped the Nyanza as extending much too far north upset Speke considerably because Burton had had in his possession, while they had been in Africa, an account by the Austrian missionary, Ignatius Knoblecher, of his travels south of Gondokoro, making clear that the trading station and mission were 200 miles north of the Nyanza. Speke told Norton Shaw angrily: '[Burton] ought not to have let my map go home without telling me that I had flooded the mission station with my Lake.'[21] To Burton himself, he wrote in great distress: 'All I can say is that for the sake of Geography it is a shocking pity you did not tell me.' Burton did not try to excuse himself by denying having read Knoblecher's book. He had wanted to make a fool of Speke and had succeeded.[22]

Another blow to outwardly friendly relations was a difference of opinion about precisely when Speke should have paid his share of the expedition's debts, over and above the £1,000 originally voted by the British government. In mid-June he offered to pay half of any sum finally owing to creditors, but only after Burton had made a request to have the money refunded by the Bombay government. The moment any request was refused, he would pay his share.[23] Burton was irritated by this delaying tactic – as he saw it – but did not get round to submitting a request for a refund from the Bombay government till late March the following year. A refusal finally came back several months later and Speke's brother Ben paid the debt for Jack who had already sailed for Africa.[24]

The argument over whether the expedition's porters and other servants ought to have been paid anything when the two explorers had returned to Zanzibar, aroused more ill-feeling than the matter of their private debt to one another. It was made more acrimonious by the involvement of Captain (eventually General) Christopher P. Rigby, who had succeeded Colonel Hamerton as British Consul on Zanzibar, and had been Burton's only rival as an exceptional East India Company linguist in India. Whether Rigby was jealous of Burton is beyond proving, but he certainly disliked him and when he knew that Speke felt the same way, it created a strong bond between them.

Burton maintained that the twelve Baluchi soldiers, who had been provided by Sultan Majid, had been given 'no regular pay, as they were servants of the prince'. Each man had been paid 'an advance' of 20 Maria Theresa dollars; and, when first engaged, they had been led to believe (and these are Burton's words) that there were 'prospects of remuneration on [their] return'.[25] Burton refused to pay them this 'remuneration' because of their 'notorious misconduct', such as disobeying orders and deserting for brief periods. Given the hardships and dangers of African travel, few porters would ever have been paid anything at all if occasional refusals to march and periodic absences had disqualified them from receiving payments after months of back-breaking work.

This was certainly the line Speke took when he wrote to Rigby on behalf of the Baluchi guards and the rest of the porters and other servants. 'The Baluchis, I told him [Burton] repeatedly, ought to be paid something.' The Sultan of Zanzibar agreed, and gave these men 2,300 dollars (£460). Speke took the same line over the ten superior slaves, whose owner, Ramji, had been 'clean robbed'. Ramji had been paid 300 dollars as an advance, and Burton later refused to pay anything for the eleven additional months these men had been with him. In his view they had been 'the most troublesome of the party'. Speke disagreed, both in their case, and in the case of Sheikh Said bin Salim, the caravan leader, who had been paid 500 dollars as an advance by Colonel Hamerton and had been promised by him 'that if he escorted the gentlemen to the Great Lake in the interior, and brought them in safety back to Zanzibar, he would be handsomely rewarded'. It had been Speke's understanding that Said would receive 1,000 dollars and a gold watch.[26] One reason Burton gave for declining to pay Said bin Salim a penny more was that he had refused to go with Speke to the Nyanza. In fact Burton had forbidden him to go there. Burton also accused Said of carelessness and dishonesty, but Speke considered this unjust and appointed Said to lead the next caravan he took into Africa.[27] According to Speke, Burton's scandalous meanness to Said had been due to his discovery that he had lied to him about being of royal blood. Being a tremendous snob, Burton had seen this deception as a heinous offence. 'This was really a blackguard business,' declared Speke who felt angry enough to provide Rigby with ammunition to send to the Secretary of State for India.

The breach between the two explorers became unbridgeable when Burton learned in early February 1860 that Speke's damaging letters to Consul Rigby on the subject of the unpaid porters had been forwarded by Rigby to the Secretary of State for India. In due course Burton was asked to answer allegations made by Rigby about his failure to pay his men. His subsequent explanations were rejected and, soon after receiving an official rebuke, Burton told Speke he no longer wished to communicate with him directly.[28]

Speke's true character shines out in a note he wrote to Burton on 16 April 1860, shortly before leaving England. Given how dangerous his journey would be, Speke knew this could be the last opportunity he would ever have to end their feud. Both men had been addressing one another as 'Sir' in recent exchanges, but Speke reverted to an earlier, friendlier form of address:

My dear Burton,

I cannot leave England addressing you so coldly as you have hitherto been corresponding, the more especially as you have condescended to make an amiable arrangement with me about the debt I owe to you.[29]

The original of Burton's reply no longer exists, only the draft he wrote out in pencil on the margins of Speke's conciliatory letter. The debt, he agreed, had been satisfactorily dealt with, then added: 'I cannot however accept your offer concerning our corresponding less coldly – any other tone would be extremely distasteful to me, I am sir . . .'[30] Whether Burton mailed this chilling reply exactly as drafted can never be known. His career as an explorer was over, and he was consumed with hatred for the man who had gone out to Africa with him as his 'subordinate' and had now supplanted and eclipsed him. As the years went by, he would neglect no opportunity to deride and undermine Speke's geographical theories and achievements.

EIGHT

Our Adventurous Friend

John Blackwood.

While waiting for the British government to come up with the £2,500 he needed for his new expedition, Speke got on with writing up his journals for publication.[1] To start with, his chosen publisher, John Blackwood, told him discouragingly that he had found 'great defects' in his work, 'principally arising from your want of practice in literary labour'. But Speke took this in good part, replying with disarming candour: 'I am a perfect green at the goose quill: my fort [*sic*] being in the field and not in the cabinet.'[2] But the middle-aged man of letters and the young soldier-turned-explorer soon came to like and respect one another. Very soon

Blackwood revised his opinion of Speke's work and admitted that he was no longer correcting it as carefully as before, because he often found himself so involved that he 'forgot to note whether you are writing good or bad English . . . There is a reality about your description of the escape from the Somali which is better than the finest writing.' Despite the fact that many of his authors over-wrote – as was then almost mandatory for anyone wishing to acquire a reputation for elegant writing – he assured Speke that he meant to preserve his 'plain honest narrative & not attempt any literary adornment'.[3] Since Speke had warned him that he would find it 'intolerable if a confounded fellow' tried to make him 'talk about "azure skies"', this was just as well.[4] It was a token of Blackwood's affection for his intrepid author that to make up for the inadequacies of his formal education he sent him novels such as *The Mill on the Floss* to help him develop a taste for distinguished writing.[5] Writing about Speke, Blackwood told John Delane, the editor of *The Times*,

[My] modest, good-natured, dare-devil friend . . . is a character with a strong dash of Robinson Crusoe about him: I never met with such a mixture of simplicity and almost childish ignorance, combined with the most indefatigable energy and the most wonderful shrewdness in his own particular way.[6]

But Blackwood never patronised Speke in person and consequently the explorer would feel wholeheartedly grateful. 'Many thanks for what you have done,' he wrote, after the successful publication of his journals in *Blackwood's Magazine*. 'You have made me quite a literary character. I feel as proud as Punch . . . It's wonderful to contemplate on!'[7]

After staying with the Blackwood family at St Andrews, Speke visited his publisher's offices in Edinburgh and was shown there a copy of a map of the Bahr el-Ghazal – the complex river system to the west of Gondokoro feeding the Nile's main channel. This map was the work of a Welsh mining engineer, John Petherick, who had first gone to the Sudan to prospect for coal a decade earlier, and doubled as British honorary vice-consul at Khartoum and as an ivory trader in the regions far to the west of Gondokoro.

Speke had first met Petherick at Sir Roderick Murchison's house and now told Blackwood that he meant to get in touch with him again, since he was 'without doubt the greatest traveller in that part of Africa'.[8] Speke hoped that Petherick might be prepared – if funds could be found – to push southwards up the Nile and meet him with men and boats, somewhere between the northern shores of the Nyanza and Gondokoro, giving him essential help to pass through the hostile tribes said to inhabit this unexplored country. By then Speke hoped to have completed his northward march up the western side of the Nyanza to Uganda, and to have located the precise spot on the lake's northern shore where the Kivira – or the Nile, as he hoped it was – flowed out. He wrote with *gung-ho* enthusiasm to Norton Shaw: 'I have asked Petherick to come here for a few days, before he goes out again, that we may make arrangements for <u>ripping</u> open Africa together, he from the north & I from the south.'[9]

Petherick did indeed come to stay with Speke at his parents' imposing house in Somerset, and although a member of the English landed gentry like Speke might have been expected in this snobbish era to look down on an ivory trader from a poor background, even at their first meeting they got on well with Speke affectionately comparing the energetic manner of the big, curly-haired Welshman to that of 'a rampant hippopotamus'. He soon commended Petherick to Blackwood as a future contributor to his magazine, and made a generous subscription to the publication costs of Petherick's book *Egypt, the Soudan and Central Africa*.[10]

Unfortunately, the British government – having at last voted Speke his £2,500 – was not prepared to contribute anything towards the cost of Petherick's expedition, and so the RGS was obliged to launch a public appeal, which would close in January 1861 having failed to raise more than half the £2,000 required. Great misunderstandings would arise from this short-fall. So although the RGS told Petherick in his instructions that he should 'proceed in the direction of Lake Nyanza, with a view to succouring Captain Speke, and bringing him and his party in safety to the depot at Gondokoro', Petherick secretly doubted whether he would be able to spend anything like the two years he was being asked by the RGS to devote to waiting for Speke, way to the south of Gondokoro.[11] As Speke began to list all the sextants, artificial horizons, pocket chronometers and other equipment he would be taking, he knew nothing of Petherick's doubts. In fact it comforted him to know that burly Consul Petherick would be out there on the upper Nile with fresh supplies and equipment, waiting to help him negotiate the dangerous final quarter of his epic journey. The possibility that Petherick might fail to show up never occurred to him.

Because of his disastrous relationship with Burton, even before Speke had left Africa in 1859 he had started agonising over whom to take with him as his companion on his next expedition. Petherick would only be with him for the final phase, so Speke was going to need another colleague for the bulk of his journey. When he had been homeward-bound with Burton, an Arab caravan had disgorged a letter from Christopher Rigby, the newly appointed consul at Zanzibar. It contained the awful news that Speke's army officer brother, Edward, had been shot and killed in Delhi, soon after the outbreak of the Indian Mutiny. Only weeks earlier Speke had written to Edward in high spirits, announcing: 'I have made up my mind to return to the Nyanza, and to trace the Nile down to Egypt,' and then suggesting that his brother come 'home' as soon as possible so that, together, they could solve the Nile mystery.[12]

Denied the loyalty of an actual brother, Speke settled for a brother officer, Edmund Smythe. 'He is the hardest and toughest man in all Bengal,' he told Norton Shaw proudly, 'a wonderful pedestrian, and an astonishing cragsman, and a man of precisely my habits.' But not a man of Speke's constitution because a month later he heard that Smythe was 'feverishly inclined' like the 'feverishly inclined' Burton.[13] This was a fatal weakness; so Speke decided to take instead Captain James Grant, whom he had known and liked since 1847, when they had both been twenty-year-old Indian Army cadets. The pair had fought together in the Punjab War, and while Speke had been in Africa, Grant had been swept up in the Mutiny. Besieged in Lucknow for two months, he had been wounded, losing the thumb and forefinger of his right hand. He was an even-tempered, quietly spoken Scot, who had taken a degree in natural philosophy and maths at Marischal College, Aberdeen, but nevertheless shared Speke's love of life in the wild. Speke told the RGS that he valued Grant particularly 'for his conciliatory manner with coloured men [and] for general good temper and patience'. This would make a change from Burton, who had constantly derided Africans and had been sharp and impatient with Speke. Grant had another virtue in Speke's eyes: Georgina Speke, his mother, 'thought a lot of him'.[14]

As the time for Speke's departure approached, John Blackwood became increasingly worried about his youthful author. 'I am quite startled to think that you will soon be away from all your friends bound on your daring expedition . . . Often shall we think of you & hope that all is well with our adventurous friend.'[15] At their previous meeting, Blackwood had warned Speke that he had already 'risked his life to an extent far beyond the average dangers which the human being is likely to escape'. Shouldn't he perhaps be more sensitive to 'the feelings of those to whom he was dear?' Speke responded with a rhetorical question: 'How would I feel if any foreigner should take from Britain the honour of discovery? – rather die a hundred times!'[16]

This idea that great geographical achievements could confer *kudos* not only on the individual explorer but also on his nation had fired Sir Roderick Murchison's imagination ever since he had promoted and publicised Dr Livingstone's famous trans-Africa journey of 1853–56. Public fascination with the doctor had enabled Sir Roderick to enlist government aid for him to return to Africa, and even for Burton and Speke to go out there a year later. In August 1859, Speke had decided to ask the Queen whether he ought to call his Nyanza, the Victoria Nyanza. She had agreed, and Murchison had applauded Speke's patriotism.[17] And as if to confirm that Speke's new enterprise had national

Captain James Grant.

significance, he and Grant were invited to sail for the Cape, *en route* for Zanzibar, in the warship HMS *Forte*, which left Portsmouth on 27 April 1860.

Like Murchison and Livingstone, Speke believed that Africans would be 'wiped off the face of the earth' by the Arab-Swahili slave trade, unless Britain established in east and central

Africa a government resembling the British Raj in India.[18] But Her Majesty's Government did not share this view. Only in the 1880s would the word 'imperialism' gain its usage as a laudatory euphemism for the indiscriminate theft of territory. So although Speke and Grant were expected to bring Britain glory by solving the Nile mystery, they were not being sent out as an imperial advance party. In Palmerston's eyes the two explorers were brave, foolhardy young men, who might if they were lucky survive and increase the world's geographical knowledge.[19] Though Murchison railed at the premier's lack of imagination, he could do nothing about it as yet.

The dangers ahead were underlined for Speke and Grant on their arrival at Zanzibar when they heard that another European explorer had recently been murdered in the interior. He was a young German, Albrecht Roscher, who in October 1859 had reached Lake Nyasa from the east a few months after Livingstone had arrived on the lake's western shore. Two of Roscher's murderers were executed at Zanzibar shortly after Speke's and Grant's arrival. On the appointed day, the Sultan's death warrant did not arrive on time, so the executioner appealed to Grant, as the Sultan's senior guest, to sanction the double beheading. He did so with stolid self-assurance: 'Yes, certainly; proceed.'[20] Though Speke had been away shooting hippos and so was spared the sight of the sword's flashing descent and the gush of blood, he anticipated seeing worse things on their journey. Rigby warned him about ongoing fighting in the interior between the young Nyamwezi chief, Manwa Sera, and the Arab slave traders of Unyanyembe. The war had spread to Ugogo, where one of the principal chiefs had recently been shot dead.[21] But there could be no turning back now and the process of hiring porters began in earnest.

Sheikh Said bin Salim was at once engaged as the caravan's leader, followed by former employees Bombay and Mabruki. Consul Rigby allowed his friend to recruit Baraka, Frij and Rahan, trusted crewmen of his official launch. The highly capable Baraka would command sixty-five Wangwana – the black Swahili-speaking free people of Zanzibar. One of these men was Uledi, who later became James Grant's valet, and would one day serve H. M. Stanley with great distinction on all his major journeys. Speke had never detested the Baluchi soldiers as Burton had done, and now recruited twenty-five of them too. A hundred Nyamwezi porters, and ten Hottentots, engaged at the Cape, completed the personnel, taking the caravan's numbers to 200. Grant and Speke gave slightly different total figures, which included four women in both estimates.[22]

They started from Bagamoyo on 2 October and were soon experiencing the usual frustrations and hardships of African travel: excessive demands for *hongo* (payment for passage), deserting porters, disappearing goats and donkeys and then their first bouts of fever. Grain was scarce and at times the men refused to march. There were also numerous thefts of cloth, with which porters furtively bought extra food for themselves. So Speke and Grant were soon flogging carriers guilty of stealing the means of common survival.[23]

Passing through Uzaramo, Speke met Chief Hembé, who confessed to being the murderer of Lieutenant Maizan. The chief excused himself from full responsibility for amputating the young Frenchman's limbs and slicing off his genitals while he was still alive, on the grounds that he had been acting under the orders of Arabs who had been prepared to do anything to discourage Europeans from muscling in on their ivory trade. Being inclined to think well of Africans, Speke chose to believe that the chief would have been killed if he had disobeyed. He therefore decided not to involve the Zanzibar authorities.[24] Speke's great patience with Africans served him well when the tormenting mutual jealousy between Bombay and his deputy, Baraka, erupted into occasional violence. Since Said bin Salim was seriously ill, this rift between the caravan's two most important African captains even threatened the expedition's future. But Speke managed to reconcile them, while simultaneously bolstering Bombay's ego against future assaults from the verbally brilliant Baraka.[25]

Arriving in Ugogo, the explorers encountered famine conditions. The Unyanyembe Arabs had recently been foraging in the region, so when Speke and Grant appeared, 'the poor villagers, accustomed only to rough handling, immediately dispersed in the jungles'. Speke sent out parties with cloth to buy food, but the hiding people fired arrows at them. Meanwhile, Speke was abused by his own people for his 'squeamishness' about using his guns to persuade these villagers to give up their grain.[26] The rains swept in across Ugogo, 'worse than an Indian Monsoon', and soon desertions increased dangerously. Speke blamed them partly on the harsh conditions, partly on the threats of local people, but he also saw them as 'a judgment on us whites for the blackguard conduct of Burton in cheating the first men of the moon [Nyamwezi] who had dealings with our race'. The expedition's numbers had almost halved by early December, though the Wangwana, under Baraka's command, remained loyal. The desertion of eight of the Baluchis hurt Speke most of all since he had paid to liberate them from slavery 'and had given them muskets as an act of good faith'.[27] Speke responded to the emergency by ordering a series of forced marches, intended to reduce the time during which they were exposed to disease and war. The caravan survived because both Grant and Speke were excellent shots and able to provide flesh from small birds and animals as large as giraffe and buffalo.[28]

Both men enjoyed hunting, especially when their quarry was as dangerous as a rhinoceros. But events would make them more risk averse. Very conscious of the need to provide large amounts of meat, Speke went out one moonlit night, with a man behind him holding a second rifle for emergencies, and managed to hit a large rhinoceros bull, and then 'brought him round with a roar, exactly to the best position I could wish for receiving a second shot'. But when reaching for his second gun, Speke found that his gun-bearer had scrambled up a tree. Providentially for Speke, the rhinoceros unexpectedly 'turned right about and shuffled away'. When Speke managed to kill a second rhino, his Wangwana failed to reach the carcase ahead of local Wagogo villagers and were forced to compete with them for cuts of meat.

A more savage, filthy, disgusting, but at the same time grotesque scene cannot be conceived. All fell to work armed with swords, spears, knives and hatchets – cutting and slashing, thumping and bawling, fighting and tumbling and wrestling up to their knees in filth and blood in the middle of the carcase. When a tempting morsel fell to the possession of any one, a stronger neighbour would seize and bear off the prize in triumph.[29]

On 7 January 1861, when not far from Kazeh, Speke and Grant were electrified to hear that Manwa Sera, the Nyamwezi ruler, who was at war with the Unyanyembe Arabs, was approaching their camp with thirty armed followers. Speke ordered the remaining Baluchis to fix bayonets, and told all the porters who possessed guns to fetch them. On seeing this show of arms, Manwa Sera's men drew back, and he himself entered Speke's camp, attended only by a small bodyguard. The young king said he had heard that Speke was short of porters and offered to assist him if he would accompany him to Kazeh and then mediate on his behalf with the Arabs. Manwa Sera described how he had tried to levy a tax on all merchandise that entered his country, and had consequently been attacked by the Arabs, who had forced him to live like a fugitive and had replaced him with a puppet. But he had not surrendered. Speke 'felt very much for him' and thought him 'the very picture of a captain of the banditti of the romances'. Manwa Sera spontaneously offered to drop the tax if the Arabs would recognise him rather than the pretender, so Speke could see no reason why Snay bin Amir and his compatriots would not want to oblige the exiled ruler rather than go on fighting. However, soon after Speke's and Grant's arrival in Kazeh on 23 January, Snay and the other Arabs turned down the offer of mediation and attacked Manwa Sera with 400 men. The Nyamwezi king proved a superior tactician and routed the Arabs, killing Snay in the process. The survivors, on returning to Kazeh, begged Speke to invite Manwa Sera into Kazeh for a conference, so they could murder him. Naturally, Speke rejected their request.[30]

At Kazeh, Speke and Grant faced a crisis. All but two of their hundred Nyamwezi porters had recently deserted, as had all twenty-five Baluchis. One of the Hottentots was dead and five others so sickly that they would have to be sent to the coast. About sixty Wangwana were still with them, as were Bombay, Baraka, Uledi and Rahan. Sheikh Said bin Salim was too sick to go on, due to an old illness which Speke implied was syphilis. 'It was a sad misfortune as the men had great confidence in him.'[31] Luckily, the Indian merchant Musa Mzuri, with whom Speke would have travelled to Uganda if Burton had not prevented him, agreed to help him find porters for the next and crucial leg of his journey. There being none to be had in Unyanyembe thanks to the fighting, Musa travelled north to Rungua and returned with a disappointing thirty-nine men, 130 having deserted him on the way back due to their fear of Manwa Sera. Although Speke felt 'thrown on his beam-ends', he marched north on 16 March 1861 with the hundred or so men he had left. The months ahead were to pose the greatest test he had ever faced.

Musa, upon whom Speke depended, had been an opium addict for forty years but there was nothing wrong with his business acumen – he was charging Speke 400 per cent more for trade goods than he would have had to pay for the same items at the coast. He lived surrounded by his wives and by 300 slaves and servants, most of them Tutsis from Rwanda, who tended his orchards, vegetable gardens and his herd of cattle, besides acting as porters on his ivory trading expeditions.[32] According to Musa, all would be well when the explorers reached the court of his friend King Rumanika of Karagwe. But this monarch was 300 miles away to the north and the territory of numerous chiefs would have to be crossed *en route*. Whether Speke would be able to keep his porters with him and pay the dues demanded by these African petty-rulers was a question he was in no position to answer. He had been warned that he would never get through Usui since Chief Suwarora was so extortionate in his demands that he would 'tear him to pieces'.

After only a couple of days' travelling, the caravan reached Ukumbi where the villagers 'flew about brandishing their spears and pulling their bows in the most grotesque attitudes, alarming some of my porters so much that they threw down their loads and bolted'.[33] Most of these porters had been suffering severe bouts of fever every tenth day, which usually lasted from two to five days. Grant, who was ill himself, was jealous of Speke, 'who had been so long in Africa [that he] was not subject to them'. But Speke had other worries. He had just learned that the Watuta – Ngoni (Zulu) mercenaries employed by the Arabs – were plundering the country all around.[34]

In this dangerous situation, Speke was immensely relieved when Musa's men (though without Musa himself) unexpectedly arrived at his camp with 300 porters. Speke now sent to Kazeh for the rest of his people, including Bombay – who had succeeded the Sheikh as *cafilah-bashi* – ordering them to come on north with the supplies that they had been forced to leave behind for want of porters. But just when he should have been able to advance, news broke that the Watuta, who were renowned for their ferocity, had surrounded Rungua and were blocking the road to Karagwe and Buganda, as part of their strategy to contain Manwa Sera's Nyamwezi followers. Worse still, Musa's porters suddenly announced to Speke that they would not be allowed to travel with him for more than two marches because of the war.[35] So Speke now had no alternative but to march back to Kazeh to try to sort things out with Musa, and then confront the Arabs and demand that they stop using the Watuta against Manwa Sera. He failed to change Musa's mind about the porters, but did extract a promise that he would come with him to Karagwe, as soon as he was feeling better. He looked horribly ill, despite dosing himself with 'what he described as his training pills – small dried buds of roses with alternate bits of sugar candy'. Musa died a few days later of the combined effects of fever and his long addiction to opium. So Speke had lost the only merchant he trusted.

More bad news swiftly followed. Chief Suwarora, the first important ruler on the road to the north, was building a line of thorn *bomas* (hedges) to defend his frontier and promised 'to kill every coast-man, who dared attempt to enter Usui'. 'My heart was ready to sink as I turned into bed,' wrote Speke in his journal, 'and I was driven to think of abandoning everybody not strong enough to go on with me carrying a load.' The Cape Hottentots were certainly too ill for load-carrying. Two had already died, and the rest were yellow with jaundice, so Speke sent them to the coast to save their lives.

After his reluctant return to Kazeh, the Arabs surprised Speke by begging him once again to negotiate on their behalf with Manwa Sera, since they were being ruined by the fighting, which had trapped their ivory in Ugogo, where the porters were starving to death. Though Speke was enraged with Abdulla and Muhinna, the leading Arabs at Kazeh, for continuing to employ the Watuta, he agreed 'to write out all the articles of a treaty of peace', with sanctions against them if they broke their word to Manwa Sera. Although he and Grant detested Muhinna, who had just refused to stop beating his chained female slaves, Speke still felt he had no alternative but to try to end the war in his own interests, as well as theirs.[36] So he sent Baraka to locate Manwa Sera and bring his emissaries to Kazeh. Baraka achieved this miracle within a few days. But the negotiations foundered on the question of how much land should be restored to the African ruler. So, despite Speke's best efforts, he left Kazeh having failed to create peace in the area through which he would now be travelling. In fact, just before he marched, he heard that Manwa Sera was recruiting Wagogo and Wasukuma warriors in order to renew the struggle.

Speke was distressed to be travelling without Musa and his porters, but he felt he could wait no longer, and ignored Bombay and Baraka who both said he that he was misguided not to wait until the Arabs and their brutal mercenaries could gain a permanent advantage over Manwa Sera. Bucked by his acquisition of an experienced *kirangozi*, Speke told Baraka and Bombay about 'the perseverance and success of Columbus, who, though opposed by his sailors had still gone on and triumphed'.[37]

At Ukuni, just north of Kazeh, Speke's shortage of porters obliged him to leave behind Grant and Bombay with thirty men and the bulk of the expedition's supplies, while he and Baraka went north with just over sixty men, intending to return when enough new porters could be found.[38] Between July and September the two explorers were separated, while Speke faced a succession of rapacious chiefs and headmen without the reassurance of Grant's phlegmatic presence. Speke gave instructions to his new *kirangozi* to avoid all the chiefs on the road ahead, so he would not have to make ruinous *hongo* payments. But the man promptly led him to the *boma* (protected village) of Mfumbi, a sub-chief in Sorombo. Not only did Mfumbi ask for cloth and beads for himself, but insisted that the explorer should visit the head chief, Makaka, who lived ten miles to the west, and longed to see his first white man. Speke tried to send Baraka with a present, but of course that would not do at all. Chiefs, who had suffered losses due to the war – and all claimed they had – were not going to pass up an unrepeatable opportunity to use this white man and his possessions to bolster their depleted resources.[39] Makaka immediately demanded a silk cloak embroidered with gold lace, of a kind Speke was determined to keep for King Rumanika of Karagwe and Kabaka Mutesa of Buganda. So to avoid giving away such an expensive garment, Speke was obliged to pay out many yards of inferior cloth of the most useful kind for purchasing food.

The incompetent *kirangozi* now had the gall to explain that Mfumbi and Makaka had pretended to be chiefs but were actually 'mere officers who had to pay tribute to Suwarora'. Before learning this, Speke had agreed a massive payment in cloth, and had also consented to give the 'mere officer' a 'royal salute', in order to be released by him. 'I never felt so degraded as when I complied,' he admitted. Makaka thought the volley had been fired too slowly and shouted: 'Now fire again ... be quick, be quick ... We could spear you all whilst you are loading.' In Speke's tent, Makaka sat in his chair and stained the seat with the grease which he and his fellow tribesmen wore. He put on Speke's slippers, asked to be given his bulls-eye lantern, and demanded Lucifer matches. Speke felt almost angry enough to murder the man, but realised that if he harmed him every chief in the country would become his enemy. In his present predicament, force was not an option – only patience and a stubborn determination not to be robbed of everything. Nevertheless, the perpetual worry made Speke 'feel quite sick'. He felt worse when Baraka told him that Makaka had intimated that his superior chief, Suwarora, had captured an entire Arab caravan and would kill every member of it if the Watuta or any other strangers came any closer. Speke laughed at Baraka 'for being such a fool' as to believe such tales. 'Makaka only wishes to keep us here to frighten away the Watuta . . . Suwarora by this time knows I am coming and he will be just as anxious to have us in Usui as Makaka is to have us here, and he cannot hurt us as Rumanika is over him.'

Yet logic had no impact on Speke's porters, who were just as scared of the Watuta as was Makaka. When Speke appealed to them to march north, they refused, and nothing he could say would change their minds. Speke had no alternative but to return to Kazeh yet again to try to recruit men there. Two and a half months of effort had amounted to absolutely nothing, except the fruitless expenditure of a mass of supplies. Yet giving up never entered his mind.

By the time Speke reached Grant's camp, he was suffering from a cough so bad that he 'could not lie [down] or sleep on either side'. While climbing a hill, he 'blew and grunted like a broken-winded horse'.[40] Ill though he was, he had to press on with his search for porters or admit that he would never reach Uganda. But in Kazeh, he found that nobody would hire men to him while the war was still going on. A small exception was made by Abdulla, Musa Mzuri's son, who loaned him two guides, Bui and Nasib, 'both of whom knew all the chiefs and languages up to and including Uganda'. These men promised to accompany Bombay to Usui and to return with enough porters to enable Speke and Grant to go north together. So Speke marched back to Ukuni again and after a few days spent with Grant, marched north again to secure the porters in Usui.

After Baraka and his previously loyal Wangwana porters had let him down, Speke had begun to think that the only way to reach Uganda would be to build a raft on the lake's southern shore. But because his two new guides gave him renewed hope of succeeding by land, he abandoned the raft project. The Wangwana were also given fresh courage when a message unexpectedly arrived from Suwarora urging Speke to come to see him. Unfortunately, at this very moment Bui and Nasib heard that another local chief, Lumeresi, wanted to see their white man. Speke was determined to avoid going anywhere near another local chief, and ordered his *kirangozi* and his two new guides to steal past Lumeresi's village by night. But Bui and Nasib flatly refused to risk offending this 'savage chief' by attempting to by-pass him. Their timidity infected the Wangwana, who once again became fearful and defeatist, leaving Speke all but helpless.

He might perhaps have been able to inspire them, if his health had been better; but his cough was now so bad that he had to sleep propped up in a sitting position. His heart felt 'inflamed . . . pricking and twingeing [*sic*] with every breath'; his left arm was half-paralysed, his nostrils full of mucus, and his body was racked with pain from his shoulder blades down to his spleen and liver. In such a frail condition all he could do was repeat that he had no intention of going to Lumeresi's *boma*. But he knew he would have to give in if his men went on refusing to obey his orders. 'This was terrible: I saw at once that all my difficulties in Sorombo [with Makaka] would have to be gone through again.'[41]

Speke's first ten days as the involuntary guest of Lumeresi – really he was his prisoner – were a nightmare. The chief warned him that he would never be allowed to leave until he had parted with two *déolés* – the richly embroidered cloaks he was saving for the kings of Karagwe and Buganda. Three weeks passed and Speke was still failing to negotiate *hongo* payments satisfactory to his persecutor. At this ill-starred moment, Mfundi, who had robbed him shortly after his first departure from Kazeh, appeared in the village and declared that the road to Usui was closed, and that he personally had burned down all the villages on the path. On hearing this, Speke's new guides begged to be released, since they 'would not go a step beyond this'. Eventually, after a supreme effort of persuasion, Speke managed to get Bui, the bravest of the guides, to agree to come with him to Usui as soon as Lumeresi had agreed the *hongo* payment. Overjoyed by Bui's change of heart, Speke had his chair placed under a tree and smoked his first pipe since he had fallen ill. 'On seeing this, all my men struck up a dance, which they carried on throughout the whole night.'

None of this had any effect on Lumeresi, who had been bullying the explorer for a month now, and was as determined as ever to have a finely embroidered silk cloak. In the end, Speke had no choice but to give him the *déolé* he had saved for King Rumanika. Not even that was enough and Lumeresi insisted on his giving him double the amount of brass wire and cloth he had originally asked for. The chief's drums were beaten at last, so a poorer Speke was free to go, but now Speke found that his guides, Bui and Nasib, who also doubled as interpreters, had fled.

The shock almost killed me. I had walked all the way to Kazeh and back again [a round trip of over 200 miles] for these two men to show mine a good example – had given them pay and treble rations, the same as Bombay and Baraka – and yet they chose to desert. I knew not what to do, for it appeared that do what I would, we would never succeed; and in my weakness of body and mind, I actually cried like a child.[42]

Speke's ability to negotiate calmly, often for weeks at a time, with a succession of chiefs who clearly wished to rob him of everything, was remarkable. This, coupled with his unceasing efforts – in the face of serious illness – to keep his caravan together and find new porters (walking many hundreds of miles in the process) marked him out as a great explorer.

Only a dozen miles to the south, Grant, for a change, was suffering even greater problems. A local chief sent 200 men armed with spears and bows and arrows rampaging through his camp, stealing whatever came to hand. Only one of Grant's men stood at bay, with his rifle at full cock, in defence of his load; the rest fled. Grant himself had the terrifying experience of having the tips of assegais pressed against his chest. He was only too well aware of the danger he was in, since a few days earlier he had witnessed the execution of a man, whose genitals had been set on fire before he had been stabbed to death. But Grant was not harmed, and later that day, fifteen of fifty-six loads were returned – the chief evidently having felt that if his neighbouring chiefs had heard that he had left nothing for them to extract from the white man, he could expect to be attacked.[43]

Speke was appalled when told what had happened, but he was saved from despair by the arrival at Lumeresi's village of four men sent by Rumanika and Suwarora to say that they were eager to see him and that he should not believe anything he might have heard about them harming caravans. Lumeresi, however, sent these men away calling them frauds, and in the end only agreed to help Speke find porters for the journey north when Suwarora sent some more men bearing his mace – a long rod of brass decorated with charms. Lumeresi had remorselessly milked Speke from 23 July to 6 October 1861, when he and Grant, who had very recently joined him, were finally able to get away.[44]

Travelling north once more towards Usui, the dried-up countryside began to change for the better. Before, the only shade had been offered by the occasional fig or mango tree, but now the endless tracts of leafless scrub and burned grass were giving way to mixed woodland and green hills crowned with granite outcrops. In the valley bottoms, they walked through 'pleasant undulations of tall soft grass', and crossed streams destined for the distant Nyanza. Speke would indicate on his map that he was rarely nearer to the lake than sixty miles. His desire not to encounter more chiefs than was absolutely necessary probably accounts for his failure to visit the lake at intervals to establish whether it was a single sheet of water or several.

Close to Chief Suwarora's stronghold, they dropped down into a valley 'overhung by delightfully wild rocks and crags', which Grant declared to be like 'the echoing cliffs over the Lake of Killarney'.[45] Unfortunately, the chief and his henchmen were not to prove as delightful as the country they inhabited. Despite their earlier promises to behave differently from Lumeresi and Makaka, they fleeced Speke in exactly the same way and left him and Grant to pitch their tents in a place where rats, fleas and vicious ants made their nights a misery. Grant described Suwarora himself as 'a superstitious creature, addicted to drink, and not caring to see us, but exacting through his subordinates the most exorbitant tax we had yet paid'.[46]

Speke felt slightly happier about his situation when he met an Arab trader, Masudi, who had taken over a year to travel the 150 miles from Kazeh to Suwarora's *boma* at Usui and *en route* had been obliged to pay even more than he and Grant had done. Since leaving Kazeh, Speke and Grant had been on the road a mere eight months. Yet, while it seemed easily explicable that slave-trading Arabs should be ill-treated, it struck them as extraordinary that people who had never seen Europeans before, or ever been harmed by them, should treat them in a similar way.

Left to wait for weeks outside the chief's fenced enclosure, in patchy jungle with no shady trees, Speke and his men were robbed even by ordinary villagers – the most audacious theft being the abduction of two women attached to the caravan. Most of Speke's captains had acquired additional wives and concubines during the journey. The thieves had torn off the women's clothes, hurrying them away 'in a state of absolute nudity'. This was too great an insult to be endured, and Speke gave orders that the next thief should be fired at. The following night an intruder was indeed shot at close range. 'We tracked him by his blood, and afterwards heard he had died of his wound.'[47]

He and Grant finally escaped the clutches of Suwarora on 15 November 1861 and began their march to Karagwe – a region which Grant would soon compare, rhapsodically, with the English Lake District. For Speke it was 'truly cheering' to reflect that they 'now had nothing but wild animals to contend with before reaching Karagwe'.[48] By the end of November they had reached a country of grassy hills, most of them 5,000 feet tall, and from the top of one called Weranhanjé, they saw far below them a beautiful lake, which Speke and Grant thought very like England's Lake Windermere. On a plateau overlooking the water was the palace enclosure, shielded by a screen of trees. This kingly residence was on a larger scale than anything they had yet seen, with many huts and interlinked courtyards. To honour the king, Speke ordered his men to fire a volley outside the palace gate. To their surprise, Rumanika invited them in at once, without obliging them to wait for weeks for the honour of an audience.[49]

From their first sight of him, both explorers were captivated. Rumanika, said Grant, was 'the handsomest and most intelligent sovereign they had met with in Africa. He stood six foot two inches in height, and his countenance had a fine, mild, open expression'.[50] Speke described the first greetings of the king as being 'warm and affecting . . . [and] delivered in good Kiswahili'. It was clear from the start that the king felt himself fortunate to meet these strangers from afar and had no plans to fleece them. In fact he would rebuke his brother when he begged for a gun, and would never demand anything for himself, although Speke and Grant would voluntarily give him many presents. 'He had been alarmed he confessed, when he had heard we were coming to visit him, thinking we might prove some fearful monsters, that we were not quite human, but now he was delighted beyond all measure by what he saw of us.' He asked intelligent questions, such as whether 'the same sun we saw one day appeared again, or whether fresh suns came every day'. But while Speke answered this question in a straightforward and factual way, when Rumanika asked him to explain the decline of kingdoms (it pained the king that Karagwe no longer ruled over Burundi and Rwanda) the explorer told him that Britain maintained its power in the world because Christianity gave a sense of moral entitlement. In the spirit of wishing to share this bounty, Speke offered to take one of the king's children back to England to be educated in a Christian school, so that he could return to Karagwe to impart to others what he had learned. In contradiction of what he had said earlier about Christianity, Speke went on to say that science was the branch of knowledge best adapted to increase a nation's wealth, and he cited the impact of the electric telegraph and the steam engine. Rumanika's intelligence and kindness, coming after so much bullying and disrespect, made Speke feel much more optimistic about the next and most crucial phase of his journey.[51]

Speke and Grant present Rumanika with a rhinoceros' head.

Speke and Grant celebrated Christmas at Rumanika's court with his athletic sons and amazingly fat daughters, who were force-fed with milk and beef-juice until they became almost spherical, as was the fashion for women at court. Just as the crinoline in Europe demonstrated that a 'lady' did not work, these princesses were showing that they too led ornamental lives and had parents who could afford to feed them prodigiously. In exchange for showing one of the princesses his bare arm, Speke persuaded this young woman, who 'was unable to stand except on all fours', to allow him to measure her. The circumference of her upper arm was an amazing two feet, and that of her thigh almost three feet. Her rolls of flesh made him think of gigantic puddings.[52]

Early in the New Year of 1862, the explorers received news which, wrote Speke, 'drove us half wild with delight for we fully believed Mr Petherick was indeed on his road up the Nile, endeavouring to meet us'. The members of a diplomatic mission, sent by Rumanika some months earlier to Bunyoro (to the north of Buganda), had just returned, bringing news that foreigners in boats had arrived in Gani, north-east of Bunyoro. These foreigners had apparently been driven off to the north. Because Speke was convinced by this intelligence that Petherick and his party had just failed to get through, he wrote the Welshman a letter of encouragement, which was taken north by Baraka, Uledi and a small bodyguard provided by Rumanika. On 7 January an Indian ivory trader called Juma arrived in Karagwe with news that King Mutesa of Buganda was sending some officers to greet Speke and Grant and escort him back to his kingdom.

Just when their final push towards the source of the Nile seemed to be beginning, Grant's health threatened his participation. His right leg, above the knee, had become stiff, swollen and alarmingly inflamed. He could neither walk nor leave his hut. The intense pain was only eased by his making incisions to release the fluid. Yet fresh abscesses would form within days. In his desperate situation, he was ready to try any cure suggested by the locals, including a cow-dung poultice and having a paste like gunpowder rubbed into the cuts. One theory was that he had been bitten by a snake when sleeping. It seems more likely that he was suffering from a bacterial infection of the deep tissues, which today would be treated with antibiotics. Although Grant did not know it, months of suffering lay ahead while his immune system rallied to fight the infection.[53] So when, on 10 January, Maula, a royal officer from Buganda, strode into Rumanika's palace enclosure, followed by a smartly dressed escort of men, women and boys, and announced that Kabaka Mutesa was eager to see the white men, the uncomplaining Grant had to be left behind. He seemed content with Speke's assurances that they would be re-united as soon as his leg improved. Rumanika had warned both men that Mutesa never allowed sick people to enter his country.

As Speke and his men followed Maula across a swampy plain towards the deep and strongly flowing Kagera river, he sensed that what he had been told about the Kagera on his first visit to the Nyanza had been right – namely that this was the lake's principal feeder and that it rose far to the west in the Mountains of the Moon.[54] This feeling was not entirely intuitive, since in June 1858 Snay bin Amir had told him that he had 'found it emanating from Urundi, a district of the Mountains of the Moon'.[55] In fact it originated well to the south of the Ruwenzoris (Mountains of the Moon) from two distinct sources in remote highland regions of Rwanda (close to Lake Kivu) and Burundi (close to Lake Tanganyika), but was, nonetheless the Victoria Nyanza's main provider.

Speke wrote in his journal at the start of his march to Buganda: 'I am perfectly sure . . . that before very long I [shall] settle the great Nile problem for ever.' But this would depend entirely upon how he fared in Buganda, where, unknown to him, the *kabaka* had just sacrificed over 400 people in a vast ritual massacre to celebrate the coming of the white man. Kabaka Mutesa possessed the largest army in central Africa and was ruler of a kingdom that had been centralised and socially stratified since the fifteenth century. Rumanika warned Speke that Mutesa hated Bunyoro and its king, Kamrasi, and therefore never let anyone leave his country travelling in a northerly direction. This would make following any river north from Buganda extremely dangerous. In any case, Speke knew that he would be taking his life in his hands by placing himself in the power of an unpredictable feudal autocrat. But he had never lacked courage, as he was about to show many times during his long sojourn in Buganda.[56]

NINE

As Refulgent as the Sun

—∞∞∞—

During Speke's six-week march to Buganda, as he came closer to the Nyanza, he and his men had to wade chest deep across a succession of swampy valleys where the water's surface was only broken by large termite mounds, each topped with its own euphorbia candelabra tree. Towards the end of January, for the first time on this journey, he caught a glimpse of the glittering Nyanza from a place called Ukara; but neither on this occasion, nor when he came closer still on 7 February, did he choose to visit the lakeside itself to check whether the water seemed to be continuous. Certainly, he was restricted by the orders of his royal escort, but this lack of scientific thoroughness would come to haunt him later. Possibly he took it for granted that the lake was one immense inland sea because everyone he met said that it was.[1]

In late January, after sending messengers to the *kabaka* to learn his wishes, Maula – who, unknown to the explorer, was Mutesa's chief spy and torturer – told Speke that it would be ten days or more before they would be able to continue their journey and in the meantime he meant to visit friends. While he was gone, local villagers subjected Speke to two days and nights of 'drumming, singing, screaming, yelling and dancing'. In their own eyes, they were frightening away the devil – aka the ghostly-looking white man – though Speke gave no indication that he made the connection. After several days of this hubbub, he was delighted to receive an unexpected visit from N'yamgundu, the brother of the dowager queen of Buganda. This nobleman promised to return at sunrise to escort him and his followers to Mutesa's palace.

When N'yamgundu failed to turn up early next morning, Speke ordered Bombay to strike his tent and begin the march. Bombay objected on the excellent grounds that without N'yamgundu, they had nobody to guide them. Frustrated and disappointed, Speke shouted: 'Never mind; obey my orders and strike the tent.' When Bombay refused, Speke pulled it down over his head. 'On this,' wrote Speke, 'Bombay flew into a passion, abusing the men who were helping me, as there were fires and powder boxes under the tent.' But Speke was beyond reason. Recalling all the insults, delays, untruths, disloyalties, thefts and losses he had endured without venting his fury, Speke's self-control finally cracked. 'If I choose to blow-up my property,' he roared, 'that is my look-out; and if you don't do your duty I will blow you up also.' Bombay still refused to obey him, so Speke delivered three sharp punches to his head. Bombay squared up as if about to fight back, but changed his mind and did not lay a finger on his attacker. Showing amazing self-restraint, he simply declared that he would no longer serve him as caravan leader. When Speke offered Bombay's job to Nasib, the older of his two indispensable interpreters, he declined it. Instead, in Speke's words, 'the good old man made Bombay give in'.

Speke later rationalised the bludgeoning he had administered by saying that he could not have 'degraded' Bombay by allowing an inferior officer to strike him for disobeying a direct order from his leader. But really, Speke had behaved outrageously and knew it – especially since he respected Bombay more than any other man in his employ. 'It was the first and last time I had ever occasion to lose my dignity by striking a blow with my own hands.'[2] It is some mitigation of the offence that virtually every other European explorer of Africa handed out thrashings from time to time in order to preserve a semblance of discipline – even Dr Livingstone. The endless vexations of African travel, and the hypersensitivity caused by repeated attacks of malaria, could sting the most patient of men into violent over-reaction.

While this row had been going on, N'yamgundu unexpectedly arrived and the caravan moved off soon afterwards. Two days later, several of the *kabaka*'s shaven-headed pages turned up carrying three sticks representing the three charms or medicines, which Mutesa hoped the white man would give him. The first was a potion to free him from his dreams of a deceased relative; the second was a charm to improve his erections and his potency; and the third a charm to enable him to keep his subjects in awe of him. Though daunted by these outlandish requests, Speke's confidence was boosted when a royal officer joined the caravan as it reached the northern shores of the lake and told Speke that 'the king was in a nervous state of excitement, always asking after [him]'.[3] While the explorer's principal interest still lay in locating the northern outlet of the Nyanza, he was also gripped by the drama of arriving at a unique feudal court and meeting a king whose ancestors had been monarchs since the fifteenth century.

As he came closer to the royal palace, Buganda itself began to charm him. 'Up and down we went on again, through this wonderful country, surprisingly rich in grass, cultivation and trees.' All the watercourses were bridged now with poles or palm trunks. Because the lake brought rain all the year round, the hills were as green as English downs, though larger, and their tops were grazed by long-horned cattle rather than sheep. Through banana plantations and woods, Speke caught tantalising glimpses of *his* shimmering lake.

On 18 February, the caravan was at last close to the *kabaka*'s palace. 'It was a magnificent sight,' enthused Speke in his journal. 'A whole hill was covered with gigantic huts, such as I had never seen in Africa before.' Indeed they were fifty-feet-tall conical structures, bound onto cane frames which were covered with tightly woven reeds. Speke had hoped to be summoned at once, but to his dismay was shown into a small and dirty hut to await the *kabaka*'s pleasure. N'yamgundu explained gently that a *levée* could not take place till the following day because it had started to rain.

Speke began the manuscript of his book *Journal of the Discovery of the Source of the Nile* with a first sentence that would be deleted by his publisher:

Our motto being: 'Evil to him who evils thinks,' the reader of these pages must be prepared to see and understand the negroes of Africa in

The road to the *kabaka*'s palace.

their natural, primitive, or naked state; a state in which our forefathers lived before the forced state of civilization subverted it.

John Blackwood advised that this account of a 'forced' civilisation 'subverting' a more desirable and 'natural' way of life, should be replaced with a banal passage in which Speke could suggest that tribal faults and excesses might be viewed compassionately because Africans had been excluded from the Christian dispensation that gave Europeans their moral compass.[4] As will become apparent, the omitted sentence reflected his true feelings.

But to begin with, to gain respect, he planned to claim that he was a royal prince in his own country and therefore the *kabaka*'s social equal. Personal vanity in part explains this pretence, though practical considerations were also involved. To enter a self-contained world – which had remained, despite the arrival of Arab slave traders two decades before, almost exactly as it had been four centuries earlier – offered Speke, as this world's first white visitor, an extraordinary opportunity. As the first of his race ever to be seen by the *kabaka* and his courtiers, Speke knew he would seem a marvel – and this would not only be personally gratifying, but would also make it easier for him to gain the *kabaka*'s support for his Nile mission. Or so he hoped. But the charm of his novelty might be lost were he to allow himself to be outshone or humiliated by the *kabaka*. So he gave much thought to the figure he ought to cut when marching from his humble hut to the royal enclosure where his audience was scheduled to take place the following day: 20 February 1862.

The Union Flag was carried in front of him by his *kirangozi*, while, just behind him, a twelve-man guard of honour, dressed in red flannel cloaks and carrying their arms sloped, followed. The rest of his people came next, each carrying a present. The little procession was led past huts 'thatched as neatly as so many heads dressed by a London barber, and fenced all round with the common Uganda tiger-grass'. In one nearby court, musicians were playing on large nine-stringed harps, like the Nubian *tambira*, and on immense ceremonial drums. Within a separate enclosure lived the *namasole*, or queen-dowager, with Mutesa's three or four hundred wives, many of whom stood chatting as the little procession went by. In the next fenced court, Speke was presented to courtiers of high dignity: the *katikiro*, or prime minister, the *kamraviona* (properly *kamalabyonna*) or commander-in-chief; the *kangaawo* and the *ppookino* ('Mr Pokino' and 'Colonel Congow' to Speke), who were governors of provinces; as well as meeting the admiral-of-the-fleet, the first- and second-class executioners, the commissioner in charge of tombs, and the royal brewer. The *kabaka*'s cabinet of senior advisers, the *lukiiko*, 'wore neat bark cloaks resembling the best yellow corduroy cloth . . . and over that, a patchwork of small antelope skins, which were sewn together as well as any English glovers could have pieced them'.

Mutesa's musicians.

Then, just when an audience with the *kabaka* seemed imminent, Speke was asked to sit on the ground and wait outside in the sun, as Arab traders were obliged to do. 'I felt,' recalled Speke, 'that if I did not stand up for my social position at once, I should be treated with contempt . . . and thus lose the vantage ground of appearing rather as a prince than a trader.' So he turned on his heel and stalked off in the direction of his hut, while his men remained sitting on the ground, in a state of terror lest he be killed. But something very different happened. Several courtiers dashed after him, fell upon their knees, and implored him to return at once, since the king would not eat until he had seen him. But Speke turned his back on them and entered his hut as if mortally offended. Soon other courtiers arrived, humbly informing him that the king wished to be respectful and that Speke would be allowed to bring his own chair to the audience, 'although such a seat was exclusively the attribute of the king'. Speke kept them waiting for his decision, while he smoked his pipe and drank a cup of coffee.

He found the *kabaka* waiting for him in his 'state hut', surrounded by numerous squatting courtiers and by some of his wives:

The king, a good-looking, well-figured, tall young man of twenty-five, was sitting on a red blanket spread upon a square platform of royal grass ... The hair of his head was cut short, excepting on the top, where it was combed up into a high ridge, running from stem to stern like a cockscomb. On his neck was a very neat ornament – a large ring of beautifully worked small beads, forming elegant patterns by their various colours ... On every finger and every toe he had alternate brass and copper rings; and above the ankles, halfway up to the calf, a stocking of very pretty beads. Everything was light, neat, and elegant in its way; not a fault could be found with the taste of his 'getting-up'.

When Speke was permitted to sit opposite the monarch, he wanted to open a conversation, but thought better of it on observing that no courtier dared speak, or even lift his head for fear of being accused of eyeing the royal wives. 'So the king and myself sat staring at one another for full [*sic*] an hour,' without exchanging a single word. Eventually, the king commanded Maula to ask Speke 'if [he] had seen him'. 'Yes, for full [*sic*] one hour,' replied the explorer, which, when translated, cannot have pleased the *kabaka*, who had expected a fulsome tribute to his good looks and magnificence. So he made no offer of food and walked away in his most formal manner, imitating the strides of a lion – a gait which had been affected by Bugandan kings for many generations. Speke's porters were awed, but Speke thought it made Mutesa look unintentionally ridiculous, though not quite as silly as his own men who were shuffling away like frightened geese.

An hour later he and Mutesa met again and spoke to one another – a difficult procedure involving Bombay translating his words into Kiswahili, then Nasib rendering them into Luganda, and finally, Maula conveying them directly to the king, 'for it was considered indecorous to transmit any message to his majesty except through the medium of one of his officers'. The *kabaka* wanted to know what messages had been sent by Rumanika, and after being told, turned to Speke and asked him again, with great intensity, whether he had *seen* him. This time Speke made up for his earlier tactlessness and told the *kabaka* he was 'very beautiful, as refulgent as the sun, with hair like the wool of a black sheep, and legs that move as gracefully as a lion's'.[5]

Before Speke could mention his plans for exploration, the king asked whether he would show him some of his guns. So Speke's followers laid out the firearms brought as presents, including a Whitworth's rifle – in Speke's opinion 'the best shooting gun in the world' – and a revolver, three carbines, three sword-bayonets and several boxes of ammunition and gun-caps. Mutesa 'appeared quite confused with the various wonders as he handled them', and sat poring over his presents until the light began to fail. The four rich silk cloths, ten bundles of rare beads, several sets of cutlery, an iron chair and a gold chronometer, received less attention. Speke probably saw no irony in the fact that the first white visitor's most valuable presents conferred no peaceful arts, but rather the capacity to kill more effectively than the *kabaka* had hitherto dreamed of.[6]

Three days later, after meetings on each of the preceding days, the king summoned Speke and asked him to shoot the four cows that were walking about the court. Having brought no weapon, he borrowed the revolver he had given to the *kabaka*, and succeeded in killing all four with five rapidly fired shots. 'Great applause followed this *wonderful* feat.' But what followed showed Mutesa in a darker light. The king loaded one of the carbines Speke had given him, and handing it 'full-cock to a page, told him to go out and shoot a man in the outer court; which no sooner accomplished than the little urchin returned to announce his success with a look of glee'. A horrified Speke observed in his journal: 'There appeared no curiosity to know what individual human being the urchin had deprived of life.'[7] It would not be long before Speke began to see,

nearly every day ... one, two or three of the wretched palace women, led away to execution, tied by the hand, and dragged along by one of the bodyguard, crying out as she went to premature death, 'Hai Minangé!' ['O my lord!'] at the top of her voice in utmost despair.

This was indeed a world of extraordinary ambivalence. While Baganda society worked better administratively than any other he had seen in Africa – with courtyards kept clean, hunger unknown and plantations well cared for – the other side of the coin was that people lived in fear lest for some trivial offence, they might be handed over to one of Mutesa's executioners to be bludgeoned to death or decapitated.[8]

Speke, by contrast, was treated with courtesy and rarely felt in danger, though he soon realised that he was getting nowhere with his plans to enlist the *kabaka*'s assistance. Even when Mutesa agreed to send an officer by boat to the Kagera river to collect Grant, and to send another officer to Gani, where it was believed that Petherick was detained, Speke doubted whether a channel of communication with Petherick would actually be established. The plain fact was that Mutesa wished to keep Speke with him for as long as possible, and did not want him to leave in order to search for the Nyanza's outlet. Speke hoped that if he could lure Mutesa away from the palace on an elephant-hunting trip, he would have a better opportunity to explain his plans to him man to man. So he showed the *kabaka* how to aim and fire from the shoulder, simply so that the monarch would want him to teach him how to shoot elephant and rhinoceros in the countryside. When Mutesa was feverishly eager to set out with him, the explorer refused to play ball unless the *kabaka* agreed to 'open the road outwards'. Grudgingly, he consented 'to call all his travelling men of experience together' so that Speke could show them a map and explain where he wished to go. This was to the place where Petherick was reputed to be held up.

Contriving a meeting with Petherick had become an obsession with Speke since it seemed to guarantee him a safe return down the Nile. But though a consultation with the 'travelling men' took place, afterwards Mutesa would not hear of Speke going anywhere with them.[9] But the explorer did not give up, and was delighted to be permitted to call on the *namasole* (whom he called the Queen Mother). He hoped to make her his ally in his struggle to get the *kabaka* to back his exploring aims.

In the first few years of Mutesa's reign, the Prime Minister and the Queen Mother had ruled the country, allowing the young *kabaka* little influence, but after several years of apprenticeship Mutesa had wrested control from them. Yet his mother still wielded considerable influence, which Speke hoped to exploit. Having heard that the Queen Mother suffered from various medical complaints, he brought his medicine chest with him, as well as presents of copper wire, blue egg beads and sixteen cubits of chintz. He guessed that the woman who greeted him had been good-looking before she became fat, and supposed she must be about forty-five. For a while Speke sat close to her, drinking 'the best *pombé* [beer] in Uganda' and smoking his pipe while she smoked hers. Quite soon, she dismissed the musicians and all but three of her *wakungu* (courtiers), and put on a *déolé*, so he could admire her in it. Then she leaned closer to him and begged his aid. Her liver, she said, was sending shooting pains all over her body, and she was often disturbed by dreams of her late husband, Sunna. Could her visitor cure her? Speke said that only by marrying again would she escape her dreams of her late husband. As for her physical ailments, he needed to see her tongue, feel her pulse and touch her sides. Her *wakunga* insisted that she could not be examined without the king's permission, but she dismissed their interference robustly: 'Bosh! I will show my body to the Mzungu.' They were then ordered to close their eyes while she disrobed and lay prostrate. Speke examined her, and prescribed two quinine pills and told her to drink less *pombé*. Right from this first meeting, he seems to have charmed her. Despite the cumbersome arrangement of communicating via two interpreters, she told him he must visit her again, 'for she liked him . . . she could not say how much'.[10]

Over the next fortnight Speke succeeded in making the *kabaka* and his mother furiously jealous of one another, but this did not result in his being given a hut within the palace grounds, nor did Mutesa promise that any serious efforts would be made to reach Petherick at Gani, nor even that Speke might soon be allowed to visit the lake's outlet. Yet the explorer was flattered when the king dressed himself in *dhoti* trousers in order to look more like him, and his success with the Queen Mother and various women at court was another source of pride.[11] So much so that when the departure of Mutesa's men for Gani (without Speke) seemed imminent, the explorer warned Petherick in an unintentionally comical letter, that: 'The game I am now playing will oblige you to drop your dignity for the moment and to look on me as your superior officer.' Petherick was told not to bring a uniform because Speke did not have one with him.[12] Clearly, Speke did not want anyone to undermine Mutesa's and the Queen Mother's conception of him as a man of high rank and importance in his own country.

Unless Speke had by now started to find daily life at Mengo so diverting, the *kabaka*'s refusal to help him locate either Petherick or the lake's outflow would have depressed him horribly. Nor were his spirits about to take a plunge. Suddenly, just when most required, a brand new source of happiness transformed his life at court. To his amazement, Speke found himself in love.

TEN

An Arrow into the Heart

———— ⊶⊷ ————

Six weeks after his arrival at the royal palace on Mengo Hill, Speke was sitting chatting to the Queen Mother when one of her courtiers asked him what colour his children would be if he married a black woman. Speke did not record his answer, but in another passage deleted from his published journal, he described the Queen Mother, 'making a significant gesture by holding her two fists to her breasts, signifying a young budding virgin'.[1] Then 'with roars of laughter [she asked Speke if he] would like to be her son-in-law, for she had some beautiful daughters'. The courtiers told Speke matter-of-factly that when the 'daughters' arrived and 'the marriage came off', he might need 'to chain the fair one . . . until she became used to [him]'.[2]

Three days later, when Speke called on the Queen Mother, she immediately produced two 'Wahuma' girls for him to take back to his hut. Speke believed that the paler-skinned and straighter-nosed Wahuma (Hima) originally came from Ethiopia, and that many centuries before his arrival at the Nyanza, they had risen to power over the darker Bantu already settled in Buganda, Karagwe and Rwanda. Although it was true that the Hima had come from the north, they were members of a Luwo clan originally from southern Sudan, rather than from Ethiopia. But after moving south, they had indeed formed ruling dynasties around the Nyanza in the centuries after AD 1200. Thereafter, they adopted Bantu speech and were culturally absorbed by them.[3] Speke, like many Europeans of his day who followed him to Africa, would find the Hima more physically attractive than the southern Bantu, with their thicker lips and flatter noses. Though this preference would be thought racist today, in the nineteenth century for an English gentleman to find any African woman attractive would have astonished most members of Speke's class, unless they had spent time in Africa.

When comparing Speke's published journal (*Journal of the Discovery of the Source of the Nile*) with the book's original proofs and manuscript, I found that many passages had either been changed in the published version or omitted from it. From now on, I shall quote in italics altered or omitted words and passages. Describing in his published *Journal* the two girls given to him by the Queen Mother, Speke represented them as 'children', saying that one, Kahala, was twelve, while the other was 'a little older'. But in the manuscript the elder is clearly described as being *'eighteen years or so'*. The younger girl in the manuscript is too young *'for present purposes'*, which were plainly meant by the Queen Mother to be sexual. The late king, Sunna, had chosen Méri the elder girl as a wife, although he had died before consummating the marriage. Méri had then become a member of the Queen Mother's household.

Speke found the girls alarmingly high-spirited but was assured by the Queen Mother that although 'they were more difficult to break than a phunda, or donkey, when once tamed, [they] became the best of wives'.[4] Two days later, Speke thanked the Queen Mother for 'having charmed [his] house with such beautiful society' and informed her that he had not found it necessary to chain his young women as she had advised him to do, since 'cords of love [were] the only instruments white men knew the use of'.[5]

Although the Queen Mother plainly suspected that Speke did not know how to tame his young women, she had great faith in him as a confidential doctor. She explained that her periods *'had eased since Bana* [Speke] *had doctored her'*, and asked what she should do now. He recommended marriage to restore regularity. Her son, the *kabaka*, rather than miss out on intimate advice, also consulted Speke, *'for he was extremely anxious of becoming as great a family man as his father, though at present there seemed to be no hope of it'*. Speke advised him only to have intercourse with those wives who had just had their periods, *'as the seed vessels were more sensitive then, and to refrain from over-indulgences, which destroy the appetite in early youth'.* Having too much sex, explained Speke, would *'increase their veins in size by over exertion, and thereby decrease their power'.* It worried the king that his penis might not be the optimum size. Speke advised him not to worry since all sizes could do the job. But *'M'tesa could not believe in a short stick being so good as a long stick, because the long one could reach so much farther, while the short one would only knock about the doorway.'* Mutesa was perplexed that a sexual expert like Speke should have no children of his own. Although Speke replied by quoting *'the old adage that a rolling stone gathers no moss,'* Mutesa remained puzzled. What was to stop a virile man becoming a father on his travels?[6]

Speke certainly made no secret of finding the wives of courtiers attractive. On a buffalo-shoot he 'commenced flirtations with M'tesa's women, much to the surprise of everyone'. He also offered to carry several wives of courtiers across a stream piggy-back fashion. The most beautiful one was especially eager to find out,

what the white man was like, [and] with an imploring face *and naked breasts* held out her hands in such a *voluptuous*, captivating manner that though [Speke] feared to draw attention by waiting any longer [to cross], could not resist compliance . . . 'Woh, woh!' said the Kamraviona 'What wonders will happen next?'[7]

Speke found it wonderfully gratifying that most women at court were *'charmed with the beautiful appearance of myself'.* But to his grief, this was not how Méri – whom he described as *'my beautiful Venus'* – saw him. Quite often she refused to speak to him, or go for walks, or do anything 'but lie at full length all day long . . . lounging in *the most indolent manner'.* Provoked, he said, beyond endurance by her indifference, Speke *'spent the next night in taming the silent shrew'.*[8] Though this sounds suspiciously like rape, it should be remembered that in Shakespeare's *Taming of the Shrew* the final proof of the success of Petruchio's 'taming' of Kate was her ultimate willingness to go to bed with him, without being coerced. But whether Speke forced himself on Méri, or whether she consented, or whether indeed his taming involved sex at all, is beyond knowing. What *is* certain is that his feelings for the girl deepened; and by the end of the month when he was separated from her – while accompanying Mutesa on a lengthy hippo-hunt – he found himself dreaming of Méri at night, and to a lesser extent of Kahala, and *'looking fondly forward to seeing what change would have been produced by this forcible separation of one week on those I loved, though they loved not me'*.[9]

On his return in early May, Méri tried to persuade him to give her a goat as a gift – although really she meant to pass it on to her favourite *nganga* (witch doctor). Even when Speke had rumbled her, she kept on nagging for the goat. *'Oh God! Was I then a henpecked husband?'* he complained. On learning that Méri had invited the *nganga* into their hut during his absence, a jealous Speke threatened to beat the man. At this point, Méri shattered him by begging to be beaten instead.

This touching appeal nearly drove my judgment from me, but as Méri showed neither love nor attachment for me ... [and my] offers [were] indifferently accepted without grace, which broke my sleep and destroyed my rest ... I therefore dismissed her, and gave her as a sister and free woman to Uledi ... I then rushed out of the house with an overflowing heart and walked hurriedly about till after dark, when returning to my desolate abode, turned supperless into bed, but slept not one wink reflecting over the apparent cruelty of abandoning one, who showed so much maidenly modesty when first she came to me, to the uncertainties of this wicked world.[10]

So Speke, who has typically been represented as incapable of love, fell painfully for a young African woman, and was made wretched by her refusal to reciprocate. A week later, Méri came to see him, saying that she had been ill since their row, and asked, with tears in her eyes, to be taken back. Speke told her she had been very wrong *'to fight with her lord'*, to which she replied that *'the only fighting she knew anything about was the fight of love'*.[11] But though Speke wanted to persuade himself

Kahala and other young Baganda women. There is no known image of Méri.

that her unyielding behaviour had been *'the fight of love'*, he failed. She could only come back he decided, if she showed evidence of being emotionally involved. Sadly, what she told him next convinced him that the situation was hopeless. *'Her luck was very great once,'* she explained. *'She was Sunna's wife, the N'yamasore's* [Queen Mother's] *maid, then his* [Speke's] *wife; so she* [had] *never lived in a poor man's house since she was a child; and now she wished to return* [to Speke] *so that she might die in the favours of a rich man.'*[12] Unsentimental honesty was not at all what the romantic Speke had wanted to hear, and he was clearly incapable of considering things from the point of view of a young woman brought up in an African feudal society, who had offered to be his wife on terms she considered satisfactory.

Grieving over the loss of Méri (as he had wished her to be), he stopped visiting the Queen Mother, who rebuked him angrily for ignoring her after she had been considerate enough to have 'given him such a charming damsel'. Speke noted in his journal that 'she little thought as she was speaking [that] she was driving an arrow into my heart'.[13] When he finally realised that he would never be close to Méri in the way he wanted, Speke gave the young woman some valedictory gifts:

In token I ever loved her and could do so now . . . a black blanket as a sign of mourning that I never could win her heart; a bundle of gundu [giraffe-hair ankle rings inter-woven with brass wire] in remembrance of her once having asked for them . . . and I [had] thought they would ill-become her pretty ankles. Lastly there was a packet of tobacco in proof of my forgiveness, though she had almost broken my heart; and for the future I only hoped she might live a life of happiness with people of her own colour as she did not like me because she did not know my language to understand me.[14]

Because Méri had described herself as Speke's wife, and he had referred to himself as her husband, it seems likely that they were sexual partners, but whatever had passed between them, his disappointed love was clearly genuine – although given the language barrier, sexual attraction must always have been the major component. But the usual picture of Speke as a selfish and insensitive misogynist does not tally with his tender feelings for Méri, and with the fact that his sense of honour prevented him from continuing to treat her as 'his wife', as she would gladly have allowed him to do if, as she had wished, he had taken her back. With no experience of romantic love – in the European sense – Mutesa and the Queen Mother had expected Speke to use Méri for his pleasure regardless of her feelings. For the most part, later adventurers and settlers would have few moral qualms about exploiting African women. There is a rumour, which surfaces from time to time, that Speke impregnated Méri.[15] While this is possible, the fact that they were together so short a time militates against it. Speke would leave Mengo in July about three months after he described 'taming' his 'shrew' in April, so if she had been impregnated she would have known it by then, and would have had no reason not to tell him. His journal is remarkably unbuttoned in its manuscript version, and yet there is no mention of a pregnancy. But in the end there can be no certainty either way.

At first, in his anger at not being loved in the way he wanted, Speke handed Méri to Uledi and his wife, Mhmua, to be her keepers. Though he described her as 'a free woman' and 'a sister to Mhmua', the latter sometimes tied Méri to her wrist to stop her running away.[16] A few weeks later, Speke evidently felt so uneasy about her situation that he offered to try 'to marry her to one of Rumanika's sons, a prince of her own breed'. But Méri rebuffed his well-meaning efforts.[17]

Until his disappointment in love, Speke had greatly enjoyed his privileged status at court, as well as his close relationships with individual Baganda from the king and his mother at the top, right down to pages and servants. In fact his enthusiastic participation in daily events, and his easy manner with African women, differentiated him from Burton, Baker, Grant and Livingstone, all of whom maintained (in their diaries at least) a much greater distance.[18] But coinciding with his loss of Méri came a steadily increasing awareness of the darker side of Mutesa's nature, which began to mar the pleasure he had once taken in being part of Baganda high society. On one occasion the king flew into a rage with a formerly favoured wife, whom Speke had always found charming. For nothing more wicked than offering her lord and master some fruit – when it had actually been the role of a particular court functionary to feed him – she was dragged away to be executed for this minor breach of etiquette 'crying in the names of *Kamraviona* and *Mzungu*, for help and protection'. As the *kabaka*'s other wives clung to his knees, begging him to be merciful, the king began beating the condemned woman over the head with a stick. This was too much for Speke, who 'rushed at the king, and staying his uplifted arm, demanded from him the woman's life'. Well aware that he 'ran imminent risk of losing [his] own life', Speke was thankful when 'the novelty of interference made the capricious tyrant smile, and the woman was instantly released'. A royal page who misinterpreted a message from Speke to the king was less fortunate and had his ears cut off for not listening more attentively.[19] But far worse than any of this was the *kabaka*'s punishment of a wife who had run away from a cruel husband, and of the elderly man who had bravely given her shelter. Both were sentenced to be given food and water for several weeks, while they were 'dismembered, bit by bit, as rations for the vultures, every day, until life was extinct'. What horrified Speke was Mutesa's 'total unconcern about the tragedy he had enacted'. As soon as the condemned man and woman had been 'dragged away boisterously . . . to the drowning music of the *milélé* and drums', the king turned cheerfully to Speke: 'Now, then, for shooting *Bana*; let us look at your gun.'[20]

But despite his revulsion, Speke could not afford to offend Mutesa or refuse to show him his picture books, or shoot with him, or offer him medical treatment, if he requested it. He also felt obliged to obey the king when he asked for his portrait to be made. In the pencil and water colour sketch, which Speke produced of him, the king is naked, 'preparing for his blister': an archaic procedure, by which fluid was drawn from the part of the body being treated. Mutesa's expression is inscrutable, and despite the artist's limitations, the king's body looks slim and graceful, although his genitals are drawn smaller than life size, as in Greek works of art.[21] Given their earlier conversation on the subject of what made a penis the ideal size, it seems unlikely that the picture pleased the king. (*See colour plates.*)

On 14 May, Mabruki, who had been led to Bunyoro by Baganda guides, returned with the thrilling news that although Petherick had not yet arrived in King Kamrasi's country, his party was still at Gani. The fact that one of the two white men was said to be bearded, seemed to guarantee that Petherick himself was present. Mabruki explained that Baraka and Uledi, who had been sent to Bunyoro from Karagwe in late January, were still being detained by Kamrasi, and were thus unable to leave for Gani. This was extremely frustrating for Speke. Meanwhile Grant, who had hoped to survey the lakeside on his way from Karagwe to Buganda, had sent ahead a message to say he was still crippled by his ulcerated leg and was being carried and was therefore unable to make observations. While Speke longed for Grant's arrival so they could leave for the Nyanza's outlet, *en route* to Bunyoro and Gani, Mutesa remained more interested in shooting than in the white man's plans. The day after Mabruki reappeared, the *kabaka* hit and killed a large adjutant bird or great stork (*leptopilos*) and 'in ecstasies of joy and excitement, rushed up and down the potato-field like a mad bull ... Whilst the drum beat, the attendants all woh-wohed, and the women rushed about lullooing and dancing'.[22]

Grant finally arrived on 27 May 1862, after a period of four months' separation from Speke. They were, in Grant's words, 'so happy to be together again, and had so much to say, that when the pages burst in with the royal mandate that his Highness must see me tomorrow, we were indignant at the intrusion'. At his first audience, Grant was as impressed by Mutesa's person and clothing as Speke had been, but it was not long before 'a shudder of horror crept over [him]'. As the audience ended, two young women, who had had the temerity to smile at the explorers, were dragged away by the executioner. 'Could we have been the cause of this calamity?' agonised Grant, 'and could the young prince with whom we had conversed so pleasantly have the heart to order the poor women to be put to death?' He would know the answer long before hearing the cries of people being tortured whenever he passed the hut of Maula, Mutesa's chief detective. Grant admired Speke for having the courage to intervene from time to time. Once, his friend even succeeded in securing the release of the executioner's own son, who had been condemned to death.[23]

But though Mutesa became no less whimsically cruel, he pleased Speke and Grant two days after the latter's arrival, by sending emissaries to Kamrasi to ask him once again to allow Baraka and Uledi to leave for Gani. But the explorers were warned by him that they themselves could not expect to go anywhere just yet. By now it was early June and Speke had been in Buganda more than three months.[24] As he was preparing for the next phase of his great journey, Méri came to see him several times, looking he thought 'more beautiful than ever, and [she went] away sighing' because wanting to be taken back. But Speke still believed that material considerations, rather than love, had inspired these visits.[25]

At last, on 18 June, after Speke had enlisted the Queen Mother's help, the *kabaka* agreed to let him and Grant travel eastward to the lake's outlet and then north-west to Bunyoro. This permission was confirmed early in July, enabling them to leave on the 7th with a Baganda escort and sixty cows donated by the king. The king and Lubuga, 'the favourite of his harem', came to see them off, and Speke persuaded his men to *n'yanzig* for the many favours they had received. This was Speke's own verb, which he had coined to describe the extravagant forms of obeisance lavished on Mutesa, such as kneeling and throwing out the hands, while repeating the words: 'N'yanzig ai N'yanzig Mkahma', and then floundering face-downwards on the earth like fishes out of water. His men must have done this vigorously, because Mutesa complimented them warmly, before taking one last glance at the white men, and then striding away, while Lubuga 'waved her little hands and cried: "Bana! Bana!"'[26]

Royal wife led to execution.

ELEVEN

Nothing Could Surpass It!

Because Petherick could not be expected to wait indefinitely at Gani, ten days into his and Grant's journey Speke was gripped by the absolute necessity of reaching the Nyanza's outlet as soon as possible. After notching up the source, he would be free to hurry north to join hands with the Welshman, before travelling downriver with him to Gondokoro. Unfortunately, Grant's ulcerated leg was still stopping him walking well, so the two friends agreed that it would be best if Speke and a small party of a dozen Wangwana and three or four Baganda were to march immediately to the outlet, while Grant travelled more slowly to Bunyoro with the expedition's stores and the rest of the men. Once there, his task would be to gain Kamrasi's consent for their passage through his kingdom to Gani.[1]

In years to come, Speke's critics would say that he selfishly reserved for himself what he confidently believed would turn out to be the discovery of the Nile's source. But Grant would always deny this, saying he had been 'positively unable to walk twenty miles a-day, through bogs and over rough ground . . . [and so had] yielded . . . to the necessity of parting'.[2] On no occasion would he ever blame Speke. Yet though Grant believed it would have been folly to risk letting his lameness delay their eagerly anticipated meeting with Petherick, three days after he and Speke had parted company, the normally sweet-natured Grant was seized by an uncharacteristic fit of rage. A goat-boy, who had briefly lost sight of his flock, was given twenty lashes on his orders – a shocking punishment for a minor offence.[3]

Speke had been detained by Mutesa for four and a half months, while being a mere fifty miles from the Nyanza's principal outflow. This short journey proved trouble-free until his party had to cross a three-mile-wide, mosquito-infested creek, which the cattle had to swim across with the men holding their tails. Then, on 21 July 1862, Speke wrote joyfully in his journal: 'Here at last I stood on the brink of the Nile; most beautiful was the scene, nothing could surpass it!' He had not *proved* that this really was the Nile, but on seeing the 600-yard river flowing between tall grassy banks, he felt more certain than ever that he had attained the object of his search. Everything about it struck him as beautiful. The valley was shaded here and there by tall trees, and the soft grass reminded him of English parkland. Hartebeest and antelope were browsing – while, occasionally, cloudy acacia and festoons of lilac convolvuli added something exotic to the scene. When Speke, in his excitement, suggested to Bombay that he and his men ought 'to shave their heads and bathe in the holy river', the African shrugged his shoulders. 'We are contented with all the commonplaces of life,' he remarked soberly, perhaps calling to mind exotic, shaven-headed holy men in India.[4] The name of this place was Urondogani, and because it was a few miles downstream from the Nyanza, Speke tried to hire boatmen to take him and his men southwards, upstream to the precise point at which Nyanza and river met – for there, he had decided, would be the source itself. But the locals refused all help, and so he was obliged to 'plod through huge grasses and jungle' for three more days to the place called by the Baganda, 'The Stones'.

Speke admitted in his journal that 'the scene was not exactly what I [had] expected; for the broad surface of the lake was shut out from view by a spur of hill, and the falls, about 12 feet deep and 400 to 500 feet broad, were broken by rocks'. Nevertheless, despite the unspectacular nature of the place, he stared for several hours, mesmerised by the water rushing from the lake between the rocky islets and sweeping over the long ledge of rock into the river, as 'thousands of passenger-fish [barbel] leapt at the falls with all their might'. He had no doubt that this was the very point at which the lake gave birth to 'old father Nile'. Bewitched by the place, he mused that he would only need 'a wife and family, garden and yacht, rifle and rod, to make [him] happy here for life'. He also thought it the perfect location for a Christian mission. He named 'The Stones' the Ripon Falls, after the first Marquess of Ripon, President of the RGS and later viceroy of India. The stretch of water into which the lake at first funnelled, he called the Napoleon Channel out of respect for the Emperor Napoleon III. Unlike the RGS, which had only honoured Burton with its Patron's Gold Medal, the French Geographical Society had presented Speke with its Medaille d'Or for his discovery of the Nyanza, making him a Francophile for life.[5]

The Ripon Falls.

Speke dallied three days at 'the source', watching the fishermen coming out in boats and stationing themselves on the islets with rods. Hippopotami and crocodiles lay sleepily on the water and cattle came down to drink in the evening. The explorer finally tore himself away and set out downstream into Bunyoro, with his fifteen men in five flimsy boats, little better than rafts. His plans were ruined by Kasoro, the man deputed by Mutesa to guide him, but who now led a raid against some Wanyoro traders in canoes. Henceforth, Speke expected hostility *en route*, and got it the same day, when 'an enormous canoe, full of well-dressed and well-armed men' came up behind his rafts and then kept pace with them. The banks on each side grew higher and were soon lined with men thrusting their spears in his direction. The crew of the pursuing canoe paddled faster and swung their vessel across the bows of Speke's little craft. Even now, Speke was in denial about the gravity of his situation. 'I could not believe them to be serious . . . and stood up in the boat to show myself, hat in hand. I said I was an Englishman going to Kamrasi's, and did all I could, but without creating the slightest impression.'

Other canoes, full of armed men, now slid out from the rushes that lined the banks, compelling Speke to order all his boats to huddle together, so that no vessel could be picked off. But several of his captains preferred to go their own way, and one of their boats was promptly caught with grappling hooks, forcing its crew to choose between using their firearms or being boarded and stabbed to death. From across the river, Speke heard his men fire three shots, and saw two Wanyoro warriors fall, one killed outright. Fearing he would now be ambushed if he continued downstream, Speke decided to travel overland to Bunyoro. It comforted him to believe that Grant was already at Kamrasi's capital, and would have established friendly relations.

However, on 16 August, Speke was shocked to hear that Kamrasi had not allowed Grant to enter his country, and a mere five days after that, he stumbled on his companion's camp, close to the border. Soon afterwards, these two avid hunters came upon a large herd of elephants that had never heard a shot fired. The explorers' joy was short-lived. When Grant hit an old female, she merely 'rushed in amongst some others, who with tails erect commenced screeching and trumpeting, dreadfully alarmed, not knowing what was taking place'. Both men were so upset by this spectacle that they stopped firing. 'I gave up,' recorded Speke, 'because I never could separate the ones I had wounded from the rest, and thought it cruel to go on damaging more.'[6]

Now that Kamrasi had forbidden them to enter his kingdom, the explorers faced a grim dilemma. Should they nevertheless risk crossing Bunyoro uninvited in order to reach Gani, where they believed Petherick was still waiting with boats and supplies, or should they give up the idea of following the river downstream and try instead to persuade Mutesa to give them the men to travel through Masailand to Zanzibar? When they were on the point of deciding, six Wanyoro guides arrived with the wonderful news that Kamrasi would see the white men after all.[7] Shortly after this, 150 of Kamrasi's warriors arrived to escort them – a sight which made Speke's Baganda guides flee rather than risk being killed by their traditional enemy. The Baganda took with them twenty-eight panic-stricken Wangwana, leaving Speke and Grant with a mere twenty followers – far too few to guarantee them a safe journey north to Gondokoro, unless Petherick could be located and soon.[8] Though confident that he had found the Nile's source, Speke knew he would be treated sceptically unless he could describe the course of the river on its way to Gondokoro. Once again an African monarch seemed likely to determine whether his mission would be satisfactorily completed.

Kamrasi, the monarch in question, feared that some super-naturally inspired misfortune might befall him if he admitted the white men, though he had no desire to deprive himself of the gifts they might shower on him. So he kept them at arms' length, housed in huts 'in a long field of grass, as high as the neck, and half under water'. This waterlogged wedge of land was encircled by the crocodile-filled river and one of its effluents, the Kafu, thus obliging the explorers to embark in a canoe when making their long-delayed first visit to Kamrasi's audience-hut.

Their reception by the *omukama* (the traditional title of all kings of Bunyoro) took place on 9 September 1862, after a wait of nine days during which Kamrasi had weighed up the risks and benefits involved in seeing them. He greeted them coldly, giving no indication whether they would be allowed to follow the river downstream and visit Gani. In contrast to Mutesa's excitement when examining his presents, Kamrasi hardly glanced at his. He only seemed mildly interested in a double-barrelled gun and a gold chronometer watch, which he had noticed Speke take from his pocket. The *omukama* dressed more plainly than Mutesa, in local bark-cloth rather than in silk or calico. Although dourer than the *kabaka,* he turned out to be more humane, only executing murderers and letting off minor criminals with a warning.

Grant and Speke at Kamrasi's court.

Speke hoped that Kamrasi's carefully concealed interest in European factory-made goods would make him eager to open a trade route to the north, and thus willing to help his new visitors to travel north-east to Gani. Yet when this subject was broached, Kamrasi remarked dismissively that all his ivory exports were sent east to Zanzibar because he was often at war with the tribes to the north. Worse still, he insisted that his 'guests' should expect to stay with him for three to four months. Only when Speke had agreed to part with his valuable chronometer did Kamrasi agree to let Bombay and an escort of fifteen Wanyoro depart for Gani with instructions to Petherick to wait a little longer.

Kamrasi explained to Speke and Grant that they were lucky he had been foolhardy enough to receive them, since they were the first whites to visit Bunyoro, and his brothers had warned him against bringing such unpredictable people among them. How could he be sure they did not 'practise all kinds of diabolical sorcery'?[9] Naturally, he had taken the precaution of placing a river between his residence and theirs. The *omukama* continued to isolate them, even when Bombay had told him that his white masters were the sons of Queen Victoria. Kamrasi refused to see them as anything but traders, whose guns were their most desirable commodity. Bunyoro had a profitable trade in salt, and the East Coast Arabs had first reached the country forty years earlier along routes pioneered by the salt traders. So, before Speke's arrival, Kamrasi had already acquired primitive muskets from the Arab-Swahili who took his ivory to Zanzibar. But, like Mutesa, he had never until now seen modern guns that could kill a cow with a single bullet. To see this miracle performed both thrilled and scared him, making him desperate to acquire such rifles.[10] So when Speke promised to send back six modern carbines from Gani, Kamrasi appeared to be ready to allow him to leave. To hasten his release, Speke gave the *omukama* quinine and samples of every pill in his possession. This was in response to the king's heartfelt request to be given medicines so that his children need not go on dying. But there would still be prolonged sessions of haggling over other desirable items – a hair-brush, a sketching stool and some dinner-knives – before Kamrasi finally permitted the explorers to leave for Gani on 9 November, exactly two months after their arrival.

Both explorers had been deeply disappointed that the *omukama* had refused to let them travel sixty miles to the west to visit an immense lake (the Luta N'zige or dead locust lake), which they imagined must be part of the Nile's system. The great river was said to thunder into this lake over spectacular falls, and then flow out again at its northern end. But though Speke badly needed to trace the river northwards and connect it with the known Nile, Bombay's return from Petherick's supposed outpost on 1 November had ruled out any journey except the trek to Gani. For while Bombay had not actually seen the Welshman at Faloro in Gani, he had heard that he had gone downriver on an eight days' journey and was expected back there soon. So

Speke's and Grant's priority would have to be joining forces with Petherick, because success in this would greatly increase their chances of reaching Egypt alive.[11]

They began their journey downstream in a large dug-out on the Kafu river, which joined the main stream after a few miles. 'This was my first sail on the river Nile,' enthused Grant, not for a moment doubting that the locally named Kivira was Egypt's river. Being over 500 yards wide, populated with hippopotami, and fringed with tall papyrus rushes, its appearance certainly seemed to support such optimism. After floating downstream for four days on what Grant called 'the sacred waters', they abandoned the river as it turned to the west and foamed over the Karuma Falls. Steep banks, overhanging trees and occasional flashes of white water reminded Grant of 'our wildest Scottish rivers'.[12] Neither Grant nor Speke left a full explanation of why they chose not to follow the river downstream at this crucial point. But, after numerous deaths and desertions, they were down to the last twenty of their original sixty-five Wangwana followers, and so relied heavily on fifty-six porters under the orders of Kidwiga, the leader of the escort loaned to them by Kamrasi.

But it seems to have been Speke's obsessive determination not to endanger a meeting with Petherick, which decided him against following the great river westward as far as the Luta N'zige. Already, Speke had left a significant gap in his map of the river and knew that he and Grant would be told on their return to England that they had not proved the link with the Nyanza, even up to Karuma. But by missing out the unknown lake, into which the river was said to flow, they would be leaving an even larger *lacuna*.

From what Grant wrote, it is clear that if they had asked Kidwiga to accompany them to the Luta N'zige, he would have refused because Rionga, a brother of Kamrasi, was his sworn enemy and lived close to the lake. Of course, if they had somehow propitiated Rionga, and managed to reach the Luta N'zige with their twenty men, their position on returning home would have been almost unassailable. So why did they not risk it? Probably because fighting between Rionga's men and Kamrasi's had been going on for years, and they might have been killed.[13] Also, Speke was well aware that Kidwiga's men would insist on returning to Bunyoro in a few weeks. This reinforced his determination to join forces with Petherick. If he arrived too late at Faloro, he would risk having to travel north with only twenty men, through regions where slave raids had made the tribes murderously hostile.

The explorers' route from now on would be due north through Acholiland to Gani. Almost at once they were struggling through sharply pointed, head-high grass that threatened to blind them. Underfoot, the ground was swampy, with unseen rocks and ruts frequently tripping them. Since both were unwell and exhausted, they longed for a change of landscape.[14] At last, they emerged into a low, flat country of yellow grass. It was a surprise, after the civilised trappings in Buganda and Bunyoro, to see women wearing no more than a fringe of leaves suspended from the waist and a pendant of chickweed behind. The equally naked men concentrated their sartorial energies on dressing each others' hair with shells, beads and feathers. Their villages of cylindrical huts were encountered every few miles in flat grassland. For their benefit, Speke put a bullet through a buffalo and stood aside while they set about despatching it with spears 'in their own wild fashion'.[15]

On 3 December they arrived at Faloro – a trading post less than twenty miles from the river, which, though the explorers did not know it, had very recently flowed northwards out of the Luta N'zige. Here, Speke and Grant joyfully prepared to join hands with John Petherick. 'Our hearts leapt with an excitement of joy only known to those who have escaped from long-continued banishment ... to meet with civilized people and join old friends.' Yet something was wrong. Speke could not understand the appearance of three large Turkish flags at the head of the procession which was now leaving the camp to the music of fifes and drums. If Petherick was really here, the flags should surely be British? Nor did these few hundred people

A fifteenth-century reconstruction of Ptolemy's second-century world map. The White Nile is shown originating from twin sources close to a mountain range. *(See pp. 25–6)*

Richard Burton depicted as an Afghan peddler
in his wife's posthumously published biography of him.

John Speke and James Grant at Mutesa's court.

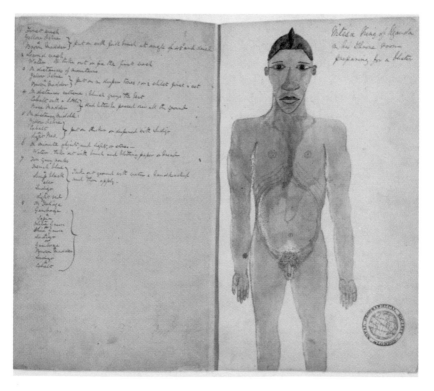

A naked Mutesa drawn by Speke.

Speke portrayed standing at the Ripon Falls source.

African birds drawn
by Speke.

Samuel Baker and Florence von Sass in a storm on Lake Albert.

Obbo warriors perform a war dance, as sketched by Samuel Baker.

Baker's sketch of himself in danger of being trampled
by an elephant.

James Gordon Bennett Jr, editor of the *New York Herald*, who was persuaded by Henry Stanley to send him to find Livingstone.

Hats worn by Livingstone and Stanley at the time of their meeting.

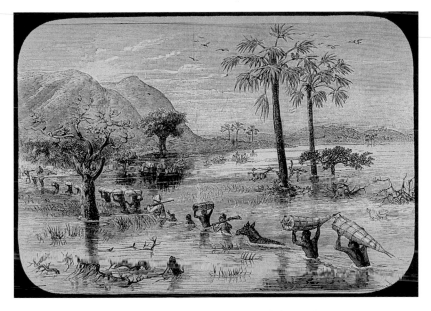

The Makata swamp crossed by Stanley.

Stanley watches a phalanx dance by Chief Mazamboni's warriors.

Livingstone's remains being carried to the coast by his men.

look like the followers of an honorary British consul. No two were dressed alike, and most of their archaic guns were different. They appeared to be Egyptians or Sudanese of African stock, presumably sent south as ivory traders. There were many slaves in the ranks from many different tribes.

Speke halted his men just before the procession reached them.

[As it did] a very black man, named Mohammed [Mohammed Wad-el-Mek], in full Egyptian regimentals, with a curved sword, ordered his regiment to halt and threw himself into my arms, endeavouring to hug and kiss me. Rather staggered at this unexpected manifestation of affection, I gave him a squeeze in return for his hug, but raised my head above the reach of his lips, and asked who was his master? 'Petrik,' was the reply. 'And where is Petherick now?' 'Oh, he is coming.' 'How is it that you have not got English colours, then?' 'The colours are Debono's. 'Who is Debono?' 'The same as Petrik.'

What this meant, Speke could only guess at, not knowing who Andrea De Bono was, and not yet realising that all these men belonged to the Maltese trader, rather than to Petherick.

Mohammed had no written orders, but said he was De Bono's *wakil* (agent), and had been instructed by him to take the two explorers to Gondokoro and to collect ivory while waiting for them to appear. So where was John Petherick and why, if he had been unable to come himself, had he not sent *his* men to meet them in his place? Public money had been subscribed for Petherick or his men to be available to help the two officers. Could he have betrayed them? Until Mohammed had appeared, Speke had been certain that Petherick was in the camp. This was because Bombay – who had been sent to Gani by Kamrasi – had brought back news a month later that Petherick's initials had been found cut into a tree not far from Faloro. So they were shocked to find that Mohammed knew nothing about Petherick having made any such journey. Indeed, he thought that 'Petrik' was at present at one of his trading stations twenty marches or more to the north.[16] Speke was appalled to hear this, having abandoned his attempt to reach the Luta N'zige largely because he had been so eager to meet Petherick.

It was exasperating to reflect that whereas Petherick could have been expected to do everything in his power to help them reach Gondokoro, this task ranked very low on Mohammed's list of priorities. For the moment, the trader's most urgent need was to secure 600 Africans as carriers for the immense amount of ivory which he and his men had stolen from the Madi people. To compel locals to become porters, he threatened to kill their families, to burn their huts and steal their possessions. And to show he meant business, he *did* burn huts, and kill people (about a dozen on this occasion). He also stole a hundred cows, but needed many more.[17] Further south Mohammed had enslaved 200 boys and women, and now would go nowhere until he had rustled enough cattle to feed these slaves and preserve their value. So for five and a half frustrating weeks the explorers had to kick their heels at Faloro, where even local marvels, such as rare butterflies and huge plums, gave them no pleasure. When Speke asked to be given guides to enable him and Grant to leave at once with their twenty men on an unassisted march through the Bari country, Mohammed refused to provide any, telling the explorers they would be murdered if they were foolish enough to travel ahead of the caravan.[18] If they slept in the open, even for a night, he warned them that they would be speared to death. Such 'revenge' attacks, the explorers discovered, were directly due to the brutality of slave traders like Mohammed himself. Nowhere else in Africa had Speke seen the inhabitants of entire villages run away at the approach of a caravan.

At last, on 11 January 1863, they were on the move again, and two days later reached Appuddo (Nimule), which was unquestionably on the White Nile, as Mohammed confirmed. The Arab took Speke and Grant to the river, where it flowed between wooded islands, and showed them the initials cut into the trunk of a nearby tamarind tree. The carver, he said, had been a bearded white man, who in 1860 had followed the Nile upstream from Khartoum, without leaving it for a day. The bark had grown inwards into the letters, obscuring most of them, leaving only two clearly defined: MI. These plainly had nothing to do with Petherick. The explorers would learn several months later that the traveller was Giovanni Miani, a Venetian trader and adventurer, who had struggled on a few miles further south from here before abandoning his attempt to reach the source of the Nile.[19]

When Mohammed's thousand followers camped a few miles outside Gondokoro, the Bari beat their drums and set fire to the surrounding grass, announcing that they meant to annihilate their enemies in the morning.[20] Fortunately for Speke and Grant this turned out to be bluster, and early next day they walked into Gondokoro without incident. Their first task was to find John Petherick and take possession of the goods and boats he had purchased for them. But when the two men called on a local trader, Khursid Agha, and asked where they might find the Welshman, 'a mysterious silence ensued'. Speke and Grant wondered what the consul could possibly be doing that was more important than coming to congratulate them after one of the greatest African journeys ever made by Europeans? Both men still clung to the hope that they would find him here.

After walking past the vessels moored along the riverbank, Speke drew level with the deserted Austrian Mission house, and saw hurrying towards him a bearded white man. For a moment he thought that this was Petherick. But when the approaching man raised his hat, and held out a hand, Speke saw at once that he was someone else entirely.[21]

TWELVE

The Nile is Settled

———— ◦◦◦◦ ————

The burly, bearded Englishman, hurrying towards the two explorers and intending to shower them with praise, was Samuel White Baker, the eldest son of a wealthy Devon family. Forty-two years old now, and uncomfortably aware of the fact, Baker was not content to have founded a thriving agricultural community in the wilds of Ceylon or even to have written two readable books about it. From the mid-1850s he had been unsuccessfully chasing the chimera of fame as an African adventurer. In 1858 he had failed to persuade Dr Livingstone that he could be of use to him on the Zambezi, and had been further mortified to hear at that time that John Speke – who, like himself, had been raised in England's West Country – had just been chosen to accompany Richard Burton to the African lakes. A brief meeting with Speke on board ship between India and the Gulf in 1854 had first alerted Baker to the younger man's interest in African exploration and had sharpened his own fiercely competitive interest in that field.[1]

But it would not be until six years later that Baker saw how to use Speke and muscle in on the search for the Nile's source. This was by writing to John Petherick and offering to join him on his mission to 'succour' Speke and Grant on the last leg of the journey they had embarked upon in the spring of 1860. Baker secretly hoped that if the pair were dead, or had been detained somewhere far to the south, he might even manage to beat them to the source. But the RGS had vetoed his joining Petherick's expedition, and had instead suggested that he explore the Ethiopian tributaries of the Blue Nile to determine the contribution these waters made to the annual flood in Egypt. So, between March 1861 and June 1862, Baker, who was rich enough to need no patronage, had explored the Ethiopian Highlands, discovering in due course that the torrential summer rains which fell there each year accounted almost wholly for the life-giving floodwaters that poured into the White Nile between June and September, irrigating the entire valley of the lower river. But this important scientific finding had in no way appeased Baker's longing to make the most glamorous discovery of all.

Just before setting out to map the Blue Nile and the Atbara, he had been asked by the Egyptian governor of Berber where he was going, and had replied without any attempt at subterfuge: 'To the source of the White Nile'. Baker had been accompanied then – and still was, on arrival at Gondokoro – by a slender white woman, dressed like himself in trousers, gaiters and a masculine shirt. Observing her youth and apparent fragility, the governor had urged the Englishman to leave her behind, since a journey up the Nile 'would kill even the strongest man'. But Baker, who loved to have his mistress with him, had no intention of heeding such advice.[2]

The way in which the nineteen-year-old came to be with him in the first place was a story in itself. Baker had purchased his 'Florence', as he called her, two years earlier at an auction of white slaves in the town of Vidin in Turkish-administered Bulgaria. Born Barbara Maria von Sass in Transylvania, then part of Hungary, Florence's parents had been killed in the 1848 Hungarian uprising, and she had later been raised by a business-minded Armenian, who expected to get a good price for her in due course. Whether desire or pity had bulked larger in Baker's decision to bid for the girl against so many prosperous Turks cannot be known, but he had soon fallen in love with her, subsequently taking a job in Romania as managing director of the Danube and Black Sea Railway solely in order to remain with her. Not that this was suspected by any of his four teenage daughters, who had been cared for in England, after their mother's premature death, by an unmarried sister and must have found their affluent father's decision to work in faraway Romania inexplicable as well as hurtful. But as a respectable widower, Samuel Baker had not even considered bringing back to England a mistress twenty years his junior and little older than his own children.

Of course, taking her to Africa, where she would meet nobody he knew (with the possible exception of Speke) had been a different matter. On the point of sailing for Alexandria in February 1861, Baker had briefly debated whether it would be safe for her to accompany him but had been unable to endure the thought of spending night after night in his tent without her. Now in March 1863 in Gondokoro – although planning disingenuously to tell Speke that he had come to Africa only in order to help him and Grant come safely home – he still had not decided how to introduce Florence.[3] But as he approached the exhausted travellers, he was able to postpone this delicate decision a little longer, since Florence had stayed aboard their boat that morning, after feeling unwell on waking.

As Baker's fellow countrymen came ever closer along the riverbank, walking beside a long line of moored vessels, he was overwhelmed with patriotic emotion. Speke with his fair hair and tawny beard was 'the more worn of the two . . . excessively lean, but in reality in tough condition . . . Grant was in honourable rags; his bare knees protruding through the remnants of trousers that were an exhibition of rough industry in tailor's work'. Yet though 'tired and feverish . . . both men had a fire in the eye that showed the spirit that had led them through'.[4] Humbled by the length of their journey from the southern to the northern hemisphere, and by their courage, Baker called out: 'Hurrah for Old England!' as he hurried up to them; but even as he embraced his compatriots, he felt chagrined that he had not managed to rescue them from 'some terrible fix' many miles further to the south of here. Gondokoro seemed suddenly rather tame, although Baker had spent lavishly to get thus far. So when Speke and Grant informed him that they had visited the Nile at enough points on its course to ensure that it originated in the Nyanza, he assumed that his own expedition was over, and felt too crestfallen to wonder if they had really proved their case.[5]

But, making the best of things, he told the explorers brightly that he had come 'expressly to look after [them]' by placing at their disposal a mass of trade goods, over forty men, camels, donkeys, a *dahabiya* (a ninety-foot Nile pleasure-boat) and two smaller vessels. Given the non-appearance of John Petherick, Grant and Speke were touched that this Good Samaritan was offering to do so much for them out of his own pocket, without having received a penny of public money. Baker now told them that Petherick, by contrast, had received almost £1,000 by public subscription raised so that he could 'succour' them.[6] Although another *dahabiya*, the *Kathleen,* and three cargo boats, had been sent to Gondokoro by Petherick and were currently moored there – and although Speke and Grant would shortly lodge their servants and their stores in the *Kathleen* – they accepted Baker's invitation to come and live with him on his *dahabiya*.[7]

On his well-appointed boat, he seated them under an awning and called for refreshments. For months, the travellers had tasted nothing even as basic as tea, sugar and bread. Not surprisingly, they eagerly consumed whatever was set before them. When a

Grant and Speke entertained by Florence and Baker on his *dahabiya*.

pretty young woman came on deck, Speke became flustered. He had heard he seemed to remember, that Baker's wife had died a few years previously. So, without thinking, he blurted out: 'I thought your wife was dead.' After an awkward silence, Baker agreed that his wife was indeed dead, and declared that Florence was his '*chère amie*'.[8] Speke's gaffe, though embarrassing to everyone, including Florence who was feverish at the time, did no harm to the esteem in which Baker was already held by the new arrivals, who considered themselves men of the world. They now described their journey, mentioning, along with much geographical information, the chiefs and rulers met on their way. But this was a mere curtain-raiser to the astonishingly generous suggestion that followed.

Suddenly, Speke proposed to Baker that he, rather than the absent Petherick, should be the one to try to 'discover' the Luta N'zige lake, which due to Kamrasi's prohibitions he and Grant had been unable to reach. This had been a severe disappointment, he explained, since they both believed that the Nile flowed into the Luta N'zige, and then out of it again to the north. This was guesswork of course, since neither had followed the river to the lake, nor seen it flow out.

Although Speke and his companion clearly thought of the Luta N'zige as at best a subsidiary reservoir of the Nile, Baker – ever the optimist – told himself it might prove 'a second source of the Nile'. Earlier, he had turned to Speke with a self-deprecating smile and asked: 'Does not one leaf of the laurel remain for me?' He was overjoyed to discover that a substantial sprig might be his for the taking, if he agreed to brave a journey bristling with dangers (although no more than 250 miles there and back). In answer to the question whether he was prepared to attempt to reach the lake, Baker handed his diary to Speke who opened it and then wrote three pages of directions, including invaluable advice about guides and interpreters.[9]

The only subject upon which Speke and Baker differed was whether Florence ought to go to the lake. As Grant recalled: 'In talking over the matter with Speke, I said: "What a shame to have so delicate a creature with him."' Speke agreed and even told Baker to his face that he ought to marry Florence on his return to England.[10] But what upset Speke much more at this time than Florence's predicament was the supposed treachery of the once well-liked Welshman, John Petherick.

Speke and Grant knew that the Welshman was an unsalaried, honorary consul who had long been obliged to trade in ivory for a living, but because he had received subscription money they were upset to learn that he was trading far to the west of Gondokoro, rather than coming to greet them. In the consul's RGS instructions, he had been told that the money had been subscribed by the public specifically to 'enable [him] to remain two years to the southward of Gondokoro ... rendering assistance to the expedition under Captains Grant and Speke'. If the explorers were not at Gondokoro on his arrival, Petherick had been instructed to leave boats there and then head south in person for the Nyanza.[11] Yet though Petherick's *wakil* had indeed left three boats at Gondokoro, Petherick himself would never set foot there until his arrival five days after Speke and Grant, nor had he or his *wakil* taken a single step further south towards the Nyanza.[12] Baker had been corresponding with Petherick and could (had he so desired) have explained that the consul had been delayed by illness and other misfortunes, but Baker chose to say nothing. Since Speke's public attacks on Petherick would later prove infinitely more damaging to *his* reputation than to Petherick's, it is important to determine whether Baker was also to blame for what happened.[13]

A daily visitor to Samuel Baker's *dahabiya* in which Baker himself, Florence and the English explorers were all staying, was a Circassian slave trader, Khursid Agha.[14] Baker was friendly with the man, despite the fact that Petherick had written telling him that Khursid had recently made a great *razzia* (slave raid) on the Dinka, along with De Bono's nephew, Amabile, and Petherick's own *wakil*, Abdel Majid. Baker also knew that Petherick, as honorary British consul in Khartoum, had attempted to enforce the *khedive*'s law against slaving by arresting both Amabile and Majid for capturing hundreds of slaves, including eighteen children.[15] Inevitably Khursid hated Petherick for arresting his friends and for handing them over to the Egyptian authorities in Khartoum, so it was probably he who mentioned to Speke, aboard the *dahabiya,* that Petherick had himself been accused of slave trading by some European traders and diplomats in Khartoum. On returning to England, Speke would use this information to make a thinly veiled attack on Petherick for slave trading.[16] Samuel Baker could easily have saved Speke from making this foolish allegation by admitting that he himself believed Petherick innocent.[17] But Baker wanted to replace Consul Petherick as the man to 'succour' the explorers, and he also hoped to ensure that when Petherick eventually arrived, Speke would not feel inclined to let the Welshman share in the glory of finding the Luta N'zige.[18] The less Speke liked Petherick, the better things would be for Baker – or so Baker appears to have calculated.

Despite being six years older than Speke and Grant, Baker got on well with both. All three had much in common in respect of background and interests, which included a shared passion for shooting, for exploration, and (with Grant at least) for painting in water colour.[19] So when Petherick, the former mining engineer and his wife, Katherine, finally appeared on 20 February, the cosy trio of English gentlemen on the *dahabiya* closed ranks against the newcomers. In his published journal, Speke claimed that he had managed to be civil to the consul and his wife soon after their arrival. 'Though naturally I felt much annoyed at Petherick – for I had hurried away from Uganda, and separated from Grant at Kari, solely to keep faith with him – I did not wish to break friendship, but dined and conversed with him.' In fact, Speke later admitted that he had spoken out in anger.[20]

As Speke saw things, unless De Bono's men had chanced to be at Faloro, he and Grant would have been murdered by the Bari before getting anywhere near Gondokoro. Petherick's apparent failure to recognise the life and death struggle they had been engaged in lay at the heart of Speke's rage. After a tense conversation with the Welshman, Speke said he could accept that the consul had been delayed by illness and accidents, but he could not understand why Petherick's *wakil* (having reached Gondokoro with his boats) had not gone on to 'search for me up the Nile'.[21] According to the consul, lack of funds was the reason. The money subscribed by the public had been only half as much as had been needed. So, according to Petherick, he and Abdel Majid had been forced to travel to the Bahr el-Ghazal to purchase tusks there 'to effect large sales of ivory' at a later date, in order to raise more cash.[22]

Unfortunately, the atmosphere on Baker's *dahabiya* was too highly charged for Petherick to describe in detail the truly dreadful events that had detained him and his wife in the Bahr el-Ghazal: such as their discovery that Abdel Majid had betrayed them and conducted a *razzia* with Khursid Agha. Then their *dahabiya* had sunk, and several hundred porters had been needed to salvage their possessions and carry them with their recently obtained ivory to Gondokoro. Dinka tribesmen had refused to act as carriers, so Petherick had tried to force them at gunpoint to carry for him. They had fought back with spears and Petherick had been obliged to shoot nine dead in self-defence. Still desperate for porters, Petherick had reluctantly decided to capture cattle from a neighbouring tribe in order to pay the Dinka for carriers in the only currency they would accept. This act of armed theft by a British consul led James Murie, a doctor accompanying the Pethericks, to complain about them to Baker. Yet for Petherick – who had been marooned hundreds of miles from his main trading station – it had been impossible to see how else he could have freed himself from his swampy prison and eventually have reached Gondokoro. But for Jack Speke, who had never shot Africans nor stolen their cattle, these bloody events when described to him by Baker, had made him feel even less sympathetic towards the consul.[23]

Petherick took some comfort from the fact that the explorers were still storing their belongings on his boat, the *Kathleen*, so he was deeply shocked when, 'without any intimation of his reasons for so doing, Speke [began] removing his effects'. The explorer told the distraught consul that 'friend Baker had offered his boats', so he would not need to use Petherick's vessels for the voyage downstream.²⁴ Since Petherick's boats had been waiting for him at Gondokoro between December 1861 and May 1862, and then from October 1862 onwards, the consul was dazed by the unfairness of Baker stepping in at the eleventh hour and usurping the role he had been given by the RGS.

John and Katherine Petherick.

In a final effort to get Speke to reverse his damaging decision to use Baker's boats and surplus stores, the Pethericks invited the two explorers and Samuel Baker to dine with them on the *Kathleen*. Katherine Petherick cooked a large ham which she had brought out from England, but this tasty peace offering failed to persuade Speke to forgive John Petherick for placing his trading activities above his 'succouring' ones. So when Katherine Petherick leaned across the dinner table in the *dahabiya*'s lamp-lit cabin and made a personal plea to Speke to accept her husband's aid, he 'drawlingly replied: "I do not wish to recognize the succour dodge."' Horrified by Speke's blunt insinuation that her husband had pocketed the subscription money, Katherine ran from the cabin.

A few months earlier Mrs Petherick had been attractive and shapely, with dark ringlets framing her face – but no longer. She had become in her own words 'a woman clad in unwomanly rags ... skin red brown, face worn and haggard, hair scorched crisp, and clad in a scanty dress of gaudy calico'. She and her husband had nearly died on the Bahr el-Ghazal, and had only been sucked into fighting the Dinka by their determination to reach Gondokoro quickly. Miraculously they had arrived a mere five days after Speke and Grant, and seventeen after Baker, who had used his advantage, in Katherine's words, 'to supplant Petherick's expedition for the relief of the Captains'.[25] She was well aware that if it became known in England that Speke had preferred Samuel Baker's aid to her husband's, his reputation would be wrecked. So she 'went to Baker's boat and implored him not to offer his boats to Captain Speke, as he, Mr Baker, well knew ... that our boats had arrived prior to his'. Affecting not to understand why she was so upset, Baker replied blandly: 'Oh, Mrs Petherick, it will be a positive service to me if he goes to Khartoum in my boats, as the men are paid in advance, and his men will serve as escort and guard.' Katherine left the *dahabiya* in tears.[26] Later, Speke sent back almost all the supplies which Petherick had bought for his use. He attached a note saying that Baker had already given him everything he needed.[27]

Speke's single-mindedness and his determination to stick to his objectives made him a great explorer, but also made him disinclined to change his opinion once he had made up his mind about a person. But despite what Baker had told him, soon after leaving Gondokoro, Speke wrote an affable, bridge-building letter to Petherick. Perhaps he dreaded the thought of another tormenting public quarrel like the one with Burton. In any case, in this letter he gave Petherick some excellent advice, which he would have been wise to have acted upon at once.

Should you feel inclined to write a full statement of the difficulties you had to contend with in going up the White river, it would be a great relief to the minds of any person connected with the incoming funds, and also to myself, as people's tongues are always busy in this middling world.

Speke seemed ready to back off if Petherick were to give a convincing account of his problems and also produce figures accounting for the funds already spent.[28]

Unfortunately, Petherick and his wife were seriously ill in June and July and so the report was not sent.[29] On 26 July, Katherine Petherick wrote telling Sir Roderick Murchison that her husband was still feverish, and added mysteriously:

I do not feel justified at present to send to you the accounts of Consul Petherick's disbursement of the £950 subscribed for his expedition under the auspices of the RGS though they have been ready many months ... we rest alone upon the consciousness of having done our best, using incredible efforts to reach Gondokoro.[30]

Yet the longer Speke was kept waiting for Petherick's disastrously late accounts and his written explanation, the more mistrustful he inevitably became. Almost a year later, he would write to the secretary of the RGS:

I asked Mr Petherick for his reports and accounts that I might bring them home, but he deferred drawing them up until he had more leisure. Since then, however, instead of using his leisure time in drawing up his accounts, he has been actively writing against me.

Not unnaturally, Speke brooded over why Petherick had been so tardy with his paperwork, and had never 'sent men above that point [Gondokoro] to look after me'.[31] The only answer that occurred to him was that Petherick had used the 'succouring' money to benefit his trading.

However, when Speke sailed downstream in 'friend Baker's' *dahabiya* in February 1863, he had other things on his mind.

He had to find words in which to announce his discovery of the Nile's source to the world. In all probability, Burton and his allies would not accept that he had proved his case, so he decided that his announcement should take the form of a gage flung down at their feet. At the British Consulate in Khartoum, he wrote out a telegram for the RGS, dated 27 March:

Inform Sir Roderick Murchison that all is well, that we are in latitude 14° 30 N upon the Nile, and that the Nile is settled.[32]

At Cairo, Speke stayed at Shepheard's Hotel, where he arranged for his nineteen Wangwana 'faithfuls' to be photographed separately and in a group, along with the four women who had accompanied them. Then he gave them all copies of these pictures to improve their chances of employment when they returned to Zanzibar. He also paid them three years' wages and made a down-payment on a vegetable garden for their use in Zanzibar, sending them more money a few months later, so that its size could be increased.[33] Bombay, Mabruki, Baraka and the others returned home via Mauritius and the Seychelles, thanks to arrangements made by Speke in concert with Colonel Lambert Playfair, who had recently replaced Christopher Rigby as British Consul at Zanzibar. When Speke said goodbye to his men at Cairo, before they boarded the Suez train, it would have amazed him if anyone had predicted that he would never see these Wangwana porters again. He certainly expected to be back again in Africa within a year or two, at most.[34]

THIRTEEN

A Hero's Aberrations

⊷

On 17 June 1863, after an absence of just over three years from their native land, Speke and Grant sailed into Southampton Water aboard the P&O Steamship *Pera*. From Buganda, Speke had written to Sir Roderick Murchison a letter which would not reach him until after its author was dead. 'As you proved yourself a good father to me by getting up this expedition, so I hope now you will consider me a worthy son, for without doubt . . . the Victoria Nyanza is the true and indisputable source of the Nile.'[1] And 'without doubt' Sir Roderick – had he received this letter in 1863 – would indeed have responded like an overjoyed father. Even after reading nothing more detailed than Speke's brisk telegram about the Nile being 'settled', he had written at once to Sir Austen Layard, Under-Secretary of State for Foreign Affairs, urging him to make sure that Lord Palmerston, the Prime Minister, was 'not stingy' when deciding how to honour the new hero for 'a feat far more wonderful than anything which has been accomplished in my life'. A knighthood at the very least, he hinted would be appropriate.[2] But Sir Roderick would be disappointed. Unimpressed by the courage and perseverance of the two men, the eighty-year-old Prime Minister grumbled to his Foreign Secretary, Lord John Russell, that,

Murchison was giving [him] no peace about Captain Speke's discovery . . . No doubt Speke has at much personal trouble, risks and expense, solved a geographical problem, which it is strange nobody ever solved before & so far he seems deserving of reward; on the other hand, as I observed to Murchison, the practical usefulness of the Discovery is not very apparent, but moreover the question arises whether there are not other African explorers, as for instance Livingstone . . . who might put forward a similar claim.[3]

A month earlier, Murchison had written to *The Times* whole-heartedly supporting Speke's claim to have found the source; and in a presidential address given a week later at the RGS, he had converted Speke's original telegram into the much shorter and triumphal sounding: 'The Nile is settled!', with its brand-new exclamation mark adding a touch of smugness.[4] But by 22 June – the date set by the RGS for Speke's and Grant's 'welcome home' celebration at Burlington House – Sir Roderick was feeling much less confident. Indeed, Lord Palmerston's surmise that Murchison's favourite explorer Dr Livingstone (who had been travelling in Africa since 1858) might believe that the source lay elsewhere, had started to trouble Murchison several weeks before the crowds began to assemble outside Burlington House for the heroic explorers' official homecoming.

Grant and Speke acclaimed at the RGS.

The two explorers expected applause from the public and got it. Indeed it was hard to get inside Burlington House so dense was the crowd on the day of their official welcome home. Several windows were broken by people pressing against them in their efforts to see inside. But explorers' reputations were frailer affairs than this hullabaloo might suggest. Men like Murchison needed to be assiduously fed with supportive nuggets of information if their patronage was to prove long-lasting.

Unfortunately, Jack Speke never understood that it was not enough to outshine other travellers in Africa. At home too, the ambitious explorer had to work out how best to convince jealous geographers and travellers that he had achieved his aims. He should at all costs avoid confrontations with people who might wish to cast doubt on his discoveries. With his fierce pride and strong sense of what was fair, Speke had already shown – especially in his quarrel with Burton – that he was not good at keeping quiet when it was strategically imperative that he do so.

Ever since Sir Roderick Murchison had written his impulsive letter to *The Times*, he had been receiving complaints from arm-chair geographers such as Dr Charles Beke and W. D. Cooley who had the unenviable distinction of being the men who had sneered at the first reports of snow-capped mountains existing in Africa. These theorists reminded Sir Roderick that as students of sixteenth-century Portuguese maps, they had been arguing for decades that the source would turn out to be in the region of lakes accessible from the East African coast. Although neither Beke nor Cooley had been within a thousand miles of Lake Tanganyika or the Victoria Nyanza, in deference to them Sir Roderick – after welcoming the explorers to Burlington House – conceded in parenthesis that a month ago he had been 'too unqualified in his praise' for Speke and Grant.

I know for example that I did not on that occasion do sufficient justice – and I am sorry for it – to able critical geographers, who had framed hypotheses or had collated data . . .

Small wonder that Speke was soon writing angrily about 'geographers who sip port, sit in carpet slippers and criticise those who labour in the field'.[5]

Sir Roderick Murchison was not the only one who let himself down at this meeting. Speke also made a serious error when he made public his suspicion that the lake might have as many as three outlets. In reality the one he had discovered was unique, and by speaking of others he devalued his 'source'. Later, it would be pointed out that he had neither sailed around the lake nor even visited the western shores when staying with Rumanika. The fact that he had stood on the southern shore of a lake at Mwanza, and then on the northern shore of a lake 200 miles to the north of that first position, did not necessarily mean, his critics would say, that he had been viewing the same stretch of water on both occasions. Even though African and Arab testimony supported the idea of a single lake, Speke had still not made it impossible for his critics to argue with some degree of plausibility that there might be two or more lakes in the intervening space. Nor had he established a foolproof link between the Nyanza and the Nile at Gondokoro.

Facing such scepticism, Speke's best policy would have been to have written a detailed report for the RGS without delay. A clear and full presentation of his arguments, accompanied by a map founded on his lunar observations would have armed Sir Roderick and his committee with just the right ammunition to confound envious critics. Unfortunately, Speke remembered offering his Somaliland diaries to the RGS in 1859, and being unofficially advised by the Society's secretary, Norton Shaw, 'not to be so liberal, but to profit by publishing a book [of his own] the same as everyone else does'.[6] Speke knew from personal experience that general publishers like Blackwood could bring an explorer's discoveries to the attention of a far wider readership than the RGS could reach through its in-house publications.[7] And since all publishers preferred to print original material that had not previously been cherry-picked by the editor of some learned journal and then leaked to the press, his course had seemed clear.

Yet with a formidable enemy like Burton due to return to England in a matter of months, Speke *should* have published *something* in an RGS journal as soon as he had conveniently been able to do so, in order to retain Sir Roderick's vital support. But, as if unaware of the importance of keeping the

RGS's white-haired president happy, he signed a book contract with John Blackwood, which committed him to a task that made it exceptionally unlikely that he would manage to publish anything else before the end of the year. Since his aim after that was to make good the omissions of his previous journey – while crossing Africa from the east coast to the west – he needed to keep Murchison and the RGS on board, since only with their endorsement would the British government be likely to fund this expensive venture.[8]

So Speke would have been well-advised to avoid unnecessary controversy. But instead, a few months later, he hinted in a speech made in Taunton, near his father's country estates, that Petherick had let him down and had been involved in the slave trade. On hearing about Speke's attack, Petherick wrote at once to *The Times* angrily protesting his innocence.[9] John and Katherine Petherick's first letters of self-exculpation reached Murchison in August 1863. Katherine gave a heartbreaking account of their tribulations, without either mentioning Petherick's theft of cattle or his attempt to force women and children to become carriers. She explained how Speke had given to Baker the task of reaching the unknown lake, ensuring that therefore 'there was to be no opening for Mr Petherick'. Such letters persuaded Murchison that the Pethericks had done everything they could to aid Speke and were being unfairly maligned by him.[10]

Only that long-awaited report from Speke might have persuaded Murchison otherwise and restored the explorer to favour. But struggling with the endless task of writing his book for Blackwood, the floundering Speke kept the committee waiting seven more months for what would turn out to be an insultingly brief account of his discoveries. Deeply aggrieved, Murchison lost much of his former enthusiasm for his protégé's project for an east–west African journey and dismissed his criticism of the Pethericks as 'Speke's visions'. 'It is very annoying to have the dispute between Speke & Petherick going on,' he complained to Grant. 'There has been much misapprehension as to what Petherick engaged to do. He, P, never engaged to go himself to relieve you – but to send boats and grain for a given time to Gondokoro.'[11] Actually, Petherick's RGS instructions *had* required him to 'proceed [in person from Gondokoro] in the direction of Lake Nyanza with a view of succouring Captain Speke'.[12] Two years later, an RGS committee of inquiry found that Petherick had not fulfilled his promise to search in person for Grant and Speke. But by then it was far too late to restore Speke in Murchison's eyes.[13]

In August 1864 – just over a year after Speke and Grant returned to Britain – a still resentful Richard Burton came home on leave from the British Consulate on the fever-ridden island of Fernando Po, West Africa. Because Burton had quarrelled with the East India Company and the Foreign Office, this obscure diplomatic posting had been the best he could obtain. The contrast between his declining fortunes, and the apparently glittering prospects of his famous former 'sub', made him seethe with jealousy. No sooner aware of the quarrel between Speke and Petherick, Burton decided to support the latter, on the age-old principle that his enemy's enemy was his friend. He formed an alliance with the armchair geographer James McQueen, who was a close friend of Petherick's brother-in-law, Peter McQuie, and began work with McQueen on their book *The Nile Basin*, which turned out to be a vitriolic and libellous attack on Speke's geographical claims *and* on his character. By the late summer of 1864, Burton had effectively become leader of all those geographers and explorers who saw Speke's account of the Nile as a threat to their own theories.[14]

In the months before Burton's arrival in England, Speke had been working on a book to follow his *Journal of the Discovery of the Source of the Nile*, which had appeared the previous December. This new book was going to cover his travels with Burton and was intended to contradict what had been said about him in Burton's *Lake Regions of Central Africa*. During many months of work, Speke inevitably relived their bitter disputes, and felt belittled by him all over again. His publisher was concerned that this new book would simply offer Burton new targets to shoot at. Speke's reply (written shortly before Burton's return to England) was not reassuring.

Don't be afraid of what I have written, for it only rests between B the B and myself whether we fight it out with the quill or the fist. I won't let him come to England quietly ... He was cut by his Regt for not accepting a challenge, and now my Regt expects me to tackle him some way or another, to say nothing of my feelings of honour. I think I have been very mild, considering the amount of injustice he has done me. I have been cautious because I can prove what I have said, whilst he, being the aggressor has brought it all on himself.[15]

It was unfortunate for Speke that just when he should have been giving his undivided attention to securing patronage for his next African expedition, he was writing about his travels with Burton and worrying about the need to counter whatever the man might say about him next.

Speke was also preoccupied with nothing less momentous than how best to help Africa and its inhabitants to prosper and progress. In January 1864, he wrote to his friend, Sir George Grey, the former Governor of Cape Colony, asking him to put his 'powerful influence [behind a] project for the regeneration of Africa'.[16] A month later, Grant was told by Speke that he 'had in view a scheme for civilizing Africa and putting a stop to the slave trade'.[17] In an astonishing departure for an army officer turned explorer, Speke published two broadsheets: 'Scheme for Opening Africa' and 'Considerations for opening Africa', and in March, he launched his new project at a meeting in the Belgravia town house of a wealthy social reformer. Although clearly influenced by Livingstone's 'civilising' formula of 'commerce and Christianity', Speke had ideas of his own and appealed to the British government to put pressure on the *khedive* of Egypt to use force to end the Egyptian and Arab slave raids on the upper Nile. He not only wanted to end the persecution of the Bari, but to use the Nile 'to open a direct trade' between Britain and the kingdoms of Buganda, Bunyoro and Karagwe. Missionaries as well as traders, he said, should be sent to the three kingdoms.[18]

Sir Roderick Murchison was no admirer of missionaries (with the single exception of Livingstone), so he found Speke's new interests puzzling and even distasteful. But the worldly RGS president had not yet given up all hope of sending Speke back to Africa, and it occurred to him that if the explorer was genuinely eager to persuade the Egyptians to crush the slave trade on the river, he might be happy to sail up the Nile with an escort of Egyptian soldiers, on his way to mapping the river's upper reaches. Murchison reckoned the British government would be delighted if the Egyptians could be shamed into paying a significant percentage of the costs of the expedition by providing its manpower.

On 12 May, Speke wrecked this plan by storming into the office of the Foreign Secretary, Lord John Russell, and telling him that the RGS had asked him 'to explore the head basin [by] forcing his way up the Nile with Egyptian troops'. He confided to Russell that he had never shot Africans or Arabs and did not intend to do so now. Instead, he wanted to enter Africa through Masai country 'as a British envoy to open a legitimate trade with the king of Bunyoro', and only after that would he fill in the gaps he had left in his earlier exploration of the Nile basin, and continue across Africa to the Atlantic.[19]

A month after Speke's visit to the Foreign Office, Lord John Russell had still not taken the hint and appointed him to a roving consulship. Nor had the RGS made him any offer of support.[20] This indifference persuaded a humiliated Speke to revert to a foolish plan he had briefly considered in February and March – which was to involve the Emperor Napoleon III of France in an Anglo-French expedition. Although France was still considered the old enemy, Speke meant to invite French explorers to set out east from Gabon on the Atlantic coast and then meet him in the region of Buganda and Bunyoro after he had reached these places either by travelling up the Nile or approaching from the East African coast. He held back at first, knowing that the plan was controversial; but in the late summer, when his relations with Murchison had become seriously strained, Speke contacted his friend Laurence Oliphant, now living in Paris, and asked him to contact the British Ambassador, Lord Cowley, about a possible meeting with the Emperor. Not perhaps understanding the full implications, Cowley obliged and Speke was granted an audience with Napoleon III on 25 August 1864. The explorer came away believing that the Emperor was ready to finance a joint expedition.[21] At this date, one French expedition was already pushing into the West African interior up the Ogowé river, and others were under way on the Niger and in Senegal. So Speke had been preaching to the converted. The Emperor was already keen to extend French influence to the east – perhaps even as far as the Sudan. That this would very likely conflict with British interests at some future date was something which Speke chose to ignore. An explorer could only explore if someone provided him with the funds to do so. If Britain denied him what he needed, he would go elsewhere.

The very idea that Speke might aid France in Africa horrified Sir Roderick and he told Austen Layard of the Foreign Office that he 'deeply regretted these aberrations, as Speke has in other respects the greatness to ensure success as a bold explorer'.[22] Murchison also wrote to Grant bemoaning his failure to persuade Speke to drop his wild schemes and limit his objectives 'to finishing off and completing much of what you [both] necessarily left in an uncertain state'.[23]

By the end of August Speke's book about his travels with Burton, *What Led to the Discovery of the Source of the Nile*, had been printed, though not as yet published. He was dividing his time between his parents' town house in Pimlico, London, and their estates in Somerset, and seemed content to be living in the countryside he loved. Of course his future was uncertain, but as a stop-gap he decided to go shooting in India for a few months in the autumn. After that, he meant to ask the East India Company for a three-year furlough so he could return to Africa if anyone had the wit to back him.[24]

Then, in early August the postman brought a letter that would have disastrous consequences.

FOURTEEN

Death in the Afternoon

—∞∞—

Sir Roderick Murchison had sent Speke a momentous letter, inviting him to address the September meeting of the British Association for the Advancement of Science. A discussion about the Nile's source was to be the principal attraction on the schedule of talks and debates mounted by the Geography and Ethnology section of the association. On 12 August, Speke replied to Murchison: 'I shall be only too glad to meet and converse with Livingstone [about the Nile], to test the matter by fair arbitration on amicable terms.' He did not mention Burton, but could not have expected to avoid debating with him too.[1] A few weeks later George Simpson, Blackwood's senior manager, wrote indignantly to his employer:

Speke's enemies are preparing a savage attack upon him at the Bath meeting, headed by Burton, aided by Livingstone. So much the better ... Speke will know how to meet them & turn the affair to the advantage of our gallant but most imprudent friend.[2]

Speke was 'imprudent' because in Simpson's opinion, he had made too many ill-judged public remarks about Petherick and Burton. Worse still, he had caused unnecessary offence to Livingstone as well as to Murchison.[3] When Speke heard that Burton was saying that the Rusizi river linked the northern end of Lake Tanganyika (Burton's own lake, as Burton saw it) with the Luta N'zige – the more northerly lake, which Baker was about to investigate – he (Speke) was very angry. To make this claim Burton had needed to 'forget' the inconvenient fact that he and Speke had been told, emphatically, by the three sons of a local chief, that the river at Tanganyika's northern end flowed *into*, rather than *out of* the lake. But since it might well be many years before any explorer managed to see this river with his own eyes, Burton appeared to have calculated that he could safely reverse the flow of the Rusizi and get away with it, perhaps for a decade – all the while undermining the claims which Speke had made for the Victoria Nyanza.

It came to Speke that he could pay back Burton for his unscrupulous *volte face* by resorting to some armchair geography of his own. Since no explorer had visited either the southern end of Lake Tanganyika, or the northern end of the more southerly Lake Nyasa, nobody in Europe could be sure whether or not a southward-flowing river linked the two lakes. If it did, the Rusizi could not possibly flow out of Lake Tanganyika to the north, or the lake would have been drained of all its water eons ago. Fortunately – from Speke's point of view – a substantial river (the Shiré) flowed out from the southern end of Lake Nyasa. So what could explain this strong southern outflow, except a comparable inflow into Nyasa from the north? This was a powerful argument for a link with Tanganyika; but it was one that, if deployed, ran the risk of aggravating the famous Dr Livingstone, who, though he had turned back before reaching the northern end of Lake Nyasa, had informed the RGS that four or five small rivers flowing into the western side of the lake, produced more than enough water to explain the Shiré's outflow.

Although, at times, Livingstone cultivated an air of saintliness, he always counter-attacked fiercely when potential rivals disagreed with his geographical theories.[4] So, when the doctor returned to Britain in July 1864, and heard what Speke had said about Lake Nyasa at the RGS a month earlier, he was apoplectic. Livingstone's reputation had been tarnished by his disastrous Zambezi Expedition, but many people still saw him as the country's greatest explorer and a man capable of extraordinary acts of self-sacrifice. So it was worse than 'imprudent' of Speke to have turned him into an enemy, and shoved him into Burton's camp. Indeed, Livingstone was soon arguing that Speke's little effluent at Ripon Falls 'would not account for the Nile', and telling his eldest daughter that Captain Speke had 'such slender mental abilities that silence in this & other matters would have better become him'.[5] Livingstone detested Burton for his contempt both for Africans and for missionaries, but despite this visceral dislike he confided to Sir Roderick Murchison, that he, like Burton, believed the Nile's source was more likely to lie in Lake Tanganyika than in the Victoria Nyanza. More precisely, Livingstone was starting to think that the true source probably lay somewhere to the west of Lake Tanganyika, and would flow into Lake Tanganyika, exiting it as the Rusizi, and then flowing on north to the Upper Nile through the Luta N'zige.[6]

Although Speke had expected to have a debate with Livingstone, Murchison had always meant him and Burton to head the bill at the big meeting in Bath. Indeed their anticipated collision was soon being advertised as 'the great Nile debate'. It seems that by pitting him against Burton, Murchison was punishing Speke for his supposed ingratitude to the RGS and for not sending in a proper report. Livingstone was expected to act as an unofficial referee, while the real battle was to be with Burton. Given the man's reputation as a debater, Speke could not have looked forward to taking him on, but he passionately believed that he had found the Nile's source, and so had no intention of giving ground. As he told Blackwood, it was a matter of honour for him to face Burton – akin to fighting a duel.[7] Speke was no coward, though he knew he would be vulnerable – and not only because he had failed to map the Victoria Nyanza.

Since the incident with the beetle, he had been deaf in one ear. Poor sight also continued to dog him, and was worse after his long literary labours. Feeling utterly exhausted, he had told Blackwood that he would 'never think again of writing a personal narration, since it only leads to getting abused when disclosing disagreeable truths'.[8] Blackwood was worried about his famous author becoming embroiled in arguments. He felt that in speeches and letters to the press 'Speke's imperfect powers of explanation [had] been more hurtful to himself than [to] anyone else', often resulting in him being 'looked upon as the reverse of the generous simple hearted fellow he was'. He begged Laurence Oliphant to do what he could 'to keep him from putting his foot in it ... He is a real good one who requires a friend.'⁹ But Oliphant – although he liked Speke – was mischievous, and made no effort to save him from the great debate. On the contrary, Oliphant egged on Burton by telling him that Speke had recently said to him that if Burton came to Bath, 'he would kick him'. Burton had replied, according to his wife Isabel: 'Well that settles it! By God, he shall kick me.' Of course Burton would have gone to Bath anyway, being eager to do Speke any harm he could. He had already applied to the Foreign Office for an extension of leave simply in order to be able to attend the meeting.¹⁰

The debate between the pair was due to take place at Bath's Royal Mineral Water Hospital on 16 September 1864; and on the 15th, Burton and Speke attended a preliminary meeting, both sitting on the platform close to Sir Roderick Murchison. Burton claimed some years later that he had been shocked by how much older Speke looked after 'his severe labours'. They glanced at one another without any sign of recognition. Someone beckoned to Speke from the hall at 1.30 p.m. and, according to Burton, he muttered: 'I can't stand this any longer!', and then left the building.¹¹

From Bath, Speke rode to Neston Park, Corsham, the house of John B. Fuller, an uncle whose estate was about ten miles away and with whom he was staying. Speke arrived at Neston Park at about 2.30 p.m. and soon afterwards went out shooting partridges with his cousin, George P. Fuller. A keeper, Daniel Davis, came with them to mark birds. Throughout his adult life, Speke had found shooting a soothing activity and he was very glad of it now.

At about 4.00, John Hanning Speke clambered over a low stone wall, holding the muzzle of his double-barrelled shotgun in one hand, using the stock like a walking-stick to help him keep his balance on the loose stones. Davis, who was 200 yards ahead, saw Speke up on the wall, and the next moment heard his gun go off. Fuller, who was considerably closer, spun round as the shot rang out, and saw his cousin tumble forwards into the field with no gun in his hand. The Lancaster breech-loader had fallen from his fingers the moment it went off, and had clattered down the side of the wall into the field he had just left. The unguarded trigger of one of the barrels seemed to have been snagged by a sapling, sending its contents into Speke's left side below the armpit. When the shotgun was retrieved, one barrel was seen to have been discharged and the hammer of the other was at half-cock.

Fuller reached Speke first and found him bleeding profusely from a large wound, which he did his best to staunch. Speke murmured feebly: 'Don't move me,' and did not utter again. Fuller duly left his cousin where he was, and went for assistance, leaving Davis with Speke, who was already lapsing into unconsciousness. He died fifteen minutes after the fatal shot was fired.[12]

The following day, at Monk's Park, Corsham – a nearby house belonging to Speke's brother, William – the local coroner held an inquest. George Fuller and Daniel Davis both gave evidence, as did Thomas Snow, the nearest available surgeon, who had been sent for by Fuller, but had arrived shortly after Speke expired. Snow told the jury that the wound was 'such as would be made by a cartridge if the muzzle of the gun was close to the body. It led in a direction upwards and towards the spine, passing through the lungs and dividing all the large blood vessels near the heart'. The unanimous verdict of the coroner's jury was that: 'The deceased died from the accidental discharge of his own gun.'[13] The verdict of accidental death was hardly surprising, since no man intending to commit suicide would have chosen to shoot himself while clambering over a rubble-stone wall, and holding his gun in a manner that made it impossible for him to reach the trigger with the fingers of either hand. Nor would anyone intending suicide have chosen to fire into his body from just below the armpit.

None of this would stop Richard Burton saying, soon after he heard the news, that the explorer had committed suicide to avoid 'the exposure of his misstatements in regard to the Nile sources'.[14] Determined to make her husband seem more humane than this allegation suggested he was, Isabel Burton wrote of him weeping about Speke's death 'for many a day'. In fact, Burton's letters to friends reveal a mood closer to gloating than to grief. Two days before Speke's burial, Burton told a fellow diplomat that: 'Captain Speke came to a bad end, but no one knows anything about it . . . The charitable say he shot himself, the uncharitable that I shot him.'[15] The idea that Speke, with the confrontation in Bath looming, might have been literally scared to death, was clearly far from displeasing to Burton.

But had Speke really been in mortal terror of the approaching debate? Two days before his death, he had started a letter to John Tinné, the brother of Alexine Tinné, the explorer of the Bahr el-Ghazal, and in it he explained the importance to Egypt, 'as well as to our own merchants, of opening up the Equatorial regions to legitimate commerce'. So his final letter is filled with hope rather than with fear.[16] Speke's married sister, Sophie Murdoch, was told by George Fuller that while he had been shooting with Speke on the fatal day, her brother had been talking shortly before the accident about his plan to persuade missionaries to come to Buganda and Unyoro – a strange topic for anyone to enthuse about minutes before ending his life.[17] Yet Burton would seek to bolster the idea of suicide, not just in letters and conversation, but by inserting into the chapter called 'Captain Speke', in his *Zanzibar: City, Island, and Coast* (1872), a number of deliberately suggestive passages. 'Before we set out [for Somaliland] he [Speke] openly declared that being tired of life he had come to be killed in Africa.'[18] Burton plucked this suicidal remark from his memory eighteen years after it was supposed to have been addressed to him. It is neither to be found in Burton's earlier *First Footsteps in East Africa*, nor in his *Lake Regions of Central Africa*, and only made its appearance after Burton had begun insinuating that Speke might have taken his own life. So did Speke really say any such thing? Habitually, he kept his thoughts to himself – as Burton had often complained – and so it is most unlikely that at a time when he was very eager to impress Burton – who was his superior officer, and whom he had just met – Speke would have let slip that he might one day kill himself, and so let down everyone connected with the expedition. James Grant after reading the 'Captain Speke' chapter, in *Zanzibar*, wrote to Rigby, describing Burton as 'this foul, false libeller . . . spitting his venom at the memory of poor Speke'.[19]

Burton and his wife were the only people who would later suggest that Speke had looked distraught in the hall the day before his death.[20] Another key passage in Burton's *Zanzibar* – much quoted by the few biographers[21] who lean towards a verdict of suicide – is as follows:

The calamity had been the more unexpected as he [Speke] was ever remarkable for the caution with which he handled his weapon. I ever made a point of ascertaining a fellow-traveller's habit in that matter and I observed that even when our canoe was shaken and upthrown by the hippopotamus, he never allowed his gun to look at him or at others.[22]

According to Speke's account, he and Burton only pursued hippopotami together in a canoe on a few days in February 1857, and during them their vessel was neither lifted up nor even struck.[23]

And had Speke really been so wonderfully experienced and cautious in the use of all manner of guns? His cousin, George Fuller, recalled that for many years Speke had shot with rifles, rather than shotguns. Indeed, when shooting with an unfamiliar double-barrelled shotgun on the day he died, Fuller observed that Speke 'did not seem to have acquired the usual precautions'. Having 'noticed this carelessness', Fuller and Davis, his game-keeper, had both 'avoided being very close to him when walking the fields . . . where the accident happened'.[24]

Speke's funeral took place in the little church of Dowlish Wake just to the south of his family's estates. With tears streaming down his face, his father led the cortege along autumnal lanes lined with villagers and estate workers. Joining the family inside the church were Sir Roderick Murchison, David Livingstone and James Grant, who 'put a small "immortelle" of violets & mignonettes on the coffin as it was borne past'. Livingstone later denied that Grant had sobbed aloud and 'had gone down into the vault' with the coffin, as had been reported in several papers.[25] Speke was thirty-seven years old on the day he died, and left less than £5,000 – most of it being the earnings from his two books.[26]

The Times, in its obituary, accepted that on balance it was likely that Speke had found the source of the Nile, but there was no unanimity about this in other papers. Livingstone doubted that the source had been found and explained why – as did Burton, who protested to *The Times* that the Nile could not be settled until a connection between his own Lake Tanganyika and the Luta N'zige had been proved or disproved.[27] So with two great explorers, and a number of lesser geographers, including the gold medallist Dr Charles Beke, unconvinced by Speke's arguments, the dead man's reputation seemed doomed to remain in a kind of limbo, perhaps for decades. Even the sales of his two books – classics of nineteenth-century travel literature – began to decline, and a second edition of *What Led to the Discovery of the Source of the Nile* would have to wait many years to make its appearance. With no explorer in the field likely to provide an early answer to the question of whether or not Speke had found the true source, uncertainty about the value of his discoveries became widespread. Sir Roderick Murchison, who despite stating in *The Times* that he and his friends proposed 'to bring about the erection of a suitable monument', had suggested to Livingstone in Bath, that he should return to Africa to solve the Nile riddle. At first Livingstone refused to commit himself, largely because a straightforward search for the source of a river – albeit the longest in the world – would never on its own persuade the public that he was returning to the 'Dark Continent' with a missionary's motives. Nor did he want to appear over-keen to compete with the likes of godless Richard Burton for geographical prizes – even the greatest prize of all.[28]

Two months after Speke's death, Burton delivered, at the RGS, the speech he had intended to give at Bath. 'Be it distinctly understood that ... I do not stand forth as an enemy of the departed,' he assured his audience; yet few of them would have been deceived. He attacked Speke's claims for all the old reasons and for some new ones too.[29] Then a month later he published this speech as Part One of his book, *The Nile Basin*, in which he claimed that Lake Tanganyika was the primary source of the Nile, despite knowing that Tanganyika's elevation above sea level was at least 1,200 feet below that of the Victoria Nyanza. He also dismissed the African testimony, which he and Speke had collected, about the direction in which the Rusizi flowed.[30] Whatever Speke's faults as a geographer – including the careless calculations in his first book that had led him to represent the Nile flowing uphill for a short distance – Burton now trumped him with his own absurdities, such as his claim that there were hills in the centre of the Victoria Nyanza and a road running through it.

Part Two of the *Nile Basin* was even worse, being a reprint of the *Morning Advertiser*'s review by James McQueen (the octogenarian armchair geographer and friend of the Pethericks) of Speke's *Journal of the Discovery of the Source of the Nile*. This review would be praised by Burton for its 'acumen and dryness of style', but in reality was a scurrilous attack on Speke's character.[31] The explorer's description of how he had measured the fat women at Rumanika's court – though little worse than similar measuring incidents involving penises in Burton's *Lake Regions* – had contained some pretty tasteless humour. But the passage did not suggest, as McQueen implied, that Speke had been sexually attracted to these immense females. Nor did Speke's honesty about his regard for Mutesa's mother, despite her heavy drinking, mean that he had 'looked on applauding the scene' when she and her ministers had been wildly intoxicated. Nor was it fair to imply that his liking for the Baganda people meant that he had condoned Mutesa's brutal acts.

Every detail of Speke's love affair with Méri had been cut from the published book, but McQueen still toyed pruriently with the idea that Speke had been actively involved in 'mixing the blood of mankind'. There should be no surprise, the old geographer declared if, at some future time, 'on one half black and white head there is seen hair like Speke's'. Wisely, given his vulnerability in this area, Speke had never considered suing for libel. That McQueen had himself been fascinated by thoughts of amorous shenanigans – and especially by the tiny triangular bark-cloth 'mbugus' which were all that concealed the female courtiers' genitals – is evident from the sheer quantity of 'mbugus' that adorns his text. But though this is obvious to anyone reading the review today, it would have been less clear at a time when sexual hypocrisy was a way of life.[32] McQueen succeeded in making people wonder whether such a libertine could have had the self-discipline to solve history's most intractable geographical mystery.

The decision to attack a remarkable man in this scabrous way, so soon after his death, says little for Burton's judgement – even though *his* words were less offensive than those of his elderly co-author. Laurence Oliphant's scathing and partisan review of the *Nile Basin* in *Blackwood's Magazine* in January 1865 resonates with anger and distaste.

We can only put Captain Burton in his true light by showing that his real object in publishing the work before us. . . is to discredit, not the discoveries of an explorer, but the memory of a deceased fellow traveller. Would it not have been the instinct of a generous mind to have allowed the controversy to slumber, rather than excite it by the disparagement of one who is no longer alive to defend himself?[33]

But Burton was soon writing. again, this time in the *Athenaeum*, continuing to distort and belittle.[34] In 1873 Dr Georg Schweinfurth, the German explorer of the Upper Nile, published a map showing the area of the Victoria Nyanza dotted with five small lakes.[35] It was a happy day for Burton, and a sad one for the memory of the man whose family had failed to preserve a single scrap of paper relating to the first twenty-seven years of his life.[36] A cloud of obscurity was fast enveloping John Hanning Speke, even before Dr Livingstone left for Africa and Samuel Baker returned to England as the new hero of the hour. With these larger-than-life, well-documented men now chasing the source, the future looked set to belong to them.

FIFTEEN

The Doctor's Dilemma

As he entered his fifties, David Livingstone was losing his teeth (due to years of an inadequately prepared African diet) and suffered terribly from piles, but he still believed that he was God's chosen instrument for opening the 'Dark Continent' to the light of the Gospel. Inevitably, he saw other explorers as interlopers trespassing on his turf. During his twenty-one years in Africa he had already 'discovered' Lake Nyasa (Malawi), although secretly fearing that the Portuguese trader, Candido de Costa Cardoso had beaten him there. But he had undoubtedly made the first authenticated crossing of the continent by a European, so Speke's claim to have done something even more remarkable – namely locating the Nile's source – had not pleased him. In fact he had been grimly determined to prove Speke wrong, even before the young explorer had enraged him by hypothesising (incorrectly, as it happened) that his account of the river system feeding Lake Nyasa was wrong.

The British Association's meeting in September 1864 had been a turning point for Livingstone. His British government-backed Zambezi Expedition had cost many lives, and had failed to open up a safe and viable district for European settlement in south-central Africa. So on arriving at Bath, wearing his famous explorers' peaked cap, Dr Livingstone might have looked the part, but in reality he had had no idea what he would be doing next, except that it would have to involve Africa. But to what purpose, and with whose backing, he could not tell.

But at the Bath meeting his imagination had been fired by the rivalry of Speke and Burton, and by their opposing views of the Nile watershed. While there, he had also learned that another contender, Samuel Baker, was travelling south towards the unknown lake, which Speke had learned about while in Bunyoro. Indeed, the day after Speke's death, a letter from the unhappy Consul Petherick – then in Khartoum – was read to the assembled geographers by Sir Roderick Murchison, informing them that in late May 1864 some men who had accompanied Baker to Shaguzi, then the capital of Bunyoro, had just returned from there to Khartoum. So Baker, it was assumed, would have reached the lake in March or April, or died in the attempt.[1] Although at Bath Livingstone had not yet accepted Murchison's informal invitation to go out to Africa to solve the Nile mystery, Sir Roderick knew that his favourite explorer had been sorely tempted to say yes. So, a few weeks later, to keep him under pressure, Murchison urged him to come to an RGS meeting scheduled for 14 November 1864, at which Richard Burton was expected to argue that the Nile originated in Lake Tanganyika.

Because the outflow from the Victoria Nyanza at Ripon Falls was so small, Livingstone had already written off Speke's claims for that lake, describing him as 'a poor misguided thing . . . [who] gave the best example I know of the eager pursuit of a foregone conclusion'.[2] The great doctor, however, saw merit in Burton's thesis when he first heard it propounded that November at the RGS's premises in Old Burlington Street. Even so, Burton's case depended entirely on whether the river at the northern tip of Lake Tanganyika flowed into the lake, or out of it. If it flowed out, then it would almost certainly continue northwards into the unknown lake (Luta N'zige), which Baker was thought to have reached in the spring, and from where it would very likely flow on into the Nile. But Livingstone had a further thought: if the Rusizi *did* flow out of Lake Tanganyika, there must be a large river pouring an equivalent amount of water into the lake. In Livingstone's judgement, this inflowing river would be very likely to rise several hundred miles to the south-west – far to the south of all the other explorers' chosen fields of investigation. So if he could only find this unknown source, he would cut out Burton, as well as the deluded Speke and the rich newcomer, Baker.

Knowing just how competitive Livingstone was, Sir Roderick clambered to his feet the moment Burton had finished speaking, and declared that his one desire was that the paper they had all just heard would lead to some 'actual exploration', rather than to yet more theorising. 'I only hope that Dr Kirk, or some person like him, may be induced to clear up the doubts that still hang over the question of the sources of the Nile.'[3] Dr Kirk, who at thirty-two was twenty years Livingstone's junior, had been the medical officer and botanist on his Zambezi Expedition and had helped Livingstone to explore Lake Nyasa. Although he was often spoken of as 'the companion of Livingstone', in private Kirk admitted that on the Zambezi he had at times doubted his leader's sanity. Murchison hoped that his elephantine hint about sending out the younger man to disentangle the Nile watershed, would finally force the touchy and competitive veteran off the fence. It did not, and six weeks later Sir Roderick wrote pushing him even harder: 'As to your future, I am anxious to know what your own wish is as respects a renewal of African exploration.' Murchison's hope, he explained, was that Livingstone would take a portable boat to the south end of Lake Tanganyika, and then sail to the northern tip of the lake, where he would be able to see with his own eyes in which direction the Rusizi flowed. If it was out, Murchison told Livingstone he 'ought to be able to reach the White Nile [!] [and would therefore] bring back an unrivalled reputation, and would have settled all the great disputes now pending'. But if Livingstone would not make up his mind, then Dr Kirk would be approached at once. Having made his threat, Murchison ended wryly: 'I cannot believe that you now think of anchoring on the mud and sand banks of England.'[4]

His letter hit the spot. Two days later, Livingstone replied: 'I should like the exploration you propose very much ... As soon as my book [about the Zambezi Expedition] is out, I shall start.' He intended, he explained, to enter Africa on the Indian Ocean coast via the Rovuma river but had no intention of going straight to the northern end of Lake Tanganyika. As he put it to Sir Roderick, even if – as they both supposed – the Rusizi flowed out to the north, 'the source would have to be sought for still, and I would be obliged to come away back to it'.[5] Disapproval of Burton was an additional reason for Livingstone's determination to find the source before doing anything else. If he were simply to establish a link between Lake Tanganyika and Baker's lake, it would make it seem that Burton's Tanganyika was the true source of the Nile. But because Livingstone loathed Burton, he was never going to let his labours reward him in this way. 'He [Burton] seems to be a moral idiot,' he told a missionary friend. 'His conduct in Africa was so bad that it cannot be spoken of without disgust – systematically wicked, impure and untruthful.'[6]

Livingstone had heard rumours that Burton had contracted syphilis in Somaliland, and had travelled with his own personal harem *en route* to Lake Tanganyika. The prospect of meeting Africans, who had been 'witnesses of his bestial immorality', appalled the godly doctor.[7] He also knew from Burton's writings that he considered Africans 'unprogressive and unfit for change', and worse still that he believed that the 'higher or lower state of a race' pre-determined their religion. If right, this would make all missionary work in Africa pointless. Since Livingstone saw no difference between the races, he detested Burton's racist condescension.[8]

But while Livingstone's eagerness to defeat Burton on the ground (and for that matter Speke and Baker too) was central to his motivation, he also believed he had to persuade the world that he was returning to Africa with missionary aims and not merely as an explorer. A purely geographical task would mean moving swiftly across country with no time even to *appear* to be planting the Gospel in people's minds. But providentially there was something else he could do – and indeed longed to.

If he started his search for the source just south of Lake Nyasa, he would be in an area of intense Arab slave-trading activity. So by reporting back on this cruel trade to the British government, he would be doing much more than simply exploring. This then was the justification he felt he needed.

The Nile sources [he told a friend] are valuable only as a means of enabling me to open my mouth with power among men. It is this power which I hope to apply to remedy an enormous evil. Men may think I covet fame, but I make it a rule not to read aught written in my praise.[9]

Though this was humbug, since Livingstone was obsessed with what was written about him, his hatred of the Arab-Swahili slave trade was genuine and passionate.

In early July 1865, when Livingstone was preparing to leave England, *The Times* published a letter from Samuel Baker to Robert Colquhoun, the Consul-General in Alexandria, stating that he had reached the Luta N'zige in March the previous year. Disappointingly, from Livingstone's point of view, this letter contained no information at all about whether the new lake was fed from Lake Tanganyika, or whether Baker had proved that the river entering the eastern side of the Luta N'zige had originated in the Victoria Nyanza, as Speke had believed.

In September 1865, on his way to Africa via India, Livingstone chanced to pass through Suez a week before a triumphant Baker and his young mistress swept through from the opposite direction. So Livingstone's inquiries about them inevitably yielded nothing.[10] Thus he began his journey knowing no more than the simple fact that Baker had reached the Luta N'zige. Nor in Bombay could he discover anything further about the lake's geography, although there was plenty of gossip about Baker's private life doing the rounds. 'Baker married his mistress at Cairo,' Livingstone misinformed a friend, 'and from all accounts she deserved it after going through all she did for him. I heard about his woman, but it was not made public, and if she turns out well, better it never should.'[11] If Livingstone had known how cynical Baker was about the abilities and intelligence of Africans, he would have considered this a far greater fault than his fornications with his young mistress. 'As to Christianity!' wrote Baker in a passage that would have enraged Livingstone had he seen it, 'the name is profaned by coupling it with the Negro.'[12] But though ignorant of such opinions, Livingstone believed he knew enough about Baker to think him selfish and unprincipled. The doctor told his daughter Agnes that: 'the great aim of Baker's journey – there can be little doubt – [was] to cut Speke and Grant out, and get to the sources first, but he cleverly turned it round to going with the intention of helping them.'[13]

The two explorers, Livingstone and Baker, who had just missed one another at Cairo, were on their way to experience very different destinies: Samuel Baker to receive a nation's acclaim and a knighthood, David Livingstone to endure great suffering and a tragic fate – although he expected great glory. Though Livingstone was probably right about Baker's motives and his cleverness in using Speke and Grant for his own ends, the triumph he shared with Florence deserved more than the grudging attention which Livingstone eventually gave it.

SIXTEEN

The Glory of Our Prize

In March 1863, eighteen months before John Speke's tragic death in an English stubble field, the ambitious Samuel Baker had watched his two benefactors glide away downstream towards Egypt, homeward bound towards their short-lived heroes' welcome. Baker's urgent desire was to leave for the lake at once, if possible without John and Katherine Petherick, who hated him for persuading Speke to refuse their goods in favour of his own. But to Baker's surprise, after a few days the Pethericks suggested that they all travel together to the lake. Of course Baker was suspicious of this olive branch. He knew that Petherick's only hope of recovering from Speke's public criticism would be to 'discover' the Luta N'zige, and he suspected that the Welshman would fail on his own because the slave traders whom he had offended would try to sabotage his expedition. But because Baker was having trouble with his own porters, he still thought it could make sense to pool resources – at any rate during the early stages of their journey.[1]

On 15 March, while still at Gondokoro, Baker and Florence were warned by Saat – a remarkable twelve-year-old orphan boy whom Florence had saved from starvation – that their men were all about to mutiny and intended, if opposed, to shoot their employer dead. Baker's immediate response was to place a travelling bedstead outside his tent, and lay upon it five double-barrelled guns, a revolver and a razor-sharp sabre. Saat and Richarn, another mission-educated boy whom Baker trusted, were provided with loaded guns to hand to him the moment he had fired both barrels of the weapon he was currently using. As Baker shouted to the mutineers to lay down their arms, Florence stood ready to point out any men attempting to strip off the protective waterproof covers from the locks of their guns. Taken aback by Baker's *chutzpah*, the mutineers wavered and then capitulated.[2] Samuel Baker's diary and his book *The Albert N'yanza* are the only sources for his and Florence's journey, but although this gave the explorer *carte blanche* to represent himself in an heroic light, more often than not the incidental detail and sheer vitality of the telling compel belief. Often he acknowledged his powerlessness.

After renewing his promise to take the consul and his wife, and their pathetic following of five loyal men, up the Nile with him, he had to backtrack: 'My men mutinously declared that if Petherick and I joined forces they would not budge, as all the people hated him.' His followers were armed and had been paid in advance, so Baker knew they could desert him at any time. 'I called my men together,' he wrote, 'and told them I would not go on with them unless they obeyed implicitly; this they promised to do, but they declared that I alone was their master and that Petherick should not join the party.' Though describing this as 'a specimen of their outrageous independence', Baker had to accept that he would never be able to leave Gondokoro for the lake if he forced the issue over Petherick. The consul understood his predicament, and reluctantly decided to return to Khartoum.[3] But before he did, Dr Murie, who was still travelling with Petherick, horrified Baker with another tale of the consul's misdeeds. After the cattle *razzia* that had resulted in the shooting dead of nine Dinka, Baker was told that: 'The heads of three of these poor devils were cut off . . . and boiled; and the skulls are to be sent home to the College of Surgeons by Mr Petherick for sale!!!'[4]

After thwarting his would-be-mutineers, Baker left Gondokoro on 26 March with seventeen porters – a wholly inadequate number. To compensate he took twenty-four donkeys, as well as several camels and horses. He had hoped that Khursid Agha, the slave and ivory trader, would furnish him with a further ten carriers, but the men Khursid had selected refused to serve Baker on the grounds that he was a spy and a madman, who would lead them all to their deaths. At this point, Khursid's mixed party of

Turks, Egyptians and Sudanese Arabs, along with their African slaves and concubines, left for the south.[5] Very fortunately for Baker and Florence, they and their small following managed to overtake the slaving party three days later, and – urged to do so by Florence – Baker persuaded Khursid's Syrian *wakil*, Ibrahim (leading the caravan in the absence of Khursid himself), to let them come along too. First, the explorer had to promise not to interfere with Ibrahim's slave raids. He swore that all he wanted to do was to reach the Luta N'zige, and that he had no interest in spying on Ibrahim's *razzias*. However, he warned the slave trader that if he or Florence were harmed, the authorities in Khartoum would hang him as the likeliest suspect. But if Ibrahim helped him, Baker promised to use his influence to obtain for him and his master the opportunity to buy ivory in any country he might 'discover'. When Ibrahim was wavering, Baker clinched the deal by handing him a double-barrelled gun and a purse of gold coins.[6]

A series of cataracts made travelling on the Nile impracticable not far south of Gondokoro, but Baker still hoped to stay close to the river. Unfortunately Ibrahim's trading activities took him away from the Nile, and with murder commonplace in the area there was no possibility that Baker and Florence could travel in safety away from the caravan. Even accompanying Ibrahim's party, Baker was constantly worried about Florence. 'I dared not think of her position in the event of my death amongst such savages. These thoughts were shared by her.'[7] Even after he had joined the larger column, Baker was warned by Saat that several of his men still wanted to kill him. Small wonder Baker was anxious.

That night I was asleep in my tent, when I was suddenly woken by loud screams, and upon listening attentively I distinctly heard the heavy breathing of something in the tent, and I could distinguish a dark object crouching close to the head of the bed. A slight pull at my sleeve showed me that my wife also noticed the object . . . [Baker would always pretend that he had married Florence before taking her to Africa.] Mrs Baker was not a screamer, and never even whispered . . . My hand had quietly drawn the revolver from under my pillow and noiselessly pointed it within two feet of the dark crouching object, before I asked, 'Who is that?' . . . 'Fadeela.' Never had I been closer to a fatal shot!

Fadeela was a female servant who had just sought refuge in Baker's tent after being flogged with a hippopotamus hide whip until her back had been pouring blood. Her 'crime' had been being absent without leave.[8]

Khursid's sixty or so African slaves and servants were treated cruelly but the local Latuka and Bari experienced much worse. Though Baker considered Africans to be 'savages quite on a level with brute nature', he wrote:

I pity these natives; they are anything but perfect, but they are angels compared with the Khartoumers, and were they kindly treated would generally behave well . . . Certainly, not as badly as white men under similar circumstances.[9]

During his journey, Baker would come across a number of independent-minded Africans, who were not overawed by the brutality of men like Khursid. One of these was Commoro, the highly intelligent chief of the Latuka. When Baker assured him that there was life after death, Commoro replied scornfully: 'When a man dies he is finished and his children take his place.' Baker argued that man was like a seed that was buried and rotted and yet gave rise to a plant. Commoro waved aside this botched analogy: 'The original grain does not rise again; it rots like the dead man, and is ended; the fruit produced is not the same grain that we buried.'[10] Commoro was incredulous to be told that Baker had come to Africa to look for a *nyanza*. Speaking to Baker with the help of a Latuka hunchback, who spoke Arabic (as did Baker), he oozed scepticism: 'Suppose you get to the great lake what will you do with it? What will be the good of it? If you find that the large river does flow from it what then?' Baker's reply about the importance of acquiring new scientific information for its own sake, and opening remote parts of the world to 'legitimate trade', did not impress the chief. 'The Turks will never trade fairly,' he exploded. Due to much suffering at the hands of men like De Bono and Khursid, Chief

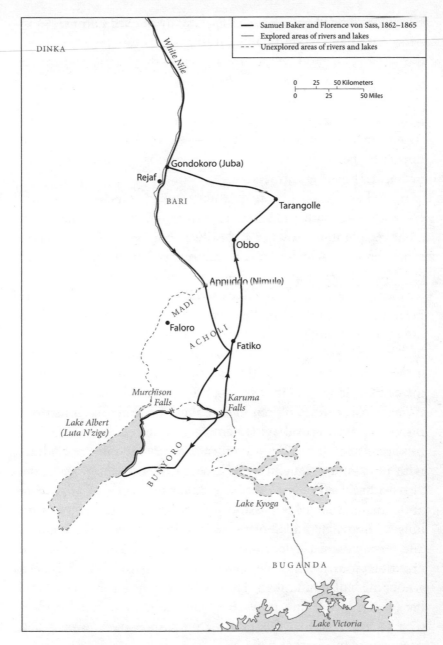

Journey of Samuel Baker and Florence von Sass.

Commoro had an unsentimental view of human nature. 'Most people are bad,' he told Baker, 'if they are strong they take from the weak. The good people are all weak; they are good because they are not strong enough to be bad.'[11]

As an analysis of the brutal life he was observing on the upper Nile, Baker understood such pessimism. But despite the dangers which he and Florence were facing, they were both natural optimists, believing that practical solutions could be found to problems, however intractable.

In Baker's case his adaptability owed much to an un-conventional youth and education. Although his father had been a banker, plantation owner and railway company director, Baker senior had not sent his sons to famous public schools, but had employed private tutors in England and Germany. So, despite his family's wealth, Sam Baker would always feel an outsider in respectable upper-middle-class society. He had worked in his father's London office, but only briefly. Finding it dull, he had begged to leave the City to run the family's sugar estates in Mauritius. Married by the age of twenty-two, he had taken his new bride with him to the island, where she had given birth to, and lost, three children. The Bakers had then established a profitable agricultural settlement in the mountains of Ceylon, but because of ill-health had returned to England in 1855, along with four young daughters. The death of his wife in the same year had seemed only to increase Baker's craving for adventure and danger, which his passion for big-game hunting could no longer satisfy. He had shot tigers in India, bears in the Balkans and elephants in Ceylon, and had brought to Africa a massive and ridiculously heavy elephant gun, 'the baby', which fired a whopping half-pound shell. Though of average height, Baker was broad-shouldered and powerfully built, and was not knocked over by the recoil of this gun, as most men were, even when propped up by another person.[12]

Sam Baker described himself as 'averse to beaten paths . . . not fitted for those harnessed positions which produce wealth; yet ever happy when unemployed, and too proud to serve'. He was dogmatic and opinionated, and thought very little of Africans in general, but he respected and liked individual black people. He hated the slave trade, taught himself Arabic and spoke it tolerably well, and wrote entertaining books. Despite many bigoted opinions, he had done something which few British gentlemen would ever have contemplated: bought a woman in a slave auction.[13] Now, he and this remarkable person, in her loosely cut breeches and knee-length gaiters, were going to attempt a journey – which had defeated Miani, De Bono, and his agent Wad-el-Mek – becoming, if successful, the first Europeans to visit the unknown *nyanza*. Driven back from a point near the present Ugandan border by repeated attacks of fever, by mutinous porters, by African revenge attacks, and by cataracts, the slave traders' failure was a warning to Baker and to Florence. Would *they* be able to rise to such a formidable challenge?

They started out with a distressing handicap. They loathed the slave trade – indeed Florence had been a slave – and yet they were going to be entirely dependent on Ibrahim and his slowly evolving plans. When he decided to make a series of raids in a particular area, instigated over several months, Baker and Florence were obliged to await his pleasure. Naturally they made the best of it – setting up 'home' together in a mud hut, keeping hens, growing lettuces, onions and yams in their garden, and trying their hand at making wine and *pombé*. Florence adopted a monkey as a pet, and later made Robinson Crusoe-like outfits for herself and her bearded lover. But whenever Ibrahim left on one of his brutal forays, Baker and Florence were compelled to come with him, lest in his absence, their own followers were overwhelmed by angry locals. 'The traders convert every country into a wasps' nest,' lamented Baker, knowing that his men would probably be killed fetching water from the river, without Ibrahim's followers being around to defend them. So Baker and Florence were obliged to accompany Ibrahim wherever his slave and ivory trading took him. 'I am more like a donkey than an explorer,' groaned the would-be discoverer of the Luta N'zige. In truth he was luckier than his real donkeys, which were already being killed by the tsetse fly. So he was daily becoming more dependent on Ibrahim for porters; and there could be no knowing whether the Syrian would eventually agree to accompany him and Florence to Bunyoro. Being logical, why would any slave trader want to go to the country of a powerful king like Kamrasi, able to place 'restrictions upon his felonious propensities'? At times Baker wondered whether he might do better to risk everything – including his life and Florence's – on a dash for the lake with as many porters as he could manage to bribe. But for all his impetuosity and pride, Baker knew how to wait when it was absolutely necessary.[14] He and Florence endured nine months of moving about within the territory of the Latuka and Obbo peoples.

They were still 200 miles from their objective, and frequently in danger, despite Ibrahim's presence (indeed partly because of it). Over again they heard the war drums ring out and were obliged to build barricades with their baggage. On one particularly menacing occasion, Florence laid out several hundred cartridges of buckshot, powder flasks and wadding on a mat, while Baker lined up his guns and rifles. Even little Saat strapped on his belt and cartouche-box and took his stand among the men, but at two in the morning, after many anxious hours of waiting, the dense crowds of armed men began to disperse. The Latuka had recently trapped a caravan of 300 Arabs, and after chasing them to the verge of a precipice, had thrust them over it with their spears. So the dangers were real enough. Meanwhile Baker's own men continued to alarm him, and he was fortunate to end a near mutiny by knocking out the ringleader with a lucky punch.[15]

Baker and Florence were in the village of the chief of the Obbo when they fell dangerously ill with malaria. Both had suffered bouts of fever before, but this time neither had the strength to help the other. They could not keep down water and were delirious. Katchiba, the old chief, was told that they were dying. On finding them lying helpless, he filled his mouth with water and squirted it about, including over the sick pair, and left confidently predicting that they would get better. Given how many European traders had died in these latitudes, his optimism was surprising. But he turned out to be right. In the travellers' hut, which was swarming with rats and white ants, Katchiba spotted Baker's chamber pot and decided it would make a perfect serving bowl for important occasions. So he was deeply disappointed when told it was 'a sacred vessel' which had to accompany Baker everywhere he went.[16]

With the Obbo that summer, Baker could not resist hunting elephant, although his horse was 'utterly unfit [and] went perfectly mad at the report of a gun fired from his back'. When thrown to the ground twenty yards from a charging elephant, Baker seemed to be facing certain death, until the animal changed direction at the last moment and thundered after his departing horse. Without knowing it, Florence had narrowly missed the fate she dreaded most of all: being left alone in the heart of Africa.[17]

Khursid re-joined his men in June, and though soon afterwards the slave trader ordered the slaughter of sixty-six local tribesmen, Baker still had no choice but to stay with him. Acts of casual brutality continued: a father who came to the camp to try to free his daughter, who had been enslaved, was gunned down and his body left for the vultures. Baker had already observed the order in which vultures fed on carrion: eating the eyes first, then the soft inner thigh and the skin beneath the arms, before consuming the tougher parts.[18] The Latukas' eating habits also intrigued him. On one occasion, he saw the head of a wild boar ('in a horrible state of decomposition') being cooked over a fire, until 'the skull became too hot for the inmates, [whereupon] crowds of maggots rushed pêle-mêle from the ears and nostrils like people escaping from the doors of a theatre on fire'. Not that this stopped the cooks 'eating the whole and sucking the bones'.[19]

At first Baker welcomed the rains since they brought down the temperature to below 100 °F:

How delightful to be cool in the centre of Africa! I was charmingly wet – the water was running out of the heels of my shoes . . . the wind howled over the hitherto dry gullies . . . It was no longer the tropics; the climate was that of old England restored to me.

But soon all his stores were covered in mildew and even with constant fires burning it was impossible to dry out his possessions. By July the rains had made the rivers too high for anyone to travel south, as he discovered during a week's reconnaissance. Only when the dry season started in October would travel become possible again. By then, he and Florence had suffered many more attacks of fever and their stock of quinine had been reduced to a few grains. Their horses and donkeys were all dead and they were too weak to walk, so there was still no hope of an early departure. Even when Baker invested in three oxen, 'Beef', 'Steak' and 'Suet', he and Florence found they lacked the strength to mount them. But at least he managed to persuade Ibrahim to come with him to Bunyoro as soon as he and Florence were able to make a start. In part this had been achieved by repetition of his promise to obtain for Khursid and Ibrahim favourable terms for acquiring ivory from Kamrasi; and in addition, Baker offered him a good supply of beads from his substantial store, with which to make his purchases. Ibrahim had few beads of his own and was already indebted to Baker for 65 lb.[20]

On 4 January 1864, Florence and Baker swallowed the last grains of quinine in their medicine chest, and prepared to head south the following day. After an hour or so of travelling, Baker's ox bolted, obliging him to walk eighteen miles on the first day, and Florence's beast was stung by a fly and plunged so suddenly that she was thrown to the ground and badly shaken up. The next day Ibrahim sold two well-behaved oxen to the exhausted Baker and his bruised mistress, who reached the Asua river, close to modern Nimule, after only four days' riding.

On their way there, on entering villages Ibrahim's men had ransacked granaries for corn, dug up yams and 'helped themselves to everything as though quite at home'. Baker made no mention in his diary of feeling any qualms about urging the agent of a notorious slave trader to enter a kingdom where the trade was not yet endemic. His hero, Speke, had not accepted help from slave traders until he had left the kingdoms of Buganda and Bunyoro and was moving towards an area already devastated by slavers. It was true that Ibrahim had promised Baker that he would not enslave people or steal cattle while in Bunyoro; but his word would mean very little in future.[21]

When Baker was twelve miles south of Faloro in the land of the Madi, he could see with his own eyes that many villages had been burned to the ground and the whole country laid waste by Mohammed Wad-el-Mek, the *wakil* of Andrea De Bono. He even noted that: 'It was the intention of Ibrahim . . . to establish himself at Shooa [south-east of Faloro] which would form an excellent *point d'appui* for operations to the unknown south.' So Baker clearly realised that his current journey would encourage Khursid Agha (Ibrahim's master) to compete with De Bono for control of the slave and ivory trade in 'the unknown south'.[22] Perhaps it eased Baker's conscience to think that Khursid would have pressed on into Bunyoro anyway. It was a token of the intensity of Baker's desire to achieve fame as an explorer that he was prepared to ignore his conscience so completely. In Khartoum, two years earlier, he had written angrily to *The Times* (25 November 1862) about the terrible evils of 'man-hunting' and the unimaginable suffering it caused.

While Baker was at Shooa, which was about eighty miles from Kamrasi's capital, a boy who had formerly worked for Mohammed Wad-el-Mek was brought to the explorer. This youth told him that soon after his master had escorted Speke and Grant to Gondokoro from Faloro, he had marched south into Bunyoro, along Speke's route at the head of a large force. De Bono, Wad-el-Mek's master, had ordered him to support Rionga in his longstanding struggle to supplant his brother, Kamrasi, as ruler. Success would provide De Bono with a compliant monarch to do business with – or so he had hoped. Kamrasi, however, had fought back and survived, although 300 of his subjects had been killed in the fighting. It struck Baker forcibly that Kamrasi would now assume, quite wrongly, that it was no coincidence that he had been attacked by the very people who had escorted Speke to Gondokoro. Inevitably the ruler of Bunyoro would suppose that Wad-el-Mek had been sent by Speke to attack him.

At Gondokoro, Speke had himself warned Baker on no account to set foot in the territory which Rionga controlled, or Kamrasi would think of him as his greatest enemy's ally and would stop him travelling to the lake.

To the south of Shooa, Baker and Ibrahim and their followers crossed a splendid granite plateau bordering a level tableland of fine grass. But from this high ground, they could see a low and interminable prairie stretching southwards as far as the eye could see, relieved only by an occasional palm tree. Their guide now lost the path, and as they struggled through ten-foot-high grass, they found themselves stumbling into deep swamps between undulations in the land. Since these morasses were numerous, the march became exhausting for man and beast – the oxen often having to be unloaded and their burdens floated across on improvised rafts. Florence was too feverish to walk and had to be carried on her bed, which proved too cumbersome to be taken across the swamps. So Baker tried to carry her on his back. He soon regretted it. 'In the middle, the tenacious bottom gave way, and I sank, and remained immovably fixed while she floundered frog-like in the muddy water ... until she was landed by being dragged through the swamp.'[23]

On 22 January they reached a broad river, flowing from east to west. From Speke's directions they assumed it must be the Nile. They were greeted by some men in a canoe, who shocked them with the news that this part of the country was Rionga's domain. As soon as the canoeists learned that Baker's and Ibrahim's men had no connection with their allies Mohammed Wad-el-Mek and Andrea De Bono, they refused to sell food or to guide Baker to the lake. But it was some compensation for the visitors, as they continued southwards, to turn their back on the swamps and enter a noble forest that ran parallel with the river, as it roared beneath them to their right in a succession of falls between high cliffs. 'These heights were thronged with natives ... armed with spears and shields ... shouting and gesticulating as though daring us to cross the river.' These men were on the Bunyoro side of the river and were clearly Kamrasi's warriors. As Baker's party reached the Karuma Falls, close to the Bunyoro ferry, the heights were just as crowded with men, who sent across a canoe to parley. Bacheeta, Baker's female translator, explained to them that Speke's brother had just arrived from his country to pay Kamrasi a visit. When asked why this brother had brought so many men with him, Bacheeta replied without hesitation that the white man's presents for Kamrasi were so numerous that they required many carriers. After this mouthwatering announcement by his interpreter, Baker dared imagine that he might soon be summoned to meet Kamrasi. Certainly he would have to look the part.

I prepared for the introduction by changing my clothes in a grove of plantains for my dressing room, and altering my costume to a tweed suit, I [then] climbed up a high and almost perpendicular rock that formed a natural pinnacle on the face of the cliff, and waving my cap to the crowd on the opposite side, I looked almost as imposing as Nelson in Trafalgar Square.

Returning to the ground, Baker ordered his and Ibrahim's men – 112 in all – to hide themselves in the plantains, in case 'the natives were startled by so imposing a force'. With Florence beside him, he then advanced to meet Kamrasi's men, who had been in the canoe and were now approaching on foot through the reeds. Their greeting was both gratifying and alarming, being expressed by 'rushing at us with the points of their lances thrust close to our faces, [while] shouting and singing in great excitement'. Baker asked Bacheeta to tell them that he hoped not to be kept waiting for weeks before meeting Kamrasi as Speke had been. They replied by recounting how Wad-el-Mek had come to Bunyoro, claiming to be Speke's friend, and had therefore been trusted and given gifts by Kamrasi, but had then returned with Rionga's people and with their help had killed many of the king's subjects. So, Baker was told, it was out of the question for him to cross the river before messengers had returned from the capital with Kamrasi's permission. After all, Baker's party might include some of the people who had behaved so treacherously several months earlier. Forewarned about Wad-el-Mek's attack, Baker had expected to be met with suspicion, but he was still disappointed by the extent of the hostility. After lengthy discussions, the headman of the district reluctantly agreed to let Baker and Florence cross the river. It was a mark of Baker's almost excessive self-confidence that he was prepared to be ferried over with only two servants and with Bacheeta, despite warnings from his men that he would be murdered if separated from them.[24]

Baker and Florence slept on the ground on straw under a Scotch plaid, having dined on ripe plantains, washed down with plantain wine that tasted like thin cider. Next day, nobody would tell them a word about the lake, although they asked numerous people. Not that the hundreds of Nyoro flocking to look at them were hostile. Indeed, the sight of Florence combing her long blonde hair created as great a stir (in Baker's phrase) as a gorilla would have done appearing on a London street.

At the end of a wearisome week of waiting, some men arrived from Kamrasi's town, Shaguzi (M'ruli). After inspecting Baker closely, they declared that he was truly 'the brother of Speke', and agreed that he and all his men could leave for Shaguzi the following day, 30 January 1864. After this announcement Baker felt more affectionate towards his hosts, and wrote in his diary about the cleverness of their blacksmiths and potters and the beauty of their women, but this benign mood would not last. Florence fell ill on the first day of the march, and for a week Baker feared she would die. On 5 February she was so ill that even travelling on a litter was more than she could bear. Baker described the country as being 'full of mosquitoes' but made no connection between their presence and the fever that so many of his people were contracting. Fadeela – the servant who had appeared in Baker's tent after being beaten – was dying and expired three days later. On that day, Baker was so weak that he had to be held upright on his ox's back by two men, and even then he fell off and had to rest under a tree for five hours.

From the contradictory messages now being received from Kamrasi, Baker could see that the ruler was deliberately trying to delay his arrival, possibly out of fear.[75] But, on 10 February, the Englishman and his party at last arrived at Shaguzi, and a man whom Baker took to be Kamrasi, accompanied by 500 warriors, came to see him. This royal visitation was due to the fact that Baker – like Florence – was too ill to walk. Later, he was carried to the royal hut where he presented the supposed *omukama* with some presents, including a large Persian carpet, a pair of red Turkish shoes, some necklaces and a double-barrelled gun. When he asked permission to travel to the lake, the man he thought was Kamrasi – who was actually Kamrasi's younger brother, Mgambi, impersonating the king under orders – told Baker that the lake was a hundred miles away and that in his weakened condition he would certainly die on the way there. Baker brushed aside this warning, and ignoring the immense danger that he and Florence would face without quinine, renewed his pleas to be permitted to set out. Baker explained that the Nile flowed northwards for an immense distance, passing through many countries from which valuable articles could be sent to Kamrasi, if he would only allow his English visitor to travel to the Luta N'zige.

Mgambi tried to make his consent conditional upon Baker agreeing to attack Rionga, which he refused to do. Ibrahim, however, agreed to become Mgambi's blood brother, licking blood from his punctured arm, and promising to act against his enemies. This pledge was made after he had been given twenty large tusks and promised more. Ibrahim was also happy, it turned out, to take all his men towards Karuma Falls and to leave Baker with only thirteen porters, and the interpreter, Bacheeta, whose freedom he was obliged to purchase with three double-barrelled guns. Mgambi, the impersonator, gave Baker and Florence the use of a hut, built on marshy ground in a mosquito-ridden meadow. They suffered from fever daily, and were appalled to be told by Mgambi that all the medicines in the chest left behind by Speke had been used up. It rained in torrents most days, and Baker feared that he and Florence would not survive if they were detained in this damp place much longer. They felt a little more hopeful after learning from an indiscreet headman that the journey was not as horrifying as it had been made out. In fact, salt traders usually reached the lake in ten days.[26]

Baker was finally given permission to leave on 23 February, but at the last moment, just as the oxen were being saddled, Mgambi, whose protuberant eyes had always disturbed Baker, said casually: 'I will send you to the lake and to Shooa, as I've promised; but you must leave your wife with me.' In his account (the only one there is), Baker thrust the muzzle of his revolver against Mgambi's chest and said he would shoot him dead if the insult was repeated. Florence in the meantime looking 'as amiable as the head of the Medusa', let fly at Mgambi in Arabic, which Bacheeta bravely translated word for word. Mgambi was astonished by all the fuss. He said he would have been perfectly happy to have offered Baker one of *his* wives. It was the custom in Bunyoro, but if Baker did not like it he was sorry. By way of compensation, he ordered all the bystanders to act as carriers for Baker, and in addition provided an escort of 300 men.[27]

They began their march through the beautiful Bugoma mimosa forest but soon arrived at the same great swamp that earlier had forced them away from the direct route to the lake. Baker and Florence were too ill to cross the morass on foot, and since their oxen could only proceed by swimming, the two invalids were placed on litters and propelled to firmer ground by two dozen men splashing in the water. In their enfeebled state, the lovers could not control their escort, whose members rushed ahead and plundered every village on their route. Nor could they compel them to start early enough to avoid the heat of the sun. On 27 February, they had to cross the Kafu river, which was covered over with thickly matted aquatic plants, forming a bridge of sorts. But to ride oxen on this trembling and uncertain surface was impossible, so even the desperately ill Florence had to walk. Baker urged her to follow him, treading exactly where he had placed his feet. At all costs, he said, she should keep moving.

Looking back, when less than halfway across, he was horrified 'to see her standing in one spot and sinking gradually through the weeds, while her face was distorted and perfectly purple'.

A moment later, 'she fell as though shot dead'. Baker and about ten men 'dragged her like a corpse through the yielding vegetation'. It was an agonising moment for him:

I laid her under a tree, and bathed her head and face with water . . . but she lay perfectly insensible, as though dead, with teeth and hands firmly clenched, and her eyes opened but fixed. . . It was in vain that I rubbed her heart and the black women rubbed her feet . . . she was carried mournfully forward as a corpse.

The only sign of life was 'a painful rattling in the throat', which seemed the prelude to death.

At the next village, he laid her down in a hut and opened her teeth with a wooden wedge, before moistening her tongue with drops of water. She was breathing, but only five times a minute, and he feared she was suffering from 'congestion of the brain'. Outside the hut, members of his escort danced and sang until Baker could bear it no longer and swore he would fire at them unless they returned to Shaguzi. Left with his own people and about twenty porters – thirty-five people in all – he continued nursing Florence all next day and night. On 1 March they carried her on a litter for a while. It was a terrible time for Baker, who blamed himself for putting his personal ambitions above his love for her.

Was she to die? Was so terrible a sacrifice to be the result of my self-exile? . . . I was ill and broken-hearted, and I followed by her side over wild parklands and streams, with thick forest and deep marshy bottoms . . . and through valleys of tall papyrus rushes, which waved over the litter like the black plumes of a hearse.

For a second night he sat by her side in a dismal hut, listening to the cry of a hyena, and imagining the animal digging up her grave.

Next day they pressed on, but had to stop when she became delirious. In the morning they started again and in the evening, after a long day's march, she had violent convulsions and it seemed 'all but over'. He lay down on a plaid beside her, while outside his men began to dig her grave. Yet at first light, 'when she opened her eyes, they were calm and clear'. The date was 4 March, and Florence slowly recovered during the coming week. She was very fortunate to be alive, and her man was lucky not to be facing a lifetime spent blaming himself for his adored lover's death.

On 14 March, on a clear day, they climbed out of a valley and toiled to the top of a hill. Below them was the lake.

The glory of our prize burst suddenly upon me! There, like a sea of quicksilver, lay far beneath, the grand expanse of water – a boundless sea horizon on the south and south-west, glittering in the noonday sun; and on the west, at fifty or sixty miles' distance, blue mountains rose from the bosom of the lake to a height of about 7,000 feet . . . It is impossible to describe the triumph of that moment . . . England had won the sources of the Nile!

He decided to name his lake Albert Nyanza, after Queen Victoria's late lamented consort. Believing his *nyanza* to be larger than Speke's, Baker's respect for the primacy of his friend's discovery speedily diminished. 'The Victoria and the Albert Lakes are the two sources of the Nile,' he declared.[28]

The zigzag path down to the lake was so precipitous that the riding oxen had to be left at the top, while Florence supported herself on her lover's shoulder and tottered down the pass on foot, resting every few minutes. The descent to the lakeside beneath the cliff took two hours. On the white pebbly beach Baker rushed into the water 'thirsty with heat and fatigue, and with a heart full of gratitude, drank deeply'. This closer view of the Luta N'zige did not lead him to reduce the height of the mountains to a more realistic 5,000 feet, nor to halve the lake's average width. But his greatest exaggeration of its size was the immense distance to which he believed it extended in the south. He allowed local reports of other lakes in that direction (in reality the separate lakes Edward and George) to lead him to suppose that these waters were an extension of his lake, which stretched, he guessed, as far as Karagwe. In time, all this would be shown to be the wishful thinking of a man who had longed for *his* lake to be the Nile's most important source. Nevertheless, since the days when Nero had sent his two centurions south, nobody travelling directly up the Nile – and many had tried – had reached any of the great lakes.

Baker did not attempt a full circumnavigation, partly because of Florence's ill-health, but also because he feared that if he failed to reach Gondokoro before the end of April, the boats left there by Petherick would have departed for Khartoum on the last southerly winds of the season. After a week of recurrent fever, enough of his men had recovered to embark the entire party in two canoes, and paddle north, close to the eastern shore. They were heading for Magungo, where a large river flowed into the lake. Baker believed this must be the river he had crossed at Karuma Falls, and which Speke had told him flowed out of the Victoria Nyanza as the Nile. Baker erected a crude awning to shelter Florence from the hot sun, and somehow resisted the temptation to shoot any of the lake's hippopotami. Had he shot one, his men would have stripped off the meat and then cooked and eaten it – the whole process delaying them all for several days.

Magungo was reached after a thirteen-day voyage, and here the lake was already narrower, its northward flow discernible. But before continuing on their course, they paddled due east into the broad reed-fringed channel of the incoming river. Just before they entered it, Baker saw in the distance, less than ten miles away, at the lake's most northerly tip, another river flowing out northward. Everyone Bacheeta spoke to at Magungo said that this second river flowed on to Appuddo on the Nile, through Madi country. Speke and Grant had travelled on from Appuddo to Gondokoro, so Baker knew that his lake was an important basin of the Nile, which either entered it from the southern shores which he had not seen, or through the river which he was now entering. Though Baker had hoped to return to Gondokoro by following the river at the Luta N'zige's northern tip, his Nyoro porters and boatmen refused to consider this because of the hostility of the people living along the banks. It was a key moment when the truly great explorer compels his men to obey

Murchison Falls.

him. But Baker and Florence were still very weak and lacked the strength and will to insist that they paddle all the way downstream to Gondokoro. Instead, he and Florence allowed their men to paddle them eastwards, confining their investigations to the river before them.[29]

During their eighteen-mile voyage upstream, Baker thought he might die. He lost consciousness, and, as darkness fell, was carried on a litter, with his 'poor sick wife, herself half dead', walking by his side to the nearest village. Next morning, both were too weak to walk and were carried to their dug-out, where they 'lay like logs while the canoes continued their voyage'. Most of Baker's men were also ill, and seeing them 'crouched together', he thought they looked like 'departing spirits being ferried across the melancholy Styx'. On the third morning, on waking, they saw a thick fog covering the surface of the water. As it cleared, they observed that the river had become narrower with the current flowing fast against them. Bacheeta announced that they were now approaching a great waterfall. Already they could hear a sound like distant thunder. As the men paddled against the flow, the water became spume-flecked and the noise of the waterfall grew louder. On the river's banks lay numerous crocodiles, many of them very large. On both sides, tall cliffs, which were clad with mature trees, rose almost vertically. At the next bend in the river, an unforgettable sight greeted them. The whole river was funnelled into a rocky cleft only twenty-four feet wide, and burst from it as if from a ruptured water-main, to cascade and tumble down the rock face for 120 feet in a foaming mass of snow-white roaring water.

As his men were paddling away from this natural marvel, Baker – ever aware of his own self-interest – decided to name it the Murchison Falls, after the man who could do more than any other for his exploring career. This might have ended prematurely, when a bull hippopotamus unexpectedly lifted their canoe half out of the water. Had it capsized, the lovers and their boatmen would have had a hard time escaping the many crocodiles watching on the banks. Yet, even when they were safely ashore, with a land journey ahead of them, their prospects were not bright. Their oxen had been bitten by tsetse fly, and the animals' staring coats and running noses showed that they were dying. While Baker managed to toil up the cliff path that brought them to the track above the falls, Florence had to be carried. They now faced seven-foot-high grass and waterlogged country choked with vegetation. It was raining and they were wet and cold. Without riding-oxen and quinine, their chances of survival looked slim, and would soon seem slimmer.

Sleeping on straw in a succession of waterlogged huts, they grew weaker and could no longer move from the positions in which they had been deposited. Ahead of them, due east, the country and the islands on the river belonged to Rionga, who had recently been attacked by Ibrahim. Rather than encounter these inevitably hostile people, Baker intended to abandon the direct route along the river to Karuma Falls, and loop south to bypass the rebels. But on the morning on which he hoped to start, he and Florence were deserted by all their porters and left helpless with less than a dozen followers – too few to carry their sick leader and his mistress. There would be hardly anyone left over to shoulder the trade goods essential for purchasing food. Since not an animal, or even a bird, was to be seen, they survived by digging up hidden grain in burned-out villages. Occasionally, the boy Saat and Bacheeta managed to buy a fowl from the rebels on their islands. Confined to a dark hut for two months, Baker wrote instructions for his headman in case he died. In that event the man was to deliver up his maps, observations and papers to the British Consul in Khartoum. If he failed to do this, all the evidence for Baker's and Florence's discoveries would be lost. By now, Baker had given up hope of reaching Gondokoro before the boats sailed for Khartoum.

'We were very nearly dead,' he recalled later, 'and our amusement was a childish conversation about the good things in England [such as] an English beefsteak and a bottle of pale ale.' Their mutual dread was that Baker would die and Florence would then fall into Kamrasi's hands to be one of his many wives, never to return to Europe again. At times they both looked upon death as 'a pleasure, affording rest, [and] . . . no more suffering'. Every week, during this two-month period 'of fever and constant starvation', one of Kamrasi's chiefs would turn up to report back on their condition to his king. It became obvious to Baker that Kamrasi had ordered the porters to desert and had deliberately kept them here as virtual prisoners. When

Kamrasi sent a courtier with the proposition that Baker and his men, with all their guns, should join him in attacking Chief Fowooka (Rionga's ally), the Englishman was almost angry enough to ally himself with Fowooka. It was plain to him that Kamrasi was using his and Florence's suffering to force them to become his allies. Baker now tried to strike the best bargain he could, though it maddened him to be in this subservient position. Through Bacheeta, he told the king's emissary that if Kamrasi wanted an alliance, he would have to deal face to face with him and send fifty men at once to transport him and his wife to the royal camp.

The men duly arrived next day with an ox for slaughter. After three days' travel, the whole party arrived at Kisoona (Kisuna), where Kamrasi had his camp. But Baker was once again met by Mgambi, who at last admitted he was the king's younger brother, and explained that because De Bono's people had fought with Rionga against Kamrasi, the king had naturally needed to be careful about which foreigners he agreed to see. Baker was disgusted to have been fobbed off with the king's brother, but concentrated on how best to make an impression on Kamrasi. To do this, he exchanged the rags he was wearing for a full-dress Highland suit with all the accessories: kilt, sporran and Glengarry bonnet. In this astonishing outfit, he was carried by ten of his men through curious crowds to Kamrasi's hut. When the real Kamrasi asked Baker why he had not come to see him sooner, he replied: 'Because I have been starved in your country, and I was too weak to walk.'

Baker thought Kamrasi handsome and beautifully dressed in a fine mantle of black and white goatskins. Yet he also found the ruler 'peculiarly sinister', perhaps because his subjects approached him on their hands and knees, touching the ground with their foreheads. From the time of their meeting, Kamrasi gave Baker an ox every week, plenty of flour, and a cow that produced copious milk. So though the lovers could not leave for Shooa, and suffered attacks of fever almost daily, they began to grow stronger on their new diet. During the next three weeks,

Kamrasi visited Baker at intervals to demand that he come at once to attack Rionga and Fowooka, and pick them off from afar with his Fletcher 24 rifle, which the king coveted. Baker claimed to be too weak to fight, until one night he was woken by a frenzied cacophony of drums and horns, and found people screaming that they were about to be attacked by De Bono and by Rionga. Mgambi dolefully informed Baker that the king would have to flee. Kamrasi himself declared that it would be futile to fight against 150 guns, even with the advantage of Baker's firepower. 'Pack up your things and run,' he advised. But, according to his own account, Baker had other ideas.

After donning his Highland costume, he hoisted the Union Jack on a tall staff, and sent men to tell Wad-el-Mek that Kamrasi was under British protection. He then wrote to Wad-el-Mek in Arabic stating that if he attacked the king, he would be arrested on his return to Khartoum. This caused Wad-el-Mek to desert his allies, enabling Kamrasi to launch a successful counter-attack on Fowooka.

By the time Baker was eventually allowed to leave Bunyoro in November 1864 – ten months after his arrival at Shaguzi – he knew that Kamrasi hoped one day to conquer Buganda with the help of Ibrahim and Khursid. The arrival of 'the Turks' in Bunyoro – largely thanks to Baker – had been a harmful development. But without Ibrahim's help, Baker knew he would not have been able to make his great discovery. And in November 1864, Ibrahim was again about to be indispensable. For he and his thousand-strong caravan would escort Baker and Florence safely through Madi country, enabling them to get home and enjoy the fame their bravery and astonishing resilience had earned them.

For Kamrasi, the consequences of Baker's visit would be less pleasing. The explorer would represent the ruler of Bunyoro as cruel, cowardly and devious; and this caricature would stick to him, and to his successor, Kabarega, with the disastrous consequence that they would be mistrusted and disliked by the British Colonial Office. In reality, as Speke had justly recorded, Kamrasi was a better ruler than Mutesa and a lot less brutal. The cultural gulf between Baker and Kamrasi had been impossible to bridge. Through cunning, and the efforts of his spies, the king had cleverly preserved his kingdom, which the more powerful ruler of Buganda had repeatedly attempted to wrest from him. Inevitably, Kamrasi had suspected that Baker, like Mutesa, had also come to steal his land, and that his tale about coming to visit a lake had been an invention. Since Chief Commoro had entertained exactly this suspicion, Baker should have expected to be mistrusted by Kamrasi. Inevitably, the king had supposed that his frightening visitor had brought along a 'wife' in order to breed sons, who could then inherit Bunyoro after their father's death.[30]

Though Baker showed no understanding of Kamrasi, he did his best to prevent injustice when it occurred in front of him. During the return journey to Gondokoro, he tried to mitigate the cruel treatment of the slaves in Ibrahim's caravan. When a young female slave and her mother were condemned to be hanged for trying to escape, Baker announced that he would use 'any force' to prevent such an act, and would report the names of the offenders to the Egyptian authorities. Meanwhile, Florence protected and fed Abbai, the two-year-old son of a Nyoro mother, who had been sold separately after attempting to run away. She also looked after four other young dependents, feeding them milk, and greasing their skin, as their mothers would have done. But in the end, when the caravan arrived at Appuddo, these children were all handed back to Ibrahim and his men, including little Abbai, who tearfully begged in broken Arabic to go home with Florence. 'Had I purchased the child to rescue him from his hard lot,' claimed Baker, 'I might have been charged with slave dealing.' Other travellers – Henry Stanley for one – would purchase the freedom of slaves, without fearing the consequences.[31]

The problem posed by these unfortunate children had been nothing to the great dilemma obsessing Baker for much of the journey down the Nile: *should he, or should he not bring Florence back to Britain with him*? In none of his letters home to family and friends, written from Khartoum, did he mention her. Only in a letter to Robert Colquhoun, the British consul-general in Cairo, who had actually met Florence, did he write that 'we are all right' – a guarded indication that she had survived. Although 500 men in Khartoum's garrison of 4,000 had recently died of plague, Baker spent two months in this place he detested, simply because he could not make up his mind what to do about Florence. Otherwise, he would have had every incentive to hurry back to England to see his family and receive the longed-for plaudits of the public. But how could he introduce Florence to his teenage daughters and to Min, his unmarried sister who had brought them up? Marrying a woman with Florence's background would certainly be scandalously unconventional. But by the time he reached Alexandria, Baker had finally decided that he would not be able to endure life without her. So he sent a telegram to one of his brothers, Captain James Baker RN, asking him to arrange a quiet marriage in London.[32]

Only after this ceremony had taken place on 4 November 1865 – without guests, and with James Baker and his wife, Louisa, the only witnesses – were Samuel White Baker and his new wife ready to step onto the public stage and tell the world what they had found in Africa.

SEVENTEEN

A Trumpet Blown Loudly

On the day of their wedding, Baker and Florence dined with Sir Roderick Murchison and found him still purring with satisfaction at being immortalised by their association of his name with one of Africa's most spectacular waterfalls. Of course Sir Roderick knew that by failing to visit and then navigate the river flowing out from the northern tip of Lake Albert, Baker had not proved the lake's connection with the lower Nile—although the oral testimony of Africans and Baker's calculations for the altitude of the lake and for the Nile at Appuddo had made the link seem almost certain. But likelihood was not proof. Also still unproven was whether Lake Albert was fed by Speke's Victoria Nyanza. Baker had only managed to travel upstream for twenty miles on the river which flowed into Albert on its eastern shore, before looping south, overland, and resuming his northward journey at Karuma Falls. More disappointing still had been his failure to find a river flowing into Lake Albert's southern shore that might link it with Lake Tanganyika. Despite this, Baker made extravagant claims for his lake, suggesting that at its widest it was ninety miles across, and in length extended two degrees south of the equator, which would place its southern shores to the west of Karagwe, on the same latitude as the centre of Victoria Nyanza.[1]

Though all this was highly speculative, Murchison needed new heroes to boost membership of the RGS and keep fees and donations flowing in. Sir Roderick felt that Speke had let him down by becoming Francophile and eccentric. So with Livingstone on his way back to Africa, and Burton and Grant no longer involved with exploration, Murchison needed someone else to galvanise the public and exert pressure on politicians to finance expeditions. So it was a great blessing that this bearded English gentleman, with his apparently warm-hearted personality and impulsive nature, should have sprung to prominence at the perfect time, claiming to be the discoverer of a great lake possibly the equal of Speke's Victoria Nyanza.[2] Baker delighted Murchison by even managing to describe his discovery without British reserve and false modesty:

The Albert is the great basin of the Nile . . . a reservoir not only receiving western and southern affluents direct from the Blue Mountains, but it also receives the supply from the Victoria and from the entire equatorial basin. The Nile as it issues from the Albert lake is the entire Nile.[3]

So on his return to England, the man who owed everything to Speke was perfectly happy to pose as a greater explorer than his dead friend. Had Speke been alive, Baker would not have dared make such claims for his lake, or have published the vainglorious map, which would later come to haunt him. It is ironic that Speke – relying solely on African information – drew and published a far more accurate map of the Luta N'zige than Baker could manage after visiting it.[4] But Sir Roderick was not worried by a few exaggerations, which were unlikely to be exposed for many years to come. In the immediate future, the manly Baker and his beautiful, suntanned wife would together attract immense publicity, from which Murchison and the RGS could expect to profit. Of course, there was a danger that Florence's background might prove embarrassing, but since only the discreet and gentlemanly James Grant, and a few equally tactful British diplomats, like Robert Colquhoun, had met Florence with Baker before their marriage, Sir Roderick believed that any scandal could be smothered at birth.[5]

Murchison wrote glowingly to a friend about Baker's 'little blue-eyed Hungarian wife, who . . . is still only 23 years of age [and who] we all like very much'.[6] To make sure that Grant went on being gentlemanly reticent, Sir Roderick told him that Florence had been 'announced by Sam Baker as Mrs Baker & received as such by all his family' and by society at large, including by the Murchisons, 'and we all like her . . .'[7]

On 13 November Baker was formally welcomed home at a meeting at the RGS's Burlington House headquarters, and Murchison announced that he had been awarded the Society's Gold Medal. Baker turned out to be a brilliant raconteur, and after he had spoken of his great discovery, and encounters with wild beasts, slave traders, 'savage' rulers, and deadly fevers, he turned to thank Murchison and the Society and declared:

There is one other whom I must thank . . . one who though young and tender has the heart of a lion and without whose devotion and courage I would not be alive today to address you tonight – Mr President, my Lords, ladies, gentlemen, allow me [*and at this moment he walked to the wings, bowed, and returned with Florence on his arm, perfectly dressed and coiffured*] to present my wife.[8]

It was his ability to pull off these dramatic effects, along with his gifts as a public speaker that blinded all but a few to his short-comings as a geographer and explorer. His literary gifts also helped. His book *The Albert N'yanza* was not just a record of a journey, but a series of well-told anecdotes and adventures. 'It was [in the words of his biographer] conversational narrative at its best: witty, opinionated, and only rarely pompous.'[9] Baker eliminated many of those passages in his diaries, in which he had all but given up hope of surviving, and instead wrote of suffering endured with good humour and fortitude. Indeed, he and Florence had been brave – almost suicidally so after their quinine had been exhausted. The book did not always concentrate on dangers, being homely too, with descriptions of tending an African garden and preparing local foods. There had been nothing like this in books by Burton and Speke. Nor had those earlier volumes contained a record of 'married' love in places where some African tribes wore no clothes to speak of and where men and women were enslaved like beasts. At a time when members of 'the fair sex' (at least those in comfortable circumstances) were not meant to be exposed to scenes of male nudity, Baker wrote in his diary about the educational value 'to young ladies' of a journey up the Nile.[10] He did not include such risqué passages in his book, which he dedicated to Queen Victoria.

The knighthood, which Murchison had failed to conjure up for Speke, in Baker's case came of its own accord in August 1866. Such was the popularity of Baker's book and his public appearances that the Prime Minister, Lord Derby, had needed no prompting to see the political benefits of the award. Christopher Rigby, still grieving two years after Speke's death, was upset by the way his friend had been eclipsed by a man whose 'statements [respecting his lake's extent] are purely conjectural'. But, as Rigby told Grant sadly:

Baker has certainly blown his trumpet rather loudly. . . he has also put his wife very prominently forward and this has taken wonderfully with the English public; had poor Speke only possessed Baker's skill with his pen what a different reception his book would have met with.[11]

Members of Speke's family were shocked by the award of a knighthood to Baker for what they believed had been a lesser journey, and a lesser discovery. 'I think it is the most shameful thing I ever heard of,' wrote Speke's brother Ben to a friend. 'None of our people are going to congratulate the knight. It hurt poor mother very much.'[12] Grant, who was made a Commander of the Bath, rather than a Knight Commander of that order, felt just as miserable: 'By God! I never heard of anything more disgusting to us!' he complained to Blackwood.[13]

Meanwhile, the appeal for a memorial which Murchison had launched soon after Speke's death had only just received, two years later, enough subscriptions to meet the building costs.[14] An obelisk of red polished granite was eventually put up in Kensington Gardens, London, in October 1866, bearing the inscription: 'In memory of Speke, Victoria Nyanza, and the Nile 1864'. Murchison's carefully chosen words fell far short of endorsing Speke's claim to have found the source.[15]

The intolerable truth, which tormented Grant, was that unless Speke had generously directed Baker to the Luta N'zige, nobody would have heard of the man who was now the toast of the town. Grant knew with absolute certainty that, whatever it might have cost him and Speke in blood and treasure, they should themselves have visited this wretched lake and established its precise relationship to the Victoria Nyanza and the Nile. But someone else would have to do that now and sort out the whole central African watershed. It might take many years. A disillusioned Grant returned to India and his old job with the military. Forgetting Africa would not be easy.

EIGHTEEN

Almost in Sight of the End

———— ✥ ————

David Livingstone was in his fifty-third year on 19 March 1866 when he landed on the East African coast 600 miles north of Quelimane and plunged inland into thick jungle. Although he joked about his smile as being 'that of a hippopotamus' and himself as 'a dreadful old fogy',[1] he was physically fit for his age and was convinced that he could achieve his astonishingly ambitious twin aims of solving the Nile mystery and shaming the British government into suppressing the Arab-Swahili slave trade.

Dr Livingstone's early years as a child worker in a Scottish cotton mill, and his struggle to educate himself and qualify as a medical doctor, made him scornful of gentlemen who had never had to strive for advancement. Unaware that his own powers of endurance were exceptional, he was intolerant of ordinary human weakness and could not understand why other more gentlemanly explorers so often collapsed when on the verge of making great discoveries. Burton and Speke, when tantalisingly close to their objective, had not managed to reach the northern end of Lake Tanganyika, and had then failed to launch a boat on the great Nyanza discovered by Speke alone. In the same situation, Livingstone believed he would have made the final death-defying push, regardless of ill-health, dwindling stores and deserting porters.

He tended to forget that his own greatest journey – that had taken him from Sesheke at the heart of Africa to Loanda on the Atlantic, and then right back across the entire continent to Quelimane on the Indian Ocean – had been achieved with the assistance of porters loaned to him by Chief Sekeletu of the Kololo. These men had been ordered to serve him under pain of death. But in 1866, at the start of a journey no less ambitious, Livingstone engaged only four men who had served him on the Zambezi. Knowing nothing about Indian customs and temperaments, he hired a dozen sepoys and a *havildar* (corporal) from the Bombay Marine Battalion. Equally experimental was his choice of eight ex-pupils from the government-run school for ex-slaves at Nasik. Added to these would be ten men from Johanna, although these islanders had a reputation for laziness and dishonesty. *En route*, about two months later, Livingstone added twenty-four men giving him a total of fifty-nine – still too few for the immense task in hand.[2]

If Livingstone had decided to start his journey at Zanzibar and Bagamoyo, he could have engaged many more experienced and dependable porters, but his over-ambitious plans had led him to reject the obvious course of travelling via Unyanyembe to Lake Tanganyika's northern end and discovering whether it supplied Lake Albert by way of the Rusizi river. Instead, assuming that the Rusizi flowed out, he intended as his first objective to find and trace the river that must flow into Lake Tanganyika. He was partly motivated by the unpleasing thought that if Tanganyika really *was* the main reservoir of the Nile, Burton would get all the credit, unless he (Livingstone) had gone one better and actually found the lake's source. But the problem with this plan was not just that Livingstone would get inferior porters by starting his journey far to the south of Zanzibar, but that Lake Tanganyika might in reality have nothing to do with the Nile.

Because Livingstone had left England shortly before Baker's return, he had no idea what the younger man and his mistress had actually found. Before sailing, he had learned from telegrams reaching the RGS that Samuel Baker had almost certainly 'discovered' the Luta N'zige (Lake Albert) by March 1864, but this had *not* told him whether Baker had managed to circumnavigate the lake and prove that it was fed by Lake Tanganyika. In fact even if a large river had been found flowing into the southern end of Baker's lake, this would still not have been certain proof that it had originated in Lake Tanganyika. So rather than assume the link, Livingstone should have gone straight to the Rusizi to solve this basic problem.

But Livingstone meant instead to march inland along the River Rovuma, and then, after passing the southern end of Lake Nyasa, to head north towards the region south and south-west of Lake Tanganyika where he expected to find the Nile's source. When his despatches reached London, he enjoyed anticipating that there would be a great many red faces.

As he and his men left the coastal belt of jungle and began to climb, he felt all the old exhilaration he had known during his transcontinental journey:

The mere animal pleasure of travelling in a wild unexplored country is very great. When on lands of a couple of thousand feet elevation, brisk exercise imparts elasticity to the muscles, fresh and healthy blood circulates through the brain, the mind works well, the eye is clear, the step is firm . . . Africa is a wonderful country for appetite.[3]

His optimism did not last long. Soon he was upbraiding the sepoys and Nasik men for deliberate cruelty to the mules and camels which he had brought to gauge whether they had greater resistance to the tsetse fly than had oxen and horses. The Nasik men, copying the sepoys, engaged local tribesmen to carry their loads on the understanding that the white man would pay. They also offered the party's Somali guide, Ben Ali, cloth and money to direct them all back to the coast. Eventually Livingstone was obliged to give one of the sepoys 'some smart cuts with a cane'.[4] Yet this was not enough to stop the thieving and the infliction of deep gashes on the baggage animals' flanks. Many of the poor creatures were dying before May was over; and Livingstone had no idea whether this was due to the tsetse or to the sepoys. Just when tensions within the party were growing worse, Livingstone began to see evidence of terrible inhumanity every few miles. On 19 June he wrote:

We passed a woman tied by the neck to a tree and dead, the people of the country explained that she had been unable to keep up with the other slaves in a gang, and her master had determined that she should not become the property of anybody else if she recovered after resting for a time.

Local people admitted that when they managed to rescue such slaves, they would only feed them up in order to sell them again.[5]

This evidence of African indifference to African suffering increased rather than lessened Livingstone's determination to end the slave trade, and at this time he wrote two well argued despatches to the British Foreign Secretary urging that Zanzibar should be blockaded at once, and the main slave market closed. He gave detailed reasons why he did not believe that this would create anarchy in Zanzibar, or cause smaller slave markets to open up along the coast. There is something extraordinarily impressive about the unemotional and logical way in which he marshalled his facts at a time when he was involved with the far from abstract misery of the slaves themselves. Every few days, he was finding little groups of corpses. Some had been shot, others stabbed, and others tied together and left to starve to death.

Meanwhile his porters dawdled, stole and threatened to desert. In July the sepoys concocted a story about how a tiger had killed and eaten the expedition's only buffalo calf. Livingstone asked whether they had seen the tiger's stripes. They eagerly agreed that they had. Since African tigers have no stripes, the doctor was unimpressed. Next day a sepoy threatened to shoot a Nasik man and another stole a large number of cartridges and cloth from the stores. At last Livingstone had had enough and gave the sepoys eighteen yards of cloth and left them at a village to wait for the next Arab caravan to the coast.[6]

On 6 August, when he reached the blue waters of Lake Nyasa, he found 'a dash in the breakers quite exhilarating'. By now, he was down to twenty-three men, less than half the number he had had in early May. A month later, when he arrived at the crossing point on the Shire river, the ten Johanna porters decided to desert *en masse*. They had learned from Arab slave traders and local Africans that the country ahead was being pillaged by the 'Mazitu' (Ngoni) and since they wished to see their families again would serve no longer. They had been almost as troublesome as the sepoys, so Livingstone did not try to detain them. In 1863, he had encountered the 'Mazitu' in the same area and knew that the dangers ahead were very real.[7]

In January 1867, shortly after the man carrying the expedition's chronometers had slipped and fallen, damaging these vital clocks and guaranteeing that all Livingstone's future calculations for longitude would be inaccurate, his medicine case was stolen by a deserter. With most of his party ill with malaria and dysentery, the second loss struck Livingstone as a possible death sentence. But despite this, and although the rains were making travel increasingly difficult, the doctor was focussed again and excited. He was heading for an unknown lake which he believed would be found to feed a river flowing into the southern end of Lake Tanganyika. This lake might therefore prove to be the source of the Nile. On 16 January he described a typical day's progress:

The rain as usual made us halt early... We roast a little grain and boil it, to make believe it is coffee ... Ground all sloppy; oozes full and overflowing – feet constantly wet ... Rivulets can only be crossed by felling a tree on the bank and letting it fall across ... Nothing but famine and famine prices, the people living on mushrooms and leaves. We get some elephant meat from the people, but high is no name for its condition. It is very bitter but it prevents the heartburn.[8]

The place where Lake Bangweulu was supposed to be was engulfed by a gigantic swamp. Hoping to find the river flowing out of it, he marched north and unwittingly passed almost 120 miles to the east of the lake proper, not realising when he crossed the Chambesi river that it flowed into Bangweulu. By the time he recognised his mistake the lake lay 100 miles to the south-west of his present position. He was ill for much of the following month; then war broke out between local Africans and Arab-Swahili slave traders. So by the time he reached Lake Tanganyika it was April. Then he was ill again. The war continued, preventing him from finding out whether there was a river flowing into the western side of Lake Tanganyika.

At this time he heard of a large lake called Moero (Lake Mweru), 100 miles to the west of where he was. His immediate thought was that it must be linked with Bangweulu, and could therefore lead him to the river he was seeking. But with the war being waged more fiercely than ever, he was unable to leave for this new lake until the end of September. By now his party numbered only a dozen men, and by necessity he was obliged to travel with the infamous slave and ivory trader Hamid bin Muhammad el-Murebi, known as Tippu Tip, who was close to establishing political and commercial control over the whole area.[9]

In November 1867 – just over a year and a half after landing on the East African coast – he and Tippu reached Lake Moero and, as he had hoped, he managed to establish from local reports that it was indeed linked with Bangweulu. Even more thrillingly, he heard that an immense river flowed out of Moero's north-western corner on a course that took it to the north, no one knew where. This river was called the Lualaba and from the moment Livingstone heard its name, he knew that he would have to follow it. He felt sure that it would either enter Lake Tanganyika, before exiting through the Rusizi and then flowing on through Lake Albert to the White Nile, or it would miss Tanganyika entirely and flow into Lake Albert directly.[10] For the remaining years of his life the Lualaba would obsess Livingstone, giving him no peace.

Livingstone's lack of porters and the exhaustion of his stores obliged him to remain with Tippu Tip until well into the New Year. He dithered about whether to go back to Lake Bangweulu (to make a map of it and Lake Moero, along with the connecting Luapula river) or whether to travel to Ujiji on Lake Tanganyika, where he would be able to replenish his stores and engage more porters. But neither Tippu nor Muhammad Salim, another slave trader, kept to the plans they had announced to him earlier, and in the end out of sheer frustration, in mid-April 1868, Livingstone set out for Lake Bangweulu with nine men, five of whom deserted on the same day. But with the remaining four, he bravely headed south, pursued by a messenger sent by Muhammad Salim to dissuade him from his suicidal venture. Livingstone ignored him and pressed on south. After months of illness and indecision, his recovery was almost superhuman. He even found it in his heart to forgive the five deserters. 'I did not blame them very severely in my own mind for absconding; they were tired of tramping, and so verily am I . . . Consciousness of my own defects makes me lenient.'[11]

During the twenty-seven days it took Livingstone to reach Kasembe's village, fifty-four miles to the south on the Luapula river, he and his men waded, at times waist deep, through 'black tenacious mud' exuding 'a frightful faecal odour' and contended with leeches that 'needed no coaxing to bite but flew at the skin like furies'.[12] Livingstone left Kasembe in mid-June with Muhammad Bogharib, the only Arab slave trader he would come to think of as a friend. Always, he believed that by using Arabs to further his geographical aims, he was increasing his chances of living long enough to do the maximum possible harm to the hateful trade. By July Livingstone was back at Bangweulu and taking new observations for longitude and latitude. On 8 July – confident that an Arab caravan would take his next packet of letters to the coast – he wrote a despatch to Lord Clarendon, the new Foreign Secretary:

I may safely assert that the chief sources of the Nile arise between 10° and 12° south latitude or nearly in the position assigned to them by Ptolemy . . . If your Lordship will read the following short sketch of my discoveries, you will perceive that the springs of the Nile have hitherto been searched for very much too far to the north. They rise some 400 miles south of the most southerly portion of the Victoria Nyanza, and indeed south of all the lakes except Bangweolo.[13]

In August Livingstone re-joined Bogharib, who was planning to visit Manyema in search of slaves and ivory. But a change of plan led the Arab to return instead to Ujiji on Lake Tanganyika. This was just as well for Livingstone, whose health collapsed soon after Bogharib's decision was made. Pneumonia and malaria might have killed him if he had been taken to Manyema on a litter. But by the summer of 1869, after four months of recuperation in Ujiji, he felt strong enough to set out once more for Manyema. It seemed an incredible piece of luck that Bogharib was leaving for that place at exactly this time.

Within a few months Livingstone expected to be on the banks
of the Lualaba, which he estimated to be 200 miles from the
western shores of Lake Tanganyika. His optimism was sadly
misplaced. He had entirely underestimated the anarchy and
mass murder going on in Manyema, now that it had become an
ivory boom area. The Arab-Swahili newcomers were far more
ruthless than men of Bogharib's generation and murdered any
villagers who tried to negotiate a reasonable price for their tusks.
As a result, widespread fighting broke out between Africans and
Arabs, and so Livingstone found it very hard to travel as soon
as Bogharib went off trading on his own. The hardest time in
Livingstone's life was just beginning.

Because his attempt, between June 1870 and July 1871, to
become the first European to reach the mighty Lualaba and
to navigate its course downstream, is a virtual compendium
of all the deadliest pitfalls that the nineteenth-century African
explorer could expect to face during an entire lifetime, I chose
this *annus horribilis* as the subject of Chapter One of this book. It
graphically demonstrates the almost superhuman determination
of the greatest explorers never to surrender – even when facing
death by drowning, malaria and tick fever. Desertions, food
shortages, droughts, floods, slave raids, threats of violence
and actual violence, all punctuated Livingstone's days in 1870
and 1871.

But, amazingly, there were rewards too during this awful
period. In March 1871, he was awed by his first sight of the broad,
brown waters of the Lualaba – 3,000 yards wide at this point
– flowing slowly and powerfully northwards between densely
forested banks. Because this immense river appeared on no maps,
and had not been described in the literature of any of the world's
geographical societies, its discovery was all the more thrilling. As
explained in Chapter One, due to his readings of Herodotus, and
the apparent confirmation given to the Greek historian's account
of the Nile's sources by Josut and Moenpembé – two well-travelled
Arabs, whom the doctor met in Manyema in 1870 – Livingstone
had become convinced that the Lualaba was indeed the Nile. His

own work in isolating the source bolstered this conclusion. So the fact that his many efforts to reach it at times came close to killing him was simply a reflection of his certainty that this was *his* moment when he must not fail, as the gentlemen explorers had done when their great moments had come.

For seven frustrating months, Livingstone was unable to move any closer to the fabled river because suffering from pneumonia and enduring the terrible pain of tropical ulcers eating into the soles of his feet. Ill-health kept him a prisoner in the town of Bambarre, midway between Lake Tanganyika and the Lualaba, until February 1871. At this time his following dwindled to three men.

Then, out of the blue, on 4 February ten porters arrived from the east coast, sent many months earlier by Acting-Consul Kirk.[14] Although these men enabled Livingstone – with additional help from several Arab slave traders – to reach the Lualaba a month later, they then did their utmost to prevent him following the river downstream. In his daily field notebooks, he railed against these new arrivals, who turned out to be slaves owned by *banians* for whose services Livingstone was being asked to pay more than if they had been free men. He thought them devious, dishonest and cowardly, since they were not prepared to accompany him in a canoe down the Lualaba. Their perfectly natural fear was that tribes along the banks, after suffering repeated raids by Arab slave traders operating from Nyangwe, would attack all strangers on the river. The 'Banian slaves', as Livingstone called them, made it impossible for him to secure canoes by telling the local Manyema that he 'wanted neither slaves nor ivory but to kill them'. Though Chuma and Susi, who had been with Livingstone since 1861 and 1863 respectively, knew what the slaves were saying about their master, they never told him.

Livingstone had little or no control over these new arrivals who absented themselves for days at a time and even murdered three Manyema villagers, apparently in emulation of the slave traders. It horrified Livingstone that the Indian owners of these murderers were British subjects.[15] The Arabs also did their best to thwart Livingstone by buying up all the available canoes, to stop him going downstream and reporting on the mayhem they were causing to the north of Nyangwe. This did not stop him hoping that he would soon manage to buy a canoe from one of these slave traders.

Then, on 15 July, Livingstone witnessed the massacre of over 400 African residents of Nyangwe, some shot down in the market place and others drowned in a nearby creek in their panic to escape. After that, Livingstone's will to continue down the river collapsed. He could no longer bring himself to beg Dugumbé and other leading Arabs to sell him the canoes he so desperately needed. So his only option was to return to Ujiji on the eastern side of Lake Tanganyika, where he expected to find fresh stores sent from the coast by Kirk. He turned his back on the river on 20 July 1871, and in deep depression began the 200-mile march to the east. His fourteen men included the ten *banian* slaves, and he was also accompanied by an unknown number of women with whom they cohabited.[16]

During the next three months, he survived two attempts to kill him by African spearmen, who took him for a slave trader. By 7 August he was 'ill and almost every step in pain'. He suffered not just from bleeding piles but also from chronic diarrhoea which left him thin and very weak.[17] He ought to have been operated on in England, but had been too busy raising funds for his expedition and had never found the time. Sorghum flour, which he had been unable to buy from villagers before mid-September, now became available and strengthened him a little. But his condition remained parlous.

I felt as if dying on my feet. Almost every step I was in pain, the appetite failed, and a little meat caused violent vomiting, whilst the mind, sorely depressed, reacted on the body. All the traders were returning successful: I alone had failed and experienced worry, thwarting, baffling, when almost in sight of the end towards which I strained.[18]

He crossed Lake Tanganyika in a hired canoe, and reached Ujiji on 23 October 'now reduced to a skeleton'. After a couple of hours, he discovered that the supplies which Kirk had sent from the coast had arrived but been stolen and sold off by the man who had brought them, and by other Arab traders in the town. The goods had been worth £600 and all were gone. All Livingstone had left with which to buy food was a few yards of calico. After fleeing from Nyangwe to avoid depending on Arabs, it was horribly ironic that he seemed doomed to have to beg from Arab slave traders in Ujiji in order to survive. To make matters worse, Sherif Bosher, who had sold off all the goods, had used the proceeds to buy ivory which was still in the town under lock and key. But none of Ujiji's three principal men would allow Livingstone to reclaim what had been bought with his stolen property. There seemed no realistic hope now that he would be able to pay for the milch goats, wheaten flour and fish needed for his recovery. As for returning to the Lualaba – that had become a pipe-dream. He admitted in a letter to a friend: 'I was like the man who went from Jerusalem to Jericho, but no Good Samaritan would come the Ujijian way.'[19]

Incredibly, he was wrong. Less than a week later a young Welshman, masquerading as an American, was camped on a hillside a few miles from Ujiji, gazing down 'as in a painted picture, at the vast lake . . . set in a frame of dimly blue mountains'. It was an ecstatic moment for him.[20] How this man came to be an explorer and then to change David Livingstone's life, and even his place in history, is a very strange story indeed. It is also an essential strand in the saga of how the Nile mystery finally came to be solved.

NINETEEN

Never to Give Up the Search
Until I Find Livingstone

John Rowlands, who would one day be known to the world as Henry Morton Stanley, was born in the small market town of Denbigh in north Wales in 1841. He was the firstborn of a feckless eighteen-year-old barmaid, Elizabeth Parry, who deserted him as a very young baby, and would go on to have five more children – by two, or possibly three other men – only the last being born in wedlock. John never knew his father, whose identity remains uncertain. He was reputed to have been either a local solicitor, or a farm labourer, both of whom became alcoholics and died prematurely.[1]

John Rowlands was brought up by his maternal grandfather, a retired butcher, who had a fatal heart attack when his grandson was five. For six months after this disaster, John was boarded out with a middle-aged couple near his old home, but his two uncles, who were prosperous local tradesmen, suddenly stopped paying for his keep, and the couple told their eldest son, Dick, to take little John Rowlands to St Asaph Workhouse. During the eight-mile walk Dick told John that he was being taken to live with an aunt, whose farm lay in the same direction. When they arrived at the doors of the workhouse, Dick rang a bell that clanged deep within the building, and then turned to leave, saying sheepishly, when asked where he was going: 'To buy cakes for you.'[2]

'Since that dreadful evening,' Stanley wrote fifty years later, 'my resentment has not a whit abated . . . It would have been far better for me if Dick, being stronger than me, had employed compulsion, instead of shattering my confidence and planting the first seeds of distrust in a child's heart.'[3] This day of betrayal was the most formative in Rowlands's young life, since it seemed to echo that earlier abandonment by his parents, reinforcing his conviction that his family thought him worthless. Certainly, nobody could possibly have imagined that this deserted, penniless boy would one day be able to attract the substantial sums required for African exploration. As a workhouse boy for nine years, Rowlands knew that in a cruelly snobbish society he was the lowest of the low but, instead of being crushed by it, this knowledge fired him with fierce determination to prove wrong all those who had rejected him.

In December 1850, when he was not quite ten, the master took him aside during the dinner-hour and, 'pointing to a woman with a coil of dark hair behind her head', asked him if he knew her.

'No, sir,' I replied.
'What, do you not know your own mother?'
I had expected to feel a gush of tenderness, but her expression was so chilling that the valves of my heart closed as with a snap.[4]

His mother had not come to the workhouse to see him, but had been admitted herself as a destitute pauper with two of her other children. Yet, far from freezing out every fond feeling for her, John vowed that he would win this aloof woman's love. As the cleverest boy in the workhouse school, this should have been possible, but his mother after her discharge a few days later never returned to see him. Even the fact of his being picked out by the master as a future trainee-teacher made no difference.

Workhouse inmates wore suits made from fustian (rough flannel); they rose at six, washed in cold water, performed menial tasks, and if admitted with parents or brothers and sisters were immediately separated from them. However, some of the abler children learned to read, write, and do simple sums. While at the workhouse, John read David Livingstone's first book, *Missionary Travels*, which made a lasting impression on him.[5] Very few of his fellow pupils could have mastered a book like that. Educational standards had been very low when Rowlands had arrived at St Asaph, but improved steadily during his long residence.[6]

People shut up for years in institutions often harbour fantasies of escape, of climbing over walls, living in woods and walking for miles towards far horizons. It is not fanciful to suppose that John's virtual imprisonment as a boy predisposed him to explore a limitless continent.[7] John was discharged from St Asaph aged fifteen, and two years later was working as a butcher's boy in Liverpool where an aunt and uncle had taken him in. They were so poor that they took his savings of a guinea and pawned his only suit. One day, when delivering meat to an American packet-ship in the docks, he decided to emigrate. He was not quite eighteen and it was one of the bravest decisions of his life.

Although Stanley would later claim that in New Orleans – where he jumped ship – he was adopted by a wealthy cotton broker called Henry Stanley, in reality he never met the man.[8] Ever since his arrival at St Asaph Workhouse, Rowlands had longed to be part of a functioning family. In America he simply pretended that his longstanding fantasy had come true. This was no ordinary lying. John's parents had denied him an identity and he had felt an overwhelming need to invent one.

On first arriving in New Orleans in February 1859, he worked in a wholesale warehouse, which supplied goods to Mississippi riverboats for delivery to upriver towns and settlements. When the owner of this business died suddenly eight months later, Rowlands lost his job, and briefly became an assistant cook on riverboats, before finding employment in an upriver store at Cypress Bends, near Little Rock, Arkansas. Here he started calling himself Henry Stanley, which was a name he had first seen printed on sacks of cotton in the wholesale warehouse. He must have liked the way it looked and sounded. Henry Hope Stanley – to give that prosperous New Orleans businessman his full name – owned most of the machinery used to compress and bag raw cotton in the city. It clearly appealed to John Rowlands to assume the name of a rich cotton broker and factory owner, partly in the belief that the name itself had the power to confer on its new user some of its original possessor's glamour. It had long been Rowlands's desire, he wrote later, to 'rid myself of the odium attached to an old name and its dolorous history'.[9]

So how did he do it? Initially, by introducing himself as Henry Stanley when applying for that job at Cypress Bends. Then, in August 1860, a census-taker called at the store, and nineteen-year-old John Rowlands gave his name as William Henry Stanley. William would be dropped within a year, but Henry Stanley would survive, only finally to be augmented with Morton as a second name in 1872.[10]

When the American Civil War started, the other shop boys at Cypress Bends at once enlisted to fight for the South. Being a foreigner, Stanley did not think of it as his war, but the arrival of an anonymous gift of female underwear – the equivalent of a white feather – changed his mind. In April 1862, he fought in the bloody battle of Shiloh, was captured, and taken to a federal prison camp outside Chicago. Large numbers of men were dying of typhoid. So when the camp commandant offered to release him on condition that he joined the Union Army, Stanley changed sides to save his life. But after a spell in hospital recovering from dysentery, he deserted once more.

Sick and penniless, he headed east, intent on working his passage back to Britain. He had heard that his mother was now the licensee of two public houses, and so was in a position to help him at last. On docking in Liverpool, he walked fifty miles to the village where his mother kept one of her pubs. On arriving, worn out and emaciated, Stanley knocked on the side door.

My mother opened it, aghast at seeing me. She said little – but what she did say will never be forgotten . . . 'Never come back to me again unless you are in far better circumstances than you seem to be in now.'[11]

Back in America, Stanley risked joining the Union Navy, calling himself Henry Stanley, under which name he had deserted from the Union army. Captured deserters were imprisoned, or even shot or hanged. On board ship, he made friends with a sixteen-year-old ship's messenger, Lewis Noe, who remembered that Stanley spent many hours every day reading travel books by authors like Richard Burton and Alexander Kinglake, and said that he would have adventures of his own. As the navy's part in the Civil War fizzled out, Noe and Stanley deserted and set about saving money from a bizarre assortment of temporary jobs – including gold prospecting and clerking for a judge – so they could go travelling. Stanley's aim was to journey through Turkey, then on to India and China. On his return he meant to write a bestselling book. But nothing went to plan. From the day of their arrival in Turkey, they were short of money and equipment. After attempting to steal a horse from a Turkish merchant, the adventurers were themselves robbed, kidnapped, beaten up, and in Noe's case raped. They would have been destitute and helpless had not the American consul in Constantinople lent them money.

Their expedition had failed spectacularly, but Stanley still meant to impress his mother. Before leaving Turkey, he paid a tailor with part of the consul's money to make a copy of a US naval officer's uniform which, on arrival in Denbigh, he wore for the best part of a month.[12] Now that he appeared to have money and rank, his mother, Elizabeth Jones, invited him to spend Christmas at the larger of her two pubs with his half-siblings and with the man she had recently married. These were the first days Stanley had ever spent with his mother, and his family.[13]

Noe had been left behind in Liverpool to await Stanley's return, and, while there, he wrote several letters to his friend, addressing him as Henry Stanley on the envelopes. Stanley had resumed calling himself John Rowlands while in Wales, but was now obliged to explain the unfamiliar name. His mother accused him of having changed his name to mask a life of crime. Because he could not admit that he had voluntarily abandoned his original Welsh name without offending his mother and other local people, he came up with the adoption story, which in any case held a deep emotional appeal for him. He said he had been treated like a beloved son by Henry Stanley, the owner of the warehouse where he had first worked in New Orleans. Indeed, he went on, Mr Stanley had given him his own name and had made him his heir – dying just too soon to give expression to his wish in a new will. When Stanley became famous, his mother told several journalists about her son's 'adoption' and how he had acquired his name. This invention then appeared in newspapers and in a number of books, so Stanley was saddled with the lie for life. He made matters more complicated for himself by taking the fib a step further, claiming that he had been raised as an American in Missouri – thus concealing his illegitimacy and workhouse background, but denying himself the admiration and support he would have enjoyed in Britain had his British identity been acknowledged.

Re-united with Lewis Noe in Liverpool in January 1867, Stanley told his young friend something that amazed him. One day, said the man whose Turkish expedition had been a complete fiasco, he would track down Dr Livingstone in Africa, and interview him for the *New York Herald*, making himself rich and famous in the process.[14]

Although Livingstone had returned to Africa only a year earlier, the British press was full of speculation about his whereabouts just when Noe and Stanley were in Liverpool.[15] Stanley told his incredulous friend that, between leaving Wales and returning to Liverpool, he had been to London for a meeting with Colonel Finley Anderson, the *New York Herald*'s bureau chief in the capital. Incredibly, this turned out to be true, although because Stanley lacked experience as a traveller, Anderson had rejected the idea. But the bureau chief had been mildly encouraging and had asked Stanley to keep in touch.[16] Stanley himself would later attribute the brilliant idea of finding Livingstone to James Gordon Bennett Jr, the evil-tempered millionaire owner of the world-famous *New York Herald*, but this would be because by then his entire career seemed to depend upon this autocrat's continuing patronage. Nor would Stanley ever wish to have it known that the inspiration for finding Livingstone had been due to his craving for fame, rather than to a philanthropic desire on his part to bring succour to the embattled explorer.

Back in America in 1867, Stanley succeeded in getting the *Missouri Democrat* to send him to report on the Indian Wars in

Nebraska. While serving in the navy, he had sold war stories to various mid-western papers, and had been told that he showed promise as a journalist. His reports on the Indian Wars would be striking enough to change his life. Other newspaper editors and owners became aware of his vivid descriptions of General Hancock's campaign. This enabled him, early next year, to travel to New York and to persuade James Gordon Bennett to send him to Africa to report on a British punitive expedition in Ethiopia. Through bribing a crucial telegraph clerk Stanley would break the news of the Ethiopian emperor's defeat and suicide days before any other correspondent had even filed his copy. Stanley next convinced Bennett that to find Livingstone in the heart of Africa would be an historic scoop. This was no mean achievement since in Bennett's opinion Americans cared nothing for Africa. In addition, Bennett feared that Stanley, after spending many thousands of dollars, would fail to find his man, and would very likely die in the wilds of the Dark Continent. Some sixth sense led Bennett to delay Stanley's departure for over a year until the autumn of 1870 – by which time Livingstone had been in Africa and seen no white face for four and a half years. No letter had been received at the coast from the missing man in eighteen months. So if Stanley could find him, it would be sure to create a sensation.

In 1869 Stanley became engaged to Katie Gough Roberts, a Welsh girl, whom he had got to know during visits to Denbigh between assignments. Stanley longed for the security of marriage but he also needed to escape his old persona through travel and adventure. In the end, Katie's solicitor father forced him to choose between the two by saying he could not marry Katie unless he began staying in Britain for long periods of time. Since this choice was forced on him at the very moment when his great idea, the Livingstone mission, was getting off the ground, Stanley chose his African quest. 'My great love for you cannot blind me; it cannot lead me astray from the path I have chalked out,' he told Katie.[17] Yet he did not give up hope that he might be able to find Livingstone and marry

Katie on his return. She, however, was not prepared to wait, and married a Manchester architectural student in September 1870 while Stanley was still abroad and sending back stories for the *New York Herald*.[18] At last, after he had reported on the opening of the Suez Canal, and visited Jerusalem, Odessa and the battlefields of the Crimea, Stanley was allowed to travel to Bombay, and from that city set sail for Zanzibar, the gateway to Africa.

On 6 January 1871, three weeks before his thirtieth birthday, he sighted the masts and rigging of the ships at anchor in the harbour, and the Sultan's blood-red banner streaming out over his unfinished palace. In Zanzibar, Stanley was horrified to find that James Gordon Bennett had sent no money as agreed, obliging him to ask the US Consul to pledge his personal credit. Stanley would only be able to spend £1,000 on his mission – half as much as Livingstone had spent on his and had thought totally inadequate. Finding it too humiliating to admit that Bennett had treated him so disrespectfully, Stanley later claimed that his boss had spent £4,000 on his journey, enabling him to engage 192 porters, whereas in fact he had only managed to hire about a hundred. Thus his insecurity led him to diminish his real achievement.[19] Bennett's perfidy told Stanley that if he failed to find Livingstone, the magnate would probably leave him to repay the US Consul, Francis Webb. Failure would therefore mean financial ruin.

Luckily, Stanley did not know about Livingstone's most recent geographical plans. Had he done so, he would have realised how slender his chances were of finding him. But when he went to see Dr Kirk on Zanzibar, Stanley found it reassuring to be told that the doctor was somewhere to the west of Lake Tanganyika and would probably return to Ujiji at some time in the future. In fact, at the very time when Stanley and Kirk were having this chat in January 1871, Livingstone was preparing to leave Bambarre for the Lualaba, and had no intention of returning to Ujiji. Blissfully unaware of this, Stanley was euphoric as he set out for Ujiji from Bagamoyo on 21 March.

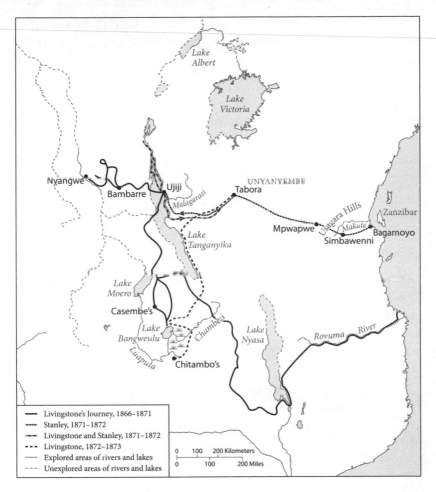

Legend:
— Livingstone's Journey, 1866–1871
---- Stanley, 1871–1872
-·- Livingstone and Stanley, 1871–1872
- - - Livingstone, 1872–1873
— Explored areas of rivers and lakes
--- Unexplored areas of rivers and lakes

0   100   200 Kilometers
0   100   200 Miles

Livingstone and Stanley.

The former workhouse boy rode into the bush on his thorough-bred stallion, resplendent in pith helmet and white flannels, while at the head of the caravan fluttered the Stars and Stripes. For a man like Stanley, who needed to prove himself after the trauma of parental rejection, Africa was a test of character that could scarcely have been bettered. His examination began within days, when the tsetse started killing his animals, including his fine stallion, and when his porters either fell ill with fever, or deserted the column. Stanley could see just how easily he might be deserted by all of them and then be left to starve, lacking the food and trade goods they had been carrying. Few Victorian explorers made greater efforts to instil discipline and to track down deserters than did Stanley, but his caravan's numbers dwindled nevertheless. Soon he quarrelled with his two white companions, John Shaw and William Farquhar, both of whom were former merchant seamen – one of them drank and the other was addicted to whores, a serious crime in Stanley's eyes, given his detestation of his mother's promiscuity. Stanley had read Speke's and Burton's books and had consequently chosen Bombay and Mabruki as his African captains because they had been Speke's most highly valued 'faithfuls'. Having studied the performance of Speke's and Burton's porters, Stanley chose mainly African Zanzibaris or Wangwana. Though they would suffer heavy casualties on all his journeys, many of the survivors would volunteer to travel with him as many as three times more – a great tribute.

John Shaw and William Farquhar.

On the way to Unyanyembe, Stanley suffered many bouts of fever, his horse and his donkeys died, and the rainy season made travel a nightmare. Farquhar died, and Shaw was so ill that he seemed certain to follow him, which he did. And worse was to come. Shortly before arriving at Tabora, only 250 miles from Ujiji, Stanley heard from members of an Arab-Swahili caravan who had been in Manyema that Livingstone was dead. Though badly shaken by this news, Stanley refused to believe it.[20] If it was true he would be ruined. But would he ever get to Ujiji or Manyema to learn the truth?

At Tabora he became enmeshed in a war being fought between the Arab-Swahili slave traders, who ran the town, and Mirambo, the marvellously named, charismatic African ruler of the Nyamwezi, who was determined to snatch control of the slave caravan route to Lake Tanganyika. Since Stanley's caravan was down to thirty men, he saw no way of getting to Ujiji unless Mirambo's warriors could be driven away from the path ahead. So, he agreed to join the Arabs in an attempt to achieve this. His Arab allies seriously underestimated Mirambo, who ordered a tactical retreat, and then ambushed them as they rushed after his warriors in hot pursuit. A few of Stanley's men were stabbed to death, and 500 Arabs were massacred in like fashion, with many of their corpses being mutilated. Stanley heard that faces were cut away, along with genitals and stomachs, and then boiled and eaten with rice. He himself had been suffering from fever at the time of the ambush, and would have been killed if his young translator, Selim, had not lifted him onto a donkey and led him back to Tabora.[21]

In late August, Mirambo attacked Tabora and burned a quarter of the town. Stanley, who had managed to add another twenty followers to his thirty, cut loopholes in the clay walls of his stockaded Arab *tembe*, and waited for what seemed sure to be a fight to the finish. Fortunately for him, Mirambo mysteriously chose to back off just when his enemies were at his mercy. Grateful to be alive, Stanley rededicated himself to his task, writing by candlelight in his diary:

I have taken a solemn, enduring oath, an oath to be kept while the least hope of life remains in me, not to be tempted to break the resolution I have formed, never to give up the search until I find Livingstone alive, or find his dead body . . . No living man or living men, shall stop me, only death can prevent me. But death – not even this; I shall not die, I will not die, I cannot die![22]

He now planned to avoid the war entirely, by marching south and south-west for ten days and only then starting to head north to Ujiji. On 21 September 1871, with thirty-four men, most of whom had spent the night before in 'one last debauch', Stanley left Tabora, suffering from malaria, yet again. Apart from the shakes and aches and sweats, he saw hideous faces and experienced shockingly rapid changes of mood. It still tormented him to think that Livingstone might be dead. His column passed through forest and marshland, and then over hills. In late October at the Malagarasi river, Stanley was overjoyed to hear that a white man with grey whiskers had just arrived at Ujiji. Nearing Lake Tanganyika, with mounting excitement, he told Selim to lay out his flannel suit, oil his boots and chalk his pith helmet. He was determined to look his best for what was destined to be the greatest day of his life so far. In truth, Stanley was very nervous, since he was haunted by John Kirk's statement that Livingstone detested other explorers – so much so that if Burton, Baker or Speke were ever to come near him, he would rapidly put a swamp between them and himself. Stanley forced himself to confront the ghastly possibility that he might refuse to be interviewed.[23]

Entering Ujiji on 10 November 1871,[24] Stanley's men fired repeated volleys – the usual ritual when a caravan entered a town – and he ordered the Stars and Stripes to be unfurled and borne aloft at the head of the column. An animated crowd surged around the advancing newcomers, and Susi, one of Livingstone's longest-serving followers, greeted Stanley ecstatically, and then ran off shouting: 'An Englishman coming! I see him!'[25] Approaching Livingstone's house, Stanley felt so excited that he longed 'to vent [his] joy in some mad freaks, such as idiotically biting [his] hand, or turning a somersault'.[26] He clambered down from his donkey's back, and saw, standing only a few paces away, a man of about sixty with a grey beard. He was wearing an old red waistcoat and tweed trousers. *This* was the scarcely imaginable moment that he had nevertheless dreamed about ever since making his impossible prediction to

Lewis Noe five years earlier. He knew that he would be famous now for the rest of his life and possibly rich too. But he had not the faintest premonition of the immeasurably more important consequences which would spring from this extraordinary meeting, affecting himself and even the history of Africa.

The Meeting, as seen in the famous engraving in Stanley's book *How I Found Livingstone*.

TWENTY

The Doctor's Obedient and Devoted Servitor

At the point in Stanley's diary where he advances towards Livingstone, three pages have been torn out, just where he ought to be saying: 'Dr Livingstone, I presume?' The only reason for tearing them out would seem to be because they had not confirmed the words of the famous greeting. Nor is the historic question to be found in Livingstone's diary, or in his notebooks, or in any of the dozen or so letters he wrote during the next couple of weeks.[1] Because Livingstone repeated Susi's far less memorable words in most of his contemporary letters, the greeting would appear to have been invented by Stanley at some point during the six months that followed the meeting. Indeed, ever since leaving Zanzibar he had been trying to work out what laconic, understated greeting an English gentleman would be likely to come up with on such a momentous occasion. With 'Dr Livingstone, I presume?' he believed he had finally found the perfect formulation. It would be a great shock when people laughed at him for not managing to say something heartfelt and spontaneous.[2]

In his book *How I Found Livingstone*, Stanley's second remark to Livingstone is recorded as having been: 'I thank God I have been permitted to see you.' And this, or some more colloquial variant, seems more likely to have been spoken.[3] But whatever was said, there can be no doubt at all that Livingstone had never been so pleased to see a white face as he was to see Stanley's. He was not exaggerating when he said: 'You have brought me new life.'[4] So the moment was one of high emotion for both men. Stanley knew from the tears in Livingstone's eyes that there was no possibility he might refuse to answer his questions. But Stanley waited till the following day before admitting that he was a special correspondent of the *New York Herald*. 'That despicable paper,' Livingstone called it, but with a smile.[5] Stanley soon grasped that the doctor was Scottish, not English as he had at first thought, and that they shared a Celtic background – though Stanley would continue to represent himself as an American.

When he described Livingstone's appearance as ordinary, 'like a book with a most unpretending binding', he put his finger on an important truth about the man. His appearance gave 'no token of what element of power or talent lay within'.[6] He looked younger than his actual age of nearly sixty; his eyes were brown and very bright; his teeth loose and irregular; his height average; shoulders a little bowed, and he walked with 'a firm but heavy tread, like an overworked or fatigued man'.[7] At once Stanley sensed that Livingstone was not the misanthrope Kirk had made him out to be. Few childhoods could rival his own for suffering and deprivation, but Livingstone's had been no picnic either. He had been a child factory worker in a cotton mill near Glasgow, and had lived with his family of six in a single room in a tenement block. Yet he had managed to put himself through medical school on his earnings as a cotton spinner.

Livingstone had first sailed for Africa in 1841 – the year of Stanley's birth – and had spent ten frustrating years as a medical missionary in Botswana, having been ordained a Congregationalist minister before leaving England. Despite the public's view of him as an unequalled missionary, in reality he made but one convert, who lapsed. After this failure, he had not been prepared to spend a lifetime as his father-in-law had done, converting a few dozen people. Livingstone understood very well why Africans considered monogamy and small families a threat to their entire way of life. A chief with many wives could give great feasts, grow large quantities of food and enjoy the support of many descendants. Why would he wish to throw this away? Failure as a conventional missionary led Livingstone to believe that only massive cultural intrusion could lead Africans to adopt the white man's customs and religion in any numbers. If traders could come up rivers into the interior in steamships, and build two-storey houses, and sell factory goods in exchange for local produce, Africans might become more respectful towards the beliefs of people who could bring them such wonders. In time, Africans might even consent to work for wages, have smaller families, limit themselves to a single wife, and consequently their loyalty to chief and tribe might weaken enough to give Christianity a chance.[8]

Livingstone sitting with Stanley outside his *tembe* in Ujiji
(from *How I Found Livingstone*).

So between 1849 and 1851, Livingstone had made three journeys aimed at opening up the continent, culminating in his trek to the Zambezi, which he had reached near Linyanti on 4 August 1851. Between 1853 and 1856, he crossed Africa from coast to coast, along the line of the Zambezi. Next, between 1859 and 1864, he tried to prove its navigability and find a location in South Central Africa suitable for missionaries and traders to settle in. Rivers would, he hoped, be 'God's Highways' into the interior.[9] But the Zambezi was choked with sandbars and blocked by rapids, which combined with malaria to destroy his dreams of a settlement. Yet rivers and lakes still lured him powerfully, as he discovered when Speke's and Burton's rival Nile theories gripped his imagination.

Normally secretive about his geographical discoveries, Livingstone paid Stanley the immense compliment of confiding to him all his ideas about the Nile's source, and then, just four days after the younger man's arrival, the older man suggested that he travel with him to the Lualaba to help him finish his work. Stanley was torn, but in the end declared that he had to do his duty to the *New York Herald* and hurry to the coast with his news of the meeting.[10]

Yet, two days later, Stanley, who had hated refusing the doctor, suggested a compromise: they should travel instead to the infinitely more accessible northern end of Lake Tanganyika. From reading the published *Proceedings of the Royal Geographical Society*, Stanley had been aware since 1865 of Burton's claim that the River Rusizi flowed northwards out of Lake Tanganyika into the southern end of Baker's Lake Albert before continuing northwards as the White Nile. This view was shared by Livingstone, as Stanley already knew from the RGS's publication of the doctor's letter to John Kirk of 30 May 1869. In this letter (the last to reach the outside world before Stanley reached Ujiji) Livingstone had said that he needed to 'go down', what he called 'the [Nile's] eastern line of drainage', by which he meant the northward-flowing river system beginning with Lake Bangweulu, and flowing on north, via Lake Moero, into the west side of Lake Tanganyika, and continuing via the Rusizi into Lake Albert.[11] But after learning more about the great Lualaba from direct experience, and realising that it flowed due north for 400 miles from its source in Lake Bangweulu, and very likely hundreds more, the doctor had lost interest in Lake Tanganyika. The Lualaba, he told Stanley was 'the central line of drainage [and] the most important line . . . [In comparison] the question whether there is a connection between the Tanganyika and the Albert N'yanaza sinks into insignificance.'[12]

But when Stanley reminded Livingstone that Sir Roderick Murchison and the RGS wanted the Rusizi to be settled, and offered to pay all the expenses of their journey to the northern tip of Lake Tanganyika, Livingstone agreed that they should go.[13] This was the very journey that had defeated Burton and Speke, but because Livingstone and Stanley refused to have anything to do with the local chief, Kannena, and instead accepted the loan of a large canoe from an Arab, Said bin Majid, and took with them only Stanley's cook, his translator, two local guides and sixteen reliable Wangwana as rowers, they always kept control over their men. Speke's and Burton's people had refused to go on because of real or imagined dangers.

Stanley and Livingstone embarked on 16 November, six days after Stanley's arrival at Ujiji.[14] Delighting in his self-acquired knowledge of Greek mythology, Stanley excitedly compared their 'cranky canoe hollowed out of the noble *mvule* tree' with Jason's ship the *Argo*. They hugged the shore and Stanley was bewitched by 'a wealth of boscage of beautiful trees, many of which were in bloom ... exhaling an indescribably sweet fragrance'. The idyllic circumstances of the people also pleased him, with their fishing settlements, palm groves, cassava gardens and quiet bays.[15] Apart from an encounter with some stone-throwers, who Livingstone mollified by showing them the white skin of his arm and asking them whether they had ever been harmed by anyone of his colour, they experienced no hostility.[16]

On reaching the head of the lake on 28 November, they found that the Rusizi flowed into Tanganyika rather than out of it. This was a major discovery and at a stroke ruled out Lake Tanganyika as being any kind of source or reservoir of the Nile. Yet even the discovery that the Rusizi flowed in would not force a retraction from Burton when he heard of it, since a river might conceivably flow out of the west side of the lake into the Lualaba and then continue northwards as the Nile. But realistically, it seemed that either the Victoria Nyanza or the Lualaba's headwaters were now the only serious candidates for being the Nile's source. However, there *was* a serious problem with the Lualaba. The height Livingstone had calculated for Nyangwe had been 2,000 feet, which was the same as Baker's height for his Lake Albert. Of course one or both of the measurements might be wrong. But if they were not, to get round these inconvenient heights (which ruled out a direct connection between the Lualaba and Lake Albert) Livingstone argued that the Lualaba could quite logically pass Lake Albert to the west and join 'Petherick's branch of the Nile', the Bahr el-Ghazal.

Stanley and Livingstone at the mouth of the Rusizi
(from *How I Found Livingstone*).

So, back at Ujiji, on 13 December, after a trip of 300 miles that had taken just under a month, the two men decided that they would march together to Kazeh. From there, Stanley would return to the coast and send back to Livingstone supplies and picked men, who would accompany the doctor to the Lualaba and trace it downstream with him until he had proved it to be the Nile.[17]

Even as they had started their trip on the lake, Stanley had written in his diary that Livingstone's manner towards him was 'benevolently paternal' and had enabled him 'to think [himself] somebody, though [he] never suspected it before'. During the voyage Stanley became seriously ill with fever and noted that 'had he been my father, he could not have been kinder'.[18] This father and son aspect of their relationship was of immense importance to Stanley, but affected Livingstone too. 'That good brave fellow has acted as a son to me,' he would tell his daughter, Agnes.[19] Livingstone's son Robert had fallen out with him, and gone to live in America under an assumed name. In the Civil War, Robert had fought for the Union and had been killed in the battle of Gettysburg. Moved to hear that Stanley had also fought for the Union in the same war (he did not of course mention his desertions), Livingstone asked him to find his son's grave and place a headstone on it. The doctor also confided how despairing he had felt after his wife's death.[20] He did not admit that Mary had become an alcoholic during her years in Britain when she had been separated from him during his major African journeys. But even this degree of self-revelation was very rare for Livingstone.

Having grown so fond of his father figure, Stanley did his best to persuade him to come home with him before returning to the Lualaba. The doctor would be able to see his children – his youngest, Anna Mary, being only twelve – and also catch up with old friends. Then there would be a chance to get his teeth fixed and have an operation to remove his piles. But Livingstone was not impressed with these arguments. If he stuck it out for another eighteen months in Africa, he would be able to sort out the Nile's watershed. His determination and his willingness to risk his life without complaint or self-pity were virtues which Stanley revered. Yet he was horrified when Livingstone told him that he did not intend to go straight to Nyangwe, but to trek hundreds of miles south instead and make a circuit around Lake Bangweulu and all the Lualaba's sources, such as the Lomani, before following the main river downstream to the north. Stanley had noticed that Livingstone suffered his worst 'dysenteric attacks' when he got wet. So wading through the Bangweulu swamps in the rainy season would be the most dangerous course open to him.[21]

After they reached Unyanyembe, and as the time for leaving grew closer, Stanley feared that he would never see his friend again after they parted. He knew that Livingstone would die in the attempt rather than turn back. 'I am not made for an African explorer . . . I detest the land most heartily,' Stanley confessed in his diary in November 1871, and three months later admitted to fearing that he would end up 'under the sable soil' of Africa if he returned there.[22] So why did Stanley, who was not conventionally religious and had suffered attacks of fever at a rate of almost one a week since mid-November, come to feel soon after returning to Britain that, if Livingstone were to die, it would be his duty to finish the dead man's work? The answer was his love and admiration for Livingstone. The impact on Stanley of this idealist with a philanthropic vision for a whole continent – for which he was ready to give up his life – was overwhelming. To be treated like a son by such a famous and unusual man was the crowning experience of Stanley's life.

Not that he suspended his critical faculties entirely. Shortly before Stanley marched for the coast, he admitted in his diary that Livingstone was 'not of such an angelic temper as I believed him to be during my first month with him'. The doctor had shocked him by expressing 'a strong contempt' for the missionaries who had come out to the Shire Highlands at his behest, and six of whom had died.[23] Yet Stanley realised that the man's weaknesses made his strengths the more remarkable – his bravery, his idealism, his struggle on behalf of victims of the slave trade, his lack of interest in money and social status. Though inclined to be dismissive towards other explorers, Livingstone treated Stanley, the journalist, as an equal. 'As if,' marvelled Stanley, 'I were of his own age or of equal experience.'[24] Stanley adored this lack of condescension. When Livingstone told him about his armchair critics within the RGS and said: 'If some of them came to Africa they would know what it costs to get a little accurate information about a river,' Stanley fumed on Livingstone's behalf.[25]

The doctor did have a saintly side to his character, as his diaries undoubtedly prove, and Stanley sensed 'something seer-like in him', as well as his 'Spartan heroism'.[26] When Livingstone told him sadly: 'I have lost a great deal of happiness I know by these wanderings. It is as if I had been born to exile,' Stanley felt a strong bond. His own peripatetic life as a journalist had been a kind of exile and had cost him the love of the woman he had hoped to marry. He also empathised with Livingstone's dedication to his work, feeling the same need in himself: 'It is in my nature to toil as it is in the other's nature to enjoy.'[27]

For all these reasons, and because the grief he experienced on parting was, in his own words, 'greater than any pains I have endured', he would represent Livingstone as a near saint in his bestseller *How I Found Livingstone*, and *this* would be the image that would go down in history. Livingstone is faultless in the book, as are his adoring longest-serving followers, despite Stanley's knowledge of their whoring, stealing and drug-taking. Fondness for Livingstone made him turn a blind eye to such things, and he also knew that it made a better story to have found a forgotten saint in Africa than an embittered recluse.

On the evening of 13 March 1872, the day before Stanley left for the coast, Livingstone poured out his thanks 'with no mincing phrases', and this caused Stanley to 'sob [like] a sensitive child of eight'. Though Stanley had suffered 'successive fevers [and] the semi-madness with which they often plagued [him]', he sensed strongly, on leaving Livingstone, that he would be the doctor's 'obedient and devoted servitor in the future, should there be an occasion when I could prove my zeal'.[28] So, already, Livingstone's personal influence had led the journalist and fame-seeker to discover within him a need to follow in his hero's footsteps – even though, when Stanley arrived safely at the coast, he was not yet fully aware of this fact. Whether he would have any chance to play his own part in the Nile quest would depend upon his reception in London.

TWENTY-ONE

Threshing Out the Beaten Straw

—— ∞∞∞ ——

On his return to Britain on 1 August 1872, Stanley expected to receive the unstinting praise and admiration of the British people for having rescued their hero. In fact he would soon learn that 'fame' was something to 'detest & shrink from'.[1] He was met at Dover, not by cheering crowds but by a first cousin and by a half-brother, both embarrassingly drunk. He would find, waiting for him at his London hotel, his Welsh step father who had come to hound him for a pension.[2] If his family shocked him, so too did his fellow journalists. Many mocked in print the absurd formality of the first words he claimed to have addressed to Livingstone, and their mirth was infectious. Dressmakers' dummies in shop-windows asked one another: 'Dr Livingstone, I presume?' and complete strangers roared at him: 'Stanley, I presume?'[3] More upsetting still was the way in which some newspapers made out that his claim to have found the explorer was fraudulent. Until Livingstone's journals, which Stanley had brought back from Africa, could be authenticated by the Foreign Office and the family, the press hinted that he might only have pretended to have found the doctor.[4]

But most serious of all – because it would affect his future prospects of getting back to Africa – was the hostility of the Royal Geographical Society. Because the RGS had despatched a 'Livingstone Relief Expedition', which had only just landed at Bagamoyo when Stanley had swept through in triumph, the council of that august body ignored the recently arrived 'American penny-a-liner' out of pique. *En route* to London, Stanley had foolishly attacked John Kirk, the British Consul in Zanzibar, in a speech he gave at a Paris banquet given for him by the American ambassador.

John Kirk.

Although Kirk had been helpful to Stanley before he began his journey, the traveller had spotted at Bagamoyo a large quantity of stores, bought for Livingstone with British government funds, which had evidently been dumped there and plundered by the men engaged to carry the sacks and boxes into the interior. According to Stanley, Kirk should have checked up at intervals, rather than discovered the situation by chance on a hunting trip to the mainland. Stanley also mentioned that the US Consul, Francis Webb, had sent him eleven packets of mail while he was with Livingstone, but that the doctor had received nothing at all from Kirk during the same period.[5] John Kirk was related by marriage to Horace Waller, who had been in the Shire Highlands with Livingstone and was on the main committee of the RGS. Unfortunately for Stanley, Sir Roderick Murchison had died a few months earlier, and the new President, General Sir Henry Rawlinson, was a close friend of Waller and was horrified to be told by him that Stanley had slandered Kirk. Rawlinson trumpeted for the benefit of journalists: 'If there has been any discovery and relief it is Dr Livingstone who has discovered and relieved Mr Stanley.'[6]

The publication of Livingstone's grateful letters put a stop to such nonsense, but when Stanley addressed the geography section of the British Association on 16 August in Brighton, the eugenicist, traveller and RGS committee member, Francis Galton, who was in the chair, insulted him by describing his speech as 'sensational stories'. He also asked Stanley directly whether he was Welsh.[7] Stories to this effect had appeared in the Welsh press, and Stanley had denied them all with such vigour that he was already being described as 'a Missourian' in various papers.[8] Yet he knew that he might in the end fail to conceal his workhouse origins and his illegitimacy, when men like Galton were so determined to discredit and belittle him. At least Livingstone stuck by him. When Livingstone heard that Kirk had been saying that Stanley was going 'to make his fortune out of him', he told his son, Oswell, that Stanley was 'heartily welcome for he saved me a wearisome tramp . . . and probably saved my life'. Nor did Livingstone ever forgive Kirk for having sent Banian slaves to Manyema rather than free men.[9]

Meanwhile Stanley lived in fear of what his enemies, and his family, might do to him. 'I am constantly apprehensive as though some great calamity impended over me . . . I have smacked my lips over the flavour of fame – but the substance is useless to me – as it may be taken away at any time.'[10] Already an enterprising London publisher, John Camden Hotten, was preparing a biography of him for the press, and had interviewed his mother and other relations. Stanley wrote at once to *The Times* to repudiate 'anything and everything he [Hotten] may relate concerning me and mine'.[11] He did make two good friends at this unhappy time: Edwin Arnold, editor of the *Daily Telegraph,* and Edward Marston, his publisher. Through Arnold's influence he was granted an audience with Queen Victoria and this late show of royal favour led the RGS to award him, albeit grudgingly, their Patron's Gold Medal for his trip with Livingstone to the Rusizi.

But the attacks in the press and the constant efforts he had been forced to make to preserve his American identity made him feel tense and unhappy. He saw more clearly than ever that Africa had actually been a sanctuary, and so might become one again.

What a contrast this world [fashionable London] is to the sinless peaceful life that I enjoyed in Africa. One brings me an inordinate amount of secret pain, the other sapped my physical strength but left my mind expanded and was purifying.[12]

In the vastness of Africa, as ruler of his small party – away from the social pettiness of north Wales, from the greed and cruelty of the slave-owning Deep South – he had felt freed from everything he had been. Hundreds of miles from any other white person, surrounded by the endless bush, with Kalulu, the African youth he had rescued from Arab slavers, and Selim, his young Syrian interpreter, and Uledi and Bombay and his other servants lying sleeping around the large campfire every night, he had felt at peace. With them he had known that he 'could talk without a chance remark being flung & broadcast before readers'.[13] They had driven him mad at times, and as was the practice of all European travellers of the period, he had beaten them for theft and attempted desertion. But when he had sailed from Bagamoyo, he had written in his diary: 'I felt strange and lonely, somehow. My dark friends, who had travelled over so many hundreds of miles, and shared so many dangers with me, were gone, and I – I was left behind.'[14] The thought of returning to Africa became increasingly attractive to him as his disillusionment with metropolitan life deepened.

Yet some good did undoubtedly come from Stanley's time in London. He had brought to England Livingstone's journals and his despatches, including his description of the Nyangwe massacre, just when a House of Commons Select Committee was considering whether to recommend abolition of the seaborne Arab trade. It did so in September 1872 in no small measure due to the arrival of Livingstone's evidence. Under threat of bombardment by the Royal Navy, the Sultan would close the Zanzibar slave market forever on 5 June 1873. This was a great step towards curing what Livingstone had described as 'this open sore of the world'.[15]

But that triumph lay many months ahead, and in October 1872, eight weeks after his return to Europe, Stanley was beginning to feel that he had made a serious mistake not to accept Livingstone's invitation to navigate the Lualaba with him. He approached Clements Markham, the secretary of the RGS, who only weeks earlier had tried, unsuccessfully, to deny him the Society's Gold Medal. Now, Markham rejected his offer to return to Africa and sort out the Nile's watershed, and purposely neglected to tell him that the RGS was about to send a young naval officer, Lieutenant Verney Lovett Cameron, to assist Livingstone. Stanley found out anyway and felt desperate enough to write humbly to Cameron offering his services. Like Markham, Cameron rebuffed 'the American'.[16]

Stanley knew that the *New York Herald* would not send him back to Africa while it was on the cards that Livingstone might solve the mystery singlehandedly, or with Cameron's help. Indeed, after Stanley had enjoyed a prolonged rest and had given some lectures in America, Gordon Bennett sent him to report on a minor British military campaign in West Africa. To be an ordinary war correspondent again came as a painful anticlimax.

The memory of his happiness with Livingstone haunted Stanley. 'I seem to see through the dim, misty, warm, hazy atmosphere of Africa, always the aged face of Livingstone, urging me on in his kind, fatherly way.'[17] Yet Stanley could see no way to help his friend again. On the sea voyage back to Britain, it seemed that all he could do was wait impotently until Livingstone or Cameron solved the mystery of the Nile. Stanley's own career as a Nile explorer seemed to be over. While lecturing in America, he had written to Louis Jennings, editor of the *New York Times*, imploring him to send him back to Africa to sort out the Central African watershed. Jennings's reply felt like the *coup de grâce* to his hopes: 'We think on careful reflection that another African expedition would be like threshing out the beaten straw. A second enterprise of that sort could not possibly equal the success of the first.'[18]

TWENTY-TWO

Nothing Earthly Will Make Me
Give Up My Work

Before Stanley had left Zanzibar on his homeward journey to England, he had taken immense pains to choose for David Livingstone fifty-six men, twenty of whom had served on his journey to Ujiji. He had equipped each man with a musket and ammunition, and had also provided flour, sugar, coffee, tea, numerous varieties of tinned food, hundreds of yards of cloth, and two riding donkeys. Stanley sent to his friend a letter, which reflected the sharp contrasts of the man himself, juxtaposing in a single paragraph affection, self-interest and exhortation for the success of his Nile mission.

My dear Doctor, very few amongst men have I found I so much got to love as yourself . . . England and America expect their people to do their duty. Do yours as persistently as heretofore & come back to your friends and country to be crowned with the laurel, and I will go forth to do mine . . . Do not forget the Herald please. The Herald will be grateful to me for securing you as a Correspondent.[1]

Livingstone had to wait almost six months for Stanley's men and goods to arrive. But on 9 August 1872 an advance party of carriers marched into Tabora. 'How thankful I am I cannot confess,' the doctor wrote in his journal.[2] With the five followers, who had been with him since 1866 – Abdullah Susi, James Chuma, Hamoydah Amoda, Mabruki (Nathaniel Cumba) and Edward Gardner – he had sixty-one men now, some of them accompanied by wives, mistresses, and even by slaves. But despite his disapproval, he knew that he had never been better supplied. In fact he felt optimistic enough about his chances of completing his work to write to a friend, asking him to find rooms for him near Regent's Park in London – 'comfortable and decent, but not excessively dear' – and to speak to a dentist 'about a speedy fitting of artificial teeth'.[3]

On his fifty-ninth birthday, 19 March, Livingstone had re-affirmed his faith in his journal:

My Jesus, my King, my life, my all; I again dedicate my whole self to Thee. Accept me, and grant, O Gracious Father, that ere this year is gone I may finish my task. In Jesu's name I ask it. Amen, so let it be. David Livingstone.[4]

His task was to reach the southern foot of Lake Tanganyika – about 450 miles away to the south-west – then march around Lake Bangweulu and the other 'four fountains of Herodotus' – another 500 miles – and finally, having pinpointed and mapped all of the river's sources, navigate the Lualaba northwards wherever it might go.

On 25 August 1872, he started on his journey, heading towards Lake Tanganyika. It was blisteringly hot, and almost at once a series of mishaps occurred. His best donkey was killed by the tsetse, which also accounted for his ten cows after they had been allowed to stray into a belt of the dreaded fly. Since milk was the only food that restored his health when he had diarrhoea, these misfortunes did not augur well. In the heat his porters became exhausted while climbing in and out of valleys, as they hugged the eastern shore of Lake Tanganyika. Soon their feet were burned and blistered by the soil. Livingstone himself was ill with fever and with dysentery by mid-October and three weeks later he was suffering from anal bleeding. With the rains approaching, he should have abandoned his plan to make a circuit of Lake Bangweulu and its surrounding swamp, but he had been as sick as this before and had suffered far worse conditions in the past, so he saw no reason not to press on.

Serious food shortages in November obliged him to abandon his attempt to pass to the east and then the south of Bangweulu, since local Africans reported even less food in that direction. So he followed his local guide directly to the northern side of the lake as the rains broke. This journey of 170 miles took a month, and with streams bursting their banks and canoes being needed to cross the larger rivers, he was lucky that it did not take longer. Unfortunately, when he had visited the lake in 1868, a damaged chronometer had led him to take inaccurate longitudes, making the lake appear far bigger than it actually was. He therefore believed he was far to the east of the position to which the guide said he had brought him, so he decided that the man was lying and refused to take his advice about the best way round the lake. So instead of heading south-west as advised (which would have taken him rapidly along the western side of the lake directly to the outflowing Luapula), he headed east, determined in future to ignore African advice. It would prove to be a fatal decision.

Four years earlier, he had decided that the lake was 150 miles from east to west, whereas in fact it was only twenty-five, with a huge area of marshland to its east, measuring about a hundred miles across. The longer he went on in an easterly direction, the more confused he became. Expecting water, he found only endless reeds and mud. When he managed to take new and accurate observations, with his undamaged chronometer, he refused to believe them because they were so different from those taken in better weather conditions in 1868. He concluded that the water had wrecked the reflectors of his sextant.[5]

They struggled on eastwards through January 1873 before turning south towards the Chambesi – the party rarely managing more than a couple of miles a day. Livingstone's health was worsening with the cold and wet and lack of decent food. Already he was too weak to ford rivers and streams. On the 24th, he wrote:

Carrying me across one of the broad deep sedgy rivers is really a very difficult task . . . The first part, the main stream came up to Susi's mouth, and wetted my seat and legs. One held up my pistol behind, then one after another took a turn, and when one sank into a deep elephant's footprint, he required two to lift him.[6]

Not long afterwards, Livingstone was attacked by leeches, which clung to his body 'as close as smallpox', yet, as a naturalist, he used the experience to note the shape and size of their mandibles.[7] His diary entries at this harrowing time contain no self-pity and no complaint. The natural descriptions were as detailed as at any time in his life.

Caught in a drenching rain, which made me fain to sit, exhausted as I was under an umbrella for an hour . . . As I sat in the rain a little tree frog about half an inch long, leaped on to a grassy leaf and began a tune as loud as that of many birds, and very sweet; it was surprising to hear so much music out of so small a musician. I drank some rainwater as I felt faint – in the paths it is now calf deep.[8]

From now on loss of blood began to affect his thinking. He became more and more obsessive about the Nile and the four fountains of Herodotus, even writing draft despatches to the Foreign Secretary as if he had found them – only dates and geographical positions being omitted. 'I have the pleasure of reporting to your Lordship that on the [blank] I succeeded at last in reaching your four remarkable fountains, each of which, at no great distance off, become a large river . . .'[9] But, as he listened to the falling rain and the screams of the fish eagle, old doubts assailed him, to do with the height of the Lualaba at Nyangwe. Might he be at the source of the Congo rather than the Nile? He soon dismissed the thought and gave all his remaining energy to acquiring canoes to take him south through the marshes. At night, in the pouring rain the doctor and his men sheltered under their upturned canoes after the wind had torn their tents from their hands. 'A man put my bed into the bilge, so I was safe for a wet night.'[10]

On 25 March he wrote: 'Nothing earthly will make me give up my work in despair. I encourage myself in the Lord my God and go forward.' The following day they crossed the Chambesi, which flowed from the east into Lake Bangweulu and would one day be confirmed to be the most remote headstream of the Lualaba. A slave girl, belonging to Livingstone's long-serving follower Hamoydah Amoda, was drowned during the crossing. On 10 April, Livingstone at last admitted the gravity of his position: 'I am pale, bloodless and weak from bleeding profusely ever since the 31st of March last: an artery gives off a copious stream and takes away my strength. Oh! how I long to be permitted by the Over Power to finish my work.'[11]

At last they were on firmer ground beyond the immense marsh, travelling south-west. Though Livingstone had been content to be carried across streams, he hated being carried over land, but there was no hiding the fact that any exertion made him dizzy, so there was no help for it. He recorded how 'unearthly' he found the voice of the fish eagle. 'It is pitched in a high falsetto key, very loud and seems as if he were calling to someone in the other world.'[12]

Livingstone travelling through marshes weeks before his death
(from his published *Last Journals*).

He was now south of Bangweulu and travelling, as he had hoped to do in November, in a broad arc around the lake's southern shore. But then he had had the strength to achieve something, whereas now everything was irretrievably changed. He was very ill and in pain all the time, which he put down to fever. 'Bleeding and most other ailments in this land are forms of it.' On 19 April, although 'excessively weak' and unable to walk, he managed to ride his last surviving donkey for an hour and a half. That evening he wrote a sublime understatement: 'It is not all pleasure this exploration.'[13]

The following day he made his last detailed observations, though he was still noting down the number of hours marched each day. On 21 April he fell from his donkey and had to be carried to a hut in the nearby village. Even so he sent men to ask the chief for guides for the following day. Death was now near but he still refused to recognise it. Twenty years earlier, he had written: 'If God has accepted my service, then my life is charmed till my work is done.'[14] And his work was definitely not yet completed. On the 25th, after four days of being carried in a litter, the dying man summoned a number of local men and asked if any knew about a hill and four adjacent fountains. To his great disappointment, all shook their heads. The last entry in his diary was written on 27 April: 'Knocked up quite and remain: recover, sent to buy milch goats. We are on the banks of the R Molilamo.'[15] But the goats could not be found, and he could not eat the pounded mapira corn offered to him.

Amazingly on the 29th, he told his men to dismantle his hut, so that the litter could be brought right up to his bed. He could not have walked to the door of the hut and yet, while life remained, was determined to continue his search for the sources. As yet, his men were prepared to carry him. Yet crossing a river on that day, he had to be transferred into a canoe and the pain in his back, caused by the pressure of his men's hands as they lifted him, was excruciating. As would be seen later, there was a blood clot the size of a man's fist obstructing his lower intestine.[16] They were now seventy miles south of Bangweulu at the village of a chief called Chitambo. This was journey's end, and here his followers built a hut, and raised his grass and sacking bed from the floor on a frame of sticks, placing his medicine chest on a packing case by his bed.

Livingstone dozed through much of the 30th, but that evening the Nile still dominated his thoughts. 'Is this the Luapula?' he asked Susi suddenly. The Luapula is the river joining Bangweulu with Lake Moero and the Lualaba. Susi told him that they were still three days from the Luapula. 'Oh dear, dear!' he sighed and then fell asleep. That night, Majwara, the boy left to watch over Livingstone, fell asleep and did not wake for three or four hours.

At four in the morning, he burst into Susi's hut and begged him to come at once. A dim glow came from the entrance of the hut. A candle stuck with its own wax on to the top of a box was still burning. Livingstone was half-dressed and kneeling on his bed with his head resting on the pillow. It looked as though he was praying. Susi and the others did not go in at once but waited for some movement. When it did not come, they went in and one of them touched the kneeling man's cheek. It was almost cold. David Livingstone had been dead for several hours.[17]

Few if any of Livingstone's followers would have understood why he had risked his life, and indeed sacrificed it, in a vain attempt to establish the relationship of widely separated rivers and lakes to the distant River Nile. They, like the chief who had ridiculed Livingstone, by replying pityingly, when asked by him insistently about the Lualaba, 'It is only water,' would have found his obsession incomprehensible given the agony it caused him.[18] But his men knew extraordinary courage and determination when they saw them and respected him as a great man.

The legend would grow up that Chuma and Susi, two of his longest-serving men, would persuade the others to help them carry his body to the coast. This version of events owes a lot to their being brought back to Britain at the expense of a rich philanthropist to help Horace Waller edit *The Last Journals of David Livingstone in Central Africa*. The truth seems to have been more remarkable. The decision to risk carrying Livingstone's body to the coast – despite the high possibility of accusations of witchcraft being made *en route* – appears to have been made as a result of a much larger number of Africans achieving a consensus. Chuma's name would not be among those carved on the tree near which Livingstone's African servants buried their master's heart and organs. But the names of Chowpereh and Manwa Sera, who had both accompanied Stanley to Ujiji, and had been chosen by him to serve Livingstone on his last journey, were on the tree, along with Susi's. These three men had been made 'heads of department' by Livingstone. Chowpereh and Manwa Sera would go on and serve Stanley, as outstanding captains on his great trans-Africa journey a decade later, and Susi would work for him on the Congo in the early 1880s. The names of the three of them were carved by Jacob Wainwright, who had been educated at Nasik, along with the five other pupils of the Bombay mission school chosen by Stanley to travel with Livingstone. These men were Christians – at least by education – unlike Chuma and Susi, who were Muslims – and they would have played a significant part in the discussions that took place. Uledi and Mabruki were also senior men. They had already served Grant and Speke, and Stanley and would serve Stanley again. So the group of Africans who gathered around the hut they had built at Chitambo's village included some of the most experienced caravan leaders and captains in Africa, who would prove their outstanding abilities again and again. Given the extraordinary hardships of Livingstone's last journey through the swamps of Bangweulu, it is a striking fact that none of these men deserted.[19]

Perhaps self-interest and the hope of a reward played some part in the decision they made, but it seems more likely that their principal motivation was to honour a great man by taking his body back to his own people along with the diaries and notebooks which he had kept with such care. Their first step, after his death, was to hide from Chief Chitambo the fact that their master was dead, and to gain the chief's consent to build a hut within a palisade outside the village. The new structure was open to the sky so they could use the sun to dry out their master's body, once they had removed and buried his organs. It was while doing this grim work that they found a blood clot of several inches diameter in his lower intestine – an obstruction that must have caused him appalling pain. The rains had just ended so they were able to make use of sunlight to dry the body for two weeks, having placed salt in the open trunk. Eventually the body was encased in bark and sewn into a large piece of sailcloth. The odour of putrefaction made it hard for them to eat, so in an attempt to stop the smell, they tarred the whole bundle.[20]

Livingstone's men reached Zanzibar in the remarkable time of five months. By then ten men had died of disease, and they had once been obliged to fight their way out of a hostile village.[21] In Unyanyembe they met Lieutenant Verney Lovett Cameron, who had been chosen by the RGS, in preference to Stanley, to lead an expedition intended to assist Livingstone and solve the Nile mystery. Blind to the magnificence of what Livingstone's carriers were doing, Cameron advised them to take no further risks with superstitious chiefs along the route and to bury the body at once. This they politely refused to do. Cameron then urged them to part with Livingstone's geographical instruments, so his party could use them. To prevent any thefts, Jacob Wainwright had written out a long and accurate inventory of all Livingstone's possessions. None of the men wished to hand over their master's sextants and chronometers, but the white man was insistent, so they did as he asked.

At Zanzibar, John Kirk was away, and the acting consul, Captain W. F. Prideaux, paid them their wages but gave them no additional reward. For men like Susi, Chuma, Gardner and Amoda, this was a disillusioning conclusion to eight years' service. It would be a year till the RGS struck a medal for these men, but by then they would have dispersed, and very few ever received it. Of those who did, it cannot have meant as much to them as a gift of cloth, beads and cattle would have done.[22] By the time Chuma and Susi arrived in England, thanks to the generosity of Livingstone's friend, James Young – the inventor of paraffin – his burial in Westminster Abbey had already taken place. Only the comparative newcomer Jacob Wainwright, whose passage was paid by the Church Missionary Society, arrived in time for the funeral.

TWENTY-THREE

Where Will You Be?
Dead or Still Seeking the Nile?

Stanley first heard of Livingstone's death at the island of St Vincent during his voyage back to England from West Africa, and received official confirmation when he reached London on 17 March 1874. His mentor's body was even now on its way to Southampton. Grief-stricken at the news, Stanley wrote to Livingstone's 27-year-old daughter, Agnes, assuring her that 'no daughter was ever beloved so deeply as you were ... How I envy you such a father. The richest inheritance a father can give his children is an honoured name.' Yet Stanley believed that the doctor had also bequeathed something of immense importance to him as well. 'The completion of your father's discoveries,' he told Agnes, '[is] like a legacy left me by Livingstone.'[1] The story of Livingstone's lonely death and his refusal to give up his work after months of anguish and struggle conjured up powerful images of self-sacrifice and devotion to duty. In Stanley's eyes the geographical task of opening Africa was also part of a wider moral obligation which he described with feeling in the obituary he wrote for the *Graphic*:

Though the heart of Livingstone ... has ceased to beat, his voice rings out loud ... He has bequeathed a rich legacy to fight the evil horror of the slave trade ... and left an obligation on the civilized nations of Europe and America, as the shepherds of the world, to extend their care and protection over the oppressed races of Africa.[2]

Although Stanley grieved as he sat in the *New York Herald*'s London office, poring over the coverage of Livingstone's death, he was stirred by the thought that the doctor's unfinished work was newsworthy again. Here then was Stanley's great opportunity to escape from the dismissive snobs of the RGS, from his grasping mother and step-father, from Katie Roberts, who for cash had shown his love letters to an unscrupulous publisher, and most of all from the delusion that fame and wealth could make him happy. His hope of future happiness lay in striving for some great purpose, 'for my own spirit's satisfaction', as he put it. At the heart of the Nonconformist Christian education of the workhouse had been the idea of redemption through suffering – becoming a new man. And what would be more likely to achieve this re-fashioning than the isolation, the hardships and the pain he would endure while completing the work of his hero, David Livingstone? 'I was not sent into this world to be happy; I was sent for a special work,' he would write twenty years later.[3]

While Livingstone's death – and his burial in Westminster Abbey at which Stanley was a pall-bearer – did not determine the future course of Stanley's life, they certainly strengthened his existing determination to solve the Nile problem. He approached the proprietors of the *Daily Telegraph* and the *New York Herald* in such a positive spirit that they each offered £6,000 towards the cost of solving the age-old mystery. The journey he outlined to them would be the most ambitious ever attempted by a land explorer. First he intended to circumnavigate Lake Victoria in a portable boat to see if it was a single body of water and the primary source of the river that flowed out at Speke's Ripon Falls. It might turn out to be, as Burton had predicted, three or more lakes of little individual consequence. Then he meant to sail around Lake Tanganyika to see what other rivers – apart from the Rusizi – flowed into and out of it. This, he expected, would establish once and for all whether Tanganyika was part of the Nile's system. Then, finally, he would attempt to navigate the Lualaba from where Livingstone had left it at Nyangwe, to see whether it was the upper Nile or the Congo – potentially a 7,000-mile journey dwarfing all earlier African expeditions.

Just as he began the detailed planning of his epic journey, Stanley fell in love with a spoilt young heiress. Alice Pike was the seventeen-year-old daughter of one of America's richest men, who owned real estate, distilleries and two opera houses. Stanley met Alice while they were both staying at London's exclusive Langham Hotel. Although twice her age, the infatuated explorer soon proposed and was accepted, although he thought Alice 'the very opposite of my ideal wife . . . However pretty, elegant etc. she may be, she is heartless and a confirmed flirt.'[4] Given his sensitive nature, Stanley was risking emotional catastrophe and knew it.

Alice Pike.

While he was pursuing Alice, scores of gentlemen and officers were pursuing *him* in the hope of being taken on his expedition. But the 'gentlemen' of the RGS had already ensured that Stanley would choose working-class companions. The three he selected were young brothers, Frank and Edward Pocock, oystermen from the Medway, who looked after the editor of the *Daily Telegraph*'s yacht, and Frederick Barker, a clerk at the Langham Hotel, who had pestered him until he gave in. Not one of these three men had even been abroad. Kalulu, the slave boy, whom

Stanley had rescued and sent to school in Wandsworth, was told that he would be returning to his own country as his master's valet. He, of course, knew all about Africa, and was not sure that he wished to return there. These four improbable adventurers were about to embark upon one of the greatest journeys of all time. It seems unlikely that Stanley would have reminded them of the fate of Shaw and Farquhar on his last journey, or of the deaths of Cameron's two white companions, which had recently been reported.

On arriving at Zanzibar, the engagement of African porters, translators, guards and servants became Stanley's priority. These men would be more important for his survival than his trio of inexperienced Europeans. So it delighted him that Mabruki Speke, Chowpereh, Uledi and Ferajji, who had accompanied him to Ujiji, all wanted to serve him again. Also eager to come was Manwa Sera, who with Chowpereh had been leaders of the party Stanley had sent to join Livingstone on his final expedition. All these Africans were Wangwana – the black free men of Zanzibar – originally coerced or enticed from their tribal environments by slave and ivory traders operating deep in the interior. Stanley considered them 'clever, honest, industrious, docile, enterprising, brave and moral'.[5]

On 17 November 1874, he led into the interior a party of 228 people, which included sixteen wives and mistresses and ten children belonging to his African captains.[6] The expedition's first objective was to reach the Victoria Nyanza, 700 miles away, and sail round it. Just as he had done when describing his journey to find Livingstone, he would exaggerate his numbers when writing about this new expedition – claiming that he took 356 people into the interior.[7] Once again this would serve to devalue his true achievement and lead historians to see him as an entirely new type of explorer with unlimited manpower, weaponry and resources. In order to get to the Nyanza, Stanley chose to pioneer a direct route, rather than go via Tabora. The rains started in December, and the men soon began to slip and fall on the clayey path under their sixty-pound loads. By January

1875, the expedition had reached an endless tableland covered with dwarf acacia, mimosa and rank-smelling gum trees. No tree was taller than the others and the forest was so thick that it was impossible to avoid the thorns and stubby branches which threatened their eyes and faces. There was no game in the forest, and, even worse, it appeared to be waterless. After eight days in this hellish environment, five men died of dehydration and another four weakened, fell behind and could not be found.[8]

The Pocock brothers, Edward (*left*) and Frank (*right*).

Emerging at last in a land of cultivated fields and cattle, Stanley's followers believed themselves safe. But it soon became apparent that local Wanyaturu tribesmen would only come near them if 'carrying a prodigious quantity of arms – spears, bows and arrows and knobsticks'.[9] Edward Pocock contracted smallpox and died, while the local chief was issuing threats to them to leave his territory. Stanley read the burial service in a shaking voice while Frank Pocock wept over the grave. Frederick Barker, Stanley's storekeeper and clerk, was seriously ill with fever, but the Wanyaturu warriors would allow no dallying on their land. Even after a porter in the rearguard was hacked to pieces, Stanley advised against any attempts at revenge. But when another of his men was stabbed to death, and about a hundred tribesmen fired arrows into his camp, he authorised retaliation. In the fight that followed, his men disobeyed orders and chased after their attackers, killing six Wanyaturu but losing three of their own number to poisoned arrows. A further fifteen of Stanley's people were driven away, never to be seen again. At the end of this disastrous skirmish, twenty-two of his party were missing, presumed dead. By the time his caravan reached the Victoria Nyanza on 27 February 1875, Stanley had lost sixty-two men out of his original 228, either through illness, or desertion, or at the hands of hostile Africans. At this rate, he feared he would have none left long before his journey ended. But soon after this sad event, Frank Pocock raced down from the brow of a hill, shouting: 'I have seen the lake, sir, and it is grand!'

Although the morale of Stanley's men was boosted by the attainment of their first objective, he himself was depressed by private worries. Before leaving Zanzibar, he had received some worrying letters from his fiancée, Alice, who had accused him of being 'real mean about writing', and informed him that she was 'real angry with Africa', because his letters took so long to reach her. Pressed about precisely when he might return, Stanley had admitted in a letter sent from Zanzibar that his journey could last three years rather than the two he had promised when they had been in England together. Her reply had not made pleasant reading: 'And suppose you are not home then, where will you be? Dead or still seeking the Nile?'[10] The strong possibility that she might not wait filled him with foreboding, causing him to say to a journalist friend that he felt 'a careless indifference as to what fate might have in store'.[11]

Certainly his plan to sail around the lake in the twenty-four-foot *Lady Alice*, with eleven crewmen and a guide was a very brave one.[12] All the more so, since he had been shocked to find that Arab slave dhows were sailing on the Nyanza, turning every local tribe against strangers. By venturing on the water, Stanley would therefore be running a real risk of being surrounded by hostile canoes. Yet he could not hope to map the lake by travelling overland, unless he devoted a year or more to this one task. So in a boat it would have to be – although at night he and his men would have to sleep ashore, exposing themselves to attack. Furthermore, as the only white man in the boat (Frank Pocock having been left in charge of the expedition's lakeside base camp), Stanley could expect to be murdered if his men ever mutinied. But, under the command of Wadi Safeni, and Uledi, his steersman, he believed his crew to be not merely loyal but exceptionally intrepid. 'Their names,' he declared, 'should be written in gold.'

Local people at Kagehyi (Kayenzi), where the expedition had first reached the lake, warned his rowers that they would meet 'people gifted with tails; enormous fierce dogs of war; cannibals who preferred human flesh above all'. His men were also told that the lake was so large that it might take two years to trace its shores, and that few of them were likely to survive that long. It is a great tribute to Stanley's leadership that his men were prepared to embark with him on 7 March.[13]

Indeed, when sailing northwards up the eastern side of the lake, the *Lady Alice* was trapped by thirteen canoes and Stanley was only able to engineer their escape by shooting at and sinking one of these vessels, killing three men.[14] By the time Stanley reached the north-eastern corner of the lake, on 27 March, he had established that from north to south the lake measured more than 200 miles. He and his men had sailed almost 500 miles in all, greatly assisted by southerly winds, which had enabled them to sail rather than row for much of their voyage at a rate of over twenty miles per day. This was despite coming through several terrifying tropical storms.

In general Stanley mapped the lake well, with his worst two errors being to miss the deceptive entrance to the massive Kavirondo Bay, and to fail to get close enough inshore to gauge the true size of the lake's south-western corner. But by late March he had proved that Burton, Schweinfurth and the garrulous armchair theorist, McQueen, had been plain wrong to have argued against the Nyanza being a single sheet of water. Suspecting from the start that this would prove to be the case, Stanley had named the substantial bight at the lake's south-eastern corner, Speke Gulf. He found no outflow anywhere during his voyage along the eastern shore; and the first he came to, after reaching the north-eastern corner, was Speke's Ripon Falls.

Here, on 28 March, Stanley ordered his men to take down their sails and row to the falls, 'the noise of whose rushing waters sounded loud and clear in our ears'. Stanley told readers of the *New York Herald* that 'Speke had been most accurate in his description of the outgoing river.' But neither in this despatch, nor in his diary did Stanley positively indentify this river as the Nile – the closest he came was to call it 'the great river outflowing [*sic*] northwards'.[15]

Of course it was still possible that the Lualaba might join the Nile to the north and west of Lake Albert (indeed this was what Livingstone had believed), and Stanley was determined to address this possibility in due course. But for the present, Speke's claim that the White Nile flowed out from Victoria Nyanza was an assertion which Stanley took very seriously.

On 4 April 1875 the *Lady Alice* sailed on westwards along the northern shore of the Nyanza, arriving later that day at the king of Buganda's lakeside hunting resort of Usavara. Mutesa was still *kabaka* – as he had been when Speke had stayed in Buganda. On hearing of Stanley's approach, the *kabaka* sent six canoes to meet his white visitor, and ordered 2,000 warriors to greet him at the shore and then accompany him to the royal residence. There Stanley was presented with ten oxen, sixteen sheep and three dozen chickens. The Mutesa, whom Stanley believed he now got to know, was very different from the violent and sadistic young man Speke had written about. Stanley attributed the *kabaka*'s surprisingly gentlemanly manner to his being a dozen years older, and to the influence of Khamis bin Abdullah al-Barwani, an Arab ivory trader, who had lived at court for a year. Stanley had met Khamis at Tabora and had found him the most personally attractive of all the Arabs there.[16]

A few months earlier, Stanley had written in his diary that 'he often entertained lofty ideas concerning regenerative civilization, and the redemption of Africa'.[17] If Livingstone had ever been in his present situation, Stanley was sure he would have summoned Christian missionaries to Mutesa's court. If the country became the first in central Africa to embrace Islam, there would be profound consequences for the whole continent. Stanley suspected that Mutesa's claim to be a Muslim did not run much deeper than his courtiers' liking for Arab daggers and embroidered jackets, and he was determined to test his theory. This was not primarily a religious issue for him. The shocking truth was that Mutesa had allowed his country to become 'the northern source of the [East African] slave trade';[18] so if nothing were done, a link would inevitably be formed between Buganda and the Muslim slave traders in Sudan, with the terrible consequence that the land of the Acholi, the Madi and the Dinka would become a slave-producing wasteland. Stanley's determination that this should not happen would make his visit to Buganda not simply a defining moment in Africa's exploration, but a major event in its history.

As soon as Stanley could obtain the *kabaka*'s permission for such a course, he wrote a letter to the *New York Herald* and the *Daily Telegraph* appealing for missionaries to come to Buganda.[19] By an extraordinary coincidence, a few days after Stanley's landing at Usavara, another white man arrived at Mutesa's court. He was Colonel Ernest Linant de Bellefonds, who had been sent by the Egyptian government on a diplomatic mission. This French officer was under the direct orders of Colonel Charles Gordon, known to the British public as 'Chinese Gordon' due to his earlier victory over the Taiping rebels. Now Gordon was serving the *khedive* of Egypt, Ismail Pasha, as governor of Sudan's most southerly province, Equatoria. De Bellefonds was therefore able to take Stanley's letter of appeal north with him, and guarantee its early arrival in Britain. Within weeks of its appearance in the *Daily Telegraph*, £24,000 would be raised for a Bugandan mission, and a year later the first British missionaries would arrive, with momentous consequences – as will be seen – for that country's future.

The well-provisioned Frenchman gave Stanley a supper of *pâté de foie gras* and sardines in his tent and then handed him a letter from Gordon, written four months earlier. The Governor of Equatoria explained that, at the time of writing, he was steaming up the Nile, south of Gondokoro, constructing trading stations as he voyaged upstream towards Lake Albert.[20] It was still Stanley's intention, when he returned to Buganda with his whole party, to travel north-west to Lake Albert to explore it thoroughly, as Baker had failed to do. So it piqued him to think that by now Gordon had probably already circumnavigated the lake. De Bellefonds could shed no light on this, but he did tell Stanley that in June 1874 another subordinate of Gordon, Colonel Charles Chaillé-Long, an American of French ancestry, had been sent to Buganda to see whether it might be possible to annexe the country to Egypt and incorporate it into the Sudan. (This news meant that Stanley was the fourth white man to have reached Buganda and not the third – after Speke and Grant – as he had previously imagined.) De Bellefonds explained that it was Khedive Ismail's dream to extend his empire southwards along the entire length of the Nile, up to its supposed source, the Victoria Nyanza. In 1874, Colonel Chaillé-Long had sailed downstream from the Ripon Falls to become the first white man to see straggling Lake Kyoga, and its surrounding area of water-lily wetlands. Although he had not navigated his way through this shallow lake to establish a link with Lake Albert, Stanley was sure that Gordon would soon send someone who would.[21]

Before meeting de Bellefonds, Stanley had been aware that Mutesa was at odds with the king of Bunyoro and wanted modern European guns in order to bring him to heel, but his conversations with the Frenchman established that Mutesa's more urgent need of weapons was to enable him to oppose Gordon's advances into his territory. Despite his liking for de Bellefonds, Stanley loathed the idea of Buganda and its surrounding territories becoming part of Muslim Egypt's empire. So he sympathised with the *kabaka*'s hope that by attracting more white men to his country, he would be able to buy guns from them and gain their help against the autocratic Khedive Ismail. Mutesa's longing for such weapons became keener still after he saw Stanley shoot dead a baby crocodile at a distance of more than a hundred yards. No Arab gun, he was sure, could have achieved this magical result. Although knowing that the *kabaka*'s motive for allowing missionaries to enter his country was part of a planned strategy, Stanley, for his own purposes, exaggerated Mutesa's enthusiasm for Christianity in his newspaper despatches. The explorer was not gullible, and was perfectly aware that an African ruler with 300 wives would be no pushover for missionaries insisting upon strict monogamy. But if Stanley had admitted to his readers in Britain that Mutesa had his own agenda, and was not as 'civilised' as he had suggested in print, the missionaries might well have had second thoughts about coming. The future of the whole region was at stake, and he knew he was lucky that Mutesa had given his permission for Christian missionaries to come. Ironically, Ismail's employee de Bellefonds had played a crucial part in convincing the *kabaka* that Christianity was not a sect but the religion of all white men. A Calvinist himself, the Frenchman had helpfully kept quiet about religious divisions in Europe.[22]

Stanley left Buganda on 21 April 1875 and sailed southwards down the western shore of the Nyanza, after waiting in vain for Mutesa to provide a promised escort of thirty canoes. In these vessels, he had hoped to transport all his men back across the lake to Buganda from Kagehyi on the southern shore, so they could accompany him to Lake Albert.

The *Lady Alice* was two-thirds of the way to Kagehyi, when Stanley became embroiled in the first act of a two-part tragedy that would dog him for the rest of his life. For three days his crew had been rowing into a strong headwind, with their sails furled. The only food they had managed to purchase for forty-eight hours had been a few fish. So when a large island, Bumbireh, came into view, they prayed that they would be able to buy food there. But as they ran their boat up on a sandy beach, they heard war cries and saw about sixty spearmen rushing across the sand towards them. Stanley raised his revolver, but his men begged him not to fire because they were too hungry to face the lake again. Against his better judgement, Stanley offered no resistance as his boat was dragged up the beach, with him and his crew inside it. Warriors clustered around the *Lady Alice*, pointing spears, pulling at their hair, and jabbing at Stanley and his men with sticks and clubs.

Stanley's reception on Bumbireh.

Several terrifying hours passed, during which Stanley was constantly afraid that they were about to be massacred. But his cool-headed interpreter and coxswain, Wadi Safeni, kept talking. He seemed to have negotiated their release with a large payment of cloth and beads, when Shekka, the chief of the islanders, appeared and ordered the seizure of their oars. Stanley knew they would be killed unless they could launch their boat immediately. With the strength of absolute desperation his men manhandled their craft into the lake, and tore up the bottom boards to use as paddles, working as arrows fell in the water around them. Meanwhile, Stanley fired at their pursuers with his elephant gun, killing one man and seriously wounding another.

Disastrously for his future reputation, Stanley believed that all newspaper editors liked to offer their readers buckets of blood, as his own had done during the American Indian Wars. His memory of this persuaded him to tell the readers of the *Daily Telegraph* and *New York Herald* that he had killed nine or ten people, and not an unexciting one or two. Pleasing editors apart, Stanley's lifelong insecurity meant that he was never able to let people think that anyone had ever got the better of him.[23]

On his return to Kagehyi, Stanley's pressing problem remained how to transport to Buganda the 155 men whom Frank Pocock had fed and kept together while he had been away. Frank was now his only white companion, since Frederick Barker, the hotel clerk, had died of malaria two weeks earlier. After his horrifying experience on Bumbireh, Stanley wanted to travel overland to Buganda. But this became impossible when the rulers of two lakeside kingdoms announced that they would fight him if he attempted the land route. He was therefore obliged to look for canoes, eventually managing to purchase twenty-three frail and leaky specimens. In these, he embarked most of his men on 20 June. Two days later, a storm sank five, and proved to Stanley that he could not risk heading out into the middle of the Nyanza to avoid passing the island where he and his men had narrowly escaped death. So there seemed no alternative to sailing through the strait between the island and the equally hostile mainland. Even when Mutesa sent fifteen fully crewed dugouts to assist him, Stanley still feared attack by a superior number of lighter, more manoeuvrable Bumbireh canoes when he entered the narrows.

To gauge the mood of the islanders, he sent a delegation to buy food. These men were met with a hail of spears and arrows, which killed one of them, and mortally wounded six others.[24] Since the men of Bumbireh had just been reinforced by Antari, ruler of the lakeside kingdom opposite, Stanley and his Baganda (Bugandan) allies felt they either had to abandon the attempt to reach Buganda, or make a pre-emptive strike to ensure that they themselves were not overwhelmed in the strait.[25] So Stanley ordered the crew of the *Lady Alice* to sail close to the shore of

Bumbireh, enabling his riflemen to pick off warriors who had gathered to prevent a landing. These tribesmen with their bows and arrows posed no risk to Stanley and his men, but thirty-three of them were killed; and this undeniable fact left Stanley vulnerable to accusations of murder.

At the time – so convinced was he that he would have put his entire party at risk unless administering this violent shock – he did not anticipate serious objections to his behaviour on his return to Britain. In West Africa, he had recently witnessed General Sir Garnet Wolseley's army kill 2,000 spear-carrying Asante warriors with the latest European field artillery and receive no censure on its return. Yet Stanley knew that unlike Sir Garnet, he had acted only for himself, without the sanction of any government. 'We went into the heart of Africa self invited,' he wrote later, 'therein lies our fault. But it was not so grave that our lives [when threatened] should be forfeited.'[26] Claiming self-defence, he went on to write openly in his newspaper despatches about the numbers killed on his second visit to Bumbireh.

Colonel Gordon was regularly involved in hostile encounters with the Bari tribe in southern Sudan. Indeed the Bari murdered Ernest Linant de Bellefonds shortly after he had delivered Stanley's letter. So Gordon knew that there were often occasions when travellers faced a situation of kill or be killed. 'These things may be done but not advertised,' the future martyr of Khartoum confided to Richard Burton.[27] The mauling Stanley received in the British liberal press was destined to damage his moral reputation so seriously that his unique journey, revealing so many of the secrets of the African central watershed, would never win for him the praise and recognition it would otherwise have done.

The expedition reached Buganda in mid-August to find that Mutesa was at war with his neighbours to the east (the Wavuma), so Stanley was denied all help for four months and only travelled north-west in early January 1876. But he and his Baganda escort were driven back from Lake Albert by a large party of Bunyoro warriors. Stanley had no alternative but to head south for Lake Tanganyika – his next objective.

En route, he spent several weeks exploring the Kagera river, which flowed into the western side of Lake Victoria. Stanley had first seen this rapidly flowing river before meeting Mutesa the previous April. Over eighty feet deep in places and 120 yards wide, he suspected that the Kagera was 'the real parent of the Victoria Nile' and was therefore eager to trace it into Rwanda. But, once again, he was driven back by hostile Africans, when correctly believing himself on the brink of 'another grand discovery'.[28] Two months later, still travelling south towards Lake Tanganyika, Stanley met Mirambo, the Nyamwezi ruler, whom he dubbed 'the African Napoleon'. Mirambo had with him an army of 15,000 men, including child soldiers, and was reputed to have killed many thousands of people, so Stanley must have been scared. He sensibly raised no objections when invited to become the warlord's blood brother.

On 27 May 1876, Stanley reached Ujiji, and although distraught to find no letters from Alice, he did receive other good news, which he at once put in a letter to Edward Levy-Lawson, the owner of the *Daily Telegraph*:

We have obtained a signal triumph over Cameron, the Protégé of the RGS, whose attainments were said to be vastly superior to those of Burton, Speke, Livingstone & Baker – if Markham [secretary of the RGS] was to be believed . . . By crossing the Lualaba and striking off in the wrong direction he [Cameron] has left the question of the Lualaba where Livingstone left it.[29]

Cameron had bowed to pressure from the notorious Arab slave trader Tippu Tip, and had abandoned his aim of following the Lualaba north from Nyangwe. Instead he had marched south-west on a trans-continental journey of no particular geographical significance. So if Stanley could avoid dying, *he* would be the one to finish Livingstone's work and become, in a century of great explorers, the greatest.

He completed in a mere fifty-one days the circumnavigation of Lake Tanganyika, which Speke and Burton, and Cameron had all failed to achieve. Stanley confirmed Cameron's surmise that the River Lukuga was the lake's only outflow and apparently drained into the Lualaba. This fact – in conjunction with the relative heights of Tanganyika, Victoria and the Lualaba at Nyangwe – made him suspect that Lake Tanganyika was very likely part of the Congo's system, rather than the Nile's. If so, he could expect a far longer and more dangerous journey to the Atlantic than the one he might otherwise have taken down the Lualaba to the Bahr el-Ghazal and then the Nile. So he sat down to write Alice what he believed might well be the last letter she ever received from him, 'until I meet you or death meets me'.[30]

TWENTY-FOUR

The Unknown Half of Africa
Lies Before Me

—⊗⊗⊗—

In London, six months before Stanley left Lake Tanganyika for the Lualaba, Christopher Rigby, Speke's devoted friend, had walked all over the City in an attempt to get hold of copies of the edition of the *Daily Telegraph* which contained Stanley's first despatches from Lake Victoria. Colonel Rigby's search had ended in frustration, since 'every copy had been bought at once'. In the end, he had been obliged to go to the RGS where he had read the newspaper and had then been shown 'Stanley's original map of the Victoria Lake', which overjoyed him by being 'in shape so very near to what Speke made it'.[1]

Richard Burton was another early visitor to the RGS. He came again on 29 November 1875, well-prepared for the debate on Stanley's discoveries. But if Rigby had expected that 'B the B', as Speke had called Burton, would apologise for having poured scorn so groundlessly, for over a decade, on his travelling companion's account of the Nyanza, he must have been thunderstruck to hear Burton say that he 'still regarded it as possible that the Tanganyika might be connected with the Nile [because] by some curious possibility the Lukuga would be found to be the ultimate source'. Burton hypocritically 'expressed his heartfelt sorrow that his old companion had not been spared ... to see the *corrections* [my emphasis] which Mr Stanley had made with regard to his [Speke's] wonderful discovery of that magnificent water that sent forth the eastern arm of the Nile'. The western arm, Burton still maintained, would spring from *his* Lake Tanganyika – his hope being that the Lukuga would flow into the Lualaba, which would in turn join the Nile somewhere above Lake Albert, as Livingstone had believed it would.[2]

Meanwhile, in Africa, Stanley had not quite ruled out such a scenario. As he marched through Manyema towards the Lualaba, he still yearned for that river to be the Nile – not for Burton's sake of course – but to vindicate the hopes of his honorary father, David Livingstone. Before crossing Lake Tanganyika, Stanley had been plagued by desertions so his party was now down to 132 individuals, most of them terrified by the dangers that might lie ahead on the river. Kalulu, the youth whom Stanley had rescued and educated, was one of the deserters. After he was recaptured, Stanley would not be able to forgive him. Yet, in the end, it would be clear that Kalulu's decision to escape had been the right one. He would surely have reached adulthood, if he had only managed to avoid recapture.[3]

On 17 October 1876, the expedition arrived on the banks of the Lualaba, and Stanley saw, for the first time, an immense pale-grey river winding its way slowly northwards into the unknown, between densely wooded banks. For the sake of the Lualaba, Livingstone had sacrificed himself, but, like Cameron, had failed to follow it beyond Nyangwe. Stanley had no means of knowing how far it would flow to the north before deviating to east or west, declaring its kinship to the Nile or to the Congo.

The following day he met the most important Arab-Swahili slave trader in Manyema, Hamid bin Muhammad el-Murebi (whose nickname Tippu Tip was supposed to mimic the sound of bullets; a grandmother had been the daughter of a Lomani chief, explaining his African appearance). He had the power to guarantee or to deny Stanley the canoes and other supplies which were essential for his voyage downstream. So the explorer felt he had no choice but to do a deal with him, rather than be stopped from following the river. The Arab also had men to spare as an escort to protect Stanley's people from hostile tribes along the Lualaba immediately to the north of Nyangwe. These tribes were dangerous to strangers because of slave raids made by men like Tippu Tip, but Stanley would still need protection and was prepared to pay him the amazing sum of $5,000 (the entire cost of his Livingstone quest) to accompany him with 140 armed men for sixty marches north of Nyangwe. If he failed to reach agreement with the Arab, Stanley knew he would fail in his mission. Cameron had tried to cut a similar deal, but Tippu Tip had turned him down. Stanley's deal did not mark a lessening of his hatred for slave traders. In a despatch written at this time, he urged Britain to act militarily against 'a traffic especially obnoxious to humanity – a traffic founded on violence, murder, robbery and fraud'.[4]

Tippu Tip.

The agreement was that Tippu Tip's men would part company with Stanley after about 200 miles, and thereafter the explorer and his 146 followers, only 107 of whom were contracted men, would take their chances on their own. Inevitably, death by drowning, disease, starvation, and by African attacks would reduce their numbers by journey's end. Before marching out of Nyangwe with Tippu Tip on 5 November 1876 into the Mitamba forest, Stanley wrote to a friend admitting that he feared he might share the fate of the explorer Mungo Park, who had been speared to death on the Niger.

But I will not go back ... The unknown half of Africa lies before me. It is useless to imagine what it may contain ... I cannot tell whether I shall be able to reveal it in person or it will be left to my dark followers. In three or four days we shall begin the great struggle with this mystery.[5]

For weeks, Stanley's people and their Arab-Swahili escort struggled along the eastern bank of the great river, beneath the canopy of the tropical forest, sweating in the dark hothouse air. On this side of the river, it would be impossible for him to miss any eastward-flowing branch which the river might throw out towards the Nile via the Bahr el-Ghazal. Since the Lualaba seemed large enough to supply both the Nile and the Congo, Stanley still did not discount the possibility of such a branch existing: 'It may be so, as there are more wonders in Africa than are dreamed of in the common philosophy of geography.'[6] After two weeks spent hacking their way through the forest, his followers embarked upon the Lualaba itself, having recently made the gruesome discovery of charred human bones near recently extinguished cooking fires.[7] But cannibals or not, Stanley was distressed to see men, women and children of the Wenya people running away whenever they caught sight of Tippu Tip's men and his own.

In December, while still paddling due north, they were involved in a series of small skirmishes which Stanley foolishly dramatised as 'fights' in his despatches to the *New York Herald*.[8] Two days after Christmas, Tippu Tip broke his agreement and returned to Nyangwe. He had just lost three of his wives to smallpox, and in a five-day period seven of his soldiers died of tropical ulcers and fever. Since they were now only 125 miles north of Nyangwe, rather than the 200 they had agreed to travel together, Stanley paid Tippu half the agreed sum.[9] In order to persuade his entire party to embark in the twenty-three canoes he had just bought for them, Stanley had to get Tippu Tip to threaten to shoot them if they did not. Otherwise, most would have begged the Arab to take them back to Nyangwe – such was their terror of sailing on the river. And who can blame them? From its banks, they often heard the cry: "*Niama, niama* [meat, meat]', and the inhabitants

313

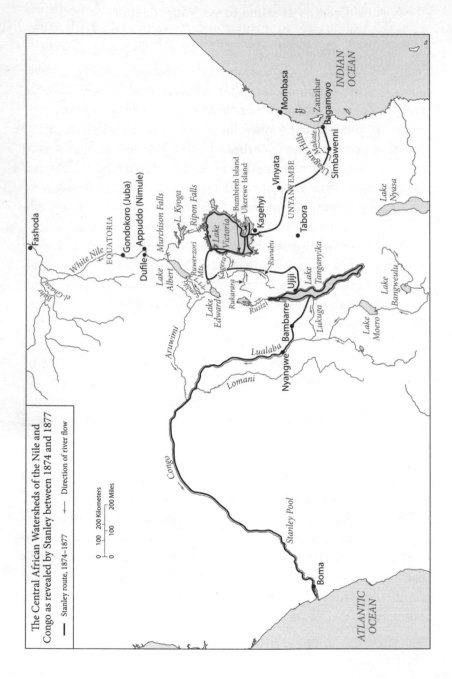

The Central African Watersheds of the Nile and
Congo as revealed by Stanley between 1874 and 1877

—— Stanley route, 1874–1877   ◄— Direction of river flow

0   100   200 Kilometers
0   100   200 Miles

of one village tried to catch an entire boat's crew in a large net. 'They considered us as game to be trapped, shot, or bagged at sight,' wrote Stanley. But he knew there was nothing he could do to allay the suspicions his presence provoked. The slave traders had seen to that. So, whenever aggressively pursued by canoes propelled by more paddlers than his own and therefore faster, he felt obliged to shoot rather than let his vessels be boarded.[10]

On 6 January, after travelling 500 miles due north from Nyangwe, they came to the first cataract in a chain of seven that extended for sixty miles. Now all his boats had to be taken out of the water and dragged overland past each one of these seven cataracts, most of which extended for several miles. The noise of the river crashing over rocks and funnelling through gorges was so loud that his men could not hear each other speak, even when standing side by side. Their progress along the falls took twenty-four days. Now at last the truth became apparent. Soon after passing the final cataract, Stanley realised that the river had turned sharply westwards.

Then, on 7 February 1877, for the very first time, he heard the river referred to as 'Ikuta Yacongo'. This was an historic moment. Two years and two months into his extraordinary journey, Stanley had proved that the Lualaba was the Upper Congo and not the Nile. The Lualaba's northward drive for a thousand miles from its source, where Livingstone had died, to the point where it turned decisively westwards would never again deceive geographers and explorers. But whether he would live to bring this news home in person, or 'whether it would be left to [his] dark followers to reveal it', was far from certain. He was still 850 miles from the Atlantic.[11]

Speke's case was proved, and Burton's and Livingstone's had been destroyed. Stanley was glad for Speke's memory and deplored how the RGS had turned against him after his death. But his deepest emotions were reserved for:

that old, brave explorer ... [and] the terrible determination which [had] animated him ... Poor Livingstone! I wish I had the power of some perfect master of the English language to describe what I feel about him.[12]

*

But had Stanley really unravelled the entire mystery that had baffled every generation since the ancients? When he had expressed his belief that the Kagera was probably 'the parent of the Victoria [White] Nile', had he meant to downgrade the importance of Speke's outlet at Ripon Falls? In a despatch to the *New York Herald* dated August 1876, Stanley repeated the question originally posed by Speke: 'What should be called the source of a river – a lake which receives the insignificant rivers flowing into it and discharges all by one great outlet, or the tributaries which the lake collects?'[13] Stanley suggested that if the tributaries were favoured, it would be but one step further to see 'sources' in the moisture and vapour which the clouds absorb. So he gave his vote to Speke.

Speke had first seen the Kagera in 1861, when staying with King Rumanika, and had called it the Kitangule. The explorer knew that this important river formed a series of small lakes, and deduced that its origins lay in springs and in rain precipitated on the mountains of Rwanda. One evening, he glimpsed what he called 'bold sky-scraping volcanic cones' fifty miles to the west. Showing astonishing insight, he described these mountains as 'the turning point of the central African watershed', as indeed they are, along with the more northerly Ruwenzori Mountains.[14]

So what of the Kagera and its highland sources, which Speke had dismissed with his rhetorical question about the respective merits of 'one great outlet [and] the tributaries which the lake collects'? It would not be until 1891 – when Burundi, Rwanda and Tanzania were classified as constituent parts of German East Africa – that an Austrian ethnographer and explorer, Dr Oscar Baumann, traced what appeared to be the most southerly tributary of the Kagera, the Ruvubu, to a point in southern Burundi about fifty miles to the south of the northern tip of Tanganyika and twenty miles east of the lake. In 1935, Dr Burckhardt Waldecker, who had fled the persecution of the Jews in Nazi Germany, found a marginally more southerly source on nearby Mount Kikizi. But being further south was not the only quality required to gain the prize. In 1898, Dr Richard Kandt, a German physician, scientist and poet, had traced the main line of the Kagera – judged by volume of water – via its Rukarara tributary to Mount Bigugu, near the southern end of Lake Kivu. This spring was alleged to be thirty-six miles further from the Mediterranean than the Kikizi source – a tiny superiority given the Nile's total length of just over 4,200 miles. But given the huge technical difficulty of calculating the length of such a long river, a definitive result will always elude geographers. A complex delta and the shifting channels in Lake Kyoga and the Sudd's floodplain pose particular problems.[15]

During the last fifty years, the line of the Rukarara has been shown to extend a little further into the Nyungwe Forest than Kandt had demonstrated. But in a marshy area of many springs, it is hard to pick out an unassailable Kagera source. Although Neil McGrigor and his Anglo-New Zealand party claimed to have added another sixty miles to the Nile with the help of GPS in 2006, it should be noted that similar claims to have extended the river beyond Kandt's source had been made in the 1960s on behalf of Father Stephan Bettentrup, a German priest living in Rwanda. Then, at the end of the last decade, a Japanese party from Waseda University also claimed to have outdistanced Kandt.[16] In my opinion, to add a few miles to the shifting upper springs and streamlets of the Rukarara does not dethrone Richard Kandt, let alone threaten the achievements of the Victorian explorers who entered Africa without maps, wheeled transport, or effective medicines, and yet solved the mystery of the entire central African watershed.

In 1875–76, when Stanley proved Speke right about Lake Victoria, the possibility had existed that a river flowing northwards into the southern end of Lake Albert might originate somewhere in the region of Lake Tanganyika (though unconnected with that lake) making it a convincing rival to the headwaters of the Kagera as the ultimate source. Indeed, such a river *did* exist. When Stanley had believed himself to be approaching Lake

Albert in 1876, he had glimpsed a significant expanse of water, shortly before being chased away by Nyoro tribesmen. He had not known it at the time, but this was a small 'undiscovered' lake, linked to a larger one, together constituting the source of the Semliki river which flowed on northwards until entering the southern end of Lake Albert. Amazingly, the Semliki was not investigated in 1876, when Lake Albert was circumnavigated by Gordon's temperamental lieutenant, Romolo Gessi.[17] Eventually, it would fall to Stanley, in 1889, to map the Semliki and explore the two lakes – Edward and George – which were its sources.

Over a dozen years before the mapping of the Semliki, Stanley's companion Frank Pocock had spotted something of great significance: 'a fine mountain crowned with snow'. The two men and their party had been camped near Lake Edward. Unfortunately, Frank had been ill and had failed to mention the snow to Stanley, so a major discovery had to wait over a decade.[18] Misty weather would prevent Baker, Gessi and Emin Pasha from seeing the Ruwenzori Mountains in 1864, 1876 and 1884 respectively. But in 1888 and 1889, Stanley and two of his officers, Dr Thomas Parke and Arthur Mounteney Jephson, all caught sight of the snow-capped Ruwenzoris, which they immediately linked to Ptolemy's Mountains of the Moon. While tracing the course of the Semliki southwards towards its source, Stanley crossed almost sixty torrents flowing into this river from the foothills of the mountains. He recognised at once the mountains' rain-making role and saw that melting snow, as well as precipitation, supplied the Nile via the Semliki and Albert. But the Semliki's twin sources turned out to be on the same latitude as the northern shores of Lake Victoria, so although the river's considerable volume made a very important contribution to the White Nile, it could not outrank the Kagera's twin branches.

What militates most against the Kagera and its tributaries being considered the true source of the Nile – rather than the principal feeder of Lake Victoria – is that the Kagera's outflow into Victoria is separated from Speke's Ripon Falls by 120 miles of lake, and so cannot with justice be said to be part of a continuous river. So,

David Livingstone in 1866 before his last
departure from Britain.

Richard Burton posing in Arab clothes in 1865,
a year after Speke's death.

James S. Jameson, who sketched a girl being killed, cooked and eaten.

Major Edmund Barttelot, who flogged men to death and was murdered.

Stanley (aged forty-six) and Anthony Swinburne, his young station chief at Kinshasa, who saved the Congo for Leopold II of Belgium.

Captain Frederick Lugard soon
after claiming Uganda for Britain.

Kabarega of Bunyoro in old age.
He died while returning to his
country after twenty-four years
of exile.

Henry Stanley in 1892 with his close friend Sir William Mackinnon,
whose Imperial British East Africa company financed Britain's early
presence in Uganda.

Major-General Sir Horatio
Kitchener at the time of the battle
of Omdurman.

Marchand's emissaries approach
Kitchener's ship.

Commandant Marchand claimed
Fashoda on the Nile for France.

Sir Harold MacMichael, Britain's
top civil servant in Sudan
1926–33. He ignored the people
of southern Sudan with dire
consequences for the future.

where does all this leave Speke's Nile source? In Stanley's words, Lake Victoria and the Ripon Falls deserved 'a higher title' than could justly be applied to rival lakes or tributaries. Only from the Ripon Falls can the Nile be said to assume a definite course: flowing, at first, through shallow Lake Kyoga (which is more like a wide and overflowing river than a lake) then thundering over the Murchison Falls into Lake Albert, only to leave that lake a few miles away, effectively turning the narrow northern end of Albert into a river, which flows on, always to the north, through gorges and over cataracts to Dufile and Gondokoro. So once Stanley had ruled out the Lualaba as a contender, he really *had* solved the Nile mystery and had correctly awarded to Speke his posthumous prize.[19] Yet though Stanley had succeeded brilliantly in his Nile quest, his own survival remained anything but certain.

On 11 February 1877, Stanley and his men were attacked with guns for the first time since they had embarked on the river. To watch 'the smoke of gunpowder drifting away from native canoes' was a novel and alarming experience. In the ensuing waterborne sniping battle, two of his men were killed and an unknown number of his opponents were struck down. The presence of firearms in the hands of the Congolese proved to Stanley that he had arrived at the furthest point on the river to which indirect Portuguese influence had penetrated from their trading stations near the coast. A few days later, Stanley and his followers were pursued by six canoes and shots were once again exchanged and casualties suffered.[20]

In mid-March 1877 a worse ordeal began when Stanley started downriver from the vast expanse of water that would be known for almost eighty years as Stanley Pool. He was about to ask for a level of commitment from his Wangwana porters that might reasonably have been asked of soldiers in war, but hardly from contracted civilians. Without such remarkable men, Burton, Speke, Grant and Stanley would have achieved little. As Stanley told a friend, he could not have travelled more than a few days' journey 'without the pluck and intrinsic goodness of 20 men'.

Foremost among them were Uledi, Manwa Sera, Chowpereh, Wadi Safeni and Sarmini. His followers' numbers had dwindled from 228 at Bagamoyo to 129. Fourteen lives had been lost in the four and a half months since leaving Nyangwe. None of them suspected that their worst ordeal was just beginning. The first rapids below the Pool reminded Stanley of 'a strip of water blown over by a hurricane'. Yet smooth water could be deadly too. On 29 March, the steersman of the canoe in which Kalulu was travelling let his vessel drift into the fastest part of the river and condemned himself and his passengers 'to glide over the treacherous calm surface like an arrow to doom'. The canoe was whirled around several times at the lip of a fall, before plunging down into the maelstrom below, drowning all six occupants, including Kalulu.[21]

Death of Kalulu.

On 12 April, Stanley and his crew, in their eleven-foot boat, found themselves descending another set of rapids, out of control.

As we began to feel that it was useless to contend with the current, a sudden terrible rumbling noise caused us to look below, and we saw the river almost heaved bodily upward, as if a volcano had burst under it . . . Once or twice we were flung scornfully aside, and spun around contemptuously as though we were too insignificant to be wrecked.[22]

Somehow they found the strength to keep paddling through the swirling, white water. On 3 June, Frank Pocock – the last of Stanley's white companions – was drowned when his canoe capsized.[23] Wadi Safeni, whose cool head had saved Stanley and his men on their first visit to Bumbireh, suffered a breakdown during this dreadful period and wandered into the bush to die.

When, on 9 August 1877, Stanley and his party stumbled into the Portuguese trading post that was furthest up the river, only 115 people could be counted, and as Stanley recorded, they were all 'in a state of imminent starvation'. For several months, the locals had been refusing to sell them food. Only 108 men, women and children would return to Zanzibar – significantly less than half of the 228 who had set out. Their epic journey from Bagamoyo to the Atlantic coast had lasted 1,000 days. Stanley was the only one of the four Britons to survive. Although his hair had gone prematurely grey and he had lost one-third of his weight, he had retained an almost mystical self-belief.

This poor body of mine has suffered terribly [he wrote during the descent of the cataracts], it has been degraded, pained, wearied & sickened, and has well-nigh sunk under the task imposed on it, but this was but a small portion of myself. For my real self lay darkly encased, & was ever too haughty & soaring for such miserable environments as the body that encumbered it daily.[24]

Although the laurels for the discovery of the source had been shown at long last to belong to John Hanning Speke, it was inevitable, sixteen years after Speke's discovery, that it would be upon Stanley's unrivalled journey that public attention would focus. So the damage done by Richard Burton's long-sustained belittlement of his travelling companion's achievement would never be put right. It just might have been, if Burton had behaved honourably and made a statement at the RGS, or even written an honest letter to *The Times*, admitting that he had been completely wrong for nearly twenty years. But instead, he waited until 1881, and chose to bury his climb-down where nobody would see it, in a commentary on the travels of the Portuguese poet, Luis de Camoens. He wrote, almost as an inconsequential aside, and without naming Speke: 'I am compelled formally to abandon a favourite theory that the Tanganyika drained into the Nile basin via the Lutanzige.'[25] This admission was made six years after Stanley had solved the mystery. Speke's biographer claims that Burton wrote a letter on his death-bed, in which he told Grant that every harsh word he had ever uttered against Speke was withdrawn. But, since Burton died of a heart attack in the night, this seems unlikely to have been true.[26]

Because Burton promoted himself as being more wicked than he really was in order to shock respectable people, and hinted at homosexual encounters as well as numerous heterosexual ones, and because he wrote savagely amusing letters, and made unexpurgated translations of the *Kama Sutra of Vatsayana* and the *Book of the Thousand Nights and a Night,* he remains a figure of fascination today – despite, as one scholar has recently put it, the last-mentioned work being 'lurid and archaising', and less readable than Edward Lane's version of fifty years earlier.[27] Burton is also remembered for criticising British racism in India – although he was a convinced supporter of the Raj – and for his deep and genuine understanding of Arab and Indian culture. But his many repellent epithets about Africans, such as 'the quasi-gorillahood of the real "nigger"' and his references to 'their chimpanzee-like fingers'[28] have been downplayed by most of his biographers, as has his ruthless destruction of Speke's right to be remembered, despite his [Burton's] very early realisation that his 'subordinate' was almost certainly right.

Speke not only discovered the Nile's source but instinctively understood the nature of the whole watershed long before any other European had grasped it. He also enjoyed the company of Africans, much as Livingstone had done, and he relished the uniqueness of the privilege of entering the kingdom of Buganda as the first European ever to have done so. His travel books are more readable than Burton's and are not self-conscious.

Burton, for all his reputation for unconventionality, yearned for recognition by the state, and resented the fact that Speke's father had been allowed to add a hippopotamus and a crocodile to his family's coat of arms (in reality a trifling reward), and told numerous friends that *he* deserved similar changes to his arms and a knighthood as well. 'I opened the way & did the whole work of opening [the continent] from East Africa,' he complained to the historian, William Hepworth Dixon.[29] After a spirited campaign by Burton's aristocratic wife, fought with her husband's wholehearted approval, he was knighted in 1886 – not for his literary accomplishments, but for his achievements as an explorer. Isabel Burton had sent letters and memoranda to the Prime Minister and his cabinet, to MPs, senior military officers and members of the royal family.[30] The same reward had been refused to Speke twenty-two years earlier, despite his immeasurably greater achievements in Africa. Burton had been carried for the greater part of his Tanganyika expedition, and had not visited the western shores of that lake, as Speke had done, nor gone with him to Victoria Nyanza.

In confirming Speke's greatness, Stanley had upstaged him with his own incomparable journey. Yet his homecoming would be no happier than had been his return to London after his successful search for Livingstone. At Zanzibar he expected to find letters from Alice, his fiancée. Indeed there *were* letters from her, but all were dated 1874. So he remained agonisingly uncertain whether he would be returning to happiness, or to the misery of rejection. A letter from his publisher, Edward Marston, made clear which it was to be.

I now come to a delicate subject which I have long debated with myself whether I should write about or wait for your arrival. I think however I may as well tell you at once that your friend Alice Pike is married! Some months ago I received the enclosed letter saying that Miss Pike is now Mrs Barney! . . . It will I fear prove another source of trouble to your sensitive nature.[31]

For a man who dreaded rejection, it was a terrible blow. Mr Barney was both younger and richer than him, being heir to a huge rolling-stock fortune. Nor was romantic anguish Stanley's only source of unhappiness. Thanks to his foolish exaggeration of hostile encounters on the river, and his failure to give a proper context to the bloody events on Bumbireh Island – he would return to England to face accusations of brutality from an RGS gold medallist, Henry Yule, and his ally, the socialist writer H. M. Hyndman. Their campaign would be so passionately prosecuted and so prolonged that his moral reputation would be seriously damaged although his critics acknowledged that his journey had been 'the greatest feat in the history of discovery'.[32] Unfortunately for Stanley, six years earlier, in 1872, he had made enemies in the British establishment by falling out with the committee members of the RGS and with Dr Kirk. Consequently, the British government refused to consider commissioning Stanley to go back to the Congo.

After his betrayal by Alice, it kept him sane to dream of transforming Africa and simultaneously destroying the slave trade along the lines which Livingstone had laid out. He had hoped to return to make a commercial and geographical assessment of the Congo as a Livingstonian 'highway' along which missionaries and traders would travel on their way into the interior. Before leaving Africa's Atlantic coast, Stanley had written for the benefit of his *Daily Telegraph* readers:

I feel convinced that the Congo question will become a political question in time. As yet, no European power seems to have the right of control. Portugal claims it because she discovered its mouth; but the great powers – England [sic], America and France refuse to recognize her right . . . The question is: What Power shall be deputed in the name of humanity to protect the youth of commerce in this little known world? . . . Let England arrange with Portugal at once to proclaim sovereignty over the Congo River to prevent the sensibilities of the world being shocked some day when least expected.[33]

His final sentence would turn out to have been remarkably prescient. So, with the British government turning its back on him, who might be prepared to send Stanley to Africa again?

He had written in his final Congo diary of his fervent hope that the river might in future become 'a torch to those who sought to do good'.[34] Tragically, the man most eager to pick up that torch was secretly contemplating measures that would be the reverse of 'good'. He was King Leopold II of Belgium, who, in November 1877, wrote in confidence to his ambassador in London: 'I do not wish to miss a good chance of getting us a slice of this magnificent African cake.'[35]

The following January, on his way back to London from the Congo, Stanley was approached, on the echoing railway platform at Marseilles, by two diplomats sent to intercept him by the Belgian king. The job of Baron Jules Greindl, a career diplomat, and Henry Shelton Stanford, a Florida landowner and former US consul in Brussels, was to secure the services of 'this able and enterprising American' for a royal project in Africa. The Nile Search would have many historic consequences, but none greater than those that would spring from this encounter in a French railway station at the end of Stanley's Nile mission.

PART 2

THE CONSEQUENCES

TWENTY-FIVE

Shepherds of the World?

———⬦⬦⬦———

Even before Stanley left Zanzibar at the start of his great journey, the early consequences of the Nile explorers' discoveries were being felt in the wider world. David Livingstone might have failed in his quest for the Nile's source, but it was *his* life story and *his* sense of mission that now inspired a whole wave of African initiatives. When his last African journals were published in 1874, the public absorbed the horrors of the East African slave trade as never before and learned of the doctor's determination to ensure that African chiefs be given the opportunity to buy the factory goods they craved from European traders, rather than from Arabs who insisted on being paid with slaves. 'It is the fault of the Arabs who tempt us with fine clothes, powder and guns,' one African chief had told Livingstone. 'I would fain keep all my people to cultivate more land, but my next neighbour allows his people to kidnap mine and I must have ammunition to defend them.'[1]

Livingstone's lonely death in the swamps of Bangweulu, and his followers' heroism in bringing his body to the coast, conjured up images so powerful that British Anglicans, Nonconformists and even Liberals (who might have been expected to oppose colonial ventures) felt an urgent need to act in order to bring liberty and change to Africa. Stanley summed up this feeling in his obituary in the *Graphic* when saying that the doctor had 'left an obligation on the civilized nations of Europe and America, as the shepherds of the world, to extend their care and protection over the oppressed races of Africa'.[2] Although the politicians seemed unmoved, the editors of newspapers sensed that the thousands of ordinary men and women who were suddenly donating to philanthropic societies with African connections ought not to

Livingstone's remains landed at Southampton.

be ignored. Perhaps the moment had come to give 'Christianity and Commerce' a trial. 'The work of England for Africa must henceforth begin where Livingstone left it off,' declared the editor of the *Daily Telegraph*.[3]

James Stewart, a young missionary representative of the Free Church of Scotland had become so disillusioned with Livingstone during the Zambezi Expedition (not least for driving Mary Livingstone to drink) that he had flung his copy of *Missionary Travels* into the Zambezi, with the words: 'So perish all that is false in myself and others.'[4] But during the doctor's funeral in Westminster Abbey he experienced, as it seemed to him, a miraculous change of heart and decided to found a mission on the shores of Lake Nyasa. He would call his settlement Livingstonia. The established Church of Scotland also sent a party – not to the lake – but to the Shire Highlands. Their settlement would be named Blantyre, after Livingstone's birthplace. Today, Blantyre is Malawi's business centre and its most populous city. Roger Price of the London Missionary Society had nearly lost his life in a Livingstone-inspired mission in the Barotse valley, which had turned out to be a death trap; but he, like Stewart, had a transforming change of heart and went out to Lake Tanganyika to search for sites for new missions. Scottish businessmen took up the 'commerce' part of the African challenge. John and Frederick Moir started an enterprise, later to become the world-famous African Lakes Company. One of the men subscribing capital was William Mackinnon, who would go on to become a key figure in the colonial history of East Africa. In 1887, fourteen years after Livingstone's death, Arab-Swahili slave traders attacked the missionaries and the workers of the African Lakes Company. After a spirited campaign on their behalf in England and Scotland, a Protectorate was declared over Nyasaland (Malawi) in 1891. The colony which Livingstone had first dreamed of in the 1850s eventually came into existence eighteen years after his death.

These informal and voluntary responses to Livingstone's life and work by groups of philanthropic people were paralleled by interventions of a more calculated and formal kind, in which rulers sent expeditions to Africa, *as if* in response to humanitarian pressure, but really to carry out rapacious, self-interested agendas of their own in the territories revealed by the Nile explorers.

Sir Samuel Baker – a very different kind of explorer to Livingstone – led the first expedition into equatorial Africa at the behest of a powerful ruler. Baker's plan for creating colonial order bore no resemblance to the gradual process Livingstone had wanted to try out in the Shire Highlands until thwarted by slave raids and famine. The missionaries summoned by the doctor had been dying fast before he could begin his second phase and introduce traders. So he never planned an actual administration. Baker, by contrast, believed in immediate 'military occupation and despotism' as the necessary first step before 'the first seeds of civilization' could be planted.[5] Apart from holding deeply pessimistic views about Africans, he differed from Livingstone, Speke and Stanley in another crucial way. He did not mind whether or not the area he had explored became a British protectorate or colony. A country closer to hand, he thought would do just as well.

As early as June 1867 (a decade before Stanley solved the Nile mystery), Baker had told Sir Roderick Murchison that Africa could only be opened to European influence 'by annexing to Egypt the Equatorial Nile basin'.[6] This opinion would have been music to Khedive Ismail's ears. The modernising Europhile ruler of Egypt had already dreamed at that time of extending his African empire through the immense hinterland of Sudan (Africa's third largest country) as far south as to incorporate the source of the Nile.[7] One of the *khedive*'s motives for wishing to employ Sir Samuel to extend his territory was to rebut claims that the slave trade was about to be extended rather than curbed – as would have been suggested if any Egyptian officer had been given command of an expedition to the far south. Whatever his other faults, Baker hated slavery and had written spirited diatribes against the slave trade in his book, the *Albert N'yanza*.[8]

In June 1868 Baker met Nubar Pasha, the *khedive*'s foreign minister, on a visit to London. Together, they discussed, in

Baker Pasha.

detail, Sir Samuel's return to Africa to annexe the upper Nile, to promote commerce there and root out the slave trade.[9] Baker was offered a staggering salary of £40,000, spread over four years, which must have more than made up for the doubts he must have felt about the venture. From the beginning he knew that the Egyptians were great slave owners, along with all their officials in Khartoum. So help from them was never going to amount to much.

In September 1870, a speaker at the geographical section of the British Association suggested that 'if this expedition was successful, Mohammedanism [on the upper Nile] would be triumphant and Christianity extinguished'. Another complained that Muslims would take control of Bunyoro and Buganda in the far south.[10] Baker was to have three substantial steamers, 800 Egyptian troops, 500 Sudanese and 200 Sha'iqi cavalry and fourteen cannon. So his expedition had to be taken very seriously.

The permanent acquisition of an immense region in the interior of tropical Africa by a technologically advanced state had not been attempted before and could clearly not be compared with earlier more hand-to-mouth expeditions. Even before Livingstone's death, it had caused adverse comment among Nonconformists and Liberals that the person chosen to establish the first foreign administration in central Africa was not a humanitarian.

In answer to a note from the Foreign Secretary, Lord Clarendon, about Baker's mission, Prime Minister William Gladstone wrote that Baker should 'be told that HMG [will] undertake no responsibility whatever for the consequence of it [the expedition] either as regards themselves or as regards any matters connected with it'.[11] But Baker was immune to the 'Grand Old Man's' disapproval. 'My dear little wife,' he told a close friend, 'is full of determination to launch once more on the Albert Nyanza – this time we have a steamer of 130 tons and a little army instead of thirteen men . . .'[12] His dear little wife would soon be facing difficulties and dangers almost as extreme as those encountered on the way to the Luta N'zige.

TWENTY-SIX

Creating Equatoria

⊸⊷⊶

During February and March 1870, Sir Samuel Baker KCB, the *khedive*'s newly appointed Governor-General of the Equatorial Nile Basin, possessing powers of life and death over his men, was temporarily defeated by rafts of aquatic plants in the shifting channels of the Sudd. Somehow he had to get through the White Nile's most famous obstacle in order to reach Gondokoro and the still more distant kingdoms of Bunyoro and Buganda. Many of his men were 'up to their necks in water' for days at a time, trying and failing to cut through the dense web of papyrus with hoes, billhooks and rakes. Seven men died in the two months of trying, and 170 were so sick afterwards that they had to be sent back to Khartoum, forcing Baker to retreat downstream to Taufikia, where he remained stuck until December 1871. Fifty smaller boats were needed merely to transport Indian millet, the expedition's staple food. So with camels, horses, donkeys, Arab boat builders, and 1,500 soldiers also needing transport, the logistical problems caused by the lengthy hold-up threatened the future of the whole enterprise.

Baker finally escaped the Sudd seven months after first entering it, and only managed to reach Gondokoro (Ismailia, he would shortly rename it) on 14 April 1871.[1] By then there were only two years of his contract left to run, but at least he had arrived at the northern frontier of the vast territory over which he was expected to establish Egyptian rule. His *firman* from the *khedive* authorised and instructed him:

To organize and subdue to our authority the countries situated to the south.

To suppress the slave trade. To introduce a system of regular commerce.

To open to navigation the great lakes of the Equator and to establish a chain of military stations and commercial depots, distant at intervals of three days march.[2]

This absurdly ambitious programme largely rested on his ability to reach an understanding with local Africans. He had hoped that the tribe in the neighbourhood of Gondokoro, the Bari, would gratefully accept his protection against the agents of the foremost slave trader in the region, Muhammad Ahmad al-Aqqad. He could not imagine they would not. But to his horror, he found that the Bari chief, Alloron, had recently allied himself with the slavers – his people voluntarily acting as al-Aqqad's porters and mercenaries. So when Baker tried to buy foodstuffs, he was turned down. Evidently, it suited the interests of the Bari to gain immunity by coming to an accommodation with the ruling caste of Arabs permanently settled in the south. Baker had disliked these people on his earlier passage through their territory and now pronounced them 'naturally vicious and treacherous'.[3]

But though the Bari posed a serious problem, Baker experienced a worse one in his own camp, as Florence confided to her diary: 'I must confess that I am rather disgusted with the whole expedition together with the natives, and as to the soldiers, they are perfect brutes in every way – I know it worries Sam very much to have to command such troops.' Florence was shocked to hear the soldiers boasting of the numbers of Africans they had killed. One man deserted after breaking the sight on his rifle, and when recaptured, Baker sentenced him to a horrifying 200 lashes. Another received the same punishment for the far greater crime of murdering a prisoner. Baker was even shamed at times by members of his scarlet-shirted, élite corps of black Sudanese Arabs, whom he had affectionately nicknamed the 'Forty Thieves'. Florence saw one of them capture a girl of ten in order to make her his slave. When told what she had seen, Baker tore off the man's clothes, took away his gun and told him he would be shot if he offended again.[4] Baker genuinely wanted to end the slave trade and be seen as a liberator by Africans, but their natural dislike of his association with the slave-owning Egyptians doomed his efforts from the start.

Nevertheless, in May 1871, Baker hoisted the Egyptian flag over Gondokoro, renaming it Ismailia and simultaneously proclaiming the surrounding country – as far south as Buganda and Lake Albert – to be part of a new Egyptian province which he called 'Equatoria'. This would prove a highly significant moment in the region's history.

Raising the flag at Gondokoro (from Baker's *Ismailia*).

By December, Baker had violated his own principles and stolen corn and cattle from local tribesmen in order to feed his hungry soldiers. But the amount of food captured was too little and he had no alternative but to order 800 men back to Khartoum, with 300 of their 'dependents'. After trying for nine months to impose Egyptian rule on the Bari, he was forced to move south with a mere 502 soldiers and fifty-two sailors, leaving Alloron's people as determined in their opposition as they had been when he had first arrived.[5]

But when Baker arrived at Fatiko – seventy-five miles north of Karuma Falls – his luck briefly changed. The local people, the Acholi, sided with him against the local Arab slave traders and helped him to obtain porters for the rest of the journey to Bunyoro. To reward them, he garrisoned local forts and enabled the Acholi to remain independent at a critical time. Today, Baker is revered in Acholi traditions, as is his wife Florence, who is still known as *Anyadwe*, or 'Daughter of the Moon', on account of her long blonde hair.[6]

But, despite the support of the Acholi, by the end of 1871 Baker had abandoned any idea of incorporating Buganda within Equatoria. However, he still hoped to achieve this feat with Bunyoro. But given how much he had been mistrusted by Kamrasi, the previous *omukama* of Bunyoro, he was naive to imagine that he might somehow pull the wool over the eyes of his successor, Kabarega.

Kabarega's return visit to Baker (from Baker's *Ismailia*).

Baker reached Masindi, Bunyoro's present capital, on 25 April 1872. Since he only had an escort of a hundred men, he ran the risk of being detained or even murdered should Kabarega decide that he had come to steal his country. But his first meeting with the *omukama* – whom he described as 'very well clad, in beautifully made bark-cloth striped with black' – seemed to go well. But when the twenty-year-old Kabarega returned the visit, nothing that Baker could say would persuade the young man to enter his hut. Clearly the monarch suspected possible foul play. An incensed Baker called him 'an unmannerly cub' and 'a gauche, undignified lout'. The cub was in fact the twenty-third of his dynasty and had come to the throne after his father's death, as the successful claimant after a bloody succession struggle.[7] Kabarega could not reasonably be blamed for being suspicious of a man whom his father had mistrusted, and who came as the representative of a distant government. But in reality Baker was the one who had walked into danger. A crowd of 2,000 people had accompanied Kabarega, 'making a terrific noise with whistles, horns, and drums'. The king brushed aside talk of trade and civilisation, and told Baker that all he needed was military help against his rebel uncle, Rionga.

On 14 May, Baker, in his own words, 'took formal possession of Unyoro in the name of the Khedive of Egypt'. This involved nothing more troublesome than putting on his governor-general's uniform, parading his men, and then hoisting the Egyptian flag. In response to this insulting ceremony, Kabarega sanctioned the construction of huts and fences which hemmed in Baker's camp-site on both sides. He also declined to cut back the long grass which offered cover to any warrior who might wish to approach the camp without being seen.[8]

On 31 May, Lieutenant Julian Baker RN, who had come to Africa as his uncle's second-in-command, foolishly led most of the expedition's soldiers into Kabarega's town to drill them in an open space. Florence described the *omukama*'s response to this tactless provocation: 'In about ten minutes I should think that quite 5,000 or 6,000 men turned out with their shields and arms and not one of the spears had a sheath on.' The massacre of Baker's entire party seemed imminent. Somehow remaining calm, Baker waved to a senior chief whom he recognised in the armed

339

throng, and walked towards the lowered spear tips, calling out through his translator: 'Well done. Let's all have a dance!'[9] He then ordered his scratch band to play and told his men to dance, which they did to the bafflement of the warriors. As the dancing continued, Baker ordered some men to creep forward with fixed bayonets, covering his flanks. Then, feeling rather more secure, he demanded to see Kabarega. The young king duly appeared and called off his warriors.

Baker knew that his quick-thinking had only gained him a little time. Kabarega believed with good reason that Baker meant 'to eat' his country, and not simply trade with him. So the young ruler's next move, a week later, was to try to kill both the Bakers and their men with a gift of poisoned cider and grain. This attempt was foiled by Florence, who immediately mixed an emetic with vast quantities of mustard and salted water.[10]

The 'Battle of Masindi' (from Baker's *Ismailia*).

The next morning Baker was shot at by men creeping up close through the long grass. His sergeant walking just behind him was hit in the chest and died on the spot. Another member of the 'Forty Thieves' was hit in the leg. Managing to summon sixteen of his élite corps with a bugle call, Baker ordered them to return fire. Meanwhile other men were told to set fire to Kabarega's town, including the *omukama*'s audience hut. Monsoor, Baker's favourite officer, was killed early in the fighting, along with three others. 'I laid his arm gently by his side,' wrote Baker, 'for I loved Monsoor as a true friend.' Throughout the fight, Baker was plied with loaded rifles by Florence, whom he called his 'little colonel'. She also fired rockets into the town.[11] Four days later, the Bakers had no choice but to evacuate Masindi, although they knew that this was an acknowledgement of total failure.

The retreat to Fatiko (from Baker's *Ismailia*).

During the march to Fatiko, through many miles of tall grass, his column suffered numerous ambushes, leading Florence to vow that if her husband died, she would shoot herself rather than risk capture. The boy leading Baker's horse was transfixed by a spear, and crawled up to him to ask: 'Shall I creep into the grass, Pasha? Where shall I go?' The next moment, he fell dead at his master's feet. Baker's greatest fear was that Kabarega's army would overwhelm his men by force of numbers. Luckily for him, he managed to keep ahead of his pursuers. Even so, the losses on the retreat from Masindi were ten killed and eleven wounded – heavy casualties for a force barely a hundred strong.[12]

En route to Fatiko, Baker sought out Kabarega's rebel uncle, Rionga, on his island in the Nile, to pledge to him Egypt's future support in his struggle to supplant his royal nephew.[13]

Travelling back to Khartoum on the Nile, after defeating a determined group of slave traders who attacked his fort at Fatiko, Baker intercepted three boats containing 700 slaves – hardly confirming his later claims to have rid the river of the trade in human beings.[14] In fact, the overland movement of slaves to Darfur and Kordofan – following the discovery of the Bahr el-Ghazal waterway – had for a decade dwarfed the number of slaves being transported on the Nile by a ratio of six or seven to two.[15] From Ismailia, Sir Samuel wrote to his brother John, intending the letter to be released to the press:

All obstacles have been surmounted. All enemies have been subdued – and the slavers who had the audacity to attack the troops have been crushed. The slave trade of the White Nile has been suppressed – and the country annexed, so that Egypt extends to the equator.[16]

Far from being subdued, Kabarega had been left as independent and obdurate as before, and al-Aqqad and the other slavers had merely received a temporary check at Fatiko. Nor had Baker ever travelled as far south as the Equator – let alone 'annexed' anything there. Florence's hyperbole exceeded her husband's. 'After great difficulties and trials,' she told her sister-in-law, 'we have conquered and established a good Government throughout the country'.[17] Khedive Ismail, Baker's employer, was not taken in by the self-promotion, declaring that 'the success [of the expedition] has been much exaggerated' and that Baker, though 'brave' had been 'too prone to fighting . . . giving rise to a general feeling of hostility towards Europeans and my government in Upper Egypt'.[18]

Nevertheless, on returning to Britain, Baker's optimistic letters were read aloud in both Houses of Parliament, and caused *The Times* to gush: 'The undertaking stands out in the tame history of our times as a bold and romantic episode . . . Nothing recorded of the Spaniards in Mexico exceeds in stirring interest the story of the retreat from Bunyoro.'[19] The adventurous aspects of Sir Samuel's enterprise even dazzled the Liberal Foreign Secretary, Lord Derby, who wrote praising him for 'having extended British influence in Egypt' and for accelerating 'the rapid progress which we are making in opening-up Africa'. It was almost as if, in 1874, Derby foresaw that within a decade Britain would dismiss the bankrupt *khedive* and become the new ruler of Egypt and its territories on the Nile.[20] But while this Liberal statesman succeeded in sensing the direction in which the winds of history were starting to blow, he failed to recognise that Baker's recipe for creating new colonies, with a few steamers and a regiment or two, had little to do with adventure and a lot to do with brushing aside legitimate African rulers, whose only crime was to have indicated that they wished to remain independent in the face of superior might. In reality, Baker's 'adventurous' retreat from Bunyoro had been a victory for Kabarega, the 'unmannerly cub'. While Baker could justifiably claim to have been attempting to liberate the Upper Nile from the slave trade, he could not claim to have been similarly motivated in his invasion of Bunyoro, which had never been devastated and turned into an anarchic killing field by the slavers.

To many people in public life in Europe, Baker's expedition was the first to reveal the strategic and economic possibilities of alien rule in tropical Africa. It therefore brought closer the 'Scramble for Africa'. Baker claimed that by creating peaceful conditions on the Upper Nile, he had opened the way for immense crops of cotton, flax and corn to be grown in future, guaranteeing lasting prosperity to the region's inhabitants and profit to those who came to trade with them.[21] He had certainly focussed attention on Africa just when the Kimberley diamond fields were providing would-be colonists with another tempting reason to give it their attention. On 9 December 1874, the editor of *The Times* gave voice to sentiments which would have enraged Kabarega and Mutesa had they ever heard about them:

It is not long since central Africa was regarded as nothing better than a region of torrid deserts or pestiferous swamps . . . there now seems reason to believe that one of the finest parts of the world's surface is lying waste under the barbarous anarchy with which it is cursed.

Sadly, Baker's unsuccessful efforts to make Equatoria a reality and to extend Egypt's borders – and thus Sudan's – as far south as Bunyoro would be taken up by others with greater success and would prove utterly disastrous to the wider region in the long term.

TWENTY-SEVEN

An Unheard of Deed of Blood

——— ∞∞ ———

Henry M. Stanley had visited Mutesa, the *kabaka* of Buganda, in April 1875, while trying to determine whether Livingstone and Burton had been right to dismiss Speke's claim to have located the source of the Nile in Lake Victoria. So the Nile search was responsible for this nation-changing meeting between the *kabaka* and the explorer. Although Stanley would not say so, his success in persuading the king to invite Christian missionaries to come to Buganda owed less to Mutesa's interest in Christ's teaching, than to the monarch's expectation that he would be able to buy breech-loading rifles from any Europeans who might choose to come to his country as a result of his invitation. Mutesa had long feared that without such weapons to help him, the Egyptians would 'eat' his country.

Stanley had been shocked to find that Arab slave traders at Mutesa's court were buying enough slaves from the *kabaka* to make Uganda, in his words, 'the northern source of the [East African] slave trade'. So his purpose in asking Mutesa to summon Christian evangelists had been to counter the influence of slave-trading Muslims at court.[1]

The arrival in Buganda of the white-suited, Tyrolean hat-wearing, Alexander Mackay of the British Church Missionary Society (CMS) in November 1878 opened a new chapter in the history of that country and its neighbouring kingdoms. Seven missionaries had been sent a year earlier but only one survivor had been there to greet Mackay. Two had been killed near the lakeside by fishermen, one had died of fever and three had retreated to Zanzibar to recuperate from fever.[2] Mackay was small, dapper, resourceful, and very courageous. As a former engineer, he was well placed to teach boat-building and carpentry

345

Alexander Mackay.

and to set up a printing press. He was also a knowledgeable horticulturalist. In 1879, he started to translate St Matthew's Gospel into Luganda, along with short texts and prayers. In the same year, a group of French 'White Fathers' arrived under their leader Father Simeon Lourdel.

During the early 1880s the British and French missionaries made their first converts, mainly among the young pages sent to court by their families to learn leadership. These boys and other youngsters serving the missionaries made it fashionable to learn to read. They would become known collectively as 'readers'.

A number of chiefs also became converts and formed a distinct group at court. By 1884, there would be roughly a hundred Baganda Christians, with four times that number being converted in the next two years.[3] Throughout this extraordinary process, which was almost without parallel in Africa, Mutesa remained ominously aloof and expressed anger that the missionaries *only* taught his people about God, although Stanley had led him to believe that they would teach the Baganda 'how to make powder and guns'. His people needed this knowledge, he explained to Mackay, because the Egyptians were 'gnawing at [his] country like rats'.[4]

The Arabs already resident at court had everything to lose if the missionaries established themselves, since they would dissuade Mutesa from continuing the slave raids outside his borders, which enabled him to pay the slave traders with slaves for their cloth and other goods. Naturally they did their best to poison Mutesa's mind against the new arrivals, saying that the white men were only interested in 'eating up the country' and were fugitives from justice in their own lands.[5]

By 1884, Mutesa was dying of an incurable disease, and on the advice of his *ngangas* he sacrificed thousands of people to appease the ancestral spirits. As many as 2,000 were executed in a single day. Mackay called him 'this monster' and declared: 'All is self, self, self. Uganda exists for him alone.'[6] The *kabaka* was succeeded by his headstrong, nineteen-year-old son, Mwanga, who under Mackay's restraining influence decided not to murder his brothers, as his predecessors had traditionally done. But Mwanga remained deeply suspicious of the missionaries. He had heard that white men were moving inland from the East African coast, making treaties as they went. These were Germans led by the imperialist Dr Karl Peters. Mwanga had also heard that the British had taken power in Egypt after a big battle there. Since he was unsure of the differences between European nations, he gained the impression that these white men had put their heads together to steal his country. It was a natural conclusion to have drawn.

General Gordon, the Governor-General of the Sudan, had sent a small party of soldiers to Uganda in 1876, and now there was news of another Briton unexpectedly arriving at the north-east corner of Lake Victoria. Joseph Thomson had just pioneered a route through Masailand, and as ill-chance would have it, his arrival convinced Mwanga that his country was being over-whelmed from all directions. When the missionaries said they only wanted to teach his people their religion, he did not believe them and still suspected that they wanted their countrymen to come and take away his kingdom.[7] Mackay learned that several chiefs who had become Muslims were urging Mutesa to kill the Christian converts and drive the missionaries out of the country. The slave traders – named by Mackay as Kambi Mbaya (Rashir bin Shrul) and Ahmed Lemi – were apparently foremost in urging the *kabaka* to kill the missionaries.[8]

In January 1885, Mwanga arrested Mackay with three of his young readers. He was placed under guard, but his protégés were dragged off to a swamp outside the royal town of Mengo. Mackay hurried to the court and protested that they were guilty of no crime, but on Mwanga's orders the boys' arms were hacked off by his chief executioner, and then they were slowly roasted on a spit. After being released, Mackay bravely upbraided Mwanga for this appalling act.[9] The whole mission was now in acute danger.

It was at this disastrously inauspicious moment that the jovial Bishop James Hannington arrived with fifty followers at the north-eastern corner of the lake having travelled through Masai country on Mwanga's forbidden route. The adventurous and optimistic Oxford-educated cleric had been sent to Buganda by the CMS to take up residence as the first Bishop of Eastern Equatorial Africa. He would never reach his destination. On 21 October 1885, he was arrested in Busoga, with his fifty Wang-wana porters. A shocked Mackay went to the court on three consecutive days to petition Mwanga for the bishop's life. His French rival, Father Lourdel also pleaded for mercy to be shown. None would be. After eight days of incarceration in a dark and verminous hut, Bishop Hannington was taken out into a forest clearing, stripped naked and stabbed to death along with all his porters, except for four who managed to escape. One of them reported Hannington's last words as having been: 'Tell the king that I am about to die for his people, that I have bought the road to Buganda with my life.'[10] For several months, Mackay came close to leaving Buganda, but the situation gradually calmed down and he resumed his secret conversions.

Then, on 30 June 1886, Mwanga struck in earnest, arresting and executing forty-five Protestant and Catholic converts in almost equal proportions. Several he strangled with his own hands. Others were castrated, before being burned alive. The chief executioner reported to the king that 'he had never killed such brave people before, and that they had died calling on God'. Mutesa's response was to say with a laugh: 'But God did not deliver them from the fire.'[11] Mackay wrote in his journal: 'O night of sorrow! What an unheard of deed of blood! Surely if they fear invasion, they must see that by such an act they give the imaginary invaders a <u>capital</u> excuse for coming in force . . . ?'[12]

At this moment of dire emergency for the missionaries, out of the blue a Russian-born explorer, Dr Wilhelm Junker, arrived at Mackay's mission after a decade spent mapping the Welle and Ubangi rivers. Junker told the missionaries something momentous which Mackay realised at once might indirectly save him and his converts if he could only involve the British press. Apparently, Emin Pasha, the Anglo-Egyptian governor of Equatoria, Sudan's most southerly province, was retreating south towards Lake Albert, pursued by the fundamentalist Muslim followers of the self-declared Mahdi or 'Expected One'. Of humble Sudanese birth, Muhammad Ahmad, the Mahdi, had harnessed deep anti-Egyptian feelings in a movement that was part religious *jihad* and part nationalist uprising. Indeed, 10,000 of his followers had recently overwhelmed Khartoum and killed General Gordon, the Governor-General of the Sudan. Because Gordon had been a British national hero, his bloody death on the steps of his own palace had aroused great grief and fury in

Britain – the public's indignation being the fiercer because the relief expedition sent by Prime Minister Gladstone had arrived just two days too late to save the besieged governor.

Muhammad Ahmad, the Mahdi.

Gordon's death led to the downfall of Gladstone's Liberal government, convincing Alexander Mackay that the new Prime Minister, the Conservative Lord Salisbury, would do anything in his power to ensure that Emin Pasha, Gordon's last surviving governor, did not share his superior officer's fate. And if Lord Salisbury chose to send a force to save Emin, the same soldiers could then go on to rescue the Christian missionaries and their converts, a mere 200 miles away in Buganda. Fortunately for Mackay he knew and liked Emin Pasha and had corresponded with him in the past. So now he reckoned that if he could get a letter to the Pasha and receive from him in reply a passionate appeal for British intervention in Equatoria and Buganda (which Mackay would then send on to the British press), Lord Salisbury would feel obliged to despatch a force to Equatoria to relieve the beleaguered Pasha.

Having found messengers prepared to run the risk of taking a letter to Emin at Wadelai on the Nile, Mackay sat down and wrote as persuasively as he knew how. The result was the arrival of a reply several months later that exceeded his most sanguine hopes. Emin wrote of his desperate struggle for survival and vowed to hold out until he and his men were either annihilated or relieved. Mackay promptly entrusted Emin's letter to the next caravan bound for Zanzibar and a few months later it was published in the London *Times*.[13] But Lord Salisbury was no pushover and would disappoint both the Pasha and Mackay. The Prime Minister and his cabinet concluded that since Emin, who knew central Africa well, thought it impossible to reach the coast with the few thousand men at his disposal, there would be little point in sending a few thousand more to rescue him. An Anglo-Egyptian force of 10,000 men led by a British general, William Hicks Pasha, had recently been massacred by the Mahdi's followers, so history might simply repeat itself; and, in any case, if a force did succeed in reaching Emin and then managed to enter Buganda, an enraged Mwanga would probably murder all the missionaries on its approach.[14] So the pragmatic Prime Minister sat on his hands.

But there *were* two people who refused to accept that nothing could be done for the missionaries and for Emin Pasha. They were Henry Morton Stanley and his close friend, the self-made shipping millionaire and philanthropist William Mackinnon. Stanley agreed to lead an expedition formed specifically to re-supply Emin Pasha and to rescue the missionaries, provided that Mackinnon succeeded in raising the £20,000 which he estimated would be needed to pay for a full-scale relief party. The Scottish entrepreneur produced the cash swiftly, enabling Stanley, who had been responsible in the first place for summoning Mackay to the shores of Lake Victoria, to play a crucial role in the bizarre and violent chain of events that would ultimately bring Uganda and the headwaters of the Nile within the purlieus of the British Empire. But before passing to these upheavals, the slightly earlier European advances in West Africa must be visited since they would exert a decisive influence on the way in which East Africa and the Nile basin were to be carved up.

TWENTY-EIGHT

Pretensions on the Congo

—◦◦◦◦◦—

Samuel Baker had demonstrated, theoretically at least, to European rulers how African territories – even remarkably inaccessible ones – could be snatched by relatively few armed men and then held by means of forts, trading posts and alliances with local people. But thanks to Ismail's precarious finances, the *khedive*'s plans for further southward advances soon juddered to a halt. So with the British government not quite ready to take over from the *khedive* in Egypt, Baker's foray failed to kick-start a European scramble for colonies along the Nile and in East Africa. It was the sudden and surprising appearance of Stanley on the Atlantic coast, almost 3,000 miles from Egypt, that would do that – in an unexpected way.

The news that Stanley had reached the Congo's mouth, at the end of his Nile quest, had caused worldwide excitement. But it was the impression this feat made upon one minor European monarch that would have the most lasting consequences. In ignorance of Leopold II of Belgium's carefully concealed plan to pillage the Congo, Stanley was persuaded by the king to return there as his Chief Agent to set up (as Stanley thought) international trading stations on the river so the Congolese would be able to exchange their ivory, hardwoods, resins and gums for factory goods brought upriver by traders of all nations. In public the king had no trouble applauding Stanley's promise 'to open up the valley of this mighty African river to the commerce of the world . . . or die in the attempt'. But in private, and in reality, Leopold meant to close the Congo to all nations but his own, just as soon as he felt he could get away with it.[1]

Between 1879 and 1884 Stanley built a road past the cataracts on the Lower Congo, launched steamers on the upper river

King Leopold II of Belgium.

and built a string of trading stations for the Belgian king. This pioneering work would lay the foundations for the future Congo Free State and so constitutes an important episode in West African colonial history. But while Stanley was working on the Congo, significant events occurred there which would also have a direct bearing upon the competitive behaviour of European nations several thousand miles away in East Africa and along the Nile.

In November 1880, while Stanley was building his road west of Stanley Pool, an Italian-born French naval officer, Lieutenant Pierre Savorgnan de Brazza, walked boldly into his camp and introduced himself. With ambitions to extend their West African possessions, the French government had funded de Brazza to pioneer a route along the Ogowé river from the Gabon coast

353

to the River Congo in the region of the Pool. Although the Frenchman admitted that he had set up a small post on the north shore of Stanley Pool, Stanley took a liking to him and refused to believe Leopold's warning that the young officer meant to found a French colony. Since Stanley wanted the river to be opened to the traders of all nations, de Brazza's new French post did not annoy him, as it did Leopold.[2]

But on 27 February 1881 Stanley learned something from two Baptist missionaries which made him feel a lot less friendly towards de Brazza. Apparently, in October 1880, before meeting him, the Frenchman had signed a treaty with Makoko, the most important paramount chief on the northern shores of the Pool. Furthermore, according to the missionaries, de Brazza was claiming this chief's territory for France. Since de Brazza had assured Stanley that he had been sent to Africa by the International African Association, a philanthropic organisation founded by Leopold, Stanley was very angry to have been duped.

De Brazza welcomed at Makoko's court.

In December 1881, he made a treaty with local chiefs to the south of the Pool. This secured for Leopold a crucial half-mile stretch of the bank at Ntamo near where the Congo flowed into Stanley Pool. Although no sovereignty was claimed, the French were effectively excluded from building at this strategically vital location.[3] During 1882 and 1883, to deny the French the best positions on the upper river, Stanley rapidly constructed four stations on the Congo above Stanley Pool. His heart was in this work since the French were protectionists, and Leopold, Stanley believed, favoured free trade. In June 1882, Stanley's agents managed to negotiate a treaty with Chief Nchuvila of Kinshasa. On land leased by him at Ntamo and Kinshasa, the city of Leopoldville (now renamed Kinshasa) would rise in later years.

Since the Pool connected the Lower to the Upper Congo and lay at the head of any future railway, its possession would be indispensable to the government of any future Congolese state. So France would have to win control of this essential stretch of water in order to lay claim to the Congo. Later in 1882 the French parliament ratified de Brazza's treaty with Chief Makoko, clearly signalling that they meant to snatch the Congo from Leopold. To forestall them the king began to employ British, rather than Belgian officers on the river, in the belief that the French would not dare provoke an incident with Great Britain. By the end of 1883, forty-one out of 117 clerks, storekeepers, engineers and officers were British.[4]

When Stanley was on the lower river on his way to Europe – having been recalled by Leopold – de Brazza judged that the perfect moment had come to seize the southern shores of the Pool. He chose not to land at Leopoldville, where the garrison was commanded by a capable British Army officer, Captain Seymour Saulez, but at neighbouring Kinshasa, where the Briton in command was a young former apprentice tea broker, Anthony Bannister Swinburne. De Brazza crossed the Pool in late May 1884 with four canoes and about fifty French-trained Senegalese sailors, all armed with modern Winchester rifles and under the orders of Sergeant Malamine, the commander of the French post on the Pool's northern shore. De Brazza also brought his secretary, Charles de Chavannes, to draw up a treaty. Just outside the settlement, de Brazza's men were forced to halt by Hassani, one of Swinburne's Wangwana, who raised his rifle threateningly after Malamine had ordered him in Swahili to let them pass since 'de Brazza was Swinburne's master'.

Guessing that the Frenchman would not risk a shoot-out, Swinburne ran straightaway to Chief Nchuvila's compound and implored him not to meet de Brazza's party without him (Swinburne) being present. The young station chief then ordered his Wangwana to load their rifles and hide in the scrub outside their camp. They were only to emerge if the French began firing. Then, he walked calmly towards the uniformed Senegalese and invited de Brazza, Malamine and de Chavannes to join him in his wooden house for a glass of brandy. Despite Swinburne's hospitality, a fierce argument soon raged about who had the right to occupy Kinshasa. With neither party giving an inch, Swinburne suggested they begin an immediate palaver with Chief Nchuvila to find out what *he* wanted. It would not be long before de Brazza discovered that the chief and his sons were ardent supporters of young Mr Swinburne and Stanley's expedition – currently known as the International Association of the Congo (AIC). Two of the chief's sons began to rant at the French intruders, and de Brazza demanded that the two men be punished for insulting him. Swinburne refused, pointing out that the chiefs had made it very clear that they would never recognise any flag but the AIC's. Then he turned to de Brazza and said: 'I have nothing more to say to you, so wish you good morning.' De Chavannes claimed that under his breath Swinburne had then called the Tricolour a rag.[5]

At any time, de Brazza could have resorted to force, but given Swinburne's British nationality and his popularity with local Africans the political risks had scared the Frenchman. If Swinburne were to die in an exchange of fire, then Britain might be drawn into the Congo as an active participant in the struggle for domination. This was the last thing de Brazza and his countrymen wanted to happen. By bravely refusing to back off when the better-armed French party advanced on Kinshasa, Swinburne had saved the Congo for Leopold and thwarted the French. But his courage would have a disastrous outcome since it made possible King Leopold's later exploitation and rape of the Congo – perhaps the most tragic indirect consequence of the Nile quest. During a brief visit to Europe in 1882, Stanley had spoken condescendingly about de Brazza at a banquet in Paris. After Swinburne's 'insult' to France, the French press angrily condemned this new mockery of a national hero by another arrogant 'Anglo-Saxon'.

Months before Stanley had made his injudicious speech in Paris a more significant event had damaged Anglo-French relations. The background to this was the bankruptcy of the *khedive* of Egypt in 1876, after which Britain and France – the owners of the fifteen-year-old Suez Canal – had assumed financial control over the country. In 1882 this European takeover provoked a group of Egyptian army officers to seize power in a nationalist *coup*. France was paralysed by internal politics at the time, so Britain acted alone. Believing that the route to India via Suez was threatened, the British government sent an army commanded by General Sir Garnet Wolseley to take on Colonel Arabi and his officers. The result was a crushing military defeat for Arabi's forces at Tel-el-Kebir in September 1882, and the installation of the British as the *de facto* rulers of Egypt. After de Brazza's defeat on the Congo, less than two years later, this was more cause for French anger. From now onwards the gratifying idea became widespread that France might one day link its West African colonies with Sudan and the River Nile. This 'bridge across Africa' became an emotive national preoccupation, seeming to offer compensation for Britain's 'theft' of Egypt, among 'perfidious Albion's' other misdeeds.[6]

In 1884, at the Berlin Conference, the greater part of the Congo was awarded to Leopold, with the French, to their mortification (thanks to German and British pressure), receiving the smaller northern region of that vast country. The 'Scramble for Africa' now began in earnest. Due directly to French and British advances in Africa, Germany claimed Togoland, Kamerun and South-West Africa. In Bismarck's opinion, Britain and France had already been too well rewarded in the 'Dark Continent'. Now it was Germany's turn – and the vast area that most interested the Iron Chancellor lay not in West Africa, but inland from Zanzibar, where it extended as far west as the great lakes. This was the region which the Arabs had kept to themselves, but which Livingstone, Stanley, Burton, Speke and Grant had opened to the eyes of the world.[7]

TWENTY-NINE

An Arabian Princess and a German Battle Squadron

———— ⊗⊗⊗ ————

In January 1887, after leaving King Leopold's employment, Stanley stood ready to risk his life in re-supplying Emin Pasha, the embattled Governor of Equatoria, and then in aiding the Scottish missionaries and their converts in Buganda. Lord Salisbury's cabinet had concluded that the remoteness of Emin Pasha's tropical location and the military strength of the Mahdists made a government rescue too dangerous to attempt.[1] But Stanley and his philanthropic friend William Mackinnon had drawn up plans to act independently. They wished to re-supply Emin and save Mackay, but also to advance Mackinnon's African trading interests and, above all, to stop the Germans snatching Tanganyika, Uganda and the Nile's source.[2]

The German Chancellor, Prince Bismarck, had recently revealed that by virtue of several treaties 'negotiated' with Tanganyikan chiefs by Dr Karl Peters – a bespectacled young German philosopher and explorer – an imperial charter or *Schutzbrief* had been granted to Dr Peters's colonising company, authorising him to establish a German protectorate over the territory extending from Zanzibar to Lake Tanganyika.[3] To ensure that the Sultan of Zanzibar accepted this high-handed confiscation of his inland empire, in August 1885 the Iron Chancellor sent a squadron of five German warships to the island.

The Germans, however, possessed a weapon subtler than brute force. On board one of these vessels was an extraordinary duo: a naturalised German woman of Arab extraction, and her son, Rudolph. They were *extraordinary* because nineteen years earlier, Rudolf's mother – who had been born Princess Salme bint Said ibn Sultan al-Busaidi and was a sister of Sultan Barghash of

Zanzibar – had had an affair with a German businessman called Heinrich Ruete resulting in her becoming pregnant.[4] It was a tragic situation since the appropriate punishment under Sharia law was that both lovers be killed, with Princess Salme being stoned to death. Ruete managed to escape, but when Princess Salme, 'a beautiful girl of about twenty-five', tried to stow away on one of the ships owned by her lover's company, she was betrayed by a servant and confined to her house by her brother.[5]

A senior officer in the Royal Navy's East African Anti-Slave Trade Squadron, Captain Thomas Malcolm Sabine Pasley,[6] was told by Dr John Kirk (at the time British Vice-Consul) that if Princess Salme remained on Zanzibar she would 'be killed sooner or later'. Taking pity on her, Captain Pasley planned a rescue, which he timed to take place on 26 August 1866, the day of a local religious festival when pious Muslims were required to go down to the sea and wash. A ship's cutter, manned by sailors from Pasley's frigate, HMS *Highflyer*, was despatched to a prearranged spot on the beach with orders to collect the princess and her servants. Pasley stood in close to the shore in the captain's gig (a smaller ship's boat) in order to be on hand should the rescue be opposed.

Dr Kirk wrote to his fiancée after it was all over:

[The princess had] got down all her boxes of [Maria Theresa] dollars safely and sprang into the boat although manned by infidels. Her two servants who knew nothing of the whole [affair] screamed, howled and roared as women will; but a bluejacket covered the mouth of one with his hand and lifted her in, nolens volens, to follow her mistress. The other unluckily got off clean away, bellowing up the street . . . Some blame the English consulate – as if the ships of war were under us . . . Oh! If you had seen the Europeans next day. Were they not in a funk . . . As to Ruete, the German, he is a fool; in more regular countries he'd get a good horse-whipping . . . It was hard to think that a girl was to suffer while he escaped, so I am right glad she is off.[7]

Pasley and his crew carried the princess and her servants by sea to the safety of the British colony of Aden. To ensure that no Muslim revenge attacks were made on Zanzibar's European population, the Admiralty arranged for a British warship to be stationed in the harbour for several months. Princess Salme wrote to Captain Pasley the following summer, enclosing her photograph and telling him that she had received Christian instruction and been baptised in Aden, and, prior to her marriage to Ruete, given the Christian name of Emily. Her letter ended sadly. She had been 'very much afflicted by the loss of little Henry [her baby], between Lyons and Paris' on the way to Hamburg. But in that city, Herr and Frau Ruete would soon be the proud parents of a son, Rudolph, and two daughters, none of whom would have existed unless Captain Pasley had saved their mother's life.[8] From the time of the incident, the German government had recognised that the Ruete family might one day be of use and therefore made sure that Rudolph was suitably educated and that his family received support, especially after his father, Heinrich Ruete, was killed by a tram in Hamburg in 1870.

SMS *Adler*.

Almost two decades after Emily's rescue, she and the fifteen-year-old Rudolph were conveyed to Zanzibar (as already mentioned) on board the German warship, the *Adler*, which was escorted by four equally imposing cruisers, including the *Gneisenau* and *Prinz Adalbert*. Rudolph's presence in the harbour enabled Bismarck to warn the new Sultan that if he refused to cede his mainland empire – with the exception of a narrow coastal fringe – Germany would replace him with his sister's son. So a British naval officer's chivalrous act had inadvertently helped Germany to put pressure on his own country to yield the lion's share of East Africa. But Captain Pasley (who, by chance, is my maternal great-grandfather) was spared the embarrassment of seeing this happen. In 1870, when recently returned to Britain from the Indian Ocean, he died from the after effects of malaria contracted during the years when he had been chasing slave dhows among the maze of coastal mangrove swamps and creeks between Kismayu and Kilwa. (During the nineteenth century, 17,000 members of the Royal Navy died as a result of their service with the West and East African Anti-Slave Trade Squadrons.)[9]

Due to the threat to replace him with his half-German nephew, Sultan Barghash felt unable to oppose the German demand for a mainland protectorate. So the German battle squadron stood down its gun crews. Emily went ashore and asked to meet her brother, only to be told: 'I have no sister, she died many years ago.'[10] So, on 24 September, mission accomplished, the *Adler* and its escorting vessels raised steam in the harbour and very soon had dwindled to specks on the horizon.

Where Stanley and Mackinnon had failed to persuade successive British governments to pursue a forward policy in East Africa, Karl Peters, Prince Bismarck, and indirectly young Rudolf Ruete, succeeded in propelling Britain into agreeing in October 1886, at Germany's suggestion, that their two countries divide the mainland into two 'spheres of influence', with Germany taking the larger southern portion of the Sultan's empire. This extended west from Usambara, just south of Mombasa, to Lakes Victoria and Tanganyika, and south to Lake Nyasa and the Rovuma. Britain took the northern sector, which stretched as far to the west as the eastern shore of Lake Victoria. This Anglo-German agreement was made almost exactly a year after the five German warships had sailed away. Uganda, 'the pearl of Africa', and Equatoria, had not been included in this Anglo-German agreement. So Stanley and Mackinnon still feared that Peters might try to sign a treaty with Mwanga of Buganda before any British representative was in a position to do so. And if Peters reached Emin Pasha before Stanley, he might end up adding Equatoria, and not just Uganda, to his country's already substantial East African portfolio.[11]

Bismarck's acquisition of the huge country that would become Tanganyika (modern Tanzania) horrified Mackinnon, who in the same year failed to persuade the British government to back his project of building a railway from Tanga on the coast to Mount Kilimanjaro. But, in May 1886, the Prime Minister approved the granting of a royal charter to Mackinnon's Imperial British East Africa Company, in line with the government's policy of 'encouraging private enterprise to peg out claims in regions of East Africa where the Germans were likely to be active'.[12] But the self-made shipping millionaire was not deterred by his knowledge that he was being used. This former grocer's boy was a Scottish Presbyterian idealist, whose yacht, grouse moors and famous friends did not give him nearly as much pleasure as the prospect of saving Equatoria and Uganda for Christianity, free trade and British rule.

Mackinnon and Stanley felt passionately about Uganda because of Britain's long association with that country, firstly through Speke and Grant and then through Stanley himself and Mackay. Furthermore, Bishop Hannington had been martyred trying to open the direct road from the coast, and a young British explorer, Joseph Thomson, had subsequently pioneered it. The two friends felt the same way about Equatoria, which had been given its name by Baker and then administered by Gordon and later by Emin Pasha, who though German had been employed by Britain and Egypt. If Germany's explorers had done as much as Britain's to explore the Nile and reveal its mysteries, then Stanley and Mackinnon might not have felt betrayed. But betrayed or not, Stanley was prepared to cancel an American lecture series and lose £10,000 thereby in order to lead the Emin Pasha Relief Expedition.[13]

Mackinnon viewed the despatch of the expedition with acute anxiety as well as with excitement. If Stanley were to arrive too late to save Emin and the missionaries, Peters would reach Uganda first; and then the sources of the Nile, and Equatoria, could be lost to Britain forever.

THIRTY

'Saving' Emin Pasha and Uganda

Emin Pasha.

In August 1887 Stanley was on the southern shores of the Pool with just under 800 men, two tons of gunpowder, 100,000 rounds of Remington ammunition, 350,000 percussion caps, 50,000 rounds of Winchester ammunition and a Maxim gun, all to be handed over to the beleaguered Emin Pasha, providing he was still alive and could be found. Because King Leopold was still paying Stanley a retainer under their old contract, his former Chief Agent had been obliged to agree to travel to Lake Albert (where the Pasha was believed to be) along the Congo, rather than by the shorter overland route through East Africa. The Belgian king wanted Stanley to approach Lake Albert from the west because from that direction he would be able to extend the boundaries of his Congo Free State by pioneering a route to the lake through the unexplored Ituri Forest in eastern Congo. As an inducement the king had offered Stanley the use of all his steamships currently on the Upper Congo.[1] Stanley would then be able to transport his men, and the supplies intended for Emin, by water for a thousand miles upstream to the east, meaning that his porters would then only have to carry their loads overland for 400 miles to Lake Albert.

Stanley knew that Leopold also expected him to lure Emin Pasha away from the service of the Cairo-based Anglo-Egyptian government with the offer of a huge salary. Equatoria could then (hoped Leopold) be swallowed up by his already bloated Congo Free State. But Stanley had no intention of allowing this to happen. The plan he had hatched with Mackinnon was that Emin and his 3,000 soldiers should be persuaded to relocate, beyond the reach of the Mahdi's Sudanese *jihadists*, in a region just to the east of Buganda where they would be well-placed to take control of that country and stop the Germans making it their colony.

However, Stanley's plan depended upon his managing to reach Emin first – before the Mahdi's forces could kill him, and (if he survived that fate) before Karl Peters could persuade the German-born Pasha to throw in his lot with his fellow-countrymen and hand Equatoria and Buganda to the Kaiser.

At this early stage it was essential that Stanley manage to keep his force together so that by the time he had rescued Emin, and reached the missionaries in Buganda, he would still have enough men to be able to act independently on Mackay's behalf, should the need arise. So when, on arrival at Stanley Pool, he learned that three of the king's four steamers were damaged or irreparable, and that the largest one, the *Stanley*, was currently being repaired, he was devastated.[2] Even if he could persuade the two largest missionary societies in the country to lend him their steamers, he would now be delayed for months and would probably reach Emin too late to save him.

Stanley knew that his namesake steamer, the *Stanley*, once repaired, would have to make several trips towing barges back and forth along the Congo before all his 800 men could be disembarked nearly a thousand miles upstream. Even with borrowed steamships a minimum of two trips from west to east would have to be made. So to have any chance of arriving in time to save Emin, he would have to split his expedition into two contingents and set up a base camp a thousand miles away to the east. A Rear Column of several hundred men would then be left behind to look after the bulk of the expedition's stores, while a fast-moving, lightly equipped Advance Column marched eastwards to find Emin Pasha and deliver enough guns and ammunition to enable him to fight off his enemies.

Steamship on the Upper Congo.

When setting up his relief expedition, Stanley had for the first time in his life decided to employ gentlemen as colleagues, rather than working-class men, as on his previous journeys. Almost from the beginning, he regretted the change. Major Edmund Barttelot, whose father was a baronet, and who had come highly recommended by senior army officers, turned out to be short-tempered and inclined to lash out at Africans for no good reason with a metal-tipped stick. Though Stanley had grave doubts about entrusting the Rear Column to him, he knew that, as second-in-command of the expedition, the major could not be expected to serve in a detached contingent under anyone's orders but his commanding officer's. It reassured Stanley somewhat to know that Barttelot's closest friend on the expedition would be left behind with him. This popular sportsman and ethnographer, James Sligo Jameson, was a member of the Irish whiskey family, and his cheerful presence seemed to exert an influence on his colleagues that was almost as soothing as the drink that had made him rich. Barttelot would have 260 Africans under him, mainly Wangwana and Sudanese, to guard the expedition's heavy stores. Stanley supervised the construction of a stockade and ditch around their camp, and told Barttelot that if Tippu Tip kept his promise to provide him with 600 carriers, the Rear Column would soon be marching eastwards in the footsteps of the Advance Column. If porters could not be obtained, then Barttelot must either stay where he was until Stanley could return for him, or he should weed his stores and march with as many porters as he could lay his hands on.[3] Barttelot's camp was just outside a village called Yambuya on the Aruwimi river. Inside his stockade there was plenty of food, both preserved and fresh.

Lieutenant Stairs hit by an arrow.

On 28 June 1887 Stanley marched eastwards from Yambuya at the head of 389 men, less than half the number he had brought to Stanley Pool. Ahead lay hundreds of miles of unexplored jungle inhabited by villagers whose only encounter with outsiders had been with Arab-Swahili slave traders. To protect them from the slavers, cunningly disguised pits had been dug in the path, and small sharpened sticks with poisoned tips had been stuck in the ground. Anyone injured by these spikes would die within days.[4] Shortly after encountering these traps, Stanley and his men found the way ahead blocked by 300 warriors with drawn bows. They stood at the end of a section of path that had been widened and sewn with scores of tiny poisoned skewers, concealed beneath a carpet of leaves. While these barbs were being carefully pulled up, a hail of arrows fell on Stanley's waiting men, who fired back with their rifles. Now there would be no hope of buying food for many miles to come.[5]

In mid-August, Stanley's most talented young officer, Lieutenant William Stairs, was struck by an arrow just below the heart. Dr Thomas Parke, the expedition's medical officer, found Stairs in shock, blood pouring from his chest. All around he could hear the 'pit, pit, pit' of arrows dropping into the undergrowth. After injecting water into the wound, Parke bravely sucked out the poison. Stairs survived, but two other men hit at the same time died horribly from lockjaw.[6] By the end of the month Stanley's carriers were eating nothing but green bananas and plantains – a wholly inadequate diet for men carrying heavy loads. In seven days, the expedition had lost thirty porters through death and desertion. As he marched beside the Aruwimi river, Stanley shot a man in a canoe as he was in the act of firing an arrow. In this man's boat, the explorer found a dozen freshly poisoned arrows and a bundle of cooked slugs. This was an indication of how little game there was in the forest.[7] Men began to starve, and Captain Nelson, one of Stanley's officers, had to be left behind in a temporary camp with fifty-two Africans who were incapable of walking any further. Their chances of surviving appeared to be very slight.[8]

Stanley emerged from the forest a hundred miles from Lake Albert, with the Advance Column reduced to 175 men. This was 214 less than the 389 who had marched out of Yambuya four months earlier. On 14 April 1888, several days march from Lake Albert, Stanley heard from members of the Zamboni people that 'Malleju' ('the Bearded One') had recently been sailing on the lake 'in a big canoe, all of iron'.[9] Two weeks later, the Pasha's steamship anchored just below Stanley's camp. Emin turned out to be a small, slim man in a red fez and a well-ironed white linen suit. He was bearded, bespectacled, and his face looked, thought Stanley, Spanish or Italian rather than German. Emin was said to command the loyalty of about 3,000 men, and to have fought off the Mahdi and his followers, unlike poor Gordon. But at their first meeting Stanley could detect 'not a trace of ill-health or anxiety' in his demeanour, and this worried him.[10] According to the Pasha's own version of events, mailed to friends in Britain two years earlier, he and his men had survived a period of intense *jihadist* pressure.

Deprived of the most necessary things, for a long time without pay, my men fought valiantly, and when at last hunger weakened them, when after nineteen days of incredible privation and suffering, their strength was exhausted, and when the last leather of the last boot had been eaten, then they cut a way through the midst of their enemies and succeeded in saving themselves.[11]

Yet, now, Emin and his officers appeared to be fit and well – a condition far removed from the traumatised state in which Stanley and his men found themselves. The Pasha seemed to have lied about his true situation. But when he responded enthusiastically to Mackinnon's plan to resettle him and his men in the district just north-east of Lake Victoria, Stanley and his officers were able to feel that their sufferings had not been pointless. It now seemed likely to Stanley that he would soon be making a treaty with Kabaka Mwanga on behalf of Mackinnon's company, before Karl Peters could enter Buganda.[12]

Unaccountably, during the coming weeks, the Pasha failed to confide to Stanley any of the secret fears that were tormenting him – the worst being that the Mahdi's *jihadist* followers had already infiltrated his two regiments, making mass mutiny a terrifying possibility. Instead, Emin pretended that his position was stable enough for Stanley to feel secure about marching east to make contact with his Rear Column, while Emin travelled to Wadelai, north of Lake Albert, to ballot his men on whether they wished to relocate. Stanley had become increasingly worried about Barttelot and Jameson and was delighted that a suitable moment seemed to have arrived for him to find out if they were all right. Having lost so many men, he badly needed the services of the Wangwana who had been left behind with the Rear Column. Without an increase in his numbers, his opportunities for independent action in Buganda would be severely limited.

Stanley reached the Aruwimi after two months and found to his horror that the Rear Column had only managed to drag itself to Banlaya, a mere ninety-five miles to the east of Yambuya, before finally collapsing. But where were all the men he had last seen in June 1887? The only people he could see walking about, or lying on the ground, resembled living skeletons. Some were also suffering from ulcers the size of plates. Of the original officers, not one was here to greet him, only Sergeant Bonny, the column's medical orderly. Within half-an-hour Bonny had revealed to Stanley 'one of the most harrowing chapters of disastrous and fatal incidents that I ever heard attending the movements of an expedition in Africa'.[13] Less than a hundred of the 271 people who had been left behind at Yambuya were still alive. Stanley scribbled into his diary some of the unbelievable things which Bonny told him:

The major caused John Henry, a mission boy, to be flogged 300 lashes. He died that night. Ward [another officer] caused a mutineer to be flogged at Bolobo so severely that he also died within a few hours . . . The major kicked his little boy Sudi – a boy of 13 years old – in the shin with an ulcer 2 by 3 inches unable to move. The major caused a Sudanese to be shot by a platoon of his comrades for stealing a piece of meat. William Bonny relates that the least thing caused the major to behave like a fiend. He had a steel pointed cypress walking staff with which he dealt severe wounds. One man, a Manyema, he stabbed 17 times with the steel point . . . The major would walk up and down the camp with his large white teeth set firm & exposed . . . At such times he would dash at people right & left – as though he were running amuck.[14]

It came as little surprise to Stanley to learn that Major Barrtelot had eventually been murdered by a Manyema porter. He was angry and bewildered that Barttelot's officers had not stood up to him when he had ordered the execution of a hungry man for stealing a piece of meat; and it appalled him that none had objected to a sentence of 300 lashes with a whip of twisted hippopotamus hide for an equally trivial 'crime'. A man would be insensible after fifty strokes and rarely lived through more than a hundred. Stanley nursed the boy, Sudi, in his own tent until his death six days later.[15] Most of the Wangwana who had died had been starved to death or poisoned. Yambuya was rich in nutritive manioc tubers, but Barttelot had worked the Wangwana so hard that they had never had time to soak the tubers in water and then leave them in the sun for several days in order to leech out the natural cyanide. In consequence, 'to satisfy their raging hunger they ate the raw poisonous stuff'. In Stanley's eyes this failure to care for the Wangwana was murder. Yet even this was not the most grotesque crime he heard about.

Bonny informed him that Jameson, the whiskey heir, while on his way to Kasongo, had purchased an eleven-year-old girl and given her to cannibals so that he could watch her being stabbed to death, cut up, cooked in a pot and eaten, while he made sketches of the whole grisly process.[16] According to Bonny, Jameson had gone downriver and would soon be returning. In fact he had died of fever on the day Stanley reached Banlaya. One of the other officers had been invalided home and another had chosen to station himself 600 miles downstream on the Congo. Bonny did not tell Stanley that he and all the other officers had purchased slave women from the local Arab slave traders. 'Our cannibal concubines', he called them in his diary.[17] The moral collapse of the Rear Column's officers and the deaths at Yambuya would haunt Stanley for the rest of his life. He knew that people back in England would assume that Barttelot and Jameson had been:

... originally wicked ... They will not reflect that circumstances changed them ... At home these men had no cause to show their natural savagery ... They were suddenly transplanted to Africa and its miseries. They were deprived of butcher's meat & bread & wine, books, newspapers, the society & influence of their friends. Fever seized them, wrecked minds and bodies. Good nature was banished by anxiety. Pleasantness was eliminated by toil. Cheerfulness yielded to internal anguish ... until they became but shadows, morally & physically of what they had been in English society.[18]

Yet Stanley could not afford to surrender to despair. Karl Peters might already be on his way to Lake Victoria and the Pasha's men had to be there ahead of him, so Stanley gave the half-starved survivors of Banlaya ten days in which to recuperate, before leaving Banlaya on 30 August 1888. Back at the lake, he was appalled to find that Emin Pasha had not yet returned from the north after consulting his men about their relocation.[19] Then Stanley received the shocking news that Emin was being held captive by mutineers from one of his own regiments. The Pasha's life seemed to be hanging by a thread. Plainly all hope that he would take his men to north-eastern Uganda had gone. At best, it appeared that Stanley would now be taking a small number of Emin's loyal soldiery to the coast *en route* to Egypt. By failing to be honest about his true situation, Emin had turned a difficult situation into a disastrous one.[20] Now, Equatoria would probably be overrun by the *jihadists* with the connivance of Emin's men, and Uganda would become a German colony. Stanley's officers felt great bitterness towards the Pasha. 'We were led,' said one, 'to place our trust in people who were utterly unworthy of our confidence and help.'[21]

At the end of December, Emin and a handful of loyal officers and soldiers arrived at Tunguro on Lake Albert, having been released unharmed from involuntary detention at Dufile, 140 miles to the north on the Nile. Although Emin claimed that a thousand men were still loyal to him, on 10 April 1889, the agreed date of departure for the coast, only 126 officers and men assembled in Stanley's camp, along with about 350 servants, wives, concubines, children, clerks and officials. To bring away these people, described by one of Stanley's officers as 'the dregs of Cairo & Alexandria', had to date cost Stanley about 400 lives, and had put back by months the date on which he could expect to reach Alexander Mackay and his missionaries and converts in Buganda. Fortunately, Stanley would soon learn that these much-persecuted people had managed to escape from Buganda to Usambiro, on the southern shores of Lake Victoria.

On arriving at the lake Stanley was moved to tears by the 32-year-old Mackay's courage. The diminutive and dapper missionary had only left Buganda with his converts when certain that they would otherwise have been killed. Mackay warned Stanley that Karl Peters was already fighting his way through Masailand. Furthermore, the Germans had recently moved inland in large numbers into their East African 'sphere of influence'. *En route* to Lake Victoria from Lake Albert, Stanley had undergone several blood brotherhood ceremonies with chiefs, and now decided to represent these to the British government as 'verbal treaties' which might possibly be used in negotiations to prevent western Uganda falling into German hands.[22]

According to Mackay, Peters was closing in on Buganda itself, leaving a trail of burned villages and murdered Masai warriors behind him.[23] But Stanley was in no position to try to reach Buganda ahead of him. With only 215 members of his own expedition to call upon, and handicapped by having to supervise Emin's straggling column of 300 enfeebled men, women and children, his column had to concentrate on its own survival. Any attempt to do more would end in disaster.

As Stanley came to the sun-bleached borders of Masailand and saw stretching ahead of him the parched, acacia-studded plain which he remembered so well from his Livingstone search, he could just discern a caravan approaching through the quivering haze. It was led by a young German officer, and Stanley was disconcerted to be hailed 'with a perfect volley of "Guten Morgens"' from the Nyamwezi porters.[24]

Despite Stanley's belief that the Pasha would accompany him to Europe, Emin had secretly resolved never to leave Africa. In

1875, on his last visit to his native Germany, he had abandoned his former Turkish mistress, Madame Hakki, and had fled to Egypt, taking her jewels and money with him. She had obtained a judgment for 10,000 marks after his disappearance, leaving Emin in no doubt about her determination to put him behind bars should he ever return to German or Turkish jurisdiction.[25] Not until reaching Cairo would Stanley learn about the scandal of Emin's Turkish mistress and her lawsuit. He buried the information in his diary and never breathed a word to anyone, knowing that Emin's criminal treatment of his mistress, if it were ever made public, would cause a storm of anger that good lives should have been lost to rescue an immoral cad.[26]

At the coastal town of Bagamoyo in early December 1889, the short-sighted Emin fell from a balcony during a celebratory dinner and gashed his head. The German officers who had organised the dinner spirited him away to their military hospital and Stanley never saw him again. A month later, Emin announced that he intended to work for Germany, and in April 1890 he marched out of Bagamoyo at the head of a well-equipped expedition. He hoped to recruit his old Sudanese soldiers, who had been left behind on the shores of Lake Albert, and with their help to claim Equatoria for Germany. But he would soon discover that his former officers had remained loyal to Egypt and Britain. So Emin vanished into the interior on a mysterious mission of his own, which ended with his capture by Kibonge, an Arab-Swahili warlord and slave trader, somewhere south of Stanley Falls on the Congo. Emin Pasha was arrested and beheaded on the orders of Kibonge. 'The very day he was kissed by his countrymen he was doomed,' remarked Stanley, drily.[27]

Emin's ingratitude underlined the complete failure of Stanley's expedition to achieve what he and Mackinnon had most wanted to do: namely strengthen Britain's strategic position in East and Central Africa. Whether Britain, Germany, or even France, was going to emerge as the guardian of the source of the Nile and its upper reaches still remained an open question.

THIRTY-ONE

The Prime Minister's Protectorate

∽

Dr Karl Peters, the slender and scholarly German explorer with a taste for shooting Africans and decapitating their corpses, had hoped to join forces with Emin Pasha in his advance on Buganda and Equatoria; but after the Pasha vanished into the interior, Peters had been obliged to act alone. Supreme gambler that he was, the bespectacled German pushed on with only sixty men, and – after stealing a march on the British traveller, Frederick Jackson, whom Mackinnon had sent in a desperate last minute effort to intercept him – arrived at Mwanga's court and persuaded the *kabaka* to sign a treaty. This *coup* was achieved with the support of the French priests, who knew that if Mackinnon triumphed, the British missionaries would be favoured in the kingdom to their detriment. The Germans, they fondly hoped, would be neutral.[1] But just when Germany seemed to have triumphed, Lord Salisbury unexpectedly decided that vital British interests were involved after all.

And what had caused the Prime Minister's eleventh hour *volte face*? The answer was his recognition that a seismic shift was taking place in the broader region. While the Mahdist fundamentalists had remained in uncontested control of the Sudan and the Upper Nile, Lord Salisbury had been confident that the ruling Caliphate could not dam or interrupt the river's flow because it lacked western-trained engineers. But when in 1889 an Italian army advanced into Abyssinia and declared it a protectorate, Salisbury informed them very publicly that Britain would bar their troops and those of all other nations from approaching the Nile itself.

In June of the same year, Count Hatzfeld-Wildenburg, the German ambassador in London, took the hint and assured

Salisbury that all places north and east of Lake Victoria were 'outside the sphere of German colonisation'. So it had been obvious to Lord Salisbury that Prince Bismarck no longer supported Karl Peters's colonial schemes. But Bismarck was dismissed in March 1890, and Salisbury was at once warned by the German Secretary of State, Baron von Marschall that no understanding existed between Germany and Great Britain about the territories to the west of Lake Victoria – the region in which Stanley had supposedly made his 'verbal agreements'.[2] Only a general European settlement in East Africa now seemed to hold out any prospect of discouraging German adventurers like Dr Peters from advancing towards the Nile through Equatoria.

On first hearing about Peters's vexing treaty with Mwanga, Salisbury knew it would take a masterstroke to snatch back Uganda and the Nile's sources. So, as if plucking a rabbit from his hat, he produced the island of Heligoland and offered it to the delighted German Emperor. Count Hatzfeld-Wildenburg, the Kaiser's negotiator, was informed by his master that this barren island in the North Sea, which had been captured by Britain during the Napoleonic Wars, was vital for the future defence of Hamburg and the Kiel Canal. *Nothing* must be done that could jeopardise its acquisition. So Peters's treaty was revoked, and Buganda – incorporating wider Uganda and Equatoria – once again seemed destined to become a British protectorate. Nor was that all. The Ruwenzori Mountains, along with half of Lake Albert, the whole of Lake George and the hinterland to the west of Lake Victoria, as far south as the Kagera river, would no longer be claimed by Germany as part of Tanganyika. So Stanley's 'blood-brotherhood treaties' were not to be thrown away. Lord Salisbury also negotiated an extension of coastal land at Witu on the Indian Ocean to seal off the Upper Nile from possible German forays.[3]

So it seemed that Mackinnon was finally to get what he had asked for all along and the 'legacy' of the Nile explorers Speke, Grant, Baker and Stanley would be saved for Britain. Another way of looking at the Heligoland Treaty was that two

Lord Salisbury.

European nations had traded a minuscule rocky island in the North Sea for a vast chunk of Africa without reference to the people who lived there. For Mackinnon and Stanley however, Mwanga's participation in the slave trade, his murder of Bishop Hannington, and the mutilation and roasting alive of scores of mission converts seemed more than sufficient justification for intervention.

Yet in nineteenth-century Africa, few arrangements made in distant places went smoothly, even when a British prime minister and a crowned German head of state had decreed they should. In reality the situation in Buganda remained remarkably volatile, even after the removal of the immediate German threat. Buganda's capital, Kampala, was a thousand miles from the coast, and Mackinnon, whose Imperial British East Africa

Company was close to bankruptcy, was nevertheless being asked to gain control of the kingdom as quickly as possible.

To achieve this, the shipping mogul and his directors sent to Central Africa Captain Frederick Lugard, an intense, dark-eyed young Indian Army officer with a floppy black moustache and a fondness for crumpled light-weight khaki uniforms. He had the classic background for a successful African adventurer, having been jilted by an adored fiancée, whom he had caught in bed with another man. So where better than Africa to re-establish his manly credentials? This he had started to do near Lake Nyasa in 1888, where he had fought bravely and been wounded while saving missionaries from death at the hands of Arab slave traders.

On arriving in Kampala at the end of 1890, Lugard found that Mwanga's sympathies lay with the powerful faction of chiefs supporting the French missionaries. So, on their advice the *kabaka* refused to sign a treaty with Lugard. After all, why should he allow any outsider to limit his powers as hereditary ruler of Buganda and take away his right to wage war, buy gunpowder and trade in slaves?[4] Only Lugard's small but disciplined force, and his Maxim gun, eventually persuaded Mwanga that he had no choice but to sign. This was not the first time that disaster had befallen the *kabaka*. The Muslims had long ago curtailed his independence, and the rivalry of the French and British missionaries and their African factions had caused a civil war in his kingdom that had driven him briefly into exile.

Shortly after curtailing Mwanga's powers, Lugard beat back a Muslim incursion into Buganda from Bunyoro. Nevertheless, the worsening antagonism between the supporters of the Catholic Mission, the Fransa, and of the Protestant Mission, the Inglesa, presented him with a more serious problem, especially since Mwanga was encouraging the Fransa to assert themselves militarily. Knowing that his men and the British mission's supporters were outnumbered by the French alliance with Mwanga, Lugard strengthened the position of Mackinnon's company by marching to Lake Albert and recruiting 200 of the Sudanese troops left there by Emin Pasha. Lugard was back in

Buganda in December 1891 and found that relations between the missions had worsened. A return to civil war seemed inevitable, with the British mission and their Bugandan adherents likely to be on the losing side. So Lugard was horrified on his return to find a letter from the directors informing him that the company was insolvent and that he must withdraw. With Lord Salisbury's majority in the Commons now down to four, and the Liberals and Irish MPs invariably voting against every Tory motion advocating government backing for a railway line to Uganda, there seemed no chance that Mackinnon's company would be making any profits in the foreseeable future.[5]

But rather than endanger the lives of the Protestant missionaries and their Inglesa converts by obeying the order to quit, Lugard vowed to stay on until a shortage of ammunition and other supplies forced him to pull out. Before that happened, some emergency fund-raising in Britain by supporters of the Church Missionary Society enabled the young officer to cling on in Buganda.

Then, on 22 January 1892, coincidentally Captain Lugard's thirty-fourth birthday, one of the Fransa chiefs who supported the French White Fathers murdered an Inglesa convert. The crime was committed in Mengo, close to the *kabaka*'s palace, and the body was left out in the sun all day. Lugard climbed the hill and demanded that the *kabaka* hand over the murderer so he could be tried and, if found guilty, executed by firing squad. Instead, Mwanga released the arrested Fransa on the grounds that he had acted in self-defence. Then the French priests incited their flock to violence by telling them that Lugard was merely the representative of a trading company and 'could be driven out with sticks'.[6] They denounced the Scottish Protestants as heretics, and refused to tell their flock to disband and disarm as Lugard asked them to do. Their leader, Monsignor Jean-Joseph Hirth, warned Captain Lugard that the French nation was watching events in Buganda very closely.

Lugard feared that unless he could force Mwanga to hand over the murderer, the *kabaka* and the Fransa would take it as a sign of weakness and be encouraged to attack the Inglesa and the company's men. Lugard sent Dualla, his trusted diplomat and interpreter (formerly Stanley's most valued assistant on the Congo) to warn Mwanga to comply or prepare for war with the company. Flanked by Fransa chiefs, Mwanga told Dualla that he and his allies would never give up the accused man and were ready to fight.[7] Hearing this, Lugard armed all his porters as well as his servants and soldiers. Even so, he was considerably outnumbered, although to compensate his 200 Sudanese soldiers were armed with modern Sniders, and he had a Maxim gun. A second Maxim had recently come up from the coast but was not in working order.

On 24 January, Lugard fixed his binoculars on the straggling lines of Fransa and Inglesa colliding in the valley between the lush hills of Rubago and Mengo. Some of the Fransa were waving an immense tricolour. Rather than let the Protestant Scots and their followers be defeated, Lugard deployed his one functioning Maxim with predictable results. The Fransa and the French missionaries fled in terror towards Bulingugwe Island. Then they declined Lugard's well-intended invitation to them to return to Mengo and begin negotiating peace terms. The *kabaka*'s rejection of this offer was a tragic mistake. Lugard ordered his second-in-command, Captain Ashley Williams, to take a detachment of Sudanese troops and his one functioning Maxim to drive them from the island. In the ensuing fight a hundred people lost their lives (many being drowned) and Mwanga fled into exile with the majority of his Catholic supporters.[8]

An understandably emotional version of events was sent to Paris by Monsignor Hirth where it aroused passionate indignation. In London, Lord Salisbury and the British press played down the incident, and defended Lugard from allegations of bad faith and brutality. It would turn out that no French missionary had been killed.[9] Soon after these events Lugard sent emissaries to invite Mwanga to return to Kampala, which he did on 30 March 1892, signing a treaty several days later. This would mark the end of Buganda's independence. The various offices of state were removed from the *kabaka*'s gift and shared out by Lugard between the religious groups, including the Muslims. Control of different parts of the country also passed to the factions, with the Protestants being treated most favourably. Yet, at this moment of apparent triumph for Lugard and Mackinnon, Lord Salisbury lost his slender majority in the House of Commons, and Mr Gladstone was invited by Queen Victoria to form a government.

The Grand Old Man was wholly against making Buganda and wider Uganda a British protectorate. He knew that to enlarge the British Empire, while he was seeking to give Home Rule to the Irish, would be wholly inconsistent. Sir William Harcourt, the new Chancellor of the Exchequer, agreed. By now Lugard was on his way home, determined to fight tooth and nail to ensure that Uganda became British rather than French, which would be its destiny if Gladstone and Harcourt were to have their way. He told Sir Gerald Portal, the newly appointed British Consul General at Zanzibar, that there would be a bloodbath if the government refused to help the Imperial British East Africa Company to stay in Uganda beyond the end of 1892. The Arabs would return, he predicted, and, in alliance with the French, would fall upon the British missionaries and the Inglesa. Portal obligingly cabled to Lord Rosebery, the new Foreign Secretary, stating that withdrawal of the company would 'inevitably result in a massacre of Christians such as the history of this country cannot show'. This communication did not impress Gladstone and Harcourt, who saw no reason to get sucked into a country stuffed with warring factions, where 'endless expense, trouble and disaster' looked to be the most likely reward for intervention.[10]

As soon as Lugard arrived in London, the question whether Britain should retain or abandon Uganda was fiercely debated up and down the country. The young army officer was joined by the veteran explorer, Henry Stanley, in numerous town halls and chambers of commerce. Again and again they asked whether the nation was to be denied a unique opportunity to increase its trade in coffee, cotton, ivory and resins simply because the government lacked the vision and courage to annexe Uganda.

Meanwhile the Church Missionary Society and its supporters organised petitions, urging people to support the company and save the Protestant missionaries from the Muslims and the Catholics.

The Liberal cabinet failed to agree how to respond to the clamour being got up in the press. The octogenarian Prime Minister was implacably opposed to colonial advances in Africa, for moral as well as practical reasons, but Lord Rosebery, his youthful Foreign Secretary and heir apparent, led the wing of the party known as the Liberal Imperialists, whose members favoured progressive policies at home but imperial advances abroad. Rosebery took the same line as Lord Salisbury on the need to secure the Nile's sources for Egypt's sake, and listened sympathetically to Lugard's dire predictions of a massacre of Protestants by Muslims, and a subsequent French take-over if the company withdrew. Rosebery warned his colleagues of the political consequences of allowing the missionaries to come to harm. It would be as damaging to the Liberals as had been their failure to aid General Gordon. Sir William Mackinnon – recently rewarded with a baronetcy by Lord Salisbury for keeping out the Germans – orchestrated a national 'Save Uganda' campaign, and although Harcourt mocked his efforts as 'the whole force of Jingoism at the bellows', the Liberal cabinet was being torn apart from within.[11]

In order to stop Rosebery resigning, the anti-Imperialists in the cabinet were obliged, against all their instincts, to grant Mackinnon's company a subsidy enabling it to remain in Uganda until the end of March 1893, and to send Sir Gerald Portal, who had already made his support for Lugard abundantly clear, as their commissioner to report on Uganda's future. Secretly, Rosebery told Portal to prepare to take over the country from the company. When Portal eventually sent in his report, it predictably contained a recommendation that the government should revoke the company's charter and place Uganda under the supervision of the British state. In addition, he advised that a railway should be built from the coast to Lake Victoria.[12]

Gladstone had surrendered to Rosebery over Uganda in the hope of remaining in power long enough to realise his dream of bringing Home Rule to Ireland. But age and infirmity, and the new imperialism against which he had fought so resolutely, brought about his resignation in March 1894 – the resigning issue being his cabinet colleagues' readiness to increase expenditure on new battleships (it could just as well have been Uganda). Five weeks after the Grand Old Man returned to private life, Rosebery informed both Houses of Parliament that Uganda would not be abandoned. It was declared a protectorate on 27 August 1894, with Equatoria being incorporated as its immense northern province. The tide seemed finally to have turned against the old mid-Victorian Liberal policies of isolation, free trade and *laissez-faire*. With Lord Salisbury's return to power in 1895 a harder more competitive era in foreign affairs had dawned.

As yet the immense territory of the Sudan and its uncharted south had not become the focus of the world's attention, as Uganda and Equatoria had just been. Speke, Grant, Baker, Gordon and his officers, had all criss-crossed this immense hinterland between Buganda and Khartoum, which seemed to offer to any European nation daring enough to grab it, the opportunity to control the Nile, despite the advantage enjoyed by Britain as the possessor of the Ugandan source. Gladstone and Lord Salisbury had ignored the whole region even after the humiliation of Gordon's death, but events would soon bring about a change of heart. The ownership of the Nile from source to sea was about to become the focus of renewed competition.

THIRTY-TWO

To Die for the Mahdi's Cause

───── ∞∞ ─────

In 1895, shortly after Uganda was made a protectorate, Britain's new Colonial Secretary, Joseph Chamberlain – with his trademark monocle in his eye and a home-grown orchid in his button-hole – spoke passionately in Birmingham of the nation's 'manifest destiny' to be 'a great civilising power'.[1] Ironically, forty years earlier, when David Livingstone had spoken of Britain's duty to 'civilise' the peoples of Africa, and had appealed to Prime Minister Palmerston to support the creation of new colonies, he had received a sharp rebuff. Back then the country's naval and industrial lead over other nations had seemed unassailable, only requiring Britain to carry on manufacturing, exporting and controlling the high seas in order to increase its power. But around 1870 Britain's industrial lead over its competitors peaked, and thereafter began to erode as the manufacturing capacity of other nations, such as the United States and Germany, began to grow more rapidly – with both these nations producing more steel than Britain by 1900. So in the 1880s and 1890s, colonial theoreticians came to regard new African colonies as an essential counterweight for island Britain to deploy when facing the massive land powers of Germany, Russia and America.

There had also been a change of moral atmosphere during the intervening decades. In the 1850s Livingstone had declared that new European colonies in Africa would 'bring peace to a hitherto distracted and trodden down race'.[2] By the 1890s, after the discovery of gold on the Witwatersrand, 'imperialism' – once a pejorative term associated by the British with the Empire of Napoleon III of France – was being used as a laudatory description of the indiscriminate acquisition of colonies. Its supporters – both Tory and Liberal Imperialists – dressed up their big idea in the philanthropic and religious phrases which were used by missionaries to justify their own intrusion into far-flung parts of the world. Sometimes the idealism was genuine – the Arab-Swahili slave trade was a great evil that undoubtedly required intervention – but philanthropy (as in the case of King Leopold) could mask baser motives for expansion: the carving out of new markets and the exploitation of minerals.

Among the Nile explorers, Livingstone had not been uniquely naive in seeing colonial advances as the way to usher in 'civilisation'. In 1858, John Speke had written of the need for concerned and 'protecting [European] governments' to reach out into Africa to prevent the strong – whether African or Arab – from exploiting the weak. But he had not wanted 'any foreign European power to upset these Wahuma [local African] governments [which ought] to be maintained as long as possible'.[3] Such gentle attitudes would have caused wry smiles in the British Colonial Office in the 1890s.

In 1896 Britain had still not fitted in the last and largest piece in the jigsaw which would give its rulers control of the Nile from source to sea. But in this year an event occurred that would make it essential, in the British government's eyes, to end the dozen years of inaction which had passed since General Gordon's death. On 1 March, Ethiopian warriors armed by the French with modern rifles, inflicted a devastating defeat on a 20,000-strong Italian expeditionary force under General Oreste Baratieri. The hapless general had been bullied by the Italian cabinet (which was in need of a pre-election colonial 'victory') into attacking the army of Emperor Menelik II, rather than waiting, as common sense demanded, in a well-defended position until the Ethiopians attacked him. In 1889 the Italians had imposed on Menelik a protectorate which he had never accepted. The expulsion of the Italians after the battle of Adowa was the first comprehensive victory in modern history by a non-white people over a European power, and was therefore inherently alarming to all colonial nations, but it shocked the British government most of all.[4] Until Adowa, the Italian presence in Ethiopia had been seen by

Chamberlain as a very satisfactory brake on French ambitions in the region. But with Baratieri's collapse the way had been opened for a two-pronged French advance from east and west into the Sudan. Apart from the old hurt of their replacement by Britain in Egypt, the French now harboured new resentments – one of which was Lugard's treatment of their missionaries in Buganda. A French attempt to claim the Sudan seemed likely soon. Sir Samuel Baker wrote to *The Times* warning that unless Britain re-established control over the Sudan, 'a civilised power' (he meant France) might dam or divert the Nile, to the utter ruin of Egypt. This disastrous scenario haunted young Winston Churchill's imagination when he compared British Egypt's predicament to that of 'a deep-sea diver whose air is provided by the long and vulnerable tube of the Nile'.[5]

So for Britain's Nile policy to succeed, French expeditions had to be stopped before they reached the river. This was a tall order, since by the early 1890s the French had pressed on from the Atlantic to Chad, and Ubangi-Shari (later the Central African Republic) which was on Sudan's western border. But if a French force were ever to span the Nile, threatening to divert its waters, members of the British cabinet believed that they would be forced to negotiate the evacuation of Egypt with the loss of the Suez Canal. So when, in the aftermath of Baratieri's defeat, the Italians appealed to Britain to assist their threatened garrison at Kassala, Chamberlain saw to it that Major-General Sir Horatio Herbert Kitchener was soon leading an Anglo-Egyptian army of 15,000 men south from Egypt towards Dongola, 200 miles upriver in the Sudan.

Lord Salisbury, it became plain, had authorised the recapture of the Sudan from the Mahdists, and on 6 September 1897 Kitchener marched into Berber, which was little more than 200 miles from Khartoum and Omdurman. With his piercing blue eyes and luxuriant moustache, the Sirdar (Commander-in-Chief of the Anglo-Egyptian army) was now forty-eight years old and at the height of his capabilities. Reputed never to have addressed a word to an enlisted man, Kitchener's only soft spots were for his young staff officers (provided they were unmarried) and for his porcelain collection.[6] His clinical efficiency did not bode well for the Mahdi's successor, Khalifa Abdullah ibn Muhammad, and his white-robed army. But the lateness of the Blue Nile surge and of the north winds delayed Kitchener, despite his eagerness to get on with the job and erase the memory of his part in the nation's failure to save General Gordon. His task would be no less difficult than Sir Garnet Wolseley's had been thirteen years earlier. He must defeat the *khalifa* first and then press on south and throw back the French force reported to be closing in on the Nile near the junction with the Bahr el-Ghazal. But Kitchener was determined not to rush as his engineers unrolled a single-track railway line towards Abu Hamed.

Of course the Sirdar had no means of knowing how extraordinarily ambitious current French plans were. This was as well for his peace of mind. In March 1897, the French cabinet had approved the departure of three expeditions, which were intended to meet at Fashoda on the White Nile. Two would set out from the Red Sea and one would march across the continent from the French possessions in west and central Africa. In the meantime, Menelik of Ethiopia had promised to assist them by advancing to the Nile with his army.[7]

In mid-January 1898, two of the *khalifa*'s most battle-hardened *amirs*, Mahmoud Muhammad and Osman Digna, united their forces to make a single army of 10,000 men. They ignored the *khalifa*'s advice to withdraw to a strong defensive position at Sabaluqua and instead advanced on Kitchener's fort at Atbara. On their arrival on the eastern bank of the dried out riverbed they built a *zariba* from thorn bushes and stakes, and waited for Kitchener to arrive from the north. On 8 April, with 12,000 men and an impressive array of field guns, the Sirdar attacked to the sound of bagpipes and fifes. The infantry had little trouble with the thorn bushes, and soon the *amirs'* men were driven down into the riverbed where, lacking cover, they were cut to pieces by the Sirdar's artillery. Three thousand were killed and four thousand wounded, while the British and Egyptians lost 560, with five British officers killed and thirteen wounded. Osman Digna managed to flee the field, but the young and handsome Mahmoud Muhammad was captured and led in chains past his captors, who, forgetting all notions of British fair play, pelted him with rubbish. Imprisoned in a tiny cell in the coastal town of Rosetta, he would die in that town in 1904. Kitchener considered *this* engagement, not the more famous battle which followed, as the turning point of his career. Afterwards, according to the young Winston Churchill, he was 'quite human for half-an-hour', actually becoming emotional as he acknowledged the cheers of his men.[8]

By July the Abu Hamed desert railway had reached Atbara, 1,000 miles from Cairo, bringing supplies for Kitchener's army, by now 26,000 strong, of whom a third were British and the rest Egyptian. On 6 August, the Sirdar's ten gunboats attacked the forts in the Sabaluqa gorge and drove out the garrisons. Then, on 1 September, the Anglo-Egyptian army halted at Kerreri, four miles north of Omdurman and Khartoum, and dug in behind *zaribas* with their backs to the Nile and their forty-eight guns ranged across their front. They were inviting the *khalifa*'s army to come and get them. Across the sand Kitchener could make out the mud walls of Omdurman dominated by the conical dome and soaring arch of the Mahdi's tomb.

The battle of Omdurman began at dawn next day. Opposite the British position, the *khalifa*'s army of 50,000 men, foot-soldiers and horsemen, advanced across a front five miles long. The *khalifa* would have been wiser to have attacked at night or to have waited for Kitchener in the desert, away from the river where the British gunboats were at anchor. For here facing one another were two armies from different centuries. Lieutenant Winston Churchill of the 21st Lancers watched in disbelief as the Arabs came closer over the flat, sandy plain with their distinguishing banners fluttering above their battalions, looking, he declared, in a phrase that would not have pleased his Muslim adversaries, 'like the old representation of the crusaders in the Bayeux tapestry'. The Arabs fired two shells from their meagre

Battle of Omdurman.

artillery which threw up clouds of sand and dust fifty yards from the *zariba*. Seconds later, 'great clouds of smoke appeared along the front of the British and Sudanese brigades ... Above the moving masses shells began to burst, dotting the air with smoke balls and the ground with bodies.' The killing was happening at a distance of two miles. Churchill felt awe and pity as he heard the gunboats add their fire to that of the land batteries.

The entire Mahdist Empire was massed on the last great day of its existence ... Twenty shells hit the white flags in the first minute ... the banners toppled over in all directions. Yet they rose again immediately as other men pressed forward to die for the Mahdi's sacred cause ... It was a terrible sight for as yet they had not hurt us at all ... About five men on the average fell to every shell, and there were many shells ... The lines of spearmen and skirmishers came on in altered formation and diminished numbers but with unaltered enthusiasm ... The further conduct of the debate was left to the infantry and the Maxim guns ... a ragged line of men was coming on, desperately struggling forwards in the face of the pitiless fire ... [The British gunners] fired steadily and stolidly without hurry or excitement.

Indeed it was more like a mass execution than a battle, and it angered Churchill to hear colleagues make deprecating comments about the 'mad fanaticism of the enemy' rather than 'credit them with a nobler motive and believe that they died to clear their honour from the stain of defeat'.[9]

Between dawn and 11.30 a.m. an estimated 10,800 Mahdists had been killed and 16,000 wounded. Kitchener lost a mere 48 killed and 382 wounded. George W. Steevens of the *Daily Mail* praised Kitchener's men for their steadiness, but admitted: 'The honour of the fight must still go with the men who died.'

The destruction of the *khalifa*'s army made Britain the effective ruler of the Sudan – although publicly the whole enterprise was said to be in partnership with Egypt. The whole length of the White Nile was now in British hands.[10]

'Remember Gordon,' Kitchener had told his men before the battle, and two days later he held a memorial service in the ruined courtyard of Gordon's palace, where he hoisted the Union Jack and the Khedival flag after the assembled regiments had sung Gordon's favourite hymn: 'Abide with me.'[11] Now Kitchener gave orders for the Mahdi's shrine to be demolished and his bones to be tossed into the Nile. As a tit-for-tat revenge for the decapitation of Gordon's dead body, the Sirdar had the Mahdi's skull brought to him. His macabre plan was to turn it into an inkstand. However, when word of his intention reached Queen Victoria's ears she forbade it, and he was obliged to pass the skull to Sir Evelyn Baring, the British Consul-General in Cairo, who buried it quietly in a cemetery in Wadi Halfa. Kitchener's more discreet intelligence chief, General Reginald Wingate, hunted down and killed the *khalifa* and made *his* skull into an inkstand, having kept his own counsel.[12]

Kitchener had known for several months that the French were finally on their way; and, while still at Omdurman, he learned from the crew of a captured Mahdist gunboat, the *Tawfiqia* (which had originally belonged to General Gordon), that in July they had been attacked by foreigners at Fashoda, 700 miles to the south. So on 8 September, Kitchener headed south in the steamer *Dal* at the head of a flotilla of four gunboats towing twelve barges accommodating two Sudanese battalions, an Egyptian battery, a company of Cameron Highlanders and four Maxim guns. Three days later, Kitchener's flotilla moored between reedy banks just north of Fashoda.

Realising that the situation was dangerous and diplomatically very delicate, the Sirdar tactfully flew the Egyptian flag rather than the Union Jack and did not press Major Jean-Baptiste Marchand, the French commanding officer, to haul down the Tricolour which was fluttering above the old regional Mahdist headquarters.[13] After the great feat of crossing the continent from Brazzaville with 150 riflemen, Marchand had found on his arrival at Fashoda that he had been let down by the other two French commanders under orders to meet him on the Nile, and also by the hard-headed Menelik.

Kitchener made clear to Marchand, who was threatening to die for the honour of France, that, whatever the Frenchman might try to do, Kitchener meant to take possession of Fashoda for the government of Egypt. He advised Marchand to 'consider the preponderance of the force at his [Kitchener's] disposal', and told him that unless he behaved sensibly the affair could develop into a full-blown war between their two countries.[14] Since the French cabinet was just then grappling with the Dreyfus scandal and its revelation of virulent anti-Semitism in the republic's army, the added difficulty of war with Britain was the last thing French politicians wanted. The inescapable fact was that the French navy was no match for the Royal Navy, and would be defeated even if the Russians were to come in on the side of France. So the French would never be given an opportunity to exploit the numerical superiority of their army. Nor could the French Foreign Minister, Théophile Delcassé – who would soon have the unenviable job of negotiating with the canny Lord Salisbury – claim that possession of the Sudan was a vital interest for his country, in the same way that Salisbury could do, as ruler of Egypt. Thanks to Kitchener's restraint and Delcassé's good sense, Marchand's men pulled out of Fashoda on 11 December 1899 without a drop of blood being shed.

To mollify France, Britain substituted on all maps the name Kodok – a nearby Shilluk village – for that of Fashoda.[15] So

A romantic French view of Marchand and his mission.

ended an incident which, had Kitchener made a false move, could have changed the course of European, as well as African history. If Marchand had led a quixotic charge on the Cameron Highlanders, and the French press had made him a martyr, there would have been no *Entente Cordiale* a few years later, and Britain's enemy in the twentieth century could well have been France rather than Germany.

By the terms of the Anglo-French Declaration signed two months after Marchand's departure, France allowed Sudan's border to be stretched westwards at its expense and to incorporate Darfur within Sudan – an arrangement not considered momentous at the time, but of immense importance a century later when an independent Arab government in Khartoum was able to practise ethnic cleansing with impunity against Darfur's black Muslims because they lived within Sudan's legal borders. Before 1898, the Sultanate of Darfur had been fully independent.

*

393

Had Livingstone lived to read about the Battle of Omdurman he would have been disgusted by the scale of the slaughter. He had hated the slave trade and had known that the Baqqara Arabs of the Sudan were inveterate slavers, but he had always made a distinction between the cruel manner in which slaves were torn from their homes and the often humane way in which they were treated by their owners. Indeed he had come to consider many Arabs his friends. Burton too would have been appalled by the use of such overwhelming force. A similar attack on Africans would have distressed him much less. Speke's and Grant's arrival in Buganda, and Stanley's appeal for missionaries, were essential early links in the chain of causation that ended at Omdurman; so what would they have thought of Kitchener's bloody completion of Britain's acquisition of the Nile?

Shocked, I believe. When Pethcrick had failed Speke, the Arab, Mohammed Wad-el-Mek, had not; indeed Speke had felt that unless Wad-el-Mek had met him at Faloro, he and Grant would never have reached Gondokoro alive. Though Speke had never shared Burton's fondness for Arabs, he had not shunned them either. Of the five great Nile explorers only Baker might have applauded the scale of Kitchener's victory if he had lived to see it. Stanley, who had written in strong terms about the wickedness of individual slave traders, and had regretted not having a Maxim with him when he had met a large party of slavers on the Upper Congo in 1883, was alive but did not applaud the manner in which Mahdism had been brought to an end. But then he had always maintained that Gordon had invited his own death.

THIRTY-THREE

Equatoria and the Tragedy of Southern Sudan

⸗⸗⸗

There can be no denying that the nationality of Burton, Speke, Grant, Baker and Stanley was one of the most significant factors determining the brief colonial 'ownership' of Sudan, Uganda and Kenya. This matters because the future of these countries would be profoundly affected by their having fallen into the colonial portfolio of a single 'great power'. Had Sudan been annexed by France say, and Uganda by Britain (as of course happened) then the precise location of the boundary between the two countries would have been matters for international arbitration rather than the *diktat* of a single nation, and in that case – with a differently drawn boundary – the tragic twentieth-century war in southern Sudan might never have happened. Nor might the north/south divide in Uganda have come into existence to cause so much bloodshed and misery in that country.

It is never easy to pick the first significant event in a long chain of consequences that end in tragedy many decades later. In the case of southern Sudan, one might argue that the first was when John Speke mentioned Lake Albert to Samuel Baker and handed him the future fame that would lead to his employment by Khedive Ismail as his new Governor-General in the Sudan. But a more convincing first event is when Baker raised the Egyptian flag at Gondokoro in 1871, declaring himself the founder of Equatoria – his name for Egypt's most southerly province. Soon Sir Samuel was claiming for the *khedive*, and for Equatoria, the land of the Bari and the Dinka, and territory as far south as Lake Albert and the kingdom of Bunyoro, with the Bahr el-Ghazal and Acholiland thrown in. In due course Equatoria would extend as far north as

Malakal on the White Nile, a place which has rightly been said 'to hang between two worlds'. In its market northern Arabs mingle with Africans: Nuer, Dinka and Shilluk. To the south stretch the swamps, the plains, the religions and languages of Africa.[1]

In the nineteenth and well into the twentieth century the inhabitants of Equatoria usually went naked, both men and women, and the males carried bows with feathered arrows and rubbed their bodies with grease and ashes. One group of Dinka, encountered by Samuel Baker, also 'stained their hair red by a plaster of ashes and cows' urine ... Of all the unearthly looking devils I ever saw,' remarked Sir Samuel, who was no ethnographer, 'these devils beat them hollow.'[2] Indeed, Equatoria was an entirely African territory in which the northern Arabs were considered invaders and exploiters. In the early 1870s, during his push south to Bunyoro and his subsequent return, Baker made determined efforts to drive the Arab slave traders away from the upper Nile. After Baker went home in 1873, General Gordon and Emin Pasha (as Governor-General of the Sudan and Governor of Equatoria respectively) consolidated and extended the borders of Equatoria, while continuing Baker's onslaughts against the slavers.[3] Under these governors, conditions in Equatoria improved steadily, so much so that Professor Robert Collins, the great historian of the Sudan, believes that the smaller tribes were saved from extinction at this time.[4]

But in 1889, after Henry Stanley had evacuated Emin Pasha in the wake of the Mahdists' southward drive, the Pasha's second-in-command, Selim Bey, stayed on at Lake Albert with several hundred Sudanese soldiers.[5] Instead of protecting the people of the region, his men began a regime of cattle theft, abduction and rape. Meanwhile, further north, the Bari and the Azande fought the Mahdists in what for them was merely the latest misfortune in a long sequence.[6] Only after Omdurman, did the British enter the Bahr el-Ghazal region of Equatoria to try to end the anarchy. They conquered with a mixture of persuasion and force, but it would be the late 1920s before anything resembling peace had been established in this ravaged and mistrustful region.[7]

Captain Henry Kelly, Royal Engineers.

Tragedy for Equatoria moved much closer when Britain allocated half the 800-mile wide and 500-mile deep territory to Uganda and the other half to Sudan. That it might have been better to preserve its unique identity as a potential nation in its own right was something the British government did not seriously consider. In 1913 Britain's Governor-General of the Sudan, General Sir Reginald Wingate, appointed a boundary commission to determine where Sudan ended and Uganda began. The commission was led by Captain Harry H. Kelly, an officer in the Royal Engineers, who also happened to be the heavyweight boxing champion of the British Army. Uganda was represented by Captain H. M. Tufnell, who had helped to overawe the tribes of southern Equatoria and was not reluctant to order the commission's fifty black soldiers to fire fusillades whenever the surveying party was opposed by hostile villagers. Kelly deplored using force and, unlike Tufnell, who wanted to go on leave, was worried that if they made hurried decisions they might split tribes unnecessarily. Though not an anthropologist, Kelly could see that the Raajok and Obbo people were 'as truly Acholi as anyone else'. Indeed the Langi, Acholi and Obbo had much in common from their shared Luo heritage. He noted in his diary that he meant to stay on for ten extra days in order 'to come to a definite conclusion based on knowledge and not on supposition' about the hill-dwelling Acholi.[8] But despite his best efforts, the Madi would be split by his commission, and the northern Acholi would also be separated from the rest of their tribe. Yet Kelly, as his diary shows, was admirably patient in carrying out his task, even after several of his men had been killed by tribesmen.[9] In truth, the problem did not lie with the men on the spot but with the Foreign Office and the Colonial Office, and with decision-makers at the highest level in Britain.

An artificial solution to the problem of what to do with 'the savages' of Equatoria had been found by senior officials and was to be acted upon without further ado. So Uganda was going to get an influx of Nilotic people, with whom the southern Bantu, such as the all-important people of Buganda (the Baganda), would feel that they had nothing in common. Similarly, the Arabs of northern Sudan would be unable to relate to the southern tribes, whose culture they already derided and whom they had long raided and enslaved. An almost incalculable amount of suffering would spring from Britain's decision to dispose of Equatoria so casually. Of course, the harm could have been mitigated if British civil servants in Khartoum had then designed policies aimed at creating understanding between Arabs and Africans within Sudan. In truth, their master plan would do the opposite, merely exacerbating feelings of alienation and hostility.

Ironically, the Sudan Political Service, Britain's executive in the Sudan, was the most highly educated ruling elite in the history of empire. Sudan has memorably been said to have been 'a land of Blacks ruled by Blues'. Indeed, one in four of its officials over fifty years had won a Blue for sporting prowess at Oxford or

Cambridge, and ten per cent had gained a first-class degree at one or other of those universities. Never more than 125 strong at any given time, they ruled effectively (at least in the north), abolishing slavery, and promoting agriculture, public health and education in Africa's largest colony.[10] Most of these intelligent young men were Arabic speakers who found the northerners, whom they met on a daily basis in Khartoum, eager for education and economic development. But the southern Sudanese appeared in a very different light, striking the most senior civil servant in the country as relics from 'the Serbonian bog into which they had drifted, or been pushed . . . [guaranteeing that] all the lowest racial elements surviving north of the equator' were to be found in southern Sudan.[11]

Sir Harold MacMichael, who wrote those words, was the top civil servant in the Sudan. With his Cambridge first in classics, his fencing Blue and his titled mother, he loved social life in Khartoum, and postponed a visit to 'the Serbonian bog' for seven years after his appointment. Eventually in 1927 he took the plunge, and his few days down south shocked him to the core. Depending upon whether it was the wet season or the dry, the whole southern region was either a gigantic swamp, or an endless mud-baked plain. The Nilotic peoples who lived in this hot and treeless wilderness – the Dinka, Nuer and the Annuak – were tall, physically graceful, proud, and absolutely determined to preserve their way of life in their remote and inaccessible habitat. MacMichael, from behind the anti-mosquito wire-netting which protected the passenger deck of his comfortable steamer, feared that it would be impossible to persuade such people to embrace 'civilisation' as the northern Arabs appeared to wish to do. In Equatoria there was no 'native administration' to build on, and little chance of initiating a system of agricultural exports that would pay for the region's development. He therefore refused to commit his administration to the expense of building roads and improving water access. Such a project ought to have been his number one priority, but instead a policy of benign (in reality malign) neglect was dreamed up. It would insultingly be known as 'care and maintenance'.[12] Nor was 'Macmic', as MacMichael was affectionately known, going to send any of his gilded young Arabists from the Sudan Political Service to sweat, and possibly be speared to death, in the mosquito-infested south.

The men chosen to 'care' for the south were described sardonically by the Khartoum elite as 'the Bog Barons'. Mainly former army officers, they treated the inhabitants of their administrative districts with a mixture of despotic arrogance and genuine affection. They took great risks in their efforts to get the Dinka and Nuer to accept the Khartoum government, and some, such as Captain V. H. Fergusson, were murdered – in his case by a Nuer who had thought, thanks to a confusion over words, that 'Fergie' had come to his village to castrate him. This murder, like all others, would unleash ferocious British punitive expeditions.[13] But Major Mervyn J. Wheatley, who was a future mayor and MP, refused to crush the Dinka by waging war and bravely set about persuading them to make peace by making personal contact. Jack Herbert Driberg was not a soldier, but he exemplified the best qualities of the Bog Barons: disdainful of Khartoum officials, this poet, boxer and one-time music critic loved the Didinga people, fought their corner vigorously, and in 1930 published a book about them: *People of the Small Arrow*. Eventually he was sacked for allowing his partisanship to lead him physically to attack the Didinga's enemies. Some barons were extremely eccentric, like the officer who dressed the crew of his private Nile steamer in jerseys embroidered with Arabic words meaning: 'I am oppressed.' Inevitably in their isolated situation a number of barons took African mistresses.[14]

For all the Bog Barons' success in winning the trust of the indigenous peoples of the south, much more was needed if their charges were ever to participate as equal partners in an independent Sudan. Above all, a better understanding was urgently required between north and south, especially in matters of education, language and culture. Yet, from as early as 1898, Sir Reginald Wingate had encouraged British missionaries to go out to Equatoria to convert the locals and teach them English. Wingate wanted to turn southern Sudan into a Christian bulwark that would protect Uganda and Kenya from the southward spread of Islam.

In 1910, Wingate went further and sanctioned the formation of a separate Equatorial Corps manned by non-Muslim Africans for military service in the south. Within seven years all northern troops had been withdrawn from the Bahr el-Ghazal area. The teaching of English and the exclusion of Arabic from southern schools had become official policy from as early as 1904, but, as Wingate had advised, it was to be implemented 'without any fuss and without putting the dots on the *is* too prominently'. So English became the *lingua franca* in the south almost by stealth, only becoming official in 1930.[15]

It might be thought that Wingate and his successors had been secretly planning to unite southern Sudan with Uganda. But no direct evidence that this was really their intention exists. Meanness does not entirely account for low spending on education in the south. There was a genuine fear among the Bog Barons that education *per se* might undermine a rich traditional way of life without putting anything of value in its place. 'It is essential,' said a speaker at an educational conference in Juba in 1933, 'that we who are concerned with education should keep clearly in mind that education is a preparation and training for life in a tribal community which still contains social virtues which we in our individualistic western civilization are losing or have lost.'[16]

It would be eleven years before the Governor-General's council finally abandoned their Arcadian view of the south. In 1944, it was reluctantly accepted that Britain had less than twenty years (in truth a dozen) in which to prepare the country for independence. The mistakes of the past were to prove impossible to put right in the midst of a world war in which Britain was fighting for survival. But the language of the north was finally introduced into southern secondary schools in 1948 in a last-ditch attempt to prevent the southern Sudanese from being gravely disadvantaged in a country that would soon be ruled by Arabic-speakers.[17]

But perhaps the south could still be saved from subordination and second-class citizenship if a brave political decision could be made. In 1943, C. H. L. Skeet, the Governor of Equatoria, still hoped that the British government would keep all options open:

The political future of the Southern Sudan cannot yet be determined, but whatever it may be, we should work to a scheme of self-government which would fit in with an ultimate attachment of the Southern peoples southwards or northwards [i.e. connected with Sudan or with Uganda] ... The policy that is being adopted makes political adhesion to the North improbable from *the Southern Point of View*.[18]

A year later, the Governor-General, Sir Douglas Newbold, tried to persuade the Sudanese nationalists, who would soon be ruling Sudan, to leave the south to the British, but he was angrily rebuffed. So, in April 1944, the Governor-General's council at last decided to embark on a regime of 'intensive economic and educational development in southern Sudan'. Since no other money was available, this would have to be paid for with northern funds. This hard fact ended 'any serious prospect of the separation of the two regions'. Of course no 'intensive' programme was going to make up for thirty years of neglect and the south was now doomed to be subservient after independence.[19] Nor was there any practical possibility of attaching the Nilotic peoples of southern Sudan to Uganda with its Bantu-dominated south. British officials and the Bagandan elite would have rejected the idea out of hand.

In reality the only way to have avoided future tragedy would have been to preserve Equatoria as a nation in its own right. Yet to attempt to redraw the 1913 border in the 1940s would probably have provoked the northern Sudanese to armed resistance. And in any case it is doubtful whether Uganda's mission-educated northerners would ever have consented to becoming part of southern Sudan – a less developed country than the one to which they were currently attached.

Yet Sudan's south was not going to accept absorption and control by the Muslim north. The rebellion that had been brewing for two decades erupted in southern Sudan on 18 August 1955, five months before independence, when the Equatorial Corps mutinied against northern Sudanese officers who had just replaced that corps' popular British commanders. The long and tragic Sudanese civil war had started. It would last, with an interval of eleven years, until 2005, by which time four decades of fighting would have cost two million lives.[20]

Of course the roll call of people individually and collectively responsible for this terrible disaster was long. Sir Reginald Wingate, Sir Harold MacMichael and successive British Colonial Secretaries must bear a share of the blame for what happened by their failure to plan the development of the south and to foresee the suffering that would ensue if the south was still part of Sudan when independence came. Nor should Sir Samuel Baker escape blame for eagerly agreeing to extend Egyptian power to the borders of the future Uganda and beyond, thus lumping together, for the very first time, Arab Sudan and African Equatoria in a union that was destined to stick. In fairness to him, Gordon and Emin Pasha followed his lead and consolidated the territory he had claimed.

The northern Sudanese were also culpable, some of them criminally so. Even at the eleventh hour, before the mutiny, Sudan's first government-elect could have heeded the south's demand for southerners to be appointed to senior positions in the administration and the police. Yet, instead of demonstrating the unity of the nation by making appointments that would have made the southerners feel included, Ismail al-Azhari and his cabinet insulted them by offering beggarly junior appointments instead of the governorships and deputy governorships that had been asked for. This fault of deliberately ignoring a federal solution in favour of a military one would be repeated by Jafar Numeiri, Sadiq al-Mahdi, and most of all by the fundamentalists Hassan al-Turabi and Omar al-Bashir.[21] In the end, despite the fact that 90 per cent of the members of Sudan's Muslim Brotherhood had been British- or American-educated, and despite the existence of multi-party politics, the religious fundamentalists engineered a coup and took over in the late 1980s after losing at the ballot box in 1986.

*

Just over a century after General Gordon had been killed on the steps of his palace, and thirty years after independence, a Sudanese general – Omar al-Bashir, now president of Sudan – addressed a rally in Khartoum, holding a Koran in one hand and a Kalashnikov in the other. It was as if the religious fundamentalism of the Mahdi, which had flowed underground for the tranquil duration of British rule, had simply re-emerged a century later. Under Bashir's Islamic dictatorship the war against the south became a *jihad* and the Sudanese government actively encouraged militias to go on slave raids there, and in Darfur. Bashir and his elderly mentor, the Islamic scholar and Sorbonne-educated lawyer, Hassan al-Turabi, welcomed to their country groups interested in joining the 'war on America'. Among those choosing Sudan as a base was the Saudi construction magnate, Osama bin Laden. His choice of location seemed to influence the language he would use against the Americans, since it bore a striking resemblance to the Mahdi's pronouncements against the British and the Egyptians a century earlier. Terrorist attacks mounted from Sudan included an attempt to kill the former Egyptian president Hosni Mubarak, and bombings in Israel, Kenya and Tanzania. Whatever the faults and omissions of the

Omar al-Bashir.

British administrators, they will forever be dwarfed by the crimes of their Sudanese successors.[22]

Now, in the eleventh year of the twenty-first century, 99 per cent of voters in southern Sudan have opted for secession from the north, as they were entitled to do under the terms of the 2005 peace treaty brokered by America and Britain. So what should have happened before Sudan's independence in 1956 has happened fifty-five years after it. The remedy, however, will be incomplete since the southern half of Equatoria will remain within Uganda. Nor is there any certainty that northern Sudan will respect the south's independent statehood in the years to come.

In 1955 and 1956, British civil servants in Khartoum had made last-ditch efforts to protect the south with safeguards, but the Suez imbroglio had defeated them.[23] T. R. H. Owen, the last British Governor of Bahr el-Ghazal, wrote an anguished verse in which he articulated a sense of betrayal, which he shared with his fellow Bog Barons:

> 'We much regret -' 'Reasons of state demand -'
> What? That our clear commitments shall not stand?
> That suave appeasement and our craven fears
> Annul the confidence of fifty years?[24]

THIRTY-FOUR

A Sin not Theirs:
The Tragedy of Northern Uganda

In Buganda the British presence had been broadly accepted since 1892 when Frederick Lugard had defeated Mwanga and the Fransa. The support of men like Apolo Kagwa – the Protestant *katikiro* or prime minister, who would soon be knighted – and the Catholic leader, Stanislas Mugwanya, provided an effective counterweight to the still volatile Kabaka Mwanga. A reconstituted *lukiko*, or *kabaka*'s council, began functioning in the mid-1890s, with Baganda Protestants, Catholics and Muslims all represented alongside traditional chiefs. The kingdom of Buganda was to be the core of the new Uganda Protectorate, and Buganda's institutions were chosen by the British as the template for other kingdoms and territories. Indeed, the cooperation of 'civilised' Buganda made it possible for Britain to govern the enlarged and wilder peripheries of the Protectorate. But how large should Uganda be and where should its northern boundaries be set?

The seeds of future disaster were planted by the British when Uganda was extended to include not only Buganda's enemies, like Bunyoro, but also ethnic groups north of Karuma Falls and Lake Kyoga in territory where Speke and Grant had been the first European visitors and where Baker had established a transitory control. Whatever the desirability or undesirability of including Bunyoro within Uganda, early in 1894 Colonel Henry Colvile, the senior military officer in the Protectorate, took matters into his own hands and, without thought for future consequences, decided that Kabarega, the *omukama* of Bunyoro, would never accept British rule until his army had been defeated. This opinion was based in part on Sir Samuel Baker's unfairly damning opinion of Kabarega, but also on Bunyoro's habit of giving asylum to *jihadist* Muslims and anyone else opposed to British rule. Colvile attacked with 450 Sudanese troops and 20,000 Baganda spearmen and riflemen, who were to prove enthusiastic allies. Kabarega withdrew northwards having burned his capital behind him, and was eventually driven from his country into Acholiland.[1]

The situation became more complicated when Kabaka Mwanga rebelled against the curtailment of his powers and formed an alliance with Kabarega. The two kings were finally defeated and captured in 1898 and exiled to the Seychelles. Mwanga had rebelled despite having signed two treaties, but Kabarega had agreed to nothing and his exile until 1923 was a wholly unjust punishment for someone who had defended his country successfully against Emin Pasha and had merely tried to do the same against Colvile. However, Kabarega was hated by his neighbours and several years before his capture had invaded the kingdom of Toro, capturing thousands of men, women and children, and murdering the two young princes closest in line of succession to the throne. Mwanga would die in exile in 1903, and Kabarega would only be permitted to go home twenty years later. He died at Jinja in Buganda before reaching his kingdom to which he had waited so long to return. One of Idi Amin's few commendable acts was to rename the Murchison Falls the Kabarega Falls.[2]

Up to 1898 British administration did not extend further than the four southern kingdoms and Busoga. They could reasonably have been expected to form a relatively harmonious nation-state. Unfortunately matters were not to remain that way. In 1899 Sir Harry Johnston, recently appointed Special Commissioner to Uganda, made a formal declaration to the effect that the northern limit of the Protectorate lay at 5° North Latitude, a line which took in most of the southern half of Baker's Equatoria. The Governor of Uganda Protectorate, Sir Hesketh Bell, was a firm believer in employing existing chiefs and kings to implement British rule, so he objected to Johnston's plan on the grounds that this extension of territory would bring within the boundaries of the Protectorate tribes who were 'without Sultans or Kings', as Speke had described them three decades earlier. Bell was sure that the absence of substantial African chiefdoms would make the north ungovernable since 'indirect rule' could not work without paramount chiefs. As late as 1920, there were still only fifty-nine British administrators in the entire country.[3]

Sir Hesketh also knew that tribes like the Acholi and Langi had little in common with the people of Buganda with their bark-cloth clothes, their ironwork, elaborately constructed houses, and their monarchy dating back four centuries. The naked Acholi belonged culturally to the Central Sudanic and Eastern Nilotic peoples of the northern frontier region rather than to the more sophisticated Bantu settled around Lake Victoria.[4] While keenly aware of the dangers of getting involved with the northern region, Bell also knew that for decades Ethiopian elephant hunters and Arab slave and ivory traders had been selling modern rifles to the Acholi and the Langi. These weapons were now being used in local feuds which he feared might spread south if left unchecked. Sir Hesketh retired before deciding what to do, but in 1911, the new Governor, Sir Frederick Jackson, concluded that unless he soon gained control over this anarchic region, it might be impossible to do so later.[5]

The British plan was to introduce a Buganda-type administration into all the northern territories, creating in every 'tribal territory' a 'central native council' consisting of the most prominent chiefs and headmen, with the district commissioner as chief executive. At a level below this council there would be county chiefs, many of whom would be British appointees brought in from Buganda.[6]

The Langi, Acholi, Madi and Karamajong had much in common, culturally and linguistically. They also shared an informal consensus-seeking style of government under many small chiefs and elders. However, the imposition of centralised government upon each individual tribe, once carried out, inevitably fostered an idea of separate identity based on ethnicity.

This would not help Uganda to develop as a united nation state.[7] The missionaries also promoted pride in tribe by developing written vernacular languages and compiling accounts of tribal history. In truth, the strengthening of tribal awareness suited the colonial power, since if different ethnic groups saw themselves as distinct from each other, they would be less likely to make common cause against their rulers.[8]

In the 1970s and 1980s a number of anthropologists and historians insisted that many 'tribes' had actually come into existence only because it had suited the colonial authorities to consolidate small, often ill-defined ethnic groups in order to create larger, more coherent units of administration.[9] But the idea that the Europeans had 'invented' new tribes and their traditions was later seen as patronising to Africans who would never, surely, have been as gullible as to accept invented identities.[10] In the context of northern Uganda, although British administrators and missionaries may well have made the Acholi feel different from the Langi and Madi, there can be no doubt that they nonetheless continued to feel a lot closer culturally to these neighbours than to the Bantu in southern Uganda.

The British saw the tall and robust northerners as potential recruits for Uganda's army and police, or as migrant labour to deploy in the more developed south; and as a result of the administration's tendency to recruit Acholi into the army in preference to members of all other tribes, the Acholi's link with the military grew stronger over the years. Indeed by the 1960s, just prior to independence, the Acholi constituted the largest single group within Uganda's army.[11] Moreover, since they had good reason to be envious of the otherwise more highly favoured Baganda, it could and should have been foreseen that, by packing the army with Acholi, a time-bomb was being primed for the future. In this way the disastrous decision to include the southern part of Equatoria within Uganda was made immeasurably worse.

After supporting the British since the beginning of the protectorate and being well rewarded for their loyalty, the Baganda and their Cambridge-educated *kabaka* viewed the approach of independence from Britain with understandable foreboding. Although the Baganda inhabited the largest single kingdom or territory in the nation-state, they only accounted for one-fifth of Uganda's total population. So they could never hope to do better than rule in an alliance with another party or parties. By 1960, Milton Obote's leadership of the Uganda People's Congress seemed likely to propel him to the premiership. Because he was the son of a chief of the northern Langi, he could count on the support of all northerners, including the Acholi with their dominant presence in the army. He could also expect the majority of votes from the Baganda's traditional enemies such as the Nyoro (people of Bunyoro). This situation did not bode well for the future. Yet after independence in 1962, four years of peace and prosperity followed.

Because Uganda was a protectorate and not a colony most of the land had remained in African ownership. In 1931 there had still only been 385 Europeans working for private companies and only 2,000 Britons working for the government, and these numbers would not change significantly. This removed any post-independence threat of conflict between black and white – of the kind which would develop into major struggles in Kenya and Rhodesia with their large white-settler populations. Also, in 1962, the Ugandan economy was sound, with exports of tea, coffee and cotton booming. However, despite this prosperity, a power struggle between the all-African constituent parts of the country looked all but certain.

Under the constitution, Buganda had federal status and was allowed to retain its own parliament and traditions, though not to be autonomous. The national government was expected to rule the whole country. In pre-independence elections, the left-leaning Milton Obote only achieved a majority in the National Assembly with the support of the *kabaka*'s political party, and so was obliged to cooperate with His Highness Sir Frederick Edward Mutesa II, 35th *kabaka* of Buganda. Obote even had to grit his teeth and approve Mutesa's appointment as head of state in 1963.[12]

Milton Obote.

Obote, however, was determined to institute one-party rule and he took a giant leap towards it in 1966 by arresting five Baganda cabinet ministers, dissolving parliament and imposing a new constitution, which denied all the kingdoms the right to have their own parliaments. This was done on the eve of a parliamentary investigation into charges that Obote and his new army commander, Colonel Idi Amin, had been smuggling gold bars out of the Republic of the Congo to turn into cash in Uganda and then re-export this money to pay for a coup in Congo's eastern province against the American-backed government. In fact much of the money would remain in Amin's bank account.

The *kabaka* protested about the arrests and tried to negotiate with Obote, pending a court case. Obote had no time for the law and simply sent Amin to storm the royal palace on Mengo Hill. With so many northerners in the army, the troops obeyed their orders in this attack on the privileged southerners. In the assault several hundred Baganda were killed, but Mutesa II avoided summary execution by scaling a back wall, jumping down into the street and hailing a taxi that happened to be passing. This lucky chance enabled him to escape to Britain via Burundi.[13]

Although British rule had always depended on Buganda's active cooperation, no financial help was forthcoming from Westminster when the exiled *kabaka* arrived in London. Fortunately for 'King Freddie' (as the UK press would always call him) after leaving Magdalene College, Cambridge, he had been for several years an officer in the Grenadier Guards. A brother officer, Major Richard Carr-Gomm, had been a close friend. The major had subsequently left the army to found a charity with his own considerable fortune, helping homeless and isolated people in the East End of London. Carr-Gomm gave the *kabaka* the use of a rent-free, two-bedroom flat in Bermondsey. Here Mutesa II would live out the last three years of his life, living (not in a council flat as was often claimed in the press) but in cramped conditions nonetheless, with his bodyguard, Major Katende, and his ADC, George Maaolo, and an admiring graduate student, Ignatius Iga, all sleeping in one bedroom, while the *kabaka* slept in the other. The former Attorney General of Buganda, Frederick Mpanga, and C. M. S. Mukasa, the former head of Buganda's Civil Service, would often visit, as would the *kabaka*'s daughter, Sarah Kagere, and his brother, Prince Harry Kimera.

On 21 November 1969, after some heavy drinking around the time of his forty-fifth birthday, the *kabaka* collapsed in the evening, and was put to bed by Major Katende, who did not check up on him until several hours later when he was found to be dead. John Simpson, then a young BBC journalist, had seen Mutesa earlier in the day and would later declare that he had been sober and apparently in good health when he spoke to him. Although a coroner gave the cause of death as 'alcohol poisoning', Major Carr-Gomm stated that Mutesa was neither a heavy drinker nor an alcoholic and that he personally suspected that the *kabaka* had been poisoned. A young Ugandan policewoman, posing as a student, but working as a spy for Obote, had visited the *kabaka*'s flat several times during the preceding couple of weeks, but Carr-Gomm could not prove that she had ever been alone with Mutesa in order to administer a slow-acting poison. Lord Boyd, who had been Secretary of State for the Colonies at the time of the Kenyan Mau Mau rebellion, went with Carr-Gomm to ask Sir John Waldron, the Commissioner of the Metropolitan Police, to launch an official inquiry, which he declined to do. The commissioner genuinely believed that the deeply unhappy *kabaka* had drunk himself to death. This was almost exactly a century after Speke had sat staring for an hour at his all-powerful grandfather in Mengo.

After a funeral in the Guards' Chapel, Wellington Barracks, Mutesa was buried in Kensal Green Cemetery. Two years later, after Idi Amin's coup against Obote, Amin offered the late

Mutesa II, *kabaka* of Buganda, at his coronation. He was known in Britain as 'King Freddie'.

kabaka a state funeral in Buganda, which his family accepted. So Mutesa II was exhumed and reburied with his ancestors at Kasubi. His family, and Carr-Gomm, who was the guardian of several of his children, attended the funeral and were struck by the irony of occasion. General Amin, who was orchestrating proceedings, would have killed Mutesa on the spot if he had caught him in his palace three years earlier.[14]

In retrospect it is easy to see that Obote, and Amin after him, used the army to make themselves the sole inheritors of the all-powerful centralised colonial state. Obote abolished democracy, and all Uganda's monarchies, after his coups of 1966 and 1967. An era of tyranny ensued. In time it would become clear that former princes and monarchs often made better rulers of independent states than the new African politicians like Kaunda, Nkrumah and Obote with their academic qualifications and scorn for the backwardness of kings and chiefs. Nelson Mandela, a Xhosa prince, Haile Selassie, the Ethiopian Emperor, and Seretse Khama of Botswana, who had come to the Tswana throne as a child, were all successful leaders.[15]

Uganda might have stood a better chance of good governance if Britain had given the kingdoms and territories something very close to autonomy. Clearly the Westminster-style first-past-the-post electoral system was wholly unsuited to Uganda's realities. Only federal power-sharing would have had any chance of working.[16] Yet with rulers like Obote and Amin determined to mobilise their northern ethnic support, which was concentrated in the army, it is hard to imagine any constitutional framework surviving their attempts to subvert it. Just as Obote had purged the army of Baganda officers and packed it with Acholi and Langi, Amin (from the north-west of the country) increased the number of West Nilers in the officer corps. To make room for these Lugbara and Kakwa, he liquidated many of Obote's Acholi and Langi officers.[17]

Once the army had become an instrument of domestic politics, the nightmare predicted by Chinua Achebe in his prophetic novel, *A Man of the People*, came to pass and a succession of

African leaders stole the state from the people and appropriated its assets for themselves. Richard Dowden, the Director of the Royal African Society, has dismissed the claim that Africa's dictators have simply been imitating their former colonial masters. The dictators have real power, whereas the power of the British governors 'was largely an illusion projected by display and ceremony'. European District Commissioners had typically 'travelled their domain by bicycle' wearing shorts and open-necked shirts. 'Their successors as local governors in many parts of Africa today wear dark suits and travel in a black Mercedes Benz escorted by heavily armed military convoys. Anyone on a bicycle is driven into the ditch.' Nor can the dictators excuse themselves because famous African rulers in history such as Shaka, Mzilikazi and Mirambo were tyrants. In pre-colonial days, the powers of lesser African chiefs had typically been limited by headmen and *ngangas*.[18]

After Amin's fall in 1979, Obote returned to preside over five more years of chaos, persecution and civil war, which only ended when the Acholi/Langi alliance within the army unravelled and General Tito Okello, an Acholi, mounted a successful coup against Obote, becoming the first ever Acholi president. His ascendancy would not last a year. A canny and dashing guerrilla leader, Yoweri Museveni, understood far better than he how to make crucial alliances, and in January 1986 he toppled the Acholi generals and seized Kampala, where he was received as a liberator. For the Acholi, the victory of this southerner from Ankole was a disaster. Massacred by Idi Amin in the 1970s, and then back in favour under the returning Obote, the Acholi once again lived in fear – this time fear lest Museveni should decide to take revenge for massacres their soldiers had committed. According to Matthew Green, a journalist, who knows Acholiland well: 'When Museveni's followers marched north, burning granaries and executing civilians, many Acholi believed he planned to wipe them out.'[19]

Indeed annihilation seemed to be the ultimate fate which the Acholi had always been doomed to experience ever since being typecast a century earlier as ideal soldiers by British governors. Once again, Britain's failure to give Baker's Equatoria its own identity was punishing another generation of northern people for a sin not theirs. In the aftermath of Museveni's victory there was widespread antagonism nationwide towards the northerners, who were often called *Anyanya*, an insulting expression deliberately implying that the Acholi and Langi were not Ugandans but southern Sudanese – as indeed, ethnically they were.[20]

As Museveni's troops hunted down Okello's soldiers, a number of rebel defence movements sprang up in Acholiland. One of these was led by an Acholi apprentice *nganga* with a wispy beard and sad eyes. The name of this 25-year-old was Joseph Kony, and his rebels would soon be called the Lord's Resistance Army (LRA). Other rebel groups were defeated by Museveni's troops but not Kony's with its ostensible purpose of establishing a Christian theocratic government based on the Old Testament. To Kony's rage, Acholiland did not rise up for him against Museveni, so he launched a campaign against Acholi 'collaborators' (in reality they were no such thing) abducting children and forcing them to commit unspeakable crimes against their own people. Noses and ears were cut off and people killed in cruel and barbarous ways. On several occasions, children were taken from Sir Samuel Baker School in Gulu, where Baker's name was still honoured for driving away the slave-trading enemies of the Acholi.

In the mid-1990s, the Sudanese government armed and paid Kony to attack the 'rebels' in southern Sudan. Though these men were fighting for their beliefs and their country, and some were even Acholi, Kony nevertheless obliged the fundamentalists in Khartoum by attacking his own kith and kin. After this shameful episode, Kony's LRA returned to ravage Acholiland afresh, abducting an estimated 30,000 children and displacing 1.6 million people by 2005.[21] In his book about Joseph Kony, *The Wizard of the Nile*, Matthew Green blames Museveni for failing, with all the military assets at his disposal, to defeat Kony's insurgents. Museveni often claimed in the press that 'the bandits had been crushed', when clearly they had not. Green blames him for prolonging the conflict for twenty years as a form of punishment for his northern enemies. Museveni never acknowledged the genuine grievances nursed by the Acholi. By 2003, 800,000 people, 70 per cent of Acholiland's population, had been placed in camps by Museveni, supposedly for their protection from the LRA, although these government camps were regularly attacked by Kony's men, and in them thousands of refugees died of disease.[22] Since 2005 the situation has steadily improved with 80 per cent of the internally displaced persons having returned home from the camps by 2010. The International Criminal Court issued a warrant for Kony's arrest in October 2006, but he is still at large, probably in the north-eastern region of the Democratic Republic of Congo.[23]

The Ugandan north–south divide is no longer at the top of Yoweri Museveni's list of intractable problems. He now faces a stern test in the south, which may, if he fails it, destroy his political future and tear Uganda apart. In 1993 he restored the monarchies of Toro, Bunyoro and Buganda, without returning to them the federal status they had enjoyed under the original 1962 constitution. Although Museveni allows individual candidates to stand at elections, they are not permitted to represent regional or political parties. This 'no party system' is very like a typical African 'one party system', and hands an immense advantage to the incumbent president. Despite this, Museveni has needed Buganda's votes in three general elections and will need them again in future.[24] As he is a southerner, the support of *all* the kingdoms and regions of the south has been vital for him politically, since he will never inspire anything but hatred from the north. His new problem is that King Freddie's son, Kabaka Ronald Mutebi, who was enthroned eight years ago, is determined to regain Buganda's federal status.

In September 2009, Kabaka Mutebi was forcibly prevented by the central government's police from travelling to a youth rally within the borders of his own kingdom. This police action was seen as gross interference by Mutebi's subjects. Riots broke out and twenty-seven people were killed and 600 arrested. Museveni claimed that the police had acted because Mutebi's safety could not have been guaranteed at the rally. The Baganda found this laughable and feared that Museveni's intervention in their affairs could presage even more unwelcome intrusions by the central state. Inevitably, there have been renewed demands for a federal Uganda with additional powers for Buganda's parliament. In recent years Museveni has become, in one commentator's words, 'increasingly autocratic, running a patronage system favouring family members and loyal supporters and obstructing any real challenge to his rule – just like other Big Men'.[25]

For Museveni, giving in to Buganda would mean agreeing to a reduction in his presidential power, and would be a blow to national unity. His recently passed Land Bill has paved the way for the imposition of regional administrations. If introduced, these will leave the kingdom of Buganda without political power. So a bitter struggle in the south is likely. Whether Museveni will ultimately reprise Obote's role, or whether he will seek a compromise with Uganda's uniquely important monarchy remains to be seen. His victory in the February 2011 Presidential Election, despite allegations of vote rigging, will have strengthened his hand.[26]

Undoubtedly, the disastrous British decision to divide Equatoria between Uganda and Sudan still causes seismic reverberations in both countries – as does the whole colonial composition of both nation-states. However, it is also clear that their leaders have chosen their own paths, and have repeatedly rejected compromise. Britain should have stayed longer in Africa, should have spent more money and better prepared Sudan and Uganda for independence; but with the USSR describing all European colonial nations as imperialist exploiters of territories which, for the most part, made no money at all, the choice had been between getting out or staying and facing a nationalist guerrilla war financed by the Soviets. The Americans too – even before they had desegregated their own Southern schools – attacked colonial rule as an affront to human dignity. On the ground, British administrators felt that they were betraying Africans by leaving prematurely. But 'one man one vote now' was not an easy refrain to argue against in the Mother of Parliaments.

The colonisation of one other country was also part of the legacy of the Nile explorers. Speke's and Grant's visit to Uganda, and more especially Stanley's, and his appeal for missionaries to come and live with the *kabaka*, had been essential links in the chain of causation that led to Lugard's intervention on the side of the Protestants and to the subsequent declaration of a Ugandan Protectorate. Before 1900, British East Africa – the future Kenya – was seen primarily as the route to Uganda. But how could the cotton, ivory, tea and coffee of Uganda be transported to the coast, and European goods and personnel be carried in the reverse direction, without involving dangerous journeys of several months' duration?

Obviously a railway would have to be built from Mombasa on the coast to Lake Victoria. This had been realised even in the 1880s. The Masai might have thwarted the building of the railway when it was stretching across the northern part of their grazing grounds, but thanks to British caution and to an incident known as the Kedong massacre, they decided to be cautious too. In a violent clash with a Kikuyu railway workers' caravan and their Swahili porters in November 1895, the Masai killed nearly 600 men. An outraged Scottish trader and former employee of the British Imperial East Africa Company, Andrew Dick, who had happened to be encamped nearby, went with two French travellers and attacked the victors, shooting a hundred dead before he too was killed. He was very likely unaware that the caravan had been attacked in response to the rape of several Masai girls. But the predominant feeling of the famous Masai *laibon*, or religious leader, Lenana, was not anger but shock that three men had been able to kill so many of his warriors.[27]

The Uganda Railway, which William Mackinnon had dreamed of constructing, was built a few years after his death, between

THE CONSEQUENCES

1896 and 1901, and would eventually reduce the cost of trans-
porting Ugandan cotton to the coast from a staggering £200 per
tonne to one per cent of that.[28] Its purpose was also to secure the
headwaters of the Nile once and for all against all comers. Africans
in the bush called the railway 'the iron snake from the coast', as
if they intuitively understood that as well as bringing goods to the
interior, it would suck resources, goods and people away from the
periphery into the towns. When it proved impossible to persuade
Africans to work on the railway (known as the 'Lunatic Line'
because of its steep gradients) the British government remained
determined to get it built somehow. With no concern for the long-
term consequences, Lord Salisbury and his colleagues decided to
risk altering the balance of East Africa's population by introducing
the 1896 Emigration Amendment Act which would permit a
massive influx of Indian labourers and their families.

Forty thousand of them built the railway, laying 582 miles
of track, constructing 162 bridges, digging 326 culverts and
erecting 41 stations. Over a hundred were eaten by two lions
– the famous man-eaters of Tsavo – which were shot after
several anxious weeks by the chief engineer, J. H. Patterson, a
tall, moustachioed young Englishman, whose diary describes the
men's refusal to go on working and his own desperation as he
lay in the dark, 'hearing the lions crunching the bones of their
victims'. Unable to see the predators, he could hear them purring
in thick undergrowth as they 'licked the skin off, so as to get
the fresh blood'.[29] Eventually Patterson shot both lions, to the
great joy of the work gangs. The Indians went on to prosper in
business – so much so that in the post-independence era, they
would be discriminated against in Kenya and expelled from
Uganda as an entire community by Idi Amin.[30] Britain took
in 30,000 Ugandan Asians in the 1970s with a further 10,000
being accepted by various European countries and by the USA
and Canada.

While the Indians had become the businessmen of East
Africa, causing tensions in the wider community as well as
creating employment and prosperity, the other great unintended

consequence of the railway was its immense £5.5 million cost to the British taxpayer. Could any of this money be recouped for the Treasury? With Africans reluctant to sell their labour, economic growth and taxes could not be expected to come from their labour for many years. The solution chosen by the colonial authorities was to encourage white settlers to come out and start farming. They could then be taxed and would bring new spending power to the country. Kenya with its elevated Rift Valley – the White Highlands – was considered more suitable for European settlement than Uganda and other equatorial countries, so large numbers were expected to arrive. They did not. Although by 1914 only 5,500 settlers had come (and by 1923 10,000), both the Masai and the Kikuyu would be dispossessed of about 60 per cent of their land. It would be this more than anything else which, as the historian Piers Brendon has put it, 'kindled a slow-burning anger that would eventually burst into flame'.[31]

If Uganda had not contained the source of the Nile, it would have lost all its value for Lord Salisbury, and there would have been no Protectorate. In that event there would have been no need for Britain to create Kenya Colony and build the Uganda Railway. It was to pay for the Lunatic Line that white settlers had been summoned, and if there had been no settlers, ultimately there would have been no Mau Mau rebellion and no brutal suppression of it. Before that, the colony's administration had been caught for decades in a political stalemate – with the settlers' opposition to all political change making it impossible for the civil servants to push on with Kenya's development.[32] Yet, despite the Uganda railway's unintended legacy, an independent Kenya would become one of Africa's most successful states, surviving not thanks to oil or diamonds, but through the intelligence, work ethic, education and entrepreneurial skills of its people.[33]

CODA

Lacking the Wand of an Enchanter

———— ⬤ ————

In less than a quarter of a century, a small group of exceptionally brave explorers and their remarkable African porters, guides, translators and servants had solved the greatest geographical mystery on earth, covering many thousands of miles in the process, mainly on foot. They had risked their lives repeatedly, had been detained for months at a time by chiefs and kings, and had survived by judging when best to be long-suffering and when assertive. Rarely, when exploring, had they found themselves in a position to impose their will. Their joint efforts lifted the veil on one of the planet's last great puzzles.

The cost in human lives had been very high, as Stanley's great trans-Africa journey illustrates. Of the 228 people who set out from Zanzibar, exactly half lost their lives.[1] Of the four Europeans, he was the only survivor. The vast majority of deaths had been suffered by the far more numerous Wangwana. 'The execution & fulfilment of all plans, and designs,' Stanley told a friend: 'was due to the pluck and intrinsic goodness of 20 men ... Take these 20 out and I could not have proceeded beyond a few days journey.'[2] Among these had been Manwa Sera and Chowpereh, who had both been with Livingstone on his last journey. With him too had been Uledi, whom Stanley valued more than any other captain on that same great 1874–77 journey.

The indispensable nature of the services of the leading Wangwana captains and carriers becomes obvious when the famous journeys they made possible are listed. Uledi had also been with Stanley on his Livingstone search and with Speke and Grant between 1860 and 1863. Sidi Mubarak Bombay had been with Burton and Speke in 1857–59, then with Speke and Grant several years later, and with Stanley on his Livingstone search.

Susi had been with Livingstone since 1863. With Chowpereh, Susi led the men who brought their master's body to the coast in 1873. He then served with Stanley on the Congo between 1879 and 1884, and was put in charge of constructing the first trading station at Leopoldville. Dualla, Stanley's great diplomat on the same expedition, would later become Lugard's most valued African caravan leader in the 1890s. Some of these men lived long enough to retire, as Bombay would do in 1885, on a Royal Geographical Society pension, but they were the lucky ones, outnumbered by those who died while travelling.

Of the principal European actors in the Nile search, only David Livingstone died in Africa. But Samuel and Florence Baker came as close to death as is possible without actually dying, thanks to pressing on across swampy, mosquito-infested country having exhausted their quinine. On one occasion Stanley entered the tunnel of light now popularly associated with near-death experiences. Richard Burton suffered so severely from malaria that he was unable to walk for the best part of a year; Speke endured an agonising illness with symptoms like acute hydrophobia, as well as bouts of fever, temporary blindness and a permanent loss of hearing in one ear. For nine months, Grant was immobilised by tropical leg ulcers, and Farquhar and Shaw, Stanley's two companions on the Livingstone search, died from complications of malaria. The Pocock brothers and Frederick Barker, on Stanley's second journey, died respectively from small-pox, drowning and malaria.

Livingstone could easily have died several years earlier than he did – and in the same violent manner in which the murdered British explorers Mungo Park and Richard Lander had met their end – but the spears hurled at *him* missed by inches. Less fortunate were Burton and Speke, who both received serious stab wounds at the hands of Somali tribesmen. European travellers were not infrequently murdered by Africans at this time. Between 1845 and 1865, the French naval officer Lieutenant Maizan, the German scientist Albrecht Roscher, and his compatriot Baron Klaus von der Decken were all killed by East African tribesmen. Stanley's friend Ernest Linant de Bellefonds was murdered by the Bari in 1876, two of Mackay's missionary colleagues in 1878, and two British Army officers, Frederick Carter and Thomas Cadenhead, were killed with sixty of their followers by Mirambo's men in 1880. Five years later, Bishop James Hannington and his followers were stabbed to death on the orders of Mwanga, the *kabaka* of Buganda, and soon after that, Emin Pasha was murdered by the warlord Kibonge. The Nile explorers might easily have shared the same fate as these unfortunate travellers.

Despite their obvious merits, Speke and Livingstone received no reward at all from the British state for their contribution to the sum of human knowledge. Grant was awarded a beggarly Companionship of the Bath, Baker was knighted and Stanley, who finally explained the geography of the entire central watershed, received the same honour many years after his geographical triumphs were over. Burton also received a knighthood thanks to his aristocratic wife's tireless campaigning. As *his* reward for a campaign that had ended in a single morning of mechanised slaughter, Major-General Sir Horatio Kitchener was made a baron and was voted the astonishing sum of £30,000 by Parliament.

Because the explorers arrived first in the interior before other whites, to be followed soon afterwards by the missionaries, and then by imperial agents, is it fair to say that the Scramble for Africa was a single seamless process? In one sense linkage is self-evident, since exploration was the essential precursor to later white rule and settlement. But what had the Nile explorers actually *wanted* to happen to Africa after they had penetrated and mapped so much of it? Such a question is not easy to answer because, with the exception of Richard Burton (who dismissed African colonies as unworkable because he considered the inhabitants of the 'Dark Continent' too primitive to absorb European culture), some of the others, though in favour of creating colonies, changed their views over time.[3] A case in point is Samuel Baker who was the explorer most directly responsible for extending the Sudan to the south with such appalling future consequences. In 1889, he performed a complete *volte face* and said that Britain should have nothing more to do with Equatoria and Uganda and should not occupy either because tropical Africa would always be a drain on the British taxpayer. Needless to say this late opinion was not listened to.[4]

David Livingstone, whose opinions and theories would influence the British general public more than those of all the other Nile explorers combined, began by doubting whether large-scale contact with whites would ever do anything but harm to Africans. 'If natives are not elevated by contact with Europeans,' he wrote, 'they are sure to be deteriorated. It is with pain I have observed that all the tribes I have seen lately [in Botswana and Cape Colony] are undergoing the latter process.'[5] He refused to condemn polygamy, saying that it could not be considered adultery. Livingstone understood at once that many wives were needed to produce the large families essential for chiefly power.[6] He also realised that because individuals were not allowed (under threat of accusations of witchcraft) to build up grain surpluses for their personal use, the tribe was better placed to feed everyone in a famine than would have been the case if grain had been privately, rather than communally owned. Yet, as a missionary, Livingstone had been obliged to rule out the possibility of leaving Africans to their own devices. His God-given duty, as he saw it, had been to save the souls of as many people as possible.

So between 1849 and 1851, he made three journeys to the far north of Botswana in an attempt to find an untouched tribe whose members might, he hoped, be more receptive to Jesus' teachings than those living close to the Boers. But to his horror he found during the early 1850s, that even the remotest tribes on the Zambezi had been visited by Portuguese slave traders, or their African agents, the Mambari. Indeed members of Livingstone's favourite tribe, the Kololo, turned out to have sold men and women to the Mambari in exchange for cloth, guns and stolen cattle.[7] It now seemed very unlikely that he would find any uncorrupted tribes along the Zambezi. In these distressing circumstances, Livingstone concluded that only widespread European intrusion would have any chance of effecting a moral change.

His position was a painfully ironic one. He had come in search of an untouched people, but having found them corrupted was now about to advocate even more contact with outsiders. But unless the Kololo were enabled to sell their animal skins, beeswax, resins and ivory to the kind of traders who would not expect to be paid with slaves for the factory goods the tribes craved, the slave trade and the gun-frontier would continue to spread on like wildfire. Livingstone believed that only 'commerce and Christianity', and in the end colonies, could prevent this disaster. He was convinced that chiefs would never abandon their customary rights to enslave captives taken from neighbouring tribes until they could *see* proof of the material superiority of European society to their own. Only the appearance of metal-hulled steamships and machinery seemed likely to create a crisis of confidence for powerful African chiefs.[8] Livingstone's earlier sympathy for African customs made it harder for him to think like this.

Yet the moment Livingstone decided that the slave trade would only ever be conquered if the Europeans created African colonies, he began to put pressure on successive British governments. He met with no success at all in the fourteen years left to him. In 1860, Lord Palmerston wrote: 'I am very unwilling to embark on new schemes of British possessions. Dr L's information is valuable, but he must not be allowed to tempt us to form colonies only to be reached by forcing steamers up cataracts.'[9] In mid-century, Britain was the workshop of the world, out-producing all its rivals, and did not need new colonies, in the eyes of its politicians, in order to increase its wealth or power.

Like David Livingstone, John Speke saw the creation of colonies as the best way to improve life for Africans. When he first reached Lake Victoria, he was shocked by the poverty of local people, given the extraordinary fertility of the land. Why were they so poor, he wondered? In part, their bountiful environment seemed responsible. They did not need to make clothes because the weather was so congenial, and the soil produced enough in its natural state to make agricultural effort unnecessary. So why build up a food surplus to sell and thus provide the means for other projects? Most of all, he blamed poverty on small local wars. 'The great cause [of poverty] is their want of a strong protecting government to preserve peace, without which nothing can prosper.' It struck him that,

... if, instead of this district being in the hands of its present owners, it were ruled by a few scores of Europeans, what an entire revolution a few years would bring forth. An extensive market would be opened to the world ... and commerce would clear the way for civilization and enlightenment.[10]

Speke, again like Livingstone, feared that Africans would be 'wiped off the face of the earth' by the Arab-Swahili slave trade, unless Britain established some African equivalent of the British Raj.[11] A few years later, he appealed for missionaries to go out to the Sudan, Bunyoro, Buganda and Rwanda to pave the way for 'legitimate commerce'. In his opinion, Africans 'considered the slave trade legitimate from the fact that slaves are purchased with European articles of merchandise'. What was required, said Speke, was that Africans themselves should be 'taught to abhor the slave trade'. Pressure, he said, should also be put on the Sultan of Zanzibar to end the trade in his dominions.[12] If Speke had not died in 1864, his voice would have been added to Livingstone's in advocating the formation of new colonies for humanitarian reasons.

Stanley would only come to believe that colonies (as opposed to internationalised rivers and trading stations) would have to be created after he came across 2,300 recently captured slaves on the upper Congo in 1883 and thought himself 'in a kind of evil dream', witnessing such 'indescribable inhumanity'. He guessed that in order to obtain this number of slaves, the Arabs would have shot the same number to prevent resistance. At this time, half a million people were being displaced or enslaved annually in central Africa.[13]

The case for intervention was a very powerful one. These explorers had not – as is sometimes suggested – broken open an unspoiled paradise and exposed it to the exploitative greed of the world's capitalists for the very first time.[14] On the upper Nile in the early 1860s, Samuel Baker had found European, Egyptian and Sudanese slave traders in the process of establishing trading posts within fifty miles of Lake Albert. Also in the 1860s David Livingstone had been shocked to find Nyamwezi chiefs selling members of neighbouring tribes and indeed their own people to a handful of alien intruders.[15] The internal slave trade of the Africans themselves provoked him to say that this 'perpetual capturing and sale of children' from subject tribes made the Portuguese and Arab trades 'appear a small evil by comparison'.[16] A decade earlier, David Livingstone had encountered the Portuguese slave trader Silva Porto in the centre of the continent on the Zambezi.

In the 1840s the Victorian passion for ivory piano keys, knife handles and the backs of brushes could no longer be met by African traders alone, so the coastal Arab-Swahili (whose Arab ancestors had arrived on the East African coast in the ninth century) had started to penetrate deeper and deeper into the interior to bring back ever greater numbers of tusks and the slaves required to carry them. Stanley wrote incredulously:

Every pound weight of ivory has cost the life of a man woman or child, for every five pounds a hut has been burned, for every two tusks a whole village has been destroyed . . . It is simply incredible that because ivory is required for ornaments or billiard games, the rich heart of Africa should be laid waste.[17]

Samuel Baker remarked sardonically that because the slave traders had made the country so dangerous, he had often had no choice but to travel with their large caravans:

It is remarkably pleasant travelling in company with these robbers, they convert every country into a wasps' nest. There's no plan of action or travelling and I being dependent on their movements am more like a donkey than an explorer.[18]

From Rwanda and Buganda in the north, to Lake Nyasa (Malawi) and the Shire Highlands in the south, the Nile explorers found that Arab-Swahili traders had preceded them by a decade or two, bringing destruction and suffering in their wake. The slave and ivory traders had also brought gunpowder and guns far into the interior – though, sadly, these were not recent imports. The Dutch had sold 20,000 tons of gunpowder annually along the West African coast from 1700 for over a century, while on the East African coast the Portuguese had first sailed into the Zambezi estuary with gunpowder and cannons in the mid-1500s.[19]

African migrations and warfare also brought widespread disruption. The northward movement of the Ngoni was witnessed by Speke and by Livingstone, who recorded the murders and the thefts of cattle near Lake Nyasa. In the 1870s Mirambo of the Nyamwezi, with his child soldiers and Ngoni mercenaries, fought the Arabs for control of the caravan routes to Lakes Tanganyika and Victoria in a prolonged war that sucked in many innocent people,[20] while Msiri, another central African ruler, was extending his power by invading his neighbours' land and by allying himself with the arch slave trader Tippu Tip. This enabled him to kill the *kasembe* of the Luba-Lunda people and consolidate his power over south-east Katanga with its copper resources.

Not that Mwata Kasembe VII had been an angel as David Livingstone had observed in 1867:

When he usurped power five years ago, his country was densely peopled; but he was so severe in his punishments – cropping the ears, lopping off the hands, and other mutilations, selling the children for very slight offences, that his subjects gradually dispersed themselves in the neighbouring countries beyond his power.[21]

If Britain, France and Germany had not established colonies and protectorates within the area investigated by the Nile explorers, the Arab-Swahili slave traders would have continued up the Nile extending their control over Bunyoro and Buganda. The fate of the tribes in Equatoria would have been annihilation.

The Sudanese Arabs would also have spread westwards through Chad, having first overwhelmed the Sultanate of Darfur. Even in Baker's and Gordon's day they had reached the Bahr el-Ghazal and Equatoria. Arabs from the south had made Lake Victoria an immense depot for the slave trade a decade before Stanley arrived. By then Tippu Tip's empire stretched from Lake Tanganyika, through Manyema to the Congo and the Lomani. Inevitably, the whole of central equatorial Africa would have become part of the Muslim world, with slavery an inescapable part of it, unless the colonial powers had come to stay. They did, and by the opening years of the twentieth century had suppressed the slave trade throughout East Africa, stopping a horrifying annual loss of people. Between 1800 and 1870 nearly two million slaves had been exported across the Sahara or by sea to Egypt, Arabia and the Gulf.[22]

In 1859, Speke had listed the benefits which in his opinion would accrue if 'a few scores of Europeans' came out to manage the southern shores of Lake Victoria, and a little later Livingstone described his ideal colonial administrator. This versatile individual would not compete with Africans in manual labour, but would 'take a leading part in managing the land . . . and extending the varieties of the production of the soil'. He would take 'a lead too in trade and in all public matters . . . [and] would be an unmixed advantage to everyone below and around him, for he would fill a place that is practically vacant'.[23] This might almost have been an advance job description for the later colonial district commissioner. Doubtless Livingstone would have approved of these men's university degrees, and their practical agricultural skills and advice-giving, but would have less admired their colonial assumption of superiority in all things. He had written of Africans in the mid-1850s in a different spirit:

With a general opinion they are wiser than their white neighbours . . . Each tribe has a considerable consciousness of goodness . . . In Africa they have less of what the Germans call philosophy to uphold their views; less diplomacy, protocols & notes . . . They have few theories but many ideas ... There is no search after the supreme good such as we are to believe the ancient philosophers engaged in ... But the African cares not at all for these utterly inane speculations. The pleasures of animal life are ever present to his mind as the supreme good, and but for his innumerable phantoms he would enjoy his luscious climate as well as it is possible for a man to do.[24]

Before the militarised expeditions of the 1890s, the Nile explorers had been on a level playing field with the people whose territory they had risked their lives to investigate. They paid in trade goods for the right of passage through tribal lands, and on many occasions were detained against their will for many months at the whim of African chiefs. Speke was detained by Mutesa for five months, Baker by Kamrasi for ten, Livingstone by Kasembe for three. Their hosts could at any moment have ended their lives. This situation was typical of that more innocent period which preceded the two decades during which the land was wrested from its owners by force.

The memorably fatalistic Chief Commoro of the Latuka had shared his disconcerting ideas on the subject of theft with Samuel Baker in 1863:

Most people are bad; if they are strong they take from the weak. The good people are all weak; they are good because they are not strong enough to be bad.[25]

Undoubtedly, in the context of the Scramble for Africa, the Europeans were strong and took land and sovereignty from the weak in the name of high-sounding principles – some of which were genuine, such as the desire to end the slave trade, and others false and exploitative. Episodes of resistance and conquest would take place in parts of almost every African colony.[26] Rulers like Kabarega, Mwanga and Prempeh of the Asante would be exiled. In most cases engagements would be small, continuing over several decades, with submission eventually occurring through a gradual process of unchallenged intrusion by small numbers of whites. Livingstone in a rare moment of pessimism wrote of the arrival of colonists as 'a terrible necessity', but still maintained that on people of British stock depended the 'hopes of the world for liberty and progress'.[27] Indeed most British imperial agents firmly believed that they were in Africa not only thanks to superior weaponry but also because they were, in their own estimation, the culturally superior representatives of an empire whose mission was to bring peace, prosperity and justice to less fortunate people. The moral inconsistency of occasionally having to kill people who resisted their 'civilising mission' did not dismay Sir Hesketh Bell, the first British Governor of Uganda, as he demonstrated when writing about some 'wild' Bagisu tribesmen in the east of the country:

I am sending two companies of the King's African Rifles to make them [the Bagisu] realise that they must come into line with the rest of the Protectorate . . . Hardly a year passes without the need of punishing these wild tribes for the slaying of unarmed and peaceful traders, and nothing but a show of force will induce them to mend their ways.

Since the Bagisu had always felt free to kill intruders on their land, they might justifiably have asked why they should suddenly change their behaviour when they had signed no agreement with anyone and not been defeated in battle. But Bell knew he would only be able to bring peace to this large country and govern it if he managed to stamp out acts of violence against people of all races. For this task he had been given a budget fit only for running a few British parishes, a tiny military force and twenty civil servants and commissioners. With these laughable resources he not only had to punish Africans who killed traders but also take on slave traders, warlords and adventurers in search of easy money.[28]

Arthur Mounteney Jephson, Stanley's favourite officer on the Emin Pasha Expedition, wrote in his diary several years before Uganda became a protectorate:

The ordinary native only grows just enough corn for the use of himself & his family; let him once see that what he grows has a very substantial value & he will cultivate more & be more hardworking & thrifty; he will not then be so ready to go to war with his neighbour . . . & the little petty wars which are the curse of Africa, will, with the coming of the railway & the consequent increase in trade, gradually cease.[29]

Men like Jephson, Mackay, Stanley and Mackinnon hoped that with the introduction of European agricultural methods by settlers, the soil would eventually yield enough for Africans to earn wages, which could one day be taxed to provide funds for railways, roads, hospitals and schools. Since missionaries were supposed to come to Africa ahead of the traders and settlers, the spiritual, as well as the material condition of Africans – so the theory went – would be improved. Livingstone, Stanley, Speke and Baker (a true warrior against the slave trade) all believed in this strategy for Africa's progress.

In Britain between the 1850s and the 1890s the population had risen by 70 per cent thanks to medical advances and to clean water and modern sanitation; literacy had become almost universal and cheaper food had improved average diets. By the 1880s most homes contained a wealth of printed and illustrative material which earlier generations would have been amazed to see. Even if the transfer of such benefits to Africa turned out to be haphazard and slow, there would have been no doubt in the explorers' minds that if future colonial authorities succeeded in crushing the Arab-Swahili slave trade, an incalculable benefit would have been conferred on millions.

Indeed, the British and French in their African colonies would do just that, and bring a brief era of relatively incorrupt government, with the rule of law and the benefits of modern medicine and hygiene enabling Africa's population to increase from 129 million in 1900 to 300 million by the 1960s when most colonies gained their independence.[30] This increase was highly desirable since low population densities had bedevilled Africa's development for centuries. At the simplest level: a food surplus was worthless unless there were enough people living within a ten-mile radius wanting to exchange grain or flour for other goods. Also any large agricultural projects would be impossible to undertake without sufficient workers. The preeminent French historian, Fernand Braudel summed up the situation succinctly with his aphorism: 'Civilisation is the daughter of numbers.'[31]

The post-Scramble colonies would be distinguished by genuine achievements and by some well-known disasters, such as the atrocities on the Congo in the 1890s, the massacre of the Hereros in German South West Africa and the British suppression of the Mau Mau uprising in Kenya. Where there had been sizeable white settler populations, such as in Kenya and Southern Rhodesia, the transition to independence would be bloody. Elsewhere in Britain's sub-Saharan colonies it would be peacefully achieved, with nothing resembling Portugal's disastrous efforts to maintain its colonial rule. Colonialism lasted just long enough to destroy the belief of many Africans in the spirit world which had hitherto enforced standards and personal responsibility, but not long enough to replace indigenous beliefs with Western social ideals and education. Inevitably African self-belief was damaged.

At least 3,000 ethnic groups ended up as forty-seven nation-states on the African mainland due entirely to decisions made during the colonial period. Undoubtedly – as in Uganda and Nigeria – the colonial boundaries enabled 'Big Men' to use ethnic conflicts, and indeed to create them, in order to underpin their power. In the mid-1990s there were thirty-one civil wars in Africa, almost all of which had arisen as a direct result of badly drawn boundaries and incitement by African politicians. The Rwandan genocide was planned from the top in every detail. The number of wars is smaller today, with armed banditry having replaced larger disturbances, except in Eastern Congo and the Niger Delta.

The most testing problem for the countries through which the Nile flows will be deciding how the river's water should be apportioned in future. Negotiations to reach an agreement have been ongoing for thirteen years and recently five of the equatorial states have come to their own agreement, excluding Egypt and the Sudan, which since the 1950s have claimed together in excess of 90 per cent of the water. At worst, there may be water wars in future on the banks of the Nile; but the mutual dependence of the seven nations on the river may yet compel cooperation as a matter of survival and usher in a more peaceful chapter in the history of the region.

The colonial period in Africa's history (which lasted in most colonies for a mere seventy-five years) seems likely to be seen in future as merely one of many contenders – along with the Cold War, superpower sponsorship of dictators, AIDS, malaria, drought, corrupt leaders, incompetent governments, ethnic civil war, and an unfair international trade system – for the title of 'principal cause' for why fifty years of independence has proved so disappointing. John Iliffe, the leading expert on colonial and post-colonial East Africa, has said that there can be too much pessimism about the after-effects of empire: 'To see colonialism as destroying tradition is to underestimate African resilience. To see it as merely an episode [in African history] is to underestimate how much industrial civilization offered twentieth century Africans.' Certainly, not many urban Africans would wish to return to how things were in the 1880s.[32]

Today in America and Europe the press inevitably focuses on disasters, ignoring the size of Africa and the fact that many millions have remained untouched throughout their lives by violence and starvation. It was the same story, of peaceful places lying just adjacent to dangerous ones, when the Nile explorers experienced grim and violent events, only to travel a few miles further and find scenes of beauty and serenity. John Speke, after his long struggle with rapacious chiefs and every imaginable hardship and shortage, had entered Karagwe, west of Lake Victoria, and been overwhelmed by the beauty of the scenery, by the herds of healthy cattle and by the plentiful supplies of food. 'We were treated like favoured guests by the chiefs of the place, who . . . brought presents, as soon as we arrived . . . The farther we went in this country, the better we liked it, as . . . the village chiefs were so civil that we could do as we liked.'[33] Rumanika, the king of Karagwe, treated Speke and Grant to 'greetings [which] were warm and affecting . . . Time flew like magic, the king's mind was so quick and enquiring.'[34]

Livingstone, although appalled by the cruelties he encountered in Barotseland, was overwhelmed by the loveliness of immemorial village scenes.

How often have I beheld, in still mornings, scenes the very essence of beauty, and all bathed in a quiet air of delicious warmth! Yet the occasional slight motion imparted a pleasing sensation of coolness as of a fan. Green grassy meadows, the cattle feeding, the goats browsing, the kids skipping, the groups of herd boys with miniature bows, arrows and spears; the women wending their way to the river with watering pots poised jauntily on their heads ... and old grey-headed fathers sitting on the ground, with staff in hand, listening to the morning gossip.[35]

Stanley, only days after being involved in fighting in which he had lost twenty-two people, found himself in 'a most beautiful pastoral country' close to Lake Victoria:

I was as gratified as though I possessed the wand of an enchanter ... I seated myself apart on a grey rock ... only my gun-bearer near me and the voices of the Wangwana came to me now and again faint by distance, and but for this, I might, as I sat there, have lost myself in the delusion that all the hideous past and beautiful present was a dream ... I revelled undisturbed in the delicious smell of cattle and young grass ... and from the hedged encircled villages there rose to my hearing the bleating of young calves and the lowing of cows ... and I could see flocks of kids and goats and sheep with jealously watchful shepherd boys close by – the whole prospect so peaceful and idyllic that it made a strangely affecting impression on me.[36]

But lacking 'the wand of an enchanter' few people in the West are able to envision today's Africa as an enchanted land, for all its natural beauty and variety and despite the humour, grace and extraordinary resilience of its people. African successes have never made headlines. The rich celebrities on television over the decades, nudging the public to open their pockets to help with some new African disaster, famine or genocide, are too imbedded in most minds for many in the West to believe that the process which the explorers set in train in the nineteenth century can deserve much celebration. It all ended like this, they say.

This attitude strikes me as unjust. The Nile explorers opened Africa to Western concern at a time when every year was bringing new devastation to ever larger areas of the continent. The courage and vision of this small group is not less praiseworthy because the next century did not bear out their hopes for the future of the regions they had revealed with so much difficulty and hardship. Nor have the ideals of nineteenth-century humanitarians lost their value because later governments in Europe and Africa did not live up to them.

Fifty Years of Books on the Search for the Nile's Source

⬥⬥⬥

In 1960 Alan Moorehead's *The White Nile* was published and became an international bestseller. The story of the search for the source of the Nile is a compelling one and Moorehead's skilful alternation of brisk biographical vignettes of the principal Nile explorers with brief accounts of the various journeys made his book eminently readable. Astonishingly, in the half-century since 1960, no attempt has been made to re-visit this unique story making detailed use of the wealth of new material – both published and in manuscript – that has accumulated during the intervening years. Christopher Ondaatje and Guy Yeoman wrote about the search in their books *Journey to the Source of the Nile* (1998) and *Quest for the Secret Nile* (2004), but in the context of their own motorised journeys to many of the key locations; and while both wrote illuminatingly about the Nile's geography, neither of them attempted to redraw the characters and relationships of the original Nile explorers in the light of all the new information that has emerged since 1960.

Indeed, post-Moorehead, an astonishing eight biographies of Burton have been published, if one includes Mary Lovell's double life of Burton and his wife, Isabel. There have been four lives of David Livingstone, six of Henry Stanley, one of Samuel Baker, one of Baker's wife, Florence, one of Samuel and Florence, and one of John Hanning Speke. So a return to the Victorian Nile story seems long overdue.

Mary Lovell, in her life of both Burtons, *The Rage to Live* (1998), revealed new facts unknown to Alan Moorehead, most notably that Burton had secretly believed Speke to have been right about the source and had written to the RGS admitting as much. Alexander Maitland with his well-researched life of Speke (1971), and the American academic, W. B. Carnochan, with his slim, incisive volume entitled: *The Sad Story of Burton, Speke, and the Nile; or, Was John Hanning Speke a Cad?* (2006) have together gone some way towards counteracting the ferociously negative slant which Isabel Burton – in her hugely influential two-volume biography, *The Life of Captain Sir Richard F. Burton* (1893) – gave to all her surmises about Speke's motives and character. Recently, Jon R. Godsall in *The Tangled Web* (2008) has done more than any previous Burton biographer to nail the many lies, inventions and distortions that had originally made their appearance in Burton's and in Isabel Burton's writings about Speke and his two journeys with her late husband.

John Speke is perhaps the most enigmatic Nile explorer. Even after I had read widely in the published literature, many questions about him still puzzled me. Had he really been suicidal when he first came to Africa as Burton claimed? Why did he and Burton fail to travel the relatively short distance from Ujiji to the Rusizi river when so much depended on it? Why did Burton hate Speke so intensely, given that he secretly agreed with his estimate of the importance of the Victoria Nyanza, and why had he not gone back with him to examine that lake when begged to do so? Because no early letters or diaries written by Speke have survived, I decided to read as many of his later communications as have been preserved in the National Library of Scotland, in particular his letters to and from his publisher. This led me to study the original manuscript of his *Journal of the Discovery of the Source of the Nile*, and also the heavily edited proofs of that book. In this way I gleaned a large amount of brand-new biographical information from reading the many excised personal passages, which had been deemed unsuitable for publication by John Blackwood – such as Speke's affecting love for one particular Bagandan woman, the sexual advice he gave to Kabaka Mutesa and to the *kabaka*'s mother, and his sympathetic view of the uninhibited sensuality of Bagandan society. All this contradicts the assertions made by many Burton biographers, including the excellent Fawn Brodie, about Speke being prim, censorious, and either sexless or a repressed homosexual.

Speke has been almost universally reviled for ruining the reputation of the British Vice-Consul at Khartoum, John Petherick, who Speke had expected to meet him with supplies and men near the northern borders of Buganda. However, the little-known diary of Petherick's wife, Katherine, in the Wellcome Library, has shown me that the charges which Speke and Baker made against Petherick – especially that he had used forced labour and had shot Africans resisting capture – were true.

After the death of Quentin Keynes in 2003, his large collection of Burton's papers and books was bought by the British Library. Although the collection's most interesting letter books, containing Burton's drafts and Speke's replies, had been privately published by Keynes in 1999 for the bibliophiles of the exclusive Roxburghe Club, under the misleading title of *The Search for the Source of the Nile*, additional papers from Keynes's collection, now in the BL, show the maverick Burton in an unexpected light. For instance they reveal that, while scoffing at the British establishment in public, in private he and Isabel wrote scores of letters in an energetic campaign to secure a knighthood for him.

Away from the world of Speke and Burton, the new material and arguments presented by me in my biographies of Livingstone (1973) and Stanley (2007) have made Moorehead's portrayal of the former as a near saint and the latter as a brash and unprincipled *condottiero* seem too stereotypical to reflect their complex motives for committing themselves to the Nile quest. That Livingstone had failed as a conventional missionary, and as a father and husband, are not facts to be found in *The White Nile*, any more than is Stanley's illegitimacy and his longing for an ideal father, which lay at the heart of his search for Livingstone. In researching *Explorers of the Nile*, I returned to Livingstone's Unyanyembe diary and field books, inspired by the recent 'imaging' work of Dr Adrian Wisnicki on the original documents from which the explorer's published *Last Journals* were transcribed. Stanley's contribution to the Nile quest during its later years was second to none and no other explorer played a more important role in involving Britain in Uganda and East Africa. All this I discovered during my research for my biography.

Moorehead wrote well about Samuel Baker, but not having had the benefit of reading Richard Hall's well-researched double biography of Baker and his wife, which appeared exactly twenty years after *The White Nile*, he was unaware of the extraordinary circumstances in which the couple had first met and of the fact that they had been unmarried during their harrowing journey to Lake Albert. I studied Baker's diary and Florence's (the first at the Royal Geographical Society and the second in Anne Baker's private collection in Salisbury) which helped me with my account of Baker's second traumatic expedition to Bunyoro that would do so much to shape the future history of the region.

John O. Udal's impressively researched two-volume work, *The Nile in Darkness* (1998 and 2005) is more concerned with the political history of Egypt and the Sudan than with the Nile search *per se*, but it contains excellent material about the explorers and a full account of Baker's Equatoria expedition in the service of Khedive Ismail Pasha and the political machinations which led to Britain's assumption of control in Egypt and finally in the Sudan, Uganda and Kenya. In this field I owe a considerable debt to the work of Professor R. O. Collins, including his chapter 'The Origins of the Nile Struggle' in Prosser Gifford's and W. R. Louis's *Britain and Germany in Africa: Imperial Rivalry and Colonial Rule* (1967) and to his books about the Sudan: *Land Beyond the Rivers: The Southern Sudan, 1898–1918* (1971) and *Shadows in the Grass: Britain in the Southern Sudan, 1918–1956* (1983).

Because my maternal great-grandfather (albeit unintentionally) played a little-known but significant part in East African history by rescuing a sister of the Sultan of Zanzibar from certain death by stoning after she had been impregnated by a German businessman, I have been able to give some new details of this strange incident that would cause the British Prime Minister, Lord Salisbury, such difficulties in dealing with Germany fifteen years later.

In describing the splitting of Equatoria between Sudan and Uganda, and the long British relationship with the Acholi and its consequences, I have been indebted to S. R. Karugire's A *Political History of Uganda* and to F. Odoi-Tanga's dissertation 'Politics, ethnicity, and conflict in post-independent Acholiland, Uganda, 1962–2006' – an illuminating study of Acholiland's role in post-independence Uganda's history. On the subject of the Sudan–Uganda border itself, G. H. Blake's *Imperial Boundary Making: The Diary of Captain Kelly at the Sudan–Uganda Boundary Commission of 1913* was invaluable. In conclusion Matthew Green's *The Wizard of the Nile,* about his hunt for Joseph Kony, R. R. Atkinson's *The Roots of Ethnicity*, concerning the Acholi and the Baganda before the colonial era, Martin Meredith's *The State of Africa: A History of Fifty Years of Independence* and Richard Cockett's *Sudan: Darfur and the Failure of an African State* all helped in preparing Chapters 33 and 34, as did John Reader's magnificent *Africa: A Biography of the Continent.*

Acknowledgements

Before mentioning my indebtedness to archivists and librarians who helped
me with my research, I wish to thank Anne Baker for allowing me to see
her collection of Samuel W. Baker's letters (and his paintings) and his wife
Florence's African diaries. Her sons Julian and David Baker also helped me,
as did their cousin Ian Graham-Orlebar, who showed me his Baker papers. I
am also grateful to Peter Speke, who lives close to the site of the house where
his famous ancestor grew up, and showed me his paintings of John Hanning
Speke and Speke's guns, sextant, watch and other effects. His son, Geoffrey
Speke, and Dan Cook let me see Speke's own copy of his book, *What Led to
the Discovery of the Source of the Nile*, with an illuminating printed coda,
which is not to be found in copies sold to the public. I would like to re-thank
the members of the Livingstone family (alive and dead) who helped me with
my biography many years ago, and the adoptive family of Henry M. Stanley,
whose life I wrote more recently.

Frances Harris, Head of Modern Manuscripts at the British Library,
kindly allowed me to study the library's recently purchased Quentin Keynes
Collection before it had been fully catalogued. I had seen many of the Burton
items when Quentin Keynes had been alive, but now read many others for
the first time. I am indebted to Sheila Mackenzie, Senior Curator in the
Manuscripts Department of the National Library of Scotland, for helping
me steer my way through the Blackwood Archive, containing, among many
fascinating letters, treasures such as Speke's original manuscript and proofs
of his *Journal of the Discovery of the Source of the Nile*, James A. Grant's
papers, and other relevant manuscripts, and then for sending me photocopies.
I should also like to thank Robin Smith of the NLS. A conversation with Dr
Adrian Wisnicki about his 'imaging' work on Livingstone's field notebooks and
journals persuaded me to investigate some of them again. Karen Carruthers of
the David Livingstone Centre put me in touch with Anne Martin, a voluntary
archivist at the Centre, who then replied to my requests for specific information
and for many verbatim extracts from Livingstone's Unyanyembe Journal and
field books and further information about differences between these texts and
passages in Livingstone's published *Last Journals*. Alan Jutzi, Chief Curator
of Rare Books at the Huntington Library, and Gayle Richardson of the same
library, answered my questions and sent me photocopies from their wide-
ranging Burton collection. Mathilde Leduc-Grimaldi of the Royal Museum of

ACKNOWLEDGEMENTS

Central Africa did the same in connection with Henry M. Stanley. Sarah Strong of the Royal Geographical Society helped me with numerous inquiries on my many visits to Kensington Gore to study letters and journals in the Society's wide-ranging archives, which contain manuscripts in the hands of all the Nile explorers. My thanks also go to Lucy McCann, archivist at the Bodleian's 'Library of Commonwealth and African Studies at Rhodes House', for sending me photocopies from Horace Waller's correspondence.

My special thanks to Julian Loose of Faber & Faber and Chris Rogers of Yale University Press for commissioning this book, and also to Kate Murray-Browne of Faber for her excellent editorial suggestions and close attention to the text and to all phases of production. My thanks too to the production team at Faber and to Donald Sommerville for his observant textual comments and eagle-eyed copy-editing. I cannot thank my wife, Joyce, enough for once again sustaining me while I was producing another demanding *magnum opus*.

Wendy Cawthorne of the Geological Society of London gave me helpful information about Sir Roderick Murchison. My thanks too to Dan Mitchell, Special Collections, University College, London, and to Jane Baxter, Local Studies Librarian, Richmond, Surrey, for answering queries about various Burton letters; Stefanie Davidson, archivist, West Yorkshire Archive Service did the same but in connection with Speke. My thanks too to Alicia Clarke, Director of the Sanford Museum, Florida, to the staff of the Wellcome Library, London Library and Public Record Office, Kew.

Sources

Manuscript Collections Consulted

National Library of Scotland, Edinburgh

John H. Speke's correspondence with his friend and publisher, John Blackwood, and letters from other members of Speke's family. The original unedited ms of Speke's *Journal of the Discovery of the Source of the Nile*, proofs of the same book with Speke's own cuts and amendments and some in the hand of his editor, John Hill-Burton. James A. Grant's journals and other papers including his African water colours and many letters to him from Speke, Baker, Stanley, Kirk, etc., etc. A very large collection of David Livingstone's papers, including family letters, diaries, notebooks etc., etc.; also letters to friends. Stanley's letters to David Livingstone, to Agnes Livingstone, to Alexander L. Bruce, to J. A. Grant, Sir John Kirk, and copies of letters to J. B. Pond. Other letters relating to the Emin Pasha Relief Expedition.

Royal Geographical Society, London

Unique collection of sequential letters from Speke, Grant, Burton, Baker and Livingstone to successive Secretaries of the RGS (many to Dr Norton Shaw) and other officials of the Society, including Presidents Sir Roderick Murchison and Sir Henry Rawlinson, with reports on journeys, original maps, details of funding, and committee notes. Samuel Baker's African journals are in the collection. So too are Speke's original maps, sketches and several notebooks containing his water colours. The papers of Laurence Oliphant. A pamphlet entitled 'Medical History of J. H. Speke' by Anton Mifsud. Letters of Stanley to the RGS, to H. W. Bates and J. S. Keltie, and also to Henry Wellcome, including letters concerning Stanley's final illness; letters from William Hoffman (Stanley's valet) to H. Wellcome, letters from Stanley to May Sheldon. Photographs, press cuttings.

British Library, London

The late Quentin Keynes's important collection of Burton material, including Richard F. Burton's letter books containing his correspondence with John H. Speke. Also in Keynes's former collection, various letters to friends, and documents connected with Burton's and his wife's campaign to acquire a knight-

445

hood for him. Livingstone's letters to family members, including an important series to his daughter Agnes during his last journeys; his letters to Edmund Gabriel; letters from A. Layard to Lord John Russell concerning Livingstone's finances in 1865. Letters to Charles George Gordon from Samuel Baker and many others. Various Stanley letters such as to J. Bolton, the cartographer, to H. W. Bates, E. M. Parker, etc. Photocopies of many exported Stanley letters, also microfilm of Stanley's exploration diaries and notebooks (originals in Brussels, and of some correspondence e.g. with Sir Samuel Baker, Mary Kingsley, etc.). Ad Ms 37463 is the earliest known letter written by Stanley. Miscellaneous letters from Speke to various correspondents, ditto Baker and Grant, mainly photocopies of exported letters.

Huntington Library, San Marino, California

Containing what survives of Richard F. Burton's once substantial library (of approximately 6,000 volumes), along with many manuscripts and other papers, formerly in the possession of the Royal Anthropological Institute. The collection was catalogued before going to America by the Institute's librarian, Miss B. J. Kirkpatrick. One of Burton's books is his heavily annotated copy of Speke's *What led to the Discovery of the Source of the Nile*. Correspondence of Burton with Verney Lovett Cameron, Charles George Gordon and many others.

Wiltshire Record Office, Trowbridge

A collection of letters, press cuttings, reviews and photographs once owned by Isabel Burton, along with scraps of Richard F. Burton's notebooks, his business and publishing correspondence, correspondence pertaining to Isabel's Will. Copies of Foreign Office documents chronicling Burton's consular career; miscellaneous letters to Burton; photographs; scrapbooks.

Anne Baker Collection, Salisbury

The diaries of Florence Baker, miscellaneous letters (and photocopies) relevant to all stages of Samuel W. Baker's life and career. Material relevant to Florence Baker's early life. The Rev. Ian Graham Orlebar, also has miscellaneous Baker letters and photographs and mementoes.

School of Oriental and African Studies, London

The London Missionary Society Archive: unique collection of letters from missionaries such as David Livingstone and Robert Moffat to successive Foreign Secretaries of the Society, most notably Dr Arthur Tidman. Stanley's letters to Sir William Mackinnon, historically important in the colonial history of East Africa and the Congo. Complete papers of the Emin Pasha

Relief Expedition Committee, under the chairmanship of Mackinnon, including letters from Stanley, from expedition members, committee members, politicians, etc.

Henry M. Stanley Archives, Royal Museum of Central Africa, Brussels

Stanley's personal papers, containing his exploration diaries, notebooks, maps, ms drafts of his autobiography, correspondence with his wife, letters from family and friends, including Livingstone, Edward S. King, Alice Pike, Lewis Noe, Alexander Bruce, Sir William Mackinnon; also correspondence with King Leopold II, James Gordon Bennett, and with members of his major expeditions, including the diary of William Bonny; and correspondence with his valet, William Hoffman. The Luwel papers contain one of only two extant original treaties, which Stanley signed with Congolese chiefs. Stanley's article about the other Nile explorers entitled 'Our Great African Travellers'.

Rhodes House, Oxford

Letters of David Livingstone to Horace Waller, including one describing Speke's funeral. A 17–page letter about Stanley from Horace Waller to Livingstone, and other correspondence about Kirk and Stanley; also correspondence of the Anti-Slavery Society connected with East Africa and the Congo. The original proofs of *Livingstone's Last Journeys in Central Africa*, containing many passages later excised by Horace Waller, the editor. The diaries of Edward and Frank Pocock – the only written records apart from Stanley's diaries and despatches of his great trans-Africa journey of 1874–77.

David Livingstone Centre, Blantyre, Scotland

Miscellaneous Livingstone diaries and journals, including his Unyanyembe Journal, and the field notebooks from which Horace Waller assembled *The Last Journals of David Livingstone in Central Africa*. Also an ms copy of *Missionary Travels*.

Peter and Geoffrey Speke's Collection, Ilminster, Somerset

Oil portraits, including the famous double portrait with Grant; Speke's guns, and some correspondence; also Speke's copy of *What Led to the Discovery of the Source of the Nile* with the added 'Tail' (this book is currently kept in London).

Wellcome Library, Euston Road, London

Diaries of John Petherick and Harriet E. Petherick shedding new light on John Petherick's bitter dispute with Speke. Letters written by Baker and Livingstone. Papers of Henry S. Wellcome (the pharmaceutical tycoon) and friend of Stanley and his wife, containing letters from them both, and from William Hoffman and A. J. Mountney Jephson.

Public Record Office, Kew

Correspondence between the principal explorers and British Premiers, Foreign Secretaries, officials in the Foreign and Colonial Offices. The opinion of Lord Palmerston on the achievements of Speke and Grant PRO 30/22, Palmerston's opinion of DL's colonial ideas PRO 30/22. DL's correspondence with Lord Clarendon FO 84/1265 and with Lord John Russell FO 63/81. Speke's Will PRO I.R. 59/68

National Archives of Zimbabwe

Letters from Livingstone to Sir Thomas Maclear and Sir Roderick Murchison; also DL's letters to FO, Dr John Kirk, Charles Livingstone; James Stewart's journals, and papers concerning the Zambezi Expedition.

Sanford Museum, Sanford, Florida

The papers of Henry S. Sanford: 48 letters from Stanley, from Leopold II's personal secretary, Count Borchgrave, from various ministers, from Sir William Mackinnon, A. B. Swinburne and E. J. Glave.

Diplomatic Archive and Africa Archive, Ministry of Foreign Affairs, Brussels

Nine alleged copies, in a secretarial hand, of treaties with Congolese chiefs purporting to be verbatim transcripts of vanished originals signed by Stanley. One original treaty bears Stanley's signature and is dated Vivi 13.06.1880.

Bibliography
(published books; also articles in learned journals mentioned in the notes)

Ajayi, J. F. Ade *Africa in the Nineteenth Century until the 1880s* (1998)
Anstruther, Ian *I Presume: H. M. Stanley's Triumph and Disaster* (1956)
Ascherson, Neal *The King Incorporated* (1963)
Atkinson, R. R. *The Roots of Ethnicity: The Origins of the Acholi and Uganda before 1800* (1994)
Baker, Anne *Morning Star: Florence Baker's Diary of the Expedition to Put Down the Slave Trade on the Nile 1870–1873* (1972)
Baker, J. N. L. 'John Hanning Speke' *Geographical Journal* CXXVIII (1962)
Baker, S. W. *The Albert N'yanza: Great Basin of the Nile and Explorations of the Nile Sources* 2 vols (1874)

_____ *Ismailia: A Narrative of the Expedition to Central Africa for the Suppression of the Slave Trade* 2 vols (1874)

Barttelot, W. G. *The Life of Edmund Musgrave Barttelot* (1890)

Beachey, R. 'The Arms Trade in East Africa in the late 19th century' *Journal of African History* iii 3 (1962)

Beachey, R. *The Slave Trade of Eastern Africa* (1976)

Beard, Peter *The End of the Game* (1965)

Bell, H. H. J. *Glimpse of a Governor's Life* (1916)

Bennett, Norman R. *Arab versus European: Diplomacy and War in Nineteenth Century East Central Africa* (1986)

_____ *A History of the Arab State of Zanzibar* (1978)

_____ *Mirambo of Tanzania* (1971)

_____ ed. *Stanley's Despatches to the New York Herald 1871–1872, 1874–1877* (1970)

Berc, R. M. 'Land and Chieftainship among the Acholi' *Ganda Journal* 19 (1955)

Berman, Bruce and Lonsdale, John *Unhappy Valley: Conflict in Kenya and Africa* (1992)

Bierman, John *Dark Safari: The Life behind the Legend of Henry Morton Stanley* (1990)

Birmingham, D. and Martin, P. M. eds *History of Central Africa* vol. 2 (1983)

Blaikie, W. G. *The Personal Life of David Livingstone* (1880)

Blake, G. H. ed. *Imperial Boundary Making: The Diary of Captain Kelly and the Sudan–Uganda Boundary Commission of 1913* (1997)

Blixen, K. *Out of Africa* (1954 edn)

Brendon, Piers *The Decline and Fall of the British Empire 1781–1997* (2007)

Bridges, R. C. 'John Hanning Speke and the Royal Geographical Society' *Uganda Journal* 26 (1962)

Brode, H. *Tippu Tip* (1906)

Brodie, Fawn *The Devil Drives: A Life of Sir Richard Burton* (1967)

Bryaruhanga, Christopher *Bishop Alfred Robert Tucker and the Establishment of the Anglican Church* (2008)

Burton, Isabel *The Life of Captain Sir Richard F. Burton* 2 vols (1893)

Burton, Richard F. *First Footsteps in East Africa; or, An Exploration of Harar* 2 vols (1856)

_____ *The Lake Regions of Central Africa* 2 vols (1860) Narrative Press Edition (2001)

_____ *Personal Narrative of a Pilgrimage to El-Medinah and Meccah* 2 vols (1856)

_____ *Zanzibar: City, Island and Coast* 2 vols (1872)

Burton, Richard F. and M'Queen, James *The Nile Basin* (1864)

Cairns, A. C. *Prelude to Imperialism: British Reactions to Central African Society 1840–1890* (1965)

Cameron, Verney L. *Across Africa* 2 vols (1877)

Carnochan, W. B. *The Sad Story of Burton, Speke, and the Nile; or, Was John Hanning Speke a Cad?* (2006)

Carr-Gomm, Richard *All Things Considered* (2005)

_____ *Push on the Door* (1979)

Casati, Gaetano *Ten Years in Equatoria and the Return with Emin Pasha* 2 vols (1891)

Catania, Charles *Andrea De Bono: Maltese Explorer of the Nile* (2001)

Chadwick, O. *Mackenzie's Grave* (1959)

Chaillé-Long, C. *Central Africa* (1876)

Chavannes, P. de *Avec Brazza: Souvenirs de la Mission de l'Ouest Africain* (1935)

Churchill, Winston *The River War: An Historical Account of the Reconquest of the Soudan* 2 vols (1899)

Cockett, Richard *Sudan: Darfur and the Failure of an African State* (2010)

Collins, Robert O. *King Leopold, England and the Upper Nile* (1968)

_____ *Land Beyond the Rivers 1898–1918* (1971)

_____ *The Nile* (2002)

_____ *Shadows in the Grass: Britain in the Southern Sudan 1918–1956* (1983)

Collins, R. O. and Deng, F. M. eds *The British in the Sudan 1898–1956* (1984)

Colville, H. E. *The Land of the Nile Springs* (1895)

Coupland, R. *The Exploitation of East Africa 1856–1890: The Slave Trade and the Scramble* (1939)

_____ *Livingstone's Last Journey* (1945)

Crone, G. R. *The Sources of the Nile: Explorers' Maps 1856–1891* (1964)

Crowe, S. E. *The Berlin West Africa Conference 1884–85* (1942)

Daly, W. M. *Darfur's Sorrow: A History of Destruction and Genocide* (2007)

_____ *Empire on the Nile* (1986)

Dawson, E. C. *James Hannington: First Bishop of East Equatorial Africa* (1887)

Debenham, F. *The Way to Ilala: David Livingstone's Pilgrimage* (1955)

Dowden, Richard *Africa: Altered States, Ordinary Miracles* (2009)

Driberg, J. H. *People of the Small Arrow* (1930)

Driver, F. 'Henry Morton Stanley and his Critics: Geography, Exploration and Empire' *Past and Present* Nov 1991

Duigan, P. J. and Gann, L. H. *Burden of Empire* (1968)

_____ *Colonialism in Africa 1870–1960* 3 vols (1970–1971).

Dunbar, A. R. *Omukama Chwa II Kabarega* (1963)

Emerson, Barbara *Leopold II of the Belgians: King of Colonialism* (1979)

Farwell, Byron *The Man who Presumed* (1957)

_____ *Burton: A Biography of Sir Richard Francis Burton* (1963)

_____ *Queen Victoria's Little Wars* (1973)

Fisher, A. B. *Twilight Tales of the Black Baganda* (1911)

Forrest, D. W. *Francis Galton, the Life and Work of a Victorian Genius* (1974)

Foskett, Reginald ed. *The Zambesi Doctors: David Livingstone's Letters to John Kirk 1858–1872* (1964)

_____ *The Zambesi Journal and Letters of Dr John Kirk 1858–1863* 2 vols (1965)

Fox-Bourne W. R. *The Other Side of the Emin Pasha Relief Expedition* (1891)

Fraser, A. Z. *Livingstone and Newstead* (1913)

Fry, Joseph A. *Henry S. Sanford: Diplomacy and Business in Nineteenth Century America* (1982)

Galbraith, J. S. *Mackinnon and East Africa 1878–1895* (1972)

Galton, Francis *Memories of My Life* (1908)

Gann, L. H. and Duignan, P. *Burden of Empire: An Appraisal of Colonialism in Africa* (1968)

Geikie, A. *Life of Sir Roderick Murchison* 2 vols (1875)

Gifford, P. and Louis, W. R. *Britain and Germany in Africa* (1967) see chapter by Jean Stengers 'King Leopold and Anglo-French Rivalry 1882–84'; also in same volume R. O. Collins 'Origins of the Nile Struggle: Anglo-German Negotiations and the Mackinnon Agreement of 1890'

Girling, F. K. *The Acholi of Uganda* (1960)

Gladstone, Penelope *Travels of Alexine* (1970)

Godsall, Jon R. *The Tangled Web: A Life of the Sir Richard Burton* (2008)

Goldsmith, F. H. *John Ainsworth: Pioneer Administrator 1864–1946* (1955)

Grant, James *A Walk Across Africa* (1864)

Gray, Sir John 'Early Treaties in Uganda 1881–91' *Uganda Journal* xii 1 (1950)

Gray, Richard *A History of the Southern Sudan 1839–1889* (1961)

Green, Martin *Dreams of Adventure, Deeds of Empire* (1980)

Green, Matthew *The Wizard of the Nile* (2008)

Griffiths, Ieuan 'The Scramble for Africa: Inherited Political Boundaries' *Geographical Journal* 152/2 (Jul 1986)

Guadalupi, Gianni *The Discovery of the Nile* (1998)

Hall, Richard *Lovers on the Nile* (1980)

_____ *Stanley: An Adventurer Explored* (1974)

Hargreaves, J. D. *Prelude to the Partition of West Africa* (1973)

Harlow, Vincent and Chilver, E. M. eds *Oxford History of East Africa* 2 vols (1963, 1965)

Harrison, J. W. *The Story of the Life of Mackay of Uganda* (1898)

Hastings, Michael *Sir Richard Burton* (1978)

Helly, Dorothy O. *Livingstone's Legacy: Horace Waller and Victorian Mythmaking* (1987)

Henderson, K. D. D. *The Making of the Modern Sudan* (1953)

Henderson, K. D. D. and Owen, T. R. H. *Sudan Verse* (1963)

Henderson, Philip *The Life of Laurence Oliphant* (1956)

Hill, Richard *Egypt in the Sudan* (1959)

Hinde, Samuel L. *The Fall of the Congo Arabs* (1897)

Hird, Frank *H. M. Stanley: The Authorised Life* (1935)

Hobsbawm, Eric and Ranger T. *The Invention of Tradition* (1983)

Hochschild, Adam *King Leopold's Ghost: A Story of Greed, Terror and Heroism in Colonial Africa* (1998)

Howell, P. P. *The Nile: Sharing a Scarce Resource* (1994)

Hughes, L. 'Malice in Masailand' Colloque International, Montpellier 'At the Frontier of Land Issues' (2006)

Iliffe, John *Africans: The History of a Continent* (1995)

Jackson, Frederick *Early Days in East Africa* (1930)

Jameson, James S. *The Story of the Rear Column of the Emin Pasha Relief Expedition* (1890)

Jeal, Tim *Livingstone* (1973)

_____ *Stanley: The Impossible Life of Africa's Greatest Explorer* (2007)

Jephson, A. J. Mountney *Emin Pasha and the Rebellion at the Equator* (1890)

Jephson, Maurice Denham *An Anglo-Irish Miscellany: some records of the Jephsons of Mallow* (1964)

Johnson, D. H. *The Roots of Sudan's Civil War* (2003)

Johnston, Harry *The Nile Quest* (1903)

_____ *The River Congo* (1884)

_____ *Livingstone and the Exploration of Central Africa* (1891)

_____ *The Story of my Life* (1923)

Jones, Emir W. *Sir Henry M. Stanley: The Enigma* (1989)

Jones, Roger *The Rescue of Emin Pasha* (1972)

Jutzi, Alan *In Search of Sir Richard Burton: Papers from a Huntington Library Symposium* (1993)

Kaggwa, Apolo *The Kings of Buganda* (1901)

Karugire, S. R. *A Political History of Uganda* (1980)

Kasozi, A. B. K. *The Social Origins of Violence in Uganda 1964–1985* (1994)

Kavas, A. 'Ottoman Empire's Relations with Southern Africa' *Journal of Ankara University History Faculty* XLVIII (2007) II

Keltie, J. S. *The Partition of Africa* (1895)

Kennedy, Dane *The Highly Civilized Man: Richard Burton and the Victorian World* (2005)

Knoblecher, Ignatius *Jahresberichte des Marienvereins* (1852–58)

Koebner R. and Schmidt, H. D. *Imperialism: The Story and Significance of a Political Word 1840–1960* (1964)

Krapf, J. L.*Travels and Researches* (1860)

Lentz, Carola 'Tribalism and Ethnicity in Africa' *Cahiers des sciences humaine* 31 II (1985)

Liebowitz, D. and Pearson C. *The Last Expedition: Stanley's Mad Journey through the Congo* (2005)

Livingstone, D. *Missionary Travels and Researches in South Africa* (1857)

_____ H. Waller ed. *The Last Journals of David Livingstone in Central Africa* (1874)

Livingstone, David and Charles *Narrative of an Expedition to the Zambezi* (1866)

Lloyd, Christopher *The Navy and the Slave Trade* (1949)

Louis, W. R. *Ruanda-Urundi 1884–1919* (1963)

Louis, W. R. & Stengers, J. *E. D. Morel's History of the Congo Reform Movement* (1968)

Lovejoy, Paul *Transformations in Slavery* (1983)

Lovell, Mary *A Rage to Live: A Biography of Richard and Isabel Burton* (1998)

Low, D. A. *The Mind of Buganda* (1971)

Lugard, Frederick *The Rise of Our East African Empire* 2 vols (1893)

Luwel, M. *H. M. Stanley, H. H. Johnston et le Congo* (1978)

_____ *Sir Francis de Winton* (1964)

Mackenzie, J. M. *Propaganda and Empire* (1984)

MacLaren, Roy ed. *African Exploits: The Diaries of William Stairs 1887–1892* (1998)

McLynn, Frank *Burton: Snow upon the Desert* (1990)

_____ *Hearts of Darkness* (1992)

_____ *Stanley: The Making of an African Explorer* (1989)

_____ *Stanley: Sorcerer's Apprentice* (1991)

MacMichael, Harold *A History of the Arabs in the Sudan* 2 vols (1922)

Magnus, Philip *Kitchener: Portrait of an Imperialist* (1958)

Maitland, Alexander *Speke* (1971)

Manning, Patrick *Slavery and African Life* (1990)

Markham, Clements *Private History of the Royal Geographical Society* (n.d.)

Maurice, Albert *H. M. Stanley: Unpublished Letters* (1957)

Meinertzhagen, Richard *Kenya Diary 1902–1906* (1957)

Melly, George *The Blue and White Nile* 2 vols (1851)

Meredith, Martin *The State of Africa: A History of Fifty Years of Independence* (2006)

Middleton, Dorothy *Baker of the Nile* (1949)

_____ *Victorian Lady Travellers* (1965)

_____ ed. *The Diaries of A. J. Mounteney Jephson* (1969)

Moir, F. L. M. *After Livingstone* (1923)

Moorehead, Alan *The White Nile* (1960)

Morel, E. D. *Great Britain and the Congo: The Pillage of the Congo Basin* (1909)

Mpangala, G. P. 'Origins of Political Conflicts & Peace Building in the Lakes Region', paper presented at Arusha Symposium (2004)

Al-Mubarak, Khalid *Turabi's 'Islamist' Venture: Failure and Implications* (2001)

Mungeam, G. H. *British Rule in Kenya 1895–1912* (1966)

Newman, J. L. *Imperial Footprints: Henry Morton Stanley's African Journeys* (2004)

_____ *The Peoples of Africa* (1995)

Nicholls, C. S. *Red Strangers* (2005)

Nyabongo, Elizabeth *Elizabeth of Toro* (1989)

Odoi-Tanga, F. 'Politics, ethnicity and conflict in post-independent Acholiland, Uganda 1962–2006' University of Pretoria PhD thesis (2009)

Oliver, Roland *The Missionary Factor in East Africa* (1965)

_____ *Sir Harry Johnston and the Scramble for Africa* (1957)

Oliver, Roland and Atmore, Anthony *Africa Since 1800* (1981)

Ondaatje, Christopher *Journey to the Source of the Nile* (1998)

Padmore, G. *How Britain Rules Africa* (1931)

Pakenham, Thomas *The Scramble for Africa* (1991)

Parke, T. H. *My Personal Experiences in Equatorial Africa* (1891)

_____ Lyons, J. B. ed. *Surgeon-Major Parke's African Journey 1887–1889* (1994)

Parker, John and Rathbone, R. *African History* (2007)

Patience, K. *Zanzibar, Slavery and the Royal Navy* (2000)

Perham, Margery *Lugard: The Years of Adventure 1858–1898* (1956)

_____ ed. *The Diaries of Lord Lugard* 2 vols (1959)

Petherick, John, and Petherick, Katherine Harriet Edlman *Travels in Central Africa* (Vol. I) *& Exploration of the Western Nile Tributaries* (Vol. II) (1869)

Peters, Karl *New Light on Dark Africa* (1891)

Pond, J. B. *Eccentricities of Genius* (1901)

Porter, Mrs Gerald *Annals of a Publishing House: William Blackwood and his sons* (Vol. III *John Blackwood*) 3 vols (1898)

Ransford, O. N. *Livingstone's Lake* (1966)

Reader, John *Africa: A Biography of the Continent* (1997)

Rees, Sian *Sweet Water and Bitter: The Ships that Stopped the Slave Trade* (2009)

Rice, Edward *Captain Sir Richard Francis Burton* (1990)

Richards, W. A. 'Import of Firearms into West Africa in the Eighteenth Century' *Journal of African History* 21 (1980)

Riffenburgh, B. *The Myth of the Explorer* (1993)

Robinson R., Gallagher, J. and Denny, A. *Africa and the Victorians* (1961)

Rodney, W. *How Europe Underdeveloped Africa* (1982)

Roeykens, P. A. *Les débuts de l'oeuvre africaine de Leopold II 1876–1879* (1955)

Rotberg, R. I. ed. *Africa and its Explorers* (1970) Robert O. Collins chapter on S. W. Baker

Rowe, J. A. *Lugard at Kampala* (1969)

Rowlands, Cadwalader (pseud. for John C. Hotten) *H. M. Stanley: The Story of his Life* (1872)

_____ *The Finding of Dr Livingstone by H. M. Stanley* (1872)

Rowley, H. *The Story of the Universities' Mission to Central Africa* (1866)

Said, Edward W. *Orientalism* (1995)

Said-Ruete, Emily *Memoirs of an Arabian Princess* (1888; reprinted 1980, 1994)

Sanderson, G. N. *England, Europe and the Upper Nile 1882–1899* (1965)

Schweitzer, G. *Emin Pasha: his life and work* 2 vols (1898)

Seaver, G. *David Livingstone: his life and letters* (1957)

Schapera, I. ed. *David Livingstone: Family Letters 1841–1856* (1959) 2 vols

_____ *Livingstone's African Journal 1853–1856* 2 vols (1963)

_____ *Livingstone's Missionary Correspondence 1841–1856* (1961)

_____ *Livingstone's Private Journals 1851–53* (1960)

Segal, Ronald *Islam's Black Slaves: The Other Black Diaspora* (2000)

Seitz, Don C. *The James Gordon Bennetts* (1928)

Sherriff, Abdul *Slaves, Spices and Ivory in Zanzibar* (1987)

Shipman, Pat *To the Heart of the Nile* (2004)

Simpson, Donald *Dark Companions* (1975)

Simpson, John *Strange Places, Questionable People* (2008)

Slade, Ruth *King Leopold's Congo* (1962)

Smith, Iain R. *The Emin Pasha Relief Expedition 1886–1890* (1972)

Southall, A. *The Illusion of Tribe* (1970)

Speke, John H. 'Captain Speke's discovery of the Victoria Nyanza lake' *Blackwood's Magazine* LXXXVI Oct 1859 Part 2

_____ 'Journal of a cruise on the Tanganyika lake and discovery of the Victoria Nyanza lake' *Blackwood's Magazine* LXXXVI Jul–Dec 1859 Part 3

_____ *Journal of the Discovery of the Source of the Nile* (1863)

_____ *What Led to the Discovery of the Source of the Nile* (1863)

Stafford, Robert A. *Scientist of Empire: Sir Roderick Murchison, Scientific Exploration and Victorian Imperialism* (1985)

Stanley, Dorothy ed. *The Autobiography of Sir Henry Morton Stanley* (1909)

Stanley, Henry M. *The Congo and the Founding of its Free State* 2 vols (1885)

_____ *How I Found Livingstone in Central Africa* (1872)

_____ *In Darkest Africa*, 2 vols (1890)

_____ *My Dark Companions and their Strange Stories* (1893)

_____ *Through the Dark Continent*, 2 vols (1878)

Stanley, Richard and Neame, Alan eds *The Exploration Diaries of H. M. Stanley* (1961)

Swann, A. J. *Fighting the Slave Hunters in Central Africa* (1910)

Taylor, Anne *Laurence Oliphant* (1982)

Thomas, H. B. 'The Death of Speke in 1864' *Uganda Journal* Vol XII (1949)

Thomson, Joseph *Through Masailand* (1885)

Tip, Tippu *The Autobiography of Tippu Tip* translated Whitely, W. H. (1966)

Troup, J. Rose *With Stanley's Rear Column* (1890)

Tvedt, Terje *The River Nile in the Age of the British* (2004)

Udal, John O. *The Nile in Darkness: Conquest and Exploration 1504–1862* Vol. I of 2 (1998)

_____ *The Nile in Darkness: A Flawed Unity 1863–1899* Vol. II of 2 (2005)

Vansina, Jan *The Tio Kingdom of the Middle Congo 1880–1892* (1973)

Vasnia, Phiroze *The Gift of the Nile: Hellenizing Egypt from Aeschylus to Alexander* (2001)

Wallis, J. P. R. ed. *The Zambezi Expedition of David Livingstone 1858–1863* (1956)

_____ *The Zambesi Journal of James Stewart 1862–1863* (1952)

Ward, Herbert *My Life with Stanley's Rear-Guard* (1890)

Werner, J. R. A. *A Visit to Stanley's Rear Guard* (1889)

West, Richard *Brazza of the Congo* (1972)

White, James P. *The Sanford Exploring Expedition* (1967)

Wilkins, W. H. and Burton, Isabel *The Romance of Isabel Lady Burton* 2 vols (1897)

Wright, Thomas *The Life of Sir Richard Burton* 2 vols (1906)

Yeoman, Guy *Quest for the Secret Nile* (2004)

Young, D. ed. *The Search for the Source of the Nile: Correspondence between Captain Richard Burton, Captain John Speke and Others, from . . . the Collection of Quentin Keynes Esq.* (1999)

Yule, H. and Hyndman, H. M. *Mr Henry Morton Stanley and the Royal Geographical Society: being the Record of a Protest* (1878)

Zulfo, I. H. (translated Clark, P.) *Karari: The Sudanese Account of the Battle of Omdurman* (1980)

Notes

Abbreviations in the Notes

Agnes, L	Agnes Livingstone
AJ	Schapera, I. ed. *Livingstone's African Journal 1853–1856* 2 vols
AN	Baker, S. W. *The Albert N'yanza: Great Basin of the Nile*
Annals	Porter, Mrs Gerald *Annals of a Publishing House: William Blackwood and his sons* (Vol. III *John Blackwood*) 3 vols
Atkinson	Atkinson, R. R. *The Roots of Ethnicity: The Origins of the Acholi and Uganda before 1800*
Bennett	Bennett, N. R. ed. *Stanley's Despatches to the New York Herald 1871–1872, 1874–1877*
Blaikie	Blaikie, W. G. *The Personal Life of David Livingstone*
Brazza	West, Richard *Brazza of the Congo*
Brendon	Brendon, Piers *The Decline and Fall of the British Empire 1781–1997*
Brodie	Brodie, Fawn *The Devil Drives: A Life of Sir Richard Burton*
BL	British Library
Cairns	Cairns, H. A. C. *Prelude to Imperialism: British Reactions to Central African Society 1840–1890*
Carnochan	Carnochan, W. B. *The Sad Story of Burton, Speke, and the Nile; or, Was John Hanning Speke a Cad?*
Catania	Catania, Charles *Andrea De Bono: Maltese Explorer of the Nile*
CD	Stanley's Congo Diaries, devoted to his work on the Congo
Collins chapter	Robert O. Collins chapter on S. W. Baker in Robert I. Rotberg ed. *Africa and its Explorers*
Cockett	Cockett, Richard *Sudan: Darfur and the Failure of an African State*
Daly	Daly, W. M. *Empire on the Nile*
Debenham	Debenham, F. *The Way to Ilala: David Livingstone's Pilgrimage*
DL	David Livingstone
DLC	David Livingstone Centre, Blantyre, Scotland

Dowden	Dowden, Richard *Africa: Altered States, Ordinary Miracles*
ET	Elizabeth Nyabongo *Elizabeth of Toro*
FF	Burton, Richard F. *First Footsteps in East Africa: or, An Exploration of Harar* 2 vols
Foskett	Foskett, R. *The Zambesi Doctors: David Livingstone's Letters to John Kirk 1858–1872*
Gifford & Louis	Gifford, P. and Louis, W. R *Britain and Germany in Africa*
Girling	Girling, F. K. *The Acholi of Uganda*
Godsall	Godsall, Jon R. *The Tangled Web: A Life of the Sir Richard Burton*
Gray	Gray, Richard *A History of the Southern Sudan 1839–1889*
Guadalupi	Guadalupi, Gianni *The Discovery of the Nile*
Hall, *Lovers*	Hall, Richard *Lovers on the Nile*
Hall, *Stanley*	Hall, Richard *Stanley: An Adventurer Explored*
Helly	Helly, Dorothy O. *Livingstone's Legacy: Horace Waller and Victorian Mythmaking*
HIFL	Stanley, H. M. *How I Found Livingstone in Central Africa*
IDA	Stanley, H. M. *In Darkest Africa*, 2 vols
Ismailia	Baker, S. W. *Ismailia: A Narrative of the Expedition to Central Africa for the Suppression of the Slave Trade* 2 vols
JB	John Blackwood
Jeal, *Livingstone*,	Jeal, Tim *Livingstone*
Jeal, *Stanley*	Jeal, Tim *Stanley: The Impossible Life of Africa's Greatest Explorer*
Jephson	Middleton, Dorothy ed. *The Diaries of A. J. Mounteney Jephson*
Johnston	Johnston, Harry *The Nile Quest*
Journal	Speke, John H. *Journal of the Discovery of the Source of the Nile*
Journal proofs	Proofs of *Journal of the Discovery of the Source of the Nile* in NLS
Journal ms	Original manuscript of *Journal of the Discovery of the Source of the Nile* in NLS
JRGS	*Journal of the Royal Geographical Society*
Jutzi	Jutzi, Alan *In Search of Sir Richard Burton: Papers from a Huntington Library Symposium*
Karugire	Karugire, S. R. *A Political History of Uganda*
Kennedy	Kennedy, Dane *The Highly Civilized Man: Richard Burton and the Victorian World*
KGR	Katie Gough Roberts
LBR	Collins, R. O. *Land Beyond the Rivers 1898–1918*

Life	Burton, Isabel *The Life of Captain Sir Richard F. Burton* 2 vols
LLJ	Waller, H. ed. *The Last Journals of David Livingstone in Central Africa* 2 vols
LMS/SOAS	London Missionary Society Archive in School of African and Oriental Studies
Lovell	Lovell, Mary *A Rage to Live: A Biography of Richard and Isabel Burton*
LPJ	Schapera, I. ed. *Livingstone's Private Journals 1851–53*
LR	Burton, Richard F. *The Lake Regions of Central Africa* 2 vols
Mackay	Harrison, J. W. *The Story of the Life of Mackay of Uganda*
McLynn	McLynn, Frank *Burton: Snow upon the Desert*
Maitland	Maitland, Alexander *Speke*
Meredith	Meredith, Martin *The State of Africa: A History of Fifty Years of Independence*
Moorehead	Moorehead, Alan *The White Nile*
Morning Star	Baker, Anne *Morning Star: Florence Baker's Diary of the Expedition to Put Down the Slave Trade on the Nile 1870–1873*
Narrative	Burton, Richard F. *Personal Narrative of a Pilgrimage to El-Medinah and Meccah* 2 vols
NAZ	National Archives of Zimbabwe
Nile Basin	Burton, Richard F. and M'Queen, James *The Nile Basin*
'Nile Struggle'	R. O. Collins 'Origins of the Nile Struggle: Anglo-German Negotiations and the Mackinnon Agreement of 1890', in Gifford & Louis
NLS	National Library of Scotland
NYH	*New York Herald*
Odoi-Tanga	Odoi-Tanga, F. 'Politics, ethnicity and conflict in post-independent Acholiland, Uganda 1962–2006' University of Pretoria PhD thesis
Ondaatje	Ondaatje, Christopher *Journey to the Source of the Nile*
Oxford	Harlow, Vincent and Chilver, E. M. eds *Oxford History of East Africa* 2 vols
Pakenham	Pakenham, Thomas *The Scramble for Africa*
Parke	Parke, T. H., Lyons, J. B. ed. *Surgeon-Major Parke's African Journey 1887–1889*
Perham	Perham, Margery *Lugard: The Years of Adventure 1858–1898*
PRGS	*Proceedings of the Royal Geographical Society*
QK/BL	The late Quentin Keynes's Burton Collection in the BL
QK book	Young, D. ed. *The Search for the Source of the Nile: [etc.]*

459

Reader	Reader, John *Africa: A Biography of the Continent*
RGS	Royal Geographical Society
RM	Sir Roderick Murchison Bart
RMCA	Royal Museum of Central Africa
SD	Stanley's Diaries and field notebooks starting in 1866 and ending in 1901
S&N	Stanley, Richard and Neame, Alan eds *The Exploration Diaries of H. M. Stanley*
Sanderson	Sanderson, G. N. *England, Europe and the Upper Nile 1882–1899*
Shadows	Collins, R. O. *Shadows in the Grass: Britain in the Southern Sudan 1918–1956*
Shaw	Dr Norton Shaw
Shipman	Shipman, Pat *To the Heart of the Nile*
Smith	Smith, Iain R. *The Emin Pasha Relief Expedition 1886–1890*
Stanley, *Auto*	Stanley, Dorothy ed. *The Autobiography of Sir Henry Morton Stanley*
TDC	Stanley, H. M. *Through the Dark Continent*, 2 vols
Travels	Petherick, John, and Petherick, Harriet Edlman *Travels in Central Africa* (Vol. I) & *Exploration of the Western Nile Tributaries* (Vol. II)
Tucker	Bryaruhanga, Christopher *Bishop Alfred Robert Tucker and the Establishment of the Anglican Church*
Udal I	Udal, John O. *The Nile in Darkness* Vol. 1 *Conquest and Exploration 1504–1862*
Udal II	Udal, John O. *The Nile in Darkness* Vol. II *A Flawed Unity 1863–1899*
Walk	Grant, James *A Walk Across Africa*
WLT	Speke, John H. *What Led to the Discovery of the Source of the Nile*
Yeoman	Yeoman, Guy *Quest for the Secret Nile*
Zanzibar	Burton, Richard F. *Zanzibar: City, Island and Coast* 2 vols

Introduction

1. *The Gift of the Nile: Hellenizing Egypt from Aeschylus to Alexander* Phiroze Vasnia 275–7.
2. *The Nile* Robert O. Collins 1, 6, 90.
3. *Stanley: The Impossible Life of Africa's Greatest Explorer* Tim Jeal [Jeal, *Stanley*] 3.
4. *Prelude to Imperialism* H. A. C. Cairns 29 n 99.
5. Ibid 26 n 82.

6. *The Devil Drives: A Life of Sir Richard Burton* Fawn Brodie [Brodie] 15 n 1.
7. *The Autobiography of Sir Henry Morton Stanley* ed. Dorothy Stanley [Stanley, *Auto*] 533.
8. *Personal Narrative of a Pilgrimage to El-Medinah and Meccah* Richard F. Burton [*Narrative*] 2 vols, I 16.
9. J. H. Speke to Norton Shaw [Shaw] 20 May 1857 JHS 1 RGS.
10. *The Albert N'yanza: Great Basin of the Nile* S. W. Baker [*AN*] 274.
11. Cairns 20 n 64.
12. *Lovers on the Nile* Richard Hall [Hall, *Lovers*] 87; Obituary of Speke *Blackwood's Magazine* Vol. XCVI Oct 1864 414–16.
13. *Hearts of Darkness: The European Exploration of Africa* Frank McLynn ix.
14. As told to Stanley in *How I Found Livingstone in Central Africa* H. M. Stanley [*HIFL*], quoted in *A History of African Exploration* David Mountfield (1976) frontispiece; *Livingstone*, Tim Jeal [Jeal, *Livingstone*] 367.
15. *The Exploration Diaries of H. M. Stanley* eds Richard Stanley and Alan Neame [S&N] 63.
16. *Zanzibar: City, Island and Coast* Richard F. Burton [*Zanzibar*] 2 vols II 222–3.
17. *The Last Journals of David Livingstone in Central Africa* ed. H. Waller [*LLJ*] 2 vols I 287.

ONE: Blood in God's River

1. *LLJ* I 17.
2. *LLJ* I 29, 70; DL to Agnes L 18 May 1866 BL Ad MS 50184.
3. DL to Agnes L Sept 1869 BL.
4. DL to Janet and Agnes L 30 Mar 1841 *David Livingstone: Family Letters 1841–1856* ed. I. Schapera 2 vols I 19.
5. *London Journal* Dec 1856.
6. *The Way to Ilala* F. Debenham [Debenham] 293–4.
7. DL to Agnes L 5 Feb 1871 BL.
8. *LLJ* II 72.
9. DL to Agnes L Sept 1869 BL.
10. *LLJ* II 72.
11. DL to Agnes L Sept 1869 BL.
12. *LLJ* II 2.
13. *LLJ* II 40–2.
14. *The Personal Life of David Livingstone* W. G. Blaikie [Blaikie] 334.
15. *Livingstone's Legacy: Horace Waller and Victorian Mythmaking* Dorothy O. Helly [Helly] 334.
16. *LLJ* II 46–7.

17. Ibid 47–8, 67.
18. Ibid 47–8, 67–8.
19. Ibid 93.
20. *LLJ* I 7.
21. *Livingstone*, Jeal 316, 319–20; *The Zambezi Doctors: David Livingstone's Letters to John Kirk 1858–1872* ed. R. Foskett [Foskett] 143.
22. *LLJ* II 37.
23. Ibid 118.
24. Ibid 38.
25. Blaikie 331.
26. *LLJ* II 99, and ed's. footnote on 100.
27. Blaikie 334.
28. *LLJ* II 98.
29. Ibid 80.
30. Ibid 86, 78.
31. Ibid 55.
32. Ibid 34; Jeal, *Livingstone* 328.
33. Blaikie 340.
34. *LLJ* II 93.
35. Ibid 239–40.
36. *The Nile in Darkness* Vol. I: *Conquest and Exploration 1504–1862* John O. Udal [Udal I] 1.
37. *LLJ* II 339, 51.
38. *Travels of Alexine* Penelope Gladstone.
39. Herodotus *Histories* Book Two Chapters 19–35: quoted *LLJ* II 49.
40. *LLJ* II 49.
41. *The Nile Quest* Harry Johnston [Johnston] 22.
42. Blaikie 333.
43. *LLJ* II 67, 64.
44. Ibid 68.
45. Ibid 99.
46. Helly 172.
47. Ibid 173; in unpublished Unyanyembe Journal (David Livingstone Centre/DLC) 13 Jun 1870. DL considered that 'the want of a chain to confine them emboldens them to impertinence'.
48. Ibid 173; Jeal, *Livingstone* 241; DL wrote: of Nassick pupils: 'They do slave duties unbidden and all they can to ingratiate themselves with the Arabs [They] would now fain be slave stealers.' 6 Jul 1870 Unyanyembe Journal.
49. Helly 173–4.
50. *LLJ* II 101.
51. Blaikie 341.
52. *LLJ* II 101.

53. Ibid 103.
54. Ibid 107.
55. Ibid 108–9.
56. Ibid 111.
57. Ibid 113–14.
58. Ibid 120, 116.
59. Unyanyembe Journal 11 Feb, 11 Mar 1871 *DLC*; *LLJ* II 124.
60. Ibid 125.
61. Ibid 130, 132.
62. Ibid 132–41.
63. Ibid 146.

TWO: A Great Misalliance

1. DL to R. Murchison [RM] 29 Nov 1865 National Archives of Zimbabwe [NAZ].
2. *The Tangled Web: A Life of the Sir Richard Burton* Jon R. Godsall [Godsall] 110.
3. Brodie 16.
4. *The Highly Civilized Man: Richard Burton and the Victorian World* Dane Kennedy [Kennedy] 71–2.
5. Burton to Shaw 16 Nov 1853 RGS.
6. *The Life of Captain Sir Richard F. Burton* Isabel Burton 2 vols [*Life*] I 104.
7. *Life* I 123, 144.
8. Brodie 74; *Life* I 135; *A Rage to Live: A Biography of Richard and Isabel Burton* Mary Lovell [Lovell] 41.
9. Lovell 10.
10. Brodie 89.
11. *Narrative* 16.
12. Burton to Shaw 16 Nov 1853 RGS.
13. Godsall 109.
14. Quoted Udal I, 493; *Travels and Researches* J. L. Krapf 478–90, 496.
15. Burton to Shaw 15 Dec 1853 RGS.
16. *Hearts of Darkness* McLynn 57–8.
17. Lovell 232.
18. Details in *The Discovery of the Nile* Gianni Guadalupi [Guadalupi].
19. *The Blue and White Nile* George Melly 2 vols.
20. *Andrea De Bono: Maltese Explorer of the Nile* Charles Catania 214.
21. Ibid, Chapter 18.
22. Udal I 487.
23. Guadalupi 241.
24. *Speke* Alexander Maitland [Maitland] 7.
25. Godsall 115.

26. *Zanzibar* I 4–5.
27. *First Footsteps in East Africa: or, An Exploration of Harar* Richard Francis Burton 2 vols [*FF*] I xxiv; Godsall 118.
28. Lovell 85, 144.

THREE: A Rush of Men Like a Stormy Wind

1. This is certainly true of Fawn M. Brodie (1967), Byron Farwell (1963), Mary S. Lovell (1998), Frank McLynn (1990) and Edward Rice (1990). A far more objective account of the two men's strengths and failures is to be found in W. B. Carnochan's book about their falling-out: *The Sad Story of Burton, Speke, and the Nile; or, Was John Hanning Speke a Cad?* [Carnochan].
2. *Zanzibar* II 379.
3. Lovell 89.
4. Brodie 1–2.
5. *What Led to the Discovery of the Source of the Nile* John H. Speke [*WLT*] 6; Speke to Grant 18 Jun 1854 National Library of Scotland [NLS] 17910.
6. *Zanzibar* II 379; *Life* I 315.
7. *Zanzibar* II 381.
8. This information about Speke is in James August Grant's Papers 17931 NLS.
9. *Zanzibar* II 377.
10. Ibid 376–7.
11. Ibid 378; Maitland 20–1; *WLT* 1–2 and n.
12. *WLT* 20.
13. Ibid 23.
14. Maitland 23 ff.
15. *WLT* 104; Maitland 31.
16. Ibid 112 n.
17. Kennedy 87.
18. *Zanzibar* II 383.
19. Burton to Shaw 25 Feb 1859 RGS.
20. Carnochan 31; *FF* II 98.
21. *WLT* 125.
22. Ibid 127–8.
23. *FF* II 100, 105.
24. *Life* I 219–20; Lt G. E. Herne to Burton April 1855 in *The Search for the Source of the Nile: [etc]* ed. Donald Young [QK book] 44 ff.
25. In *WLT* 132 Speke wrote 'retiring', rather than 'running', the word used by Burton in *Zanzibar* II 386.
26. *WLT* 133.
27. *Zanzibar* II 386; in *Life* I 220, Burton has Speke leave the tent last,

which Burton contradicts in the more convincing account given by him
in *Zanzibar* II 386.

28. *Life* I 221; Lovell 180.
29. Maitland 37; Lovell 180.
30. *WLT* 138–40.
31. *Life* I 221.
32. QK book 35.
33. *WLT* 145, 148; Maitland 43.
34. Godsall 145; *Zanzibar* II 385.
35. *WLT* 116.
36. Ibid 144; Speke to Playfair 24 Oct 1859 quoted in Maitland 49.

FOUR: About a Rotten Person

1. Lovell 182.
2. Brodie 131.
3. *Proceedings of the Royal Geographical Society* [*PRGS*] Vol. I 26 Nov and 10 Dec 1855.
4. Burton to Shaw 9 April 1856 RGS; Godsall 149.
5. Burton to Shaw 19 Apr 1856 RGS.
6. *The Life of Laurence Oliphant* Philip Henderson 52; *WLT* 150.
7. Maitland 53; *WLT* 151.
8. *WLT* 157.
9. *The Lake Regions of Central Africa* Richard F. Burton 2 vols [*LR*] I Preface 2.
10. *Zanzibar* II 376–7.
11. Maitland 14–15.
12. Georgina Speke to John Blackwood [JB] 11 Sept 1860 4154 NLS.
13. Speke to Shaw 20 n.d but either March or May 1857 RGS; Georgina Speke to JB 11 Sept 1860 4154 NLS.
14. Speke to JB 5 Nov 1859 4153 NLS.
15. Brodie 26.
16. Proofs of *Journal of the Discovery of the Source of the Nile* [*Journal proofs*] 16 April p. 58 4873 NLS.
17. Speke to JB ? Apr 1860 f 112 NLS.
18. Speke to JB 27 March 1860 NLS.
19. Brodie 152. This version of Speke's sexual nature and character would be echoed by all but one of Burton's subsequent biographers.
20. Speke to Grant n.d. but 1855 in 'Nogal Country' NLS.
21. *Burton: Snow upon the Desert* Frank McLynn [McLynn] 106; *Laurence Oliphant* Anne Taylor 67; Brodie 168–9; *The Romance of Isabel Lady Burton* W. H. Wilkins and Isabel Burton 2 vols I 144.
22. McLynn 52, 180; Kennedy 214; Lovell 36.
23. Brodie 105.

24. *Zanzibar* II 381–2.
25. Speke to Shaw 28 Oct 1859 RGS.
26. *FF* II 107, 143.
27. Maitland 54.
28. McLynn 55 describes 'Burton's rococo prose style' as 'a serious strike against him'. JB to J. Delane 8 Dec 1863 on the 'genuineness' and effectiveness of Speke's 'quaint' style, quoted in *Annals of a Publishing House* Mrs Gerald Porter 3 vols [*Annals*] III 97.
29. Lovell 220.
30 Francis Galton quoted in Brodie 42.
31. Quoted in *In Search of Sir Richard Burton: Papers from a Huntington Library Symposium* Alan Jutzi [Jutzi] 15.
32. Lovell 228.

FIVE: Everything Was to be Risked for This Prize

1. *WLT* 168.
2. *Zanzibar* I 180.
3. *WLT* 161.
4. Ibid 162, 166; *Zanzibar* II 57–8; Godsall 162–3; Rebmann to Burton 21 March 1859 Quentin Keynes Collection BL [QK/BL].
5. *WLT* 166–7. In fact on his next journey Speke went via Unyanyembe as before; Maitland 60.
6. *LR* I 75.
7. *Zanzibar* I 81.
8. *WLT* 190.
9. *Zanzibar* I 351–2.
10. Ibid 453–63; *LR* II 310 ff; Brodie 145.
11. *LR* II 308–13; McLynn 214; Speke to Grant 22 Mar 1864 17931 NLS; *WLT* 218–19; *Journal of the Discovery of the Source of the Nile* John Speke [*Journal*] 42, 45.
12. *Zanzibar* I 484; *WLT* 189; ibid 484–5.
13. Ibid 488–9; 168.
14. *Life* I 258.
15. *Zanzibar* I 260–1.
16. *Zanzibar* II 292.
17. Godsall 155.
18. *Zanzibar* I 7; Burton to Shaw 19 Apr 1856 RGS; Burton to Sec Bombay Govt 28 Apr 1854, quoted Godsall 115.
19. *WLT* 186.
20. *Zanzibar* II 179–80, 285; *Zanzibar* I 479–82; *Life* I 281; *WLT* 193, 210–12; *LR* I 121 f.
21. *LR* I 120; Godsall 168; *WLT* 197.
22. *Zanzibar* II 286–8; *WLT* 195.

23. Lovell 245; the author claims that Frost lied because Burton had offended him in some unspecified way.
24. *LR* I 46.
25. Ibid 58–71.
26. *Zanzibar* II 222–3.
27. *LR* I 78–9, 238; *WLT* 266.
28 *Life* I 110; Brodie 51; 'Captain Speke's Discovery of the Victoria Nyanza' *Blackwood's Magazine* Vol. LXXXVI Jul–Dec 1859 Part 3, 577; *Zanzibar* II 378; Lovel 254.
29. *LR* I 88, 165–6.
30. Ibid 89; *Zanzibar* II 269, 96; *LR* I 89; Lovell 260; *The White Nile* Alan Moorehead [Moorehead] 45–6; Kennedy 115.
31. *WLT* 285, 277; H. M. Stanley to Grant 23 Dec 1878 Royal Museum of Central Africa [RMCA].
32. *LR* I 388.
33. *LR* I 81; also quoted Jutzi 39–40.
34. *LR* I 172–3.
35 *Zanzibar* II 388
36. Speke to Shaw 2 Jul 1858 RGS.
37. *Blackwood's Magazine* Vol. LXXXVI Jul–Dec 1859 Part 3, 339; Burton to Norton Shaw 19 Apr 1856 RGS; *Zanzibar* II 389.
38. *Life* I 283–4.
39. *LR* I 175–6; *Life* I 285, 284.
40. Ibid 286–7.
41. *LR* I 194–7; *Life* I 287.
42. *WLT* 196–7; *LR* I 217–18.
43. Ibid 283–4.
44. McLynn 216.
45. *Journal* 72–8.
46. *WLT* 198–9.
47. Ibid 199–200.
48. *LR* I 284–5; *WLT* 200; *LR* I 336.
49. Lovell 263 and her associated notes 55, 57 and 58; *WLT* 200.
50. That command did pass to Speke is made clear by the notes which Burton made in the margins of his personal copy of Speke's *What Led to the Discovery of the Source of the Nile* (now in the Huntington Library). Where he disagreed with a statement, Burton would usually write 'rot', as when Speke claimed to have cheered him up in his sickness. On other occasions he disagreed more elaborately, or with a simple 'no'. But Burton made no comment of any kind against Speke's claim to have taken command, implying assent.
51. Burton's copy *WLT* 200.
52. *LR* I 351.
53. *LR* II 35–6.

54. Ibid 273.
55. Ibid 117; Brodie 158; Joseph Thomson's height for Lake Tanganyika is recorded in *PRGS* Vol. IV Apr 1880; *Zanzibar* II 309.
56. *LR* II 72; *WLT* 207–8.
57. *LR* II 73; *WLT* 208.
58. *WLT* 209; 'Journal of a cruise on the Tanganyika lake and discovery of the Victoria Nyanza lake' *Blackwood's Magazine* Vol. LXXXVI 1859, Part 2.
59. *WLT* 224–5.
60. *WLT* 229–45.
61. *LR* II 76; Maitland 73–4.
62. *LR* II 76; *WLT* 246; Burton at RGS, *Journal of the Royal Geographical Society [JRGS]* Vol. XXIX 23 May 1859.
63. *LR* II 78–97, 322.
64. Ibid 98–9.
65. *Zanzibar* II 303; *WLT* 247.
66. 'Our Great African Travellers' Henry M. Stanley 3, 10 RMCA.
67. *WLT* 250–1; *LR* II 112; ; *Blackwood's Magazine* Vol. LXXXVI Oct 1859 Part 2 'Captain Speke's discovery of the Victoria Nyanza lake'.
68. *JRGS* Vol. XXIX 23 May 1859.
69. *Zanzibar* II 302; Henry M. Stanley's diary 22 Nov 1871 RMCA; *WLT* 251.
70. Speke to Shaw 2 Jul 1858 RGS; *LR* II 109.
71. *WLT* 251; *Zanzibar* II 317; Burton to Shaw 24 Jun 1858 RGS; Godsall 179.
72. *LR* II 142; *Life* I 308; *Zanzibar* II 314.
73. Speke to Rigby 22 Oct 1860 NLS.
74. Speke to JB 11 Aug 1860 4154 NLS.
75. Speke to Rigby Oct 1860, quoted by Kennedy 113.

SIX: Promises and Lies

1. *WLT* 251, 261; *Zanzibar* II 315; Speke to Rigby 2 Oct 1860 17931 NLS.
2. Burton's copy of *WLT* 263 Huntington Library.
3. Speke to *Athenaeum Magazine* 19 Dec 1863.
4. *Blackwood's Magazine* Vol. LXXXVI Oct 1859, Part 2 398.
5. *WLT* 271, 287; *Blackwood's Magazine* Vol. LXXXVI Oct 1859, Part 2 303–507.
6. *WLT* 269, 275–7; *Life* I 300.
7. *Blackwood's Magazine* Vol. LXXXVI Oct 1859, Part 2 409–11.
8. *WLT* 307.
9. *Blackwood's Magazine* Vol. LXXXVI Oct 1859, Part 2 414–16; *WLT* 312.

10. Ibid 319.
11. Ibid 322–3.
12. Ibid 326.
13. Ibid 330, 307, 367–8, 341–2.
14. Ibid 370; *LR* II 172–3.
15. *WLT* 370; *Zanzibar* II 315.
16. Godsall 181, 155.
17. *WLT* 258; *Zanzibar* II 318.
18. Speke to Rigby 22 Oct 1860 NLS; *JRGS* Vol. XXXIII 22 Jun 1863 213–14.
19. *LR* II 191–3, 203.
20. Ibid 197–8; *Life* I 322–321.
21. *The Zambesi Journal and Letters of Dr John Kirk 1858–1863* ed. R. Foskett I 310; *HIFL* 160.
22. *Zanzibar* II 388; *LR* I 326.
23. *Life* I 315; *Zanzibar* II 389; Speke to JB 30 Apr 1860 41254 NLS; *Life* II 425; *Life* I 326.
24. *LR* II 199, 136, 309.
25. Burton to East India Company 11 Nov 1859, quoted in *LR* II 392.
26. *Life* I 327; Brodie 165.
27. Burton to Shaw 19 Apr 1859 RGS.
28. *Burton: A Biography of Sir Richard Francis Burton* Byron Farwell 178.
29. Godsall 184.
30. *Zanzibar* II 390; *LR* II 322.
31. *Life* I 327. Among biographers from Brodie onwards, only Godsall does not repeat these words, presumably because doubting their credibility.
32. Carnochan 70; *Zanzibar* II 390.
33. Formerly in the private collection of the late Quentin Keynes.
34. W. B. Carnochan seems to be the first author actually to have read and digested the 'Tail'. I was enabled to do the same, thanks to Dan Cook and to Peter Speke and his son, Geoffrey. The 'Tail' is pp. 373–80 appended to a specially printed copy of *What Led to the Discovery of the Source of the Nile* once owned by John Hanning Speke.
35. The 'Tail', in Speke's copy 380.
36. Disputed dialogue to be found *Life* I 327. On this issue, and in general, Godsall is indispensable where there are dubious and untrue statements in both volumes of *Life*. In the second page of his preface to *LR* I Burton referred to 'the spontaneous offer, on his [Speke's] part, of not appearing before the Society'. But Burton quoted no actual speech. A relevant lie is Isabel Burton's editorial statement in *Life* I 258 that Speke had 'completely and wilfully spoiled the first expedition as far as lay in his power'. She offered no supporting evidence of any kind.
37. Burton to Shaw 18 Apr 1859 RGS.
38. Frank McLynn in his biography of Burton and Anne Taylor in hers of

Laurence Oliphant both mentioned the 'Tail' but wrongly described its contents. Only Carnochan quoted it accurately.

39. JB to Speke 1 Jul 1864, Speke to JB 2 Jul 1864 30361 NLS.
40. Speke to G. Simpson 18 Aug 1864 Peter and Geoffrey Speke Collection.
41. Speke to JB 18 Jul 1864 30361 NLS.
42. The copy which Carnochan and I read was Speke's own copy and was bought by the family at the Quentin Keynes Christie's auction in 2004. A few other copies were privately printed by Blackwood for close family members, but whether they still exist is unknown.
43. *Zanzibar* II 391.

SEVEN: A Blackguard Business

1. *The Nile Basin* Richard F. Burton and James M'Queen [*Nile Basin*] 7–8; only Godsall of Speke's recent biographers disputes Burton's statement.
2. Godsall 186.
3. Speke to Shaw 8 May 1859 RGS.
4. Godsall 186; *Private History of the Royal Geographical Society* Clements Markham.
5. *Journal* 17.
6. *Zanzibar* II 391.
7. Speke to Shaw 19 May 1859 RGS.
8. *Zanzibar* II 390; Brodie 167; *Life* II 424–5.
9. 'Tail' 376.
10. *Nile Basin* 8.
11. *Life* II 425.
12. Only Godsall describes these events accurately.
13. *Memories of my Life* Francis Galton 199; Godsall 189.
14. *PRGS* Vol. III 23 May 1859; Godsall 188.
15. *LR* I Preface 2.
16. *Zanzibar* II 320.
17. Speke to JB 2 Sept 1859 4143 NLS.
18. Ibid.
19. *Zanzibar* II 392.
20. Ibid 308–9; see Speke's comment *WLT* 370.
21. Speke to Shaw 5 Nov 1859 RGS; *Jahresberichte des Marienvereins* Ignatius Knoblecher.
22. Speke to Burton ? Nov 1859 QK book 165; *Zanzibar* II 316.
23. Speke to Burton 17 June 1859 QK book 154–5.
24. Burton to Shaw 20 March 1860 RGS.
25. Burton to RGS 13 Oct 1859 QK book 160–2. The advance of 20 Maria Theresa dollars was worth about £4 in the money of the day. The average wage for a domestic servant in Britain was £25 per annum.

26. Speke to Rigby 17 Oct 1859 NLS; Rigby to Sec Govt Bombay 15 Jul 1859 *LR* II 382 ff.
27. *LR* II 391.
28. Speke to Rigby 17 Oct 1859 NLS; Burton to Speke ? Feb 1860 QK book 167–8; Sir Charles Wood to Burton 8 Nov 1859 *LR* II 381 f.
29. Speke to Burton 16 Apr 1860 QK book 180.
30. Burton to Speke reply drafted on side of Speke's letter of 16 Apr 1860 QK book 181.

EIGHT: Our Adventurous Friend

1. Speke to Shaw n.d. but from the period 17–25 Jan 1860 RGS.
2. JB to Speke 8 Aug 1859 30012 NLS; Speke to JB 8 Aug 1859 4143 NLS.
3. JB to Speke 27 Mar 1859 30012 NLS.
4. Speke to JB 3 Nov 1859 30012 NLS.
5. Speke to JB 17 Apr 1860 4154 NLS.
6. *Annals* III 97.
7. Speke to JB 28 Mar 1860 4154 NLS.
8. Maitland 107.
9. Speke to Shaw 28 Oct 1859 RGS.
10. Speke to JB 11 Apr 1860 4143 NLS; Speke to JB 5 Nov 1859 4143 NLS.
11. Udal I 504; Instructions for Consul Petherick's proposed expedition up the White Nile in Aid of Captains Speke and Grant 8 Feb 1861, *PRGS* Vol. IX 8 Apr 1864 256.
12. 'Tail' 376.
13. Speke to Shaw 28 Oct, 5 Nov 1859 RGS.
14. CV memorandum Grant Papers MS 17924 NLS; Maitland 111; Speke to Shaw 23 March 1860 RGS.
15. JB to Speke 27 March 1860 30012 NLS.
16. Obit *Blackwood's Magazine* Vol. XCVI Oct 1864 514–16.
17. Maitland 105; Speke to JB 26 Aug 1859, and n.d. 1859 NLS.
18. *Journal* 450.
19. PRO/30122 31 Jul 1863 173 ff.
20. *A Walk Across Africa* James. A. Grant [*Walk*] 18–19.
21. *Journal* 23.
22. Ibid 24–32; Speke to Rigby 12 Dec 1860 RGS; *Walk* 22–3.
23. Ibid 32.
24. *Journal* 39.
25. Ibid 47–8.
26. Ibid 51.
27. Speke to Rigby 12 Dec 1860 RGS.

28. *Journal* 46.
29. Ibid 60.
30. Ibid 72–74, 87; *Walk* 53; AN 298–335.
31. *Journal* 76–7; Speke to Shaw 12 Dec 1860 RGS.
32. *Walk* 48 ff; *Journal* 85.
33. Ibid 83, 89.
34. *Walk* 59; *Journal* 90–1.
35. *Journal* 93, 100.
36. Ibid 95–7.
37. Ibid 94–103.
38. Ibid 88, 100.
39. Maitland 131 ff; *Walk* 55, 77; *Journal* 109 ff.
40. Ibid 110–16.
41. Ibid 117–22.
42. Ibid 122–7.
43. *Walk* 107, 115–16, 121.
44. *Journal* 129–41.
45. *Walk* 122.
46. Ibid 94, 128.
47. *Journal* 157, 149.
48. Ibid 162.
49. Ibid 167.
50. *Walk* 138.
51. *Journal* 168–86.
52. Ibid 172, 189.
53. Ibid 198–200.
54. Ibid 215–16.
55. Quoted in *Journey to the Source of the Nile* Christopher Ondaatje [Ondaatje] 201.
56. *Journal* 200–1; Maitland 145.

NINE: As Refulgent as the Sun

1. *Journal* 218, 224; *Quest for the Secret Nile* Guy Yeoman [Yeoman] 50.
2. *Journal* 221–2.
3. Ibid 226–7.
4. *Journal* manuscript p. 1 Ms 4872 NLS (microfilm version in BL Shelfmark YC 2006.a.7908 pt 2).
5. Speke to RM n.d. but 20 Feb 1862 RGS.
6. *Journal* 232–40.
7. Ibid 241–2.
8. Ibid 289.
9. Ibid 243, 275–7.
10. Ibid 246–9; *Journal* proofs 11 4873 NLS.

11. *Journal* 253–4, 266–7, 304.
12. Speke to Petherick 26 Mar 1862 copy of letter RGS.

TEN: An Arrow into the Heart

1. *Journal* proofs 27 March 1862 NLS.
2. *Journal* 291.
3. *The Peoples of Africa* J. L. Newman; 'Origins of Political Conflicts & Peace Building in the Great Lakes Region' G. P. Mpangala.
4. *Journal* ms 1 and *Journal* book proofs p 1 30 March 1862 NLS; *Journal* 296–7.
5. *Journal* 299.
6. *Journal* ms 2, 16 Apr 1862; *Journal* book proofs 58.
7. *Journal* 304; *Journal* book proofs 7 Apr 1862.
8. *Journal* ms 11, 12 Apr 1862; *Journal* 306.
9. *Journal* book proofs 8, 10 Apr 1862.
10. *Journal* ms 2 May 1862; *Journal* 321.
11. *Journal* ms 9 May 1862; *Journal* book proofs 73.
12. *Journal* ms 2 Jun 1862; *Journal* book proofs 81.
13. *Journal* 326; *Journal* ms 6 May 1862.
14. Ibid 3 May 1862 113–15.
15. Ondaatje 200; Hall, *Lovers* 90.
16. *Journal* book proofs 73 cut from *Journal* 338.
17. *Journal* 338.
18. Maitland 158.
19. *Journal* 315–16, 318.
20. Ibid 301.
21. Speke's drawing of Mutesa in notebook at RGS; *Journal* 337.
22. Ibid 229–30.
23. *Walk* 219, 223, 227.
24. *Journal* 335.
25. *Journal* ms 10, 13 Jun 1862.
26. *Journal* 345–59, 328; *bana* or *bwana* meaning father or lord, via Swahili from Arabic *abuna* – 'our father'.

ELEVEN: Nothing Could Surpass It!

1. *Walk* 267 gives Speke's numbers.
2. Ibid 246–7; *Journal* 363.
3. *Walk* 248; Maitland 169.
4. *Journal* 364–5.
5. Maitland 170; *Journal* 369–72.
6. *Walk* 275.
7. *Journal* 381.
8. Ibid 388.

9. Ibid 399, 402, 406–08; *Walk* 285–8.
10. *Journal* 397, 404; *Africa in the Nineteenth Century until the 1880s* J. F. Ade Ajayi 109; *Walk* 287.
11. *Journal* 438, 431–2; *Walk* 299.
12. Ibid 310.
13. Ibid 312; Journal 448 f.
14. *Walk* 315, 309.
15. Ibid 319; *Journal* 449–50.
16. Ibid 448, 453–4; *Walk* 327; Catania 276 ff.
17. *Journal* 467.
18. Ibid 457; *Walk* 339.
19. Ibid 346; *Journal* 463.
20. Ibid 469–70.
21. Ibid 470.

TWELVE: The Nile is Settled

1. Hall, *Lovers* 14–15, 33.
2. DL to Agnes L Sept 1869 Ad ms 50184 BL; Udal I 505–6.
3. Hall, *Lovers* 26 ff; R. E. H. Bailey's statement about Florence 19 Jul 1971 Anne Baker Collection, Salisbury.
4. *AN* 62–3.
5. Samuel W. Baker diary [BD] 15 Feb 1863 SWB1 RGS; *Walk* 336; *Journal* 471.
6. *Journal* 470–1.
7. *Walk* 366; Udal I 529; Hall, *Lovers* 89.
8. Ibid 89; *Walk* 366; Grant to JB 22 Oct 1866 4209 NLS.
9. *AN* 64; Hall, *Lovers* 90–1.
10. Hall, *Lovers* 94.
11. Mrs Petherick's Journal written in 1861 (original in Wellcome Library), extract published in *Blackwood's Magazine* Vol. XCI Jun 1862, 560; *PRGS* Vol. VIII 25 Apr 1864.
12. BD 30 Jan 1863; Speke to JB n.d. except 1863 NLS. Baker had learned from the Austrian priest, Father Morlang, that Petherick had never come closer to Gondokoro than the Bahr el-Ghazal. Speke had been told the same thing by Khursid Agha and by Baker and so felt he had been tricked.
13. BD 27 May, 24 Oct 1862, 30 Jan 1863; Petherick's report to RM 16 Jan 1864 RGS; Udal I 527; *Journal* 427.
14. Udal I 519.
15. BD 27 May 1862; *Travels in Central Africa* (Vol. I) *& Exploration of the Western Nile Tributaries* (Vol. II) John Petherick and Harriet Edlman Petherick [*Travels*] 134–6; Udal I 460.
16. Udal I 538.

17. BD 24 Oct 1863: Baker knew the rumours in Khartoum that Petherick had been involved in slavery were false because Petherick's *wakil*, Abdel Majid, who had been imprisoned by him for slaving, had denied to Baker that his master (whom he had every reason to hate) had ever been involved.
18. Udal I 527–8.
19. Hall, *Lovers* 91.
20. *Journal* 475; Speke to *Times* 25 Dec 1863.
21. Ibid.
22. *Travels* I 72, 132; Udal I 519.
23. Ibid 460, 522ff; Katherine Petherick's Journal 19–20 May, 3–25 Jul, 28–30 Aug 1862 5788 Wellcome Library; Hall, *Lovers* 92; BD 16 Mar 1863; Udal I 534.
24. Ibid 529.
25. Hall, *Lovers* 93; Udal I 533; *Travels* I 312–13.
26. *Travels* II 19–20.
27. *Journal* 474; *Walk* 367.
28. Speke to Petherick 15 Apr 1863 RGS.
29. Katherine Petherick's Journal Jun–Jul 1863.
30. Katherine Petherick to RM 26 Jul 1863 RGS.
31. Speke to RGS Sec 19 Feb 1864 RGS.
32. *PRGS* Vol. VII 11 May 1863; Moorehead 71.
33. *Journal* 477; Speke to Grant 22 Mar 1864 17931 NLS.
34. *Walk* 447; *Journal* 477.

THIRTEEN: A Hero's Aberrations

1. Speke to RM 6 Jul 1862 RGS.
2. RM to Layard 2 May 1863 Ad ms 3906 BL.
3. Palmerston to Lord John Russell 31 Jul 1863 PRO 30/22 173.
4. *Times* 18 May 1863; *PRGS* Vol. VII 25 May 1863.
5. Udal I 547; Godsall 251; *PRGS* Vol. VII 11 May 1863, 109, 182–96, 212–23; Speke to JB n.d 1863 NLS.
6. Speke to Shaw 19 Aug 1859 RGS.
7. Maitland 182.
8. Speke to Sir George Grey 30 Mar 1863 RGS; *Journal* 477.
9. Udal I 538.
10. Correspondence between the Pethericks and RM in Petherick Papers at RGS; Katherine Petherick to RM 26 Jul 1863 RGS.
11. RM to Grant 5 May 1864 17933 NLS. Speke was not to blame for John Petherick's dismissal as a consul. Dr Murie revealed that Petherick had stolen African cattle and forced women and children to carry for him at gunpoint. Baker prevailed on Murie to inform the British Consul-General in Cairo. This and an unconnected charge of embezzlement

led to Petherick's dismissal. BD 19–22 Mar 1863 RGS; Udal I 535–7; FO Memo by W. H. Wylde Ad Ms 38990 BL; Udal I 543–4. Speke knew he might appear petty and vindictive by attacking Petherick. But he believed that by not justifying himself after Burton had publicly attacked him in *LR* (especially in the preface), he (Speke) had 'never lost ground so much'. So he would not make the same mistake again. Speke to JB 7th (no month) 1863 NLS.

12. *PRGS* Vol. VIII 25 Apr 1864 details Petherick's instructions given on 8 Feb 1861.
13. Maitland 197; RM to Layard 1 Jul 1864 Ad Ms 39111 BL.
14. Maitland 196; Udal I 540.
15. Speke to JB Jul? 1864 4193 NLS.
16. Speke to Sir George Grey 16 Jan 1864 RGS.
17. Speke to Grant 24 Feb 1864 17910 NLS.
18. Maitland 193–5; Udal I 547–8; *WLT* 344, 362, 366–7.
19. Speke to JB 16 May 1864 4193 NLS; Speke to Layard 31 May 1864 Ad Ms 39110 BL; Udal I 548–9.
20. Ibid; FO memo W. H. Wylde 11 Jun 1864 Ad ms 38990 BL; Udal I 548–9.
21. Speke to JB 25 Aug 1864 4193 NLS.
22. RM to Layard Jul 1864 Ad ms 3911 BL.
23. RM to Grant n.d. Aug 1864 17910 NLS.
24. Speke to JB 18 Jun, 16 Aug 1864 4193 NLS; Speke to Kaye 8 Sept 1863 Ad ms 45918 BL.

FOURTEEN: Death in the Afternoon

1. Speke to RM 12 Aug 1864 1066 NLS.
2. George Simpson to JB 8 Sept 1864 4193 NLS.
3. *PRGS* Vol. VIII 13 Jun 1864.
4. Ibid 256–60.
5. DL to Agnes L ? Sept 1869 Ad ms 50184 BL.
6. Jeal, *Livingstone* 284.
7. Speke to JB 6 Aug 1864 4193 NLS.
8. Speke to JB 25 Jul 1864 4193 NLS.
9. JB to Oliphant 30 Jul 1864 30361 NLS.
10. *Life* II 426; Godsall 254.
11. *Zanzibar* II 397–8.
12. Maitland 209–17 including quotations from George Fuller's and Daniel Davis's inquest evidence and Fuller's later statement 23 Jan 1914.
13. *Times* 17 Sept 1864 report of Inquest.
14. *The Life of Sir Richard Burton* Thomas Wright 2 vols I 192.
15. Burton to Frank Wilson 21 Sept 1864 QK/BL.
16. Speke to J. Tinné 14 Sept 1864 RGS.

17. Sophie Murdoch (neé Speke) to Henry M. Stanley 20 May 1876 RMCA.
18. *Zanzibar* II 382.
19. Included in Rigby's comments on Burton's chapter 'Captain Speke' in vol II *Zanzibar* 17922 NLS.
20. *Zanzibar* II 398.
21. Notably Brodie 226 ff, McLynn 233–5.
22. *Zanzibar* II 398.
23. *WLT* 173.
24. George P. Fuller quoted Maitland 215.
25. *Life of Sir Roderick I. Murchison* A. Geikie 2 vols II 168; DL to H. Waller 24 Sept 1864 Rhodes House.
26. PRO IR 59/68.
27. *Times* 19, 23 Sept 1864.
28. Jeal, *Livingstone* 283.
29. Brodie 229.
30. Maitland 221.
31. Moorehead 76.
32. *Nile Basin* 99 ff.
33. *Blackwood's Magazine* Vol. XCII Jan 1865 101–11.
34. Burton to ed. *Athenaeum* 14 Jan 1865; Brodie 228.
35. Johnston 223.
36. Benjamin Speke to Jean ? 9th no month 1874 NLS.

FIFTEEN: The Doctor's Dilemma

1. Udal I 554.
2. DL to Agnes L 6 Sept 1869 50184 BL.
3. *PRGS* Vol. IX 14 Nov 1864, 8–10.
4. RM to DL 5 Jan 1865 quoted in Blaikie 293–4.
5. Jeal, *Livingstone* 300.
6. DL to A. Tidman 25 May 1865 London Missionary Society Collection School of Oriental and African Studies [LMS/SOAS].
7. DL to RM 29 Nov 1865 NAZ.
8. Jeal, *Livingstone* 285; *Zanzibar* II 102.
9. Debenham 293–4.
10. Blaikie 304; Hall, *Lovers* 152.
11. DL to W. C. Oswell 1 Jan 1866 quoted Hall, *Lovers* 161.
12. Quoted in Cairns 203.
13. DL to Agnes L ? Sept 1869 Ad ms 50184 BL.

SIXTEEN: The Glory of Our Prize

1. Hall, *Lovers* 94–5; BD 10–15 Mar 1865 RGS.
2. *AN* 75.

3. BD 16 Mar 1865.
4. Ibid 22 Mar 1865.
5. Hall, *Lovers* 96.
6. *AN* 101–4; BD 29 Mar 1865.
7. *AN* 78.
8. Ibid 81.
9. BD 8, 10 Apr 1864; *AN* 164.
10. BD 18 Apr 1864; *AN* 143.
11. *AN* 143.
12. At the RGS I have raised this gun to my shoulder and found it all but impossible to hold steady. I was told by Julian Baker that Samuel Baker repaired the stock with the skin of an elephant that had trampled on it. *AN* 159.
13. Johnston 175; Moorehead 88–9; Hall, *Lovers* 13–15.
14. *AN* 203–23.
15. Ibid 134–5, 115–16.
16. Ibid 210.
17. Ibid 182–3.
18. Hall, *Lovers* 164.
19. *AN* 94.
20. Ibid 148, 188, 220, 222–3.
21. Hall, *Lovers* 112.
22. *AN* 233.
23. Ibid 234–8.
24. Ibid 239–44.
25. Ibid 252–4; BD 5–7 Feb 1864.
26. *AN* 256–61; BD 11–18 Feb 1864.
27. *AN* 264.
28. Ibid 267–78; BD 11–18 Feb 1864.
29. *AN* 275–97.
30. Ibid 298–335, 356–63; *Africa and its Explorers* ed. R. I. Rotberg Robert O. Collins chapter on S. W. Baker 161–2; *Twilight Tales of the Black Baganda* A. B. Fisher 157–8.
31. *AN* 373–8, 410–11.
32. Hall, *Lovers* 154, 158.

SEVENTEEN: A Trumpet Blown Loudly

1. Baker's map in *AN* 1866. Also see map on p. 219 above.
2. Hall, *Lovers* 160; *To the Heart of the Nile* Pat Shipman [Shipman] 302.
3. *AN* 392.
4. Speke's map at RGS dated 26 Feb 1863.
5. Shipman 306–7.
6. Hall, *Lovers* 160.

7. Shipman 307.
8. In Anne Baker's and Ian Graham-Orlebar's collections letter from R. E. H. Bailey 19 Jul 1971.
9. Hall, *Lovers* 163.
10. BD 29 Apr 1861.
11. Rigby to Grant 15 Feb, 1 Dec 1866 17910 NLS.
12. Benjamin Speke to Mrs Mackenzie 20 Aug 1866 17931 NLS.
13. Hall, *Lovers* 168.
14. Rigby to Grant 12 Feb 1866 17910 NLS.
15. Godsall 256.

EIGHTEEN: Almost in Sight of the End

1. DL to Agnes L 5 Feb 1871 Ad ms 50184 BL.
2. Jeal, *Livingstone* 296 and associated notes.
3. *LLJ* I 13–14.
4. Ibid 70.
5. Ibid 56, 62–3.
6. Jeal, *Livingstone* 307.
7. *LLJ* I 115.
8. Ibid 173–6.
9. Jeal, *Livingstone* 312.
10. DL to Kirk 8 Jul 1868; *PRGS* Vol. XIV November 1869, 8.
11. *LLJ* I 287.
12. DL to RM 18 Dec 1867 NAZ.
13. DL to Lord Clarendon 8 Jul 1868 *PRGS* Vol. XIV November 1869, 8–9.
14. *LLJ* II 99.
15. Unyanyembe Diary 14 May, 4 Jul, 11 Mar, 11 Feb 1871 DLC.
16. *LLJ* II 141.
17. Ibid 151.
18. Ibid 152–3.
19. Ibid 155; Jeal, *Livingstone* 334–5; DL to T. Maclear & Mr Mann *PRGS* Vol. XVII 17 Nov 1871, 172–3, 67–73.
20. Stanley, *Auto* 261–2.

NINETEEN: Never to Give Up the Search Until I Find Livingstone

1. 'Stanley: The Mystery of the Three Fathers' Emyr Wynn Jones 127–51 *National Library of Wales Journal* 1993 Vol. 28 127–51; 'Stanley's Father, I Presume' Bob Owen *Hel Achau* (1985) No. 15 23–7; Jeal, *Stanley* 492 n 36.
2. *South Wales Daily News* 14 May 1904, interview with Richard Price.
3 Stanley, *Auto* 12.
4. Ibid 29.

5. *Stanley's Despatches to the New York Herald 1871–1872, 1874–1877* ed. Norman R. Bennett [Bennett] 51.
6. Reports Relating to the Education of Pauper Children (1856) vol. XLVIII 631; XLV 207. PRO NM 12/16140.
7. Jeal, *Stanley* 23.
8. Ibid 34–41.
9. Stanley, *Auto* 124.
10. William Henry Stanley's Compiled Service Record card 46045291 26 July 1861, National Archives, USA; Jeal, *Stanley* 40, 496 n 36 and n 20.
11. Stanley to Dorothy Stanley 18 Nov 1893 RMCA; Stanley to Katie Gough Roberts [KGR] 22 Mar 1869 RMCA.
12. Jeal, *Stanley* 52–63.
13. Jeal, *Stanley* 63–4; Stanley to Noe 25 Dec 1866 RMCA.
14. *South Wales Daily News* 12 May 1904 obituary article by Owen 'Morien' Morgan; Morgan's notes of an interview with Elizabeth Parry 1886 Cardiff Public Library; Bennett 415: Lewis Noe to ed. *New York Sun* 16 Aug 1872; Jeal, *Stanley* 64–6 and associated notes.
15. Viz. *Times* 17 Dec 1866; Jeal, *Livingstone* 338 for DL's movements.
16. Finley Anderson to Stanley 3 Jan 1867 RMCA; *Stanley: An Adventurer Explored* Richard Hall [Hall, *Stanley*] 148.
17. Stanley to KGR 27 Jun 1869 Private Collection, Bath.
18. Information from Miss M. H. Stewart, Bath, about her grandmother KGR.
19. *HIFL* 68; Stanley to Gordon Bennett 17 Jan 1871 RMCA; Stanley's Diary [SD] 21, 25 Feb 1871 RMCA; Jeal, *Stanley* 91, 93–4 and 502 n 7.
20. SD 20 Jun, 18 May 1871.
21. Bennett 45–7; *HIFL* 282 ff; SD 23, 24 Aug 1871.
22. *HIFL* 411.
23. Stanley to Gordon Bennett 17 Jan 1871; SD 28 May 1871.
24. Jeal, *Stanley* 502–6 n 10; also *LLJ* II 15 and especially *HIFL* 476: 'about a week or so after my entrance into Ujiji' is the date Stanley gives for the start of his voyage on Lake Tanganyika with DL. They started on 16 November.
25. *LLJ* II 156.
26. SD 3 Nov 1871; Stanley *Auto* 264.

TWENTY: The Doctor's Obedient and Devoted Servitor

1. Stanley's original despatch describing the meeting for the *NYH* has not survived. His famous greeting first made its appearance in *NYH* 2 Jul 1872 and the first version (still existing) of the greeting in Stanley's hand was written a year after the meeting. Jeal, *Stanley* 118–19 and associated notes.

2. Jeal, *Stanley* 117.
3. *HIFL* 412.
4. Ibid 416.
5. SD 11 Nov 1871; *HIFL* 424.
6. Bennett 95.
7. *HIFL* 429.
8. Jeal, *Livingstone* 79, 84–5, 104–5.
9. Ibid 93.
10. SD 14 Nov 1871.
11. DL to Kirk 30 May 1869 in Foskett 138–9.
12. *HIFL* 427.
13. *LLJ* II 157.
14. *HIFL* 476, 479; *LLJ* II 157.
15. Ibid 478–81.
16. *LLJ* II 157–8; SD 22 Nov 1871.
17. Jeal, *Livingstone* 323–6.
18. SD 16, 27 Nov 1871.
19. DL to Agnes L 23 Aug 1872 RI
20. SD 8 Jan 1872.
21. SD 5 Mar 1872.
22. SD 7 Mar 1872, 14 Nov 1871, 24 Feb 1872.
23. SD 3 Mar; 6, 9 Jan 1872.
24. SD 16 Nov 1871.
25. SD 21 Feb 1872.
26. *HIFL* 432; SD 16 Nov 1871.
27. SD 5 Jan 1870.
28. SD 13 Mar 1872, 13 Nov 1871.

TWENTY-ONE: Threshing Out the Beaten Straw

1. SD 11 Aug 1872.
2. SD 1 Aug 1872; Stanley to Dorothy Stanley 18 Nov 1893 RMCA; *The Finding of Dr Livingstone by H. M. Stanley* Cadwalader Rowlands [pseud. for John C. Hotten] (1872) 156–70.
3. *I Presume* Ian Anstruther 146.
4. SD 1 Aug 1872.
5. DL to H. Waller 2–3 Nov 1871 Rhodes House; DL to RM 13 Mar 1872 *PRGS* Vol. XVI (1871–2) 434.
6. Rawlinson to Stanley 6 Aug 1872 RMCA; *PRGS* Vol. XVI 13 May 1872, 241.
7. SD 16 Aug 1872.
8. *Sir Henry M. Stanley: The Enigma* Emir W. Jones 25, 116.
9. DL to John L Dec 1872 QK/BL; DL to B. Braithwaite 8 Jan 1872 LMS/SOAS; DL to Dr Wilson 14 Jan. 1872 NLS.

10. SD 11 Aug 1872.
11. Stanley to *Times* 12 Nov 1872.
12. SD 11 Aug 1872.
13. Bennett 40; Stanley's Congo Diaries [CD] 1 Jan 1881 RMCA.
14. *HIFL* 677.
15. *LLJ* II 182.
16. Stanley to Markham 5 Oct 1872 RGS; Cameron to Stanley 25 Oct 1872 RMCA.
17. Quoted Hall, *Stanley* 225.
18. Louis J. Jennings ed. *New York Times* to Stanley 9 Jan 1873 RMCA.

TWENTY-TWO: Nothing Earthly Will Make Me Give Up My Work

1. Stanley to DL 27 May 1872 NLS.
2. *LLJ* II 229.
3. DL to H. Waller 2 Sept 1872 Rhodes House.
4. *LLJ* II 174.
5. Debenham 297–317.
6. *LLJ* II 269.
7. Ibid 277.
8. Ibid 242.
9. Debenham 272.
10. *LLJ* II 282.
11. Ibid 294.
12. Ibid 296.
13. Ibid 297.
14. *Livingstone's Private Journals 1851–53* ed. I. Schapera [*LPJ*] see 4 Feb 1853.
15. *LLJ* II 298–99, facsimile of DL's last entry in his journal.
16. Jeal, *Livingstone* 365.
17. *LLJ* II 299–308; Helly 111 quoting Waller's notes of his conversations with Chuma and Susi; Jeal, *Livingstone* 366.
18. Ibid 367.
19. Helly 113 ff; *Dark Companions* Donald Simpson 189–93; *LLJ* II 313.
20. Helly 112; *LLJ* II 315 ff.
21. Jacob Wainwright to Oswell Livingstone October 1873 LMS/SOAS.
22. Jeal, *Livingstone* 369.

TWENTY-THREE: Where Will You Be? Dead or Still Seeking the Nile?

1. Stanley to Agnes L 18 Mar 1874 QK/BL; Stanley to Agnes L 28 Jan 1878 RP 4900 BL.
2. *Graphic* 24 Apr 1874.

3. SD 5 Jan 1870; Stanley, *Auto* Intro xvii.
4. SD 16, 17 May 1874.
5. *Through the Dark Continent* Henry M. Stanley 2 vols [*TDC*] I 47.
6. Jeal, *Stanley* 163, 165, 196, 217; in SD 12 Nov 1874 a figure of 224 porters, guides, guards and dependents is given – 228 when Stanley and his three European assistants are added. In a muster list, in the Luwel Collection RMCA, 227 is given as the number who left Zanzibar. There is no evidence that any additional porters were recruited at Bagamoyo – see *TDC* I 72–8; also Stanley to *NYH* 13 Dec 1874 Bennett 189; for description of recruiting on Zanzibar, Bennett 159; for Stanley's detestation of Bagamoyo, Bennett 11; for Stanley's preference for recruiting porters from the Bertram Agency on Zanzibar, SD 11 Jan 1871, Bennett 157, 159, *HIFL* 22–7.
7. *TDC* I 83.
8. Ibid 108.
9. Ibid 112.
10. Alice Pike to Stanley 13 Oct & 2 Dec 1874 RMCA.
11. Stanley to J. R. Robinson 11 Nov 1874 RP 1100 BL.
12. Bennett 212.
13. S&N 63.
14. Bennett 217; S&N 69; *TDC* I 180.
15. Bennett 217; S&N 69.
16. Bennett 225.
17. Preface to 'Uganda Diary' 1875–6 RMCA.
18. S&N 70–2; Bennett 46–7, 220, 225ff Stanley to *NYH* 14 Apr 1875; Drafts of *NYH* letter 1 Jun 1876 RMCA.
19. Stanley to *NYH* 14 Apr 1875.
20. Gordon to Stanley 20 Apr 1875 RMCA.
21. Yeoman 108; *The Scramble for Africa* Thomas Pakenham [Pakenham] 73; Jeal, *Stanley* 174, 184.
22. *Central Africa* C. Chaillé-Long 310; Moorehead 140; *TDC* I 202–3; *TDC* II 166; Bennett 226–7.
23. SD 28 Apr 1875; *TDC* I 230–1; small Australian notebook 1891–2 RMCA; Bennett 246 n 3.
24. *TDC* I 285.
25. S&N 92–3.
26. CD 15 Oct 1880 RMCA.
27. Gordon to Burton 19 Oct 1877, quoted in Frank McLynn *Stanley: Sorcerer's Apprentice* (1991) 14.
28. Bennett 274.
29. Stanley to E. Levy-Lawson 13 Aug 1876 Bennett 463 ff.
30. Stanley to Alice Pike 14 Aug 1876.

TWENTY-FOUR: The Unknown Half of Africa Lies Before Me

1. Rigby to Grant 26 Oct 1876 17910 NLS.
2. *PRGS* Vol. XIX 29 Nov 1875, 49–50.
3. S&N 130.
4. Ibid 132–3; Bennett 324–7; *Private History of the RGS* Markham 401–2 RGS; *TDC* II 96–7; Bennett 324–7.
5. Stanley to E. King 31 Oct 1876 Bennett 459 ff.
6. Ibid 332.
7. *TDC* II 145 and footnote; S&N 138–9.
8. See Bennett 377, 385–6 for large exaggerations – all Stanley's self-proclaimed 32 battles on the Congo (except one bloodless brush on 9 Mar) took place between 24 Nov 1876 and 14 Feb 1877 S&N 140–64. The 'fight of fights' and penultimate 'battle' (no. 31) was on 14 Feb and Stanley massively exaggerated the number of contestants in *TDC* and in S&N 164 – for actual numbers see Jeal, *Stanley* 201–2 and 514 n 10 and 515 n 37 quoting Frank Pocock's figures. There is no evidence in Stanley's diaries that he ever destroyed '28 large towns' as he foolishly claimed. (For his psychology see Jeal, *Stanley* 94, 163, 178, 202.) He burned a few huts in three villages after being attacked. S&N gives many examples of his efforts to make peace: 18 Dec 1876, 1–2 Jan, 7 Feb, 1–2 Mar 1877. See too S&N 141.
9. S&N 137, 143; *TDC* II 170.
10. S&N 148 1 Jan 1877.
11. As per note 5 above; also Bennett 384.
12. Ibid 460.
13. Ibid 304.
14. Yeoman 173; *Journal* 175, 215 .
15. Yeoman 162–6; *The Nile* Collins 27.
16. *Searching for the Source of the Nile* Wataru Ogawa trans. Brian Small 1 Jul 2009 www.newsjanjan.jp. In 2005, a year before Neil McGrigor, two South Africans, Peter Meredith and Hendri Coetzee, navigated the Kagera to the Nyungwe Forest www.newencyclopedia.org/entry+nile+Rukarara.
17. Johnston 232–3.
18. F. Pocock to parents 18 Apr 1876 Bennett 475, 265.
19. *The Diaries of A. J. Mounteney Jephson* ed. Dorothy Middleton [*Jephson*] 352; Yeoman 174; Jeal, *Stanley* 470; Bennett 306.
20. Jeal, *Stanley* 200 n 35, 202 n 37.
21. Stanley to E. King 2 Oct 1877 RMCA; *TDC* II 336; *SD* 3 April 1877; S&N 174.
22. S&N 180; *TDC* II 361.
23. S&N 192.
24. SD after 10 May 1877.

25. Yeoman 138.
26. Maitland 223.
27. Marina Warner on Burton as translator *London Review of Books* 18 Dec 2008.
28. Kennedy 133.
29. Burton to William Hepworth Dixon 19 Jun 1866 QK/BL.
30. Undated Private & Confidential Memorandum, lists of people written to by Isabel 1885–6 QK/BL.
31. Marston to Stanley 25 Sep, 11 Oct 1877 RMCA.
32. *Saturday Review* 16 Feb 1877; *Pall Mall Gazette* 11 Feb 1877.
33. Bennett 371–2.
34. SD 1877 notebook, end pages 26 Jun 1878 RMCA.
35. King Leopold II to Baron Solvyns 17 Nov 1877 Archives du Palais Royal, Fonds Congo 100/1.

TWENTY-FIVE: Shepherds of the World?

1. *LLJ* I 62–3; DL to Lord Clarendon 20 Aug 1866 FO 84/1265.
2. *Graphic* 24 Apr 1874.
3. Quoted *HIFL* Intro. lxxviii 2nd ed.
4. *The Zambesi Journal of James Stewart 1862–1863* ed. J. P. R. Wallis (1952) 190.
5. *Times* 20 Jan 1874.
6. *Scientist of Empire: Sir Roderick Murchison, Scientific Exploration and Victorian Imperialism* Robert Stafford 183.
7. *The Nile in Darkness: A Flawed Unity 1863–1899* John O. Udal [Udal II] 111.
8. *AN* 22.
9. *Ismailia: A Narrative of the Expedition to Central Africa for the Suppression of the Slave Trade* Samuel Baker 2 vols [*Ismailia*] I 5; Udal II 112–13.
10. *Liverpool Mercury* 17 Sept 1870.
11. Udal II 115–18.
12. Hall, *Lovers* 178.

TWENTY-SIX: Creating Equatoria

1. *A History of the Southern Sudan 1839–1889* Richard Gray [Gray] 90–92.
2. *Morning Star: Florence Baker's Diary 1870–1873* Anne Baker [*Morning Star*] 44.
3. *Africa and its Explorers* ed. Robert I. Rotberg, Robert O. Collins chapter on S. W. Baker [Collins chapter] 166; Gray 95; *Ismailia* I 108–10.
4. Florence Baker's unpublished diary 27 Dec 1870, 16, 26 Feb, 14 Apr 1871 Anne Baker Collection.

5. *Ismailia* I 220–83; Gray 96–8; Udal II 129, 132; Collins chapter 166–7.
6. Collins chapter 168; *The Acholi of Uganda* F. K. Girling [Girling] 152.
7. *Ismailia* II 184, 187, 189; Collins chapter 168.
8. *Ismailia* II 242, 257–8.
9. Julian Baker's diary quoted in *Baker of the Nile* Dorothy Middleton 192; *Morning Star* 146; *Ismailia* II 269.
10. Ibid 287.
11. Ibid 293–304.
12. Hall, *Lovers* 198–201.
13. *Ismailia* II 282.
14. Gray 101–3; Baker to Gordon 27 Oct 1874 BL; Hall, *Lovers* 202.
15. Udal II 141–2.
16. Baker to John Baker 20 May 1873 quoted Gray 103.
17. Florence Baker to E. Baker 29 Jun 1873, Gray 103.
18. Udal II 141.
19. *Times* 15 Aug 1873.
20. Udal II 141.
21. Baker to Lord Wharncliffe 22 Oct 1869 Anne Baker Collection.

TWENTY-SEVEN: An Unheard of Deed of Blood

1. Drafts of *NYH* letters 1 Jun 1876 RMCA.
2. *Bishop Alfred Robert Tucker and the Establishment of the Anglican Church* Christopher Bryaruhanga [*Tucker*] 55.
3. Ibid 67–8.
4. *The Story of the Life of Mackay of Uganda* J. W. Harrison [*Mackay*] 164–5.
5. Ibid 147.
6. Ibid 187.
7. *A Political History of Uganda* S. R. Karugire [Karugire] 64–5.
8. *Mackay* 263, 285, 178.
9. *Mackay* 183f.
10. *James Hannington: First Bishop of East Equatorial Africa* E. C. Dawson 389.
11. Tucker 59; *Mackay* 282–3.
12. Ibid.
13. *The Emin Pasha Relief Expedition 1886–1890* Iain R. Smith 29–35 n 3, 4, 5.
14. Jeal, *Stanley* 317.

TWENTY-EIGHT: Pretensions on the Congo

1. Jeal, *Stanley* 238; Stanley to Strauch 8 Jan 1880 RMCA; *Scottish Geographical Society Magazine* Jan–Mar 1884, 42; Stanley to Sanford 27 Feb 1879 Sanford Museum.

2. CD 9 Nov 1880, 27 ? 1881, 9 Mar 1880; *Brazza of the Congo* Richard West [*Brazza*] 102–3.
3. Treaty signed with Chief Kimpallamballa at Ntamo (Kintamba) 31 Dec 1881 RMCA.
4. Jeal, *Stanley* 522 n 8 for a list of Britons appointed 1882–3.
5. Stanley to Strauch 11 May 1884; ibid n.d. 1884; *Brazza* 130–1; *Avec Brazza* P. de Chavannes 182–3; *Sir Francis de Winton* M. Luwel (1964) 167–9.
6. *Africa and the Victorians* R. Robinson, J. Gallagher and A. Denny for the thesis that French resentment of the British assumption of sole power in Egypt led them to seek compensation elsewhere and was an essential driver of the Scramble for Africa.
7. *Britain and Germany in Africa* P. Gifford and W. R. Louis [Gifford & Louis], see chap by Jean Stengers 'King Leopold and Anglo-French Rivalry 1882–1884'; also in same volume R. O. Collins 'Origins of the Nile Struggle: Anglo-German Negotiations and the Mackinnon Agreement of 1890' ['Nile Struggle'].

TWENTY-NINE: An Arabian Princess and a German Battle Squadron

1. Smith 43–4 quoting memo of Wolseley 2 Oct 1886; Emin Pasha to Felkin 7 and 22 Jul 1886 pub. *Times* 9 Dec 1886.
2. Quoted in *Mackinnon and East Africa 1878–1895* J. S. Galbraith 114.
3. Pakenham 290, 128.
4. *The Exploitation of East Africa 1856–1890: The Slave Trade and the Scramble* R. Coupland 56, the author in a footnote claims the German's name was Reute. But in the Princess' wedding certificate her husband's name is given as Ruete, as it is in the princess's letters to Captain T. M. S. Pasley RN, Tim Jeal Collection. John Kirk in a letter to his fiancée, Miss Nelly Cooke, 26 Aug 1866 9942/4 NLS also refers to Mr Ruete.
5. Rigby to Grant 1 Dec 1866 17910 NLS.
6. Eldest son and heir of Admiral Sir Thomas Sabine Pasley Bart., Naval Commander-in-Chief at Portsmouth in the late 1860s.
7. Kirk to N. Cooke 26 Aug 1866 (as above).
8. Emily Ruete's letters to Captain Pasley, Tim Jeal Collection.
9. *Sweet Water and Bitter: The Ships that Stopped the Slave Trade* Sian Rees.
10. *Memoirs of an Arabian Princess* Emily Said-Ruete 213–14, 220.
11. Kirk to Mackinnon 17 Aug 1886 SOAS.
12. 'Nile Struggle' 126; Smith 63–4; *England, Europe and the Upper Nile 1882–1899* G. N. Sanderson [Sanderson] 33–4.
13. *Scotsman* 28 Dec 1886; *Eccentricities of Genius* J. B. Pond 268–9.

THIRTY: 'Saving' Emin Pasha and Uganda

1. Count Borchgrave to Stanley 7 Jan 1887 RMCA.
2. A. B. Swinburne to Sanford 17 Nov 1886 Sanford Museum; SD 20 Mar 1887; Swinburne to Sanford 29 Sept 1887.
3. SD 3, 6 Oct 1887; *In Darkest Africa* H. M. Stanley 2 vols [*IDA*] I 210; *Jephson* 159; *Surgeon-Major Parke's African Journey 1887–1889* T. H. Parke, ed. J. B. Lyons [Parke] 65; *My Personal Experiences in Equatorial Africa* T. H. Parke 129–30; SD 15 Oct 1887; Stanley to Nelson 24 Oct 1887 RP 860 BL; *IDA* I 224–6.
4. Parke 51.
5. *IDA* I 137–8; *Jephson* 113.
6. *IDA* I 152, 162, 171; ; *Jephson* 13; Parke 54–6.
7. SD 29 Aug, 12 Sept 1887.
8. Ibid 3, 6 Oct 1887; *IDA* I 210.
9. Ibid 357.
10. Ibid 374.
11. *Times* 29 Oct 1886.
12. SD I May 1888.
13. Stanley to Euan Smith 19 Dec 1889 in 'Correspondence respecting Mr Stanley's Expedition for the Relief of Emin Pasha' Africa 4 (1890), C 5906 p 9. HM Stationery Office.
14. SD 24 Aug 1888.
15. William Bonny's Diary 14 Oct 1888 RMCA.
16. Ibid 26 Aug 1888.
17. Ibid 7–27 Mar 1888.
18. At end of small Jan–Jun 1889 Stanley notebook RMCA.
19. *IDA* II 111–14.
20. *Ten Years in Equatoria and the Return with Emin Pasha* G. Casati 2 vols II 159.
21. *IDA* II 126.
22. *Jephson* 346–7, 399; Mackay to Stanley 5 Jan 1890; Stanley to Mackinnon 4 Feb 1890 SOAS; 'Early Treaties in Uganda' Sir John Gray, see Smith 266.
23. Pakenham 352.
24. *Jephson* 407–9.
25. Mss of *IDA* II 515–23; Stanley's notes on Emin Pasha n.d. but 1890 RMCA.
26. Mss of *IDA* II 520–1; *African Exploits: The Diaries of William Stairs 1887–1892* ed. Roy MacLaren 298 n.
27. Stanley, *Auto* 411–12.

THIRTY-ONE: The Prime Minister's Protectorate

1. Karugire 74.
2. 'Nile Struggle' 122, 131–3.

3. Ibid 150–1.
4. Pakenham 416.
5. Karugire 77–8.
6. Ibid 79; *The Rise of our East African Empire* F. Lugard 2 vols II 660–2.
7. Ibid 332.
8. *Lugard: The Years of Adventure 1858–1898* Margery Perham 2 vols [Perham] I 198, 238, 303, 350.
9. Pakenham 429.
10. Ibid 429–30.
11. Jeal, *Stanley* 428; Harcourt to Gladstone 3 Oct 1892 44202 BL.
12. Karugire 83–4; Pakenham 433.

THIRTY-TWO: To Die for the Mahdi's Cause

1. Perham I 461.
2. *The Zambesi Expedition of David Livingstone 1858–1863* ed. J. P. R. Wallis 416.
3. WLT 367.
4. *Prelude to the Partition of West Africa* J. D. Hargreaves 338–49.
5. *The River Nile in the Age of the British* Terje Tvedt 331 n 39, 341 n 175, 367.
6. Details of Kitchener's life from *Kitchener: Portrait of an Imperialist* Philip Magnus (1958).
7. Sanderson 293.
8. Udal II 519–20; Moorehead 333.
9. *The River War: An Historical Account of the Reconquest of the Soudan* Winston Churchill 2 vols II 82 ff.
10. Udal II 524.
11. Pakenham 546.
12. Moorehead 337; *The Decline and Fall of the British Empire 1781–1997* Piers Brendon [Brendon] 204 n 144.
13. Udal II 527.
14. Dialogue from Marchand letter in *Figaro* 20 Nov 1898.
15. *Empire on the Nile* W. M. Daly [Daly] 73, 136–7.

THIRTY-THREE: Equatoria and the Tragedy of Southern Sudan

1. *Ismailia* II 242, 257–8; *Shadows in the Grass: Britain in the Southern Sudan 1918–1956* R. O. Collins [Shadows] 68.
2. BD 13 Jan 1863 RGS.
3. 'Politics, ethnicity and conflict in post-independent Acholiland, Uganda 1962–2006' F. Odoi-Tanga [Odoi-Tanga] 79.
4. *Land Beyond the Rivers 1898–1918* R. O. Collins [LBR] 67.
5. Jeal, *Stanley* 369, 375.
6. Odoi-Tanga 76.

7. *LBR* 75–8.
8. *Imperial Boundary Making: The Diary of Captain Kelly and the Sudan–Uganda Boundary Commission of 1913* ed. G. H. Blake 16, 32–3, 39.
9. Ibid 33, 91.
10. *Shadows* 209; Brendon 361.
11. Daly 399–400.
12. *Shadows* 121–2; *Sudan: Darfur and the Failure of an African State* Richard Cockett [Cockett] 39–41.
13. *Shadows* 15, 130.
14. Ibid 93–7, 37; *People of the Small Arrow* J. H. Driberg 9–86; Daly 152; Brendon 364.
15. *Shadows* 166–7, 220; *LBR* 173–9, 313–17; Cockett 39.
16. *Shadows* 230.
17. Ibid 245–6.
18. Ibid 274.
19. Ibid 277.
20. Cockett 10, 45–6; *Shadows* 332, 457.
21. Ibid 454–55.
22. *The State of Africa: A History of Fifty Years of Independence* Martin Meredith [Meredith] 588; Cockett 84, 118, 123–4.
23. *Shadows* 447.
24. *Sudan Verse* K. D. D. Henderson and T. R. H. Owen, five-stanza poem by Owen 43.

THIRTY-FOUR: A Sin not Theirs: The Tragedy of Northern Uganda

1. Karugire 89–91; Girling 148 points out that Kabarega had 300 men with him on his arrival in Acholiland; details of campaign in *The Land of the Nile Springs* H. E. Colvile.
2. *Omukama Chwa II Kabarega* A. R. Dunbar; *Elizabeth of Toro* Elizabeth Nyabongo [ET] 30.
3. Odoi-Tanga 83–7.
4. *The Roots of Ethnicity: The Origins of the Acholi and Uganda before 1800* R. R. Atkinson [Atkinson] 75–6.
5. Karugire 114.
6. *Oxford History of East Africa* eds Vincent Harlow and E. M. Chilver 2 vols [Oxford] II 104–7; 'Land and Chieftainship among the Acholi' R. M. Bere *Ganda Journal* 19 (1955) 49–56.
7. Karugire 127.
8. Atkinson 7.
9. *The Illusion of Tribe* A. Southall 35. In 1983 in their book *The Invention of Tradition* Eric Hobsbawm and Terence Ranger argued that Britain's indirect rule (mainly exercised through existing chiefs) required

nothing less than 'the invention of tradition' by the colonial masters who needed Africans to believe that these arrangements were founded on ancient African custom. Ten years later Ranger would backtrack in favour of 'the imagination of tradition': the new concept implying equal cooperation between white and black in tradition-making.

10. 'Tribalism and Ethnicity in Africa' Carola Lentz *Cahiers des sciences humaine* 31 II 1985 318; *African History* John Parker and R. Rathbone 111.
11. Odoi-Tanga 117.
12. Karugire Chaps. 5 and 6; Meredith 232–3.
13. From obituaries of Mutesa II and Milton Obote; Meredith 233.
14. *Push on the Door, All Things Considered* both by Richard Carr-Gomm; *Strange Places, Questionable People* John Simpson; *Uganda Sunday Vision* 21, 23 May, 5, 10, 26 Jun 2010.
15. *Africa: Altered States, Ordinary Miracles* Richard Dowden [Dowden] 65.
16. *ET* 117; Dowden 63–4, 72, 56.
17. Odoi-Tanga 140; *The Social Origins of Violence in Uganda 1964–1985* A. B. K. Kasozi 111.
18. Dowden 70–1.
19. *Financial Times Magazine* article about Joseph Kony by Matthew Green 9 Oct 2008.
20. Odoi-Tanga 174. The Anyanya had been a group of Sudanese separatist rebels formed in 1963.
21. Odoi-Tanga 321; *Independent* 12 Dec 2009.
22. *Wizard of the Nile* Matthew Green 312–13; Human Rights Watch: Abducted and Abused Vol. 15 No. 12A July 2003; Odoi-Tanga 323.
23. UK High Commissioner for Refugees 'Situation in Acholi and IDP Camps' (Aug 2009); 'Trail of Death' (March 2010) Human Rights Watch DRC.
24. Meredith 404.
25. Ibid 405–6.
26. *Daily Nation* 11 Sept 2009; *Ugandan Independent* 13 Oct 2009; Ugandan National Public Radio documentary 14 Feb 2010; *Daily Monitor* 20 Feb 2011.
27. *Oxford* II 13–14; *John Ainsworth: Pioneer Administrator 1864–1946* F. H. Goldsmith 26–31.
28. *Africa: A Biography of the Continent* John Reader [Reader] 568.
29. Patterson's diaries quoted in *The End of the Game* Peter Beard 97.
30. Ibid 87, 103, 106; *Oxford* II 21.
31. Ibid 299; 'Malice in Masailand' L. Hughes Colloque International 'At the Frontier of Land Issues', Montpellier 2006; Brendon 354.
32. *Unhappy Valley: Conflict in Kenya and Africa* Bruce Berman and John Lonsdale 239–44.
33. Meredith 687.

CODA: Lacking the Wand of an Enchanter

1. S&N 25; *TDC* II 124, 513–15, 477, 480; in Stanley's *My Dark Companions and their Strange Stories*; Jeal, *Stanley* 217 and associated notes.

2. Stanley to E. King 2 Oct 1877 RMCA.

3. *Zanzibar* II 101–2.

4. Girling 149.

5. DL to LMS 17 Mar 1847 in *Livingstone's Missionary Correspondence 1841–1856* ed. I Schapera 108.

6. DL to J. H. Parker 11 Mar 1844 Wellcome Library.

7. *Livingstone's African Journal 1853–1856* ed. I. Schapera 2 vols [*AJ*] II 320–1; *LPJ* 210.

8. Jeal, *Livingstone* 84–85, 103–4.

9. Palmerston to Lord John Russell, FO 63/871; Lord John Russell to DL 17 Apr 1860 NAZ.

10. *WLT* 344.

11. *Journal* 450.

12. Maitland 194–5.

13. Stanley to Strauch 8 Jul 1879, 27 Jan 1884 RMCA; *The Congo and the Founding of its Free State* H. M. Stanley 2 vols II 144–5; CD 27 Nov 1883; Jeal *Stanley* 275, 282–4, 524–5.

14. *The Last Expedition: Stanley's Mad Journey Through the Congo* D. Liebowitz and C. Pearson 337.

15. *LLJ* I 62–3; DL to Lord Clarendon 20 August 1866 FO 84/1265.

16. *LPJ* 210.

17. *IDA* 153.

18. BD 16 Jun 1863 RGS.

19. 'Import of Firearms into West Africa in the Eighteenth Century' W. A. Richards *Journal of African History* 21 (1980) 43–59; 'Ottoman Empire's Relations with Southern Africa' A. Kavas *Journal of Ankara University History Faculty* XLVIII (2007) II 11–20.

20. S&N 117–18; Stanley to Alice Pike 2 Jun 1876 RMCA.

21. *LLJ* I 265.

22. *Islam's Black Slaves: The Other Black Diaspora* Ronald Segal 56, 154–5, 160–74; *A History of Africa* J. D. Fage (1978) 257.

23. *David Livingstone: his life and letters* G. Seaver 444.

24. *AJ* I 25–6.

25. *AN* 143.

26. Reader 570, 579, citing *Cambridge History of Africa* vol. VI (1985) Chap 12: 'The European Scramble and Conquest in African History' 722.

27. *LPJ* 210; *AJ* I 234; *Missionary Travels and Researches in South Africa* David Livingstone 679.

28. *Glimpse of a Governor's Life* H. H. J. Bell 128.
29. *Jephson* 401.
30. Reader 579, 625.
31. Ibid 245.
32. *Africans: The History of a Continent* John Iliffe 212; Pakenham 680.
33. *Journal* 163.
34. Ibid 169.
35. *Missionary Travels* Livingstone 441.
36. *TDC* I 136–7.

Index